HUMAN SERVICES MANAGEMENT

HUMAN
SERVICES MANAGEMENT

ORGANIZATIONAL LEADERSHIP
IN SOCIAL WORK PRACTICE

DAVID M. AUSTIN

COLUMBIA UNIVERSITY PRESS / NEW YORK

COLUMBIA UNIVERSITY PRESS

Publishers Since 1893

New York   Chichester, West Sussex

© 2002 Columbia University Press

Library of Congress Cataloging-in-Publication Data

Austin, David M.

Human services management : organizational leadership in
social work practice / David M. Austin.

p.   cm.

Includes bibliographical references and index.

ISBN 0-231-10836-2 (alk. paper)

1. Social work administration.   2. Public welfare administration.
3. Human services—Administration.   I. Title.

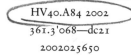
HV40.A84 2002

361.3'068—dc21

2002025650

Columbia University Press books are printed
on permanent and durable acid-free paper.

Printed in the United States of America

c 10 9 8 7 6 5 4 3 2 1

CONTENTS

FOREWORD

SOCIAL WELFARE administration has its origins in the Charities Organization Societies, which makes it the oldest practice modality in the profession. Naturally, in the nearly century and a half since the first social welfare administrators attempted to bring order to the charitable field, there have been a number of theories and practice models that have sought to guide the work of administrators. The present volume by Professor David Austin is the latest effort, and in my opinion one of the best, at providing administrators and students of administration with ways for understanding the theory and practice of contemporary social welfare administration.

I imagine that most prospective readers are not going to believe this, but for someone who's interested in this field, this book is a page-turner. Austin's command of the material is truly impressive. More importantly, he's been thinking about these ideas for a long time (at least twenty years) and has integrated and synthesized the material into an interesting "story" about social welfare management. Professor Austin is one of the finest scholars in this field. His particular strength is to combine "big think" (theoretical and conceptual approaches) with first hand knowledge of social welfare organizations. His writing is lucid, his thinking is clear, and he demonstrates an excellent command of the issues in the areas he writes about.

My understanding of the author's central theme comes from a statement he makes at the beginning of the book, in which he says that his perspective is to view the human service organization "as a social system which has very special connections to the society of which it is a part." This is a perspective that Austin has pursued over a number of years, beginning with his 1981 article on social services as "public goods." This is a point of view that I agree with and one that is reflected in my own work. I think it is an important perspective because it captures the reality of the extent to which social welfare organizations are dependent upon, and heavily influenced by, forces in the larger society. In this sense, I think of it as a *realpolitik* approach, which forces the reader to address the dilemmas and contradictions that regularly confront social welfare managers. This theme provides a framework for the entire book.

Social work is a "low paradigm" field with a low level of agreement among scholars and practitioners regarding what is "good practice," whether in clinical or nonclinical approaches. This presents a problem: what material to include in a book such as this and what to leave out. I am in agreement with the selection that Austin has made. His choice of topics provides the reader with conceptually rich material that can lead to a better understanding of the context within which the practice of management takes place. As such, it differs from the more nuts-and-bolts, hands-on approach of many texts. The author sets the tone for this approach with this quotation from Mary Parker Follett: "Of the greatest importance is the ability to grasp a total situation. . . . Out of a welter of facts, experience, desires, aims, a leader must find the unifying thread. He must see the relation between all the different factors in a situation. The higher up you go, the more ability you have to have of this kind, because you have a wider range of facts from which to seize the relations."

After a historical overview, the chapters move, roughly, from internal organizational matters to external matters. The important thing in the organization of material is that an author have a clear sense of where he wants to take the reader. This is an area in which Austin excels. The material exudes authority (in terms of mastery of the material) and confidence (as regards the clarity of the author's point of view.)

The historical overview of measuring the effectiveness of social services is an important contribution to the literature in this area. It should give the reader a helpful framework for understanding the range and complexity of issues that surround measuring the success of social programs. This perspective is especially effective when combined with the author's concern with the relationship between professionalized occupations and organizational structures. This has been, and continues to be, a major concern in the literature on social work management generally. As managed care becomes more widespread, moreover, the issues that

Austin discusses in chapter 7 will become more and more central to the management of many types of service organizations.

This book can be used effectively in a number of venues. First, and foremost, it will provide a state-of-the-art text for graduate students in social welfare administration, as well as in related human service fields, at both the master's and doctoral levels. It should provide practicing managers with the opportunity to reflect on the issues they face, and how these issues have been addressed in the past and to what effect. Finally, the wealth of material contained in this volume could provide themes for a variety of workshops and seminars for practicing managers and scholars in the field.

Professor Austin has made a major contribution to the field of human services management and administration, one that should continue to influence the field for many years to come.

> Burton Gummer, Ph.D., Professor
> School of Social Welfare
> The University at Albany
> State University of New York

PREFACE

THE LAST half of the twentieth century brought a steady expansion in all of the human service fields in which social workers, and other human service professionals, are involved—social services, education, health care, mental health care, addiction, and criminal justice. These human services have become increasingly important for the quality of life throughout American society. Human services involve the practical application of moral values that directly affect the well-being of individuals, households, and communities. Human services have increasingly become the object of critical public attention and political controversy. Some concerns about the quality and effectiveness of human service provision involve fundamental policy choices and the level of public and philanthropic expenditures. Other concerns involve the characteristics of specific service technologies. It has also become clear that many of the concerns about the effectiveness of human service programs involve questions about the quality of management leadership.

Although service technologies may be quite different, organizational and management processes across all types of human service organizations have a great deal in common. For example, there are many similarities in the management of a nonprofit adoption agency, a public school system, a community mental health center, a general hospital, and a juvenile court probation department. Moreover, many traditional distinctions among nonprofit, governmental, and for-profit human service organizations have become blurred as all three types of organizations have drawn on similar sources of funding. This book is directed to social workers, and other human service professionals, who are preparing for or who are in positions of management responsibility in social services, health care and mental health care, education, substance addiction, and criminal justice across nonprofit, governmental, and for-profit sectors.

This book does not present a prescriptive model of human services management; rather, it is an attempt to present a realistic description and analysis of those forces that shape the organizational dynamics with which every human service manager must deal. Many management textbooks deal primarily with internal organizational activities—fund-raising, financial planning and budgeting, financial control, personnel, communications, program supervision, public relations. This book deals with the social, economic, and political context of the human service organization and, in particular, with the stakeholder constituencies with which every organizational manager must deal.

This book begins with an examination of the historical development and distinctive characteristics of human service organizations, the variety of organizational and program structures found among human service organizations, and the connection of individual service organizations with service delivery networks. The central section of the book deals with key stakeholder constituencies. These include service users, service personnel—particularly service professionals, funders, the executive, and policy boards. The final two chapters focus on two increasingly important organizational processes—accountability for effectiveness and dealing with organizational changes.

An outgrowth of *The Political Economy of Human Service Programs* (1988), which dealt with the historical and societal context of human service programs, the present book has been influenced by the increasing number of publications that deal with human services management, including *Administration in Social Work* and *Nonprofit Management and Leadership*. The book has been shaped, in part, by my own studies on the historical development of social welfare institutions and on social work as an organized profession. It has benefited from the organizational experiences and insights of social work students, which have been shared through classroom discussions and individual papers. In particular, preliminary drafts of this book have benefited from critiques and classroom discussions that these students have shared with me in two doctoral seminars at the University of Texas at Austin, School of Social Work, in 1999 and 2000.

Three important writers whose creative ideas are relevant for human services management have influenced the present book. The first of these is Mary Parker Follett, a social worker and an internationally recognized management consultant in the 1920s. She explored the psychological and social dimensions of business management. The second is Rosabeth Moss Kanter, a member of the faculty at the Harvard Business School, whose analysis of the dynamics of contemporary business management reflects, in part, the writings of Follett. The third is Yeheskel Hasenfeld, a member of the faculty at the Department of Social Welfare, University of California at Los Angeles, whose application of social science concepts to the analysis of human service organizations has been important in the development of my own understanding of the organizational dynamics of human service organizations.

ACKNOWLEDGMENTS

THIS BOOK is organized around issues that were first highlighted in the Conference on Human Service Organizations and Organizational Theory held at the Center for Advanced Study in the Behavioral Sciences at Palo Alto in 1979. I participated in that conference at the invitation of Dr. Herman Stein of Case Western Reserve University. Under his leadership, that conference and the publication that followed, *Organization and the Human Services: Cross-Disciplinary Reflections*, edited by Dr. Stein, brought the insights of the social sciences—economics, sociology, and political science—to bear on the challenges of managing human service organizations. With encouragement from Dr. Stein, I continued to work on issues identified in that conference.

Critical support by Dr. Louis A. Zurcher, a former colleague at the School of Social Work at the University of Texas at Austin, led to the publication of *The Political Economy of Human Service Programs* by JAI Press in 1988, which dealt with the historical and institutional context of contemporary human service programs. In 1995, I was invited by Dr. Frederic Reamer of Rhode Island College to prepare a book on human services management as part of the Columbia University Press series, *The Foundations of Social Work*. The supportive environment of colleagues and students at the School of Social Work, The University of Texas at Austin and the encouragement of Dean Barbara W. White have been important in carrying this project through to completion. Anonymous reviewers of the completed manuscript provided important suggestions.

My wife, Zuria Farmer Austin—a graduate of the School of Applied Social Sciences, Western Reserve University; a social worker; and volunteer advocate for expanded community services—provided critical assistance. Responsibility for the final version of this book, however, is mine.

D. M. A.

ONE

INTRODUCTION

But let us look further at the essentials of leadership. Of the greatest importance is the ability to grasp a total situation. The chief mistake in thinking of leadership as resting wholly on personality lies probably in the fact that the executive leader is not a leader of men only but of something we are learning to call the total situation. This includes facts, present and potential, aims and purposes and men. Out of a welter of facts, experience, desires, aims, a leader must find the unifying thread. He must see a whole, not a kaleidoscope of pieces. He must see the relation between all the different factors in a situation. The higher up you go, the more ability you have to have of this kind, because you have a wider range of facts from which to seize the relations. —Mary Parker Follett (Graham 1995:168)

WE LIVE in a world of organizations in the United States at the beginning of the twenty-first century. Society is governed through a complex network of international, national, state, and local political/governmental organizations. Goods and services that are part of everyday living are obtained through organizational systems that reach around the world. Growing up, to a large degree, is growing up in a world of educational organizations. For most individuals, working in or with an organization is a central feature of their adult years, organizations that may be very large and impersonal or that may be small and intimate. Organizational arrangements of many types shape retirement years. In the world of organizations, the shift from an industrial society to the postindustrial society is a shift from goods-producing organizations to service-producing organizations (Bell 1973) and, increasingly, information-producing organizations.

Persons who work in, or through, human service organizations—social workers, nurses, physicians, lawyers, teachers, psychologists, counselors, clergy—spend much of their time with organizations, either the organization that they *work in*, or the organizations they *deal with* as part of their workday. In the United States, this world of human service organizations is undergoing a series of far-reaching changes (Bozeman 1987). Traditional distinctions among marketplace, for-profit firms, governmental bureaus, and nonprofit voluntary organizations are breaking down. The division of organizational responsibilities among different levels of government is changing dramatically. Traditional bureaucratic, hierarchical, "command-and-control" models of organizational management are mixed with low-profile, diffuse, and dispersed authority models (Drucker 1996, 1998).

Traditional career assumptions about long-term, stable employment in a single organization, whether marketplace, governmental, or nonprofit, are being replaced by assumptions of multiple career changes, career transformations, and continuous reeducation (Kanter 1996:142–144):

> The organization of the future requires a focus on new human resource policies. Organizations must help people gain the skills and self-reliance to master the new environment, to find security and support when they can no longer count on large employers to provide it automatically. . . . If security no longer comes from being employed, it must come from being employable. . . . Employability security comes from the chance to accumulate the human capital of skills and reputation that can be invested in new opportunities as they arise.

These changes affect everybody who is, or potentially may be, a user of the services that are produced through human service organizations. They also affect everyone who is directly involved in such organizations as an employee, a funder, a service volunteer, or a policy maker, and, in particular, organizational managers (Edwards, Cooke, and Reid 1996:468).

> In the near future, the changing political realities and their social and cultural context will bring additional challenges to the social work profession and to those who manage social work and human services organizations. . . . Social work managers must function in an atmosphere of increasing ambiguity and paradox. Managers are confronted almost daily with the need to satisfy different and sometimes competing values and stakeholder interests, all in a context of diminishing resources and organizational security within the service system.

New emphases on development of a comprehensive "continuum of service," competition among organizational service providers, quality management, and the definition and measurement of the outcomes of service provision are changing the responsibilities of organizational managers (Chism 1997). Changes in technology—teaching technology, health-care technology, information technology—make new demands on individuals in leadership roles. New rules about organizational accountability, and the role of the courts in enforcing accountability, create pressures on organizational managers and professional specialists. In particular, the complex tasks of organizational management require constant attention to events outside of the service organization that may directly affect activities within the organization. The cultural transformation of the society of the United States as a result of demographic, legal, and political changes has become a central element in the functioning of all types of human service organizations.

In this world of changing organizations, an understanding of the nature of service organizations (Fitzsimmons and Fitzsimmons 1994) and of the forces that shape such organizations is as important for front-line, direct-service, human service professional practitioners as for organizational managers and policy makers. Such an understanding is essential if professional practitioners, including social workers, nurses, school teachers, doctors, psychologists, lawyers, and other human service practitioners, are to provide responsive and high-quality services to individuals, families, and communities. An awareness of the changes that are taking place is also important, personally, for professional practitioners trying to understand the forces that will affect their ability to provide quality services and the pattern of their own professional careers.

The perspective of this book is that human services management is a complex version of the general field of organizational management in service organizations (Fitzsimmons and Fitzsimmons 1994). Human services management takes place within the nonprofit sector and the public, or governmental, sector and, increasingly, within the for-profit sector. It involves a wide variety of organizational structures through which very diverse technologies are used to produce services that directly affect the quality of life of individuals and families across the fields of social welfare services, health and mental health services, law enforcement and criminal justice, and educational services. Managers in human service organizations simultaneously carry responsibility for the quality of the services provided for individuals and families, for assuring that such services also result in benefits for communities and the society as a whole, and for making provision for the maintenance and development of the service organization. The requirements of ethical behavior in management become a central issue for managers and for other organizational participants (Reamer 1995).

The purpose of this book is to assist participants in human service organizations in developing an understanding of the dynamics that are shaping such organizations. The background of this author is primarily connected with social welfare services and with social work education. Many illustrations used in this book are drawn from social welfare organizations. The broad range of human services, however, is the context for this book, with the expectation that the content may be as relevant for the hospital administrator or the school superintendent as for the manager of a nonprofit, voluntary family service agency, a public child-welfare agency, or a community mental health center.

The development of this book has been influenced by the ideas of Mary Parker Follett, an unusual speaker and writer who was an important member of the social work community early in the twentieth century. Follett brought insights from her experience as a settlement house worker in the Roxbury community of Boston to her career in the 1920s and 1930s as a consultant on management–labor relations and as a lecturer in business management at conferences in the United States and England (Graham 1995). Follett defined the business organization as a social system, a social system that had community consequences as well as production outcomes (Graham 1995; Selber and Austin 1997). Follett's ideas are drawn on throughout this book as the human service organization is examined as a social system that has special connections to the society of which it is a part. This book also draws on the work of Rosabeth Moss Kanter, a contemporary teacher and writer on business management whose thinking, in turn, draws on the work of Mary Parker Follett (Kanter 1995).

HISTORICAL BACKGROUND

The Rationalization of Society

During the second half of the nineteenth century in the United States, a complex urban–industrial society developed that was different from societies that had existed for centuries in other parts of the world. Millions of new settlers arrived, primarily from Europe. Millions of people moved across the territory of the United States. Concentrations of new industries were established in the cities that attracted most of the new arrivals. These developments required the creation of new social organizations, transforming an earlier society organized primarily around networks of personal relationships into a society of "rational" organizations through which large numbers of strangers became parts of an operating society that had consistency and predictability.

Many of these developments were set in motion by the Civil War during the 1860s, which brought about large-scale development of business and industrial resources in the northern states as well as the organization of hundreds of thousands of men into a systematic military structure. Wartime developments in both business and government created the framework required for mobilizing resources for the expansion of urban settlements across the continent. The outcome of the Civil War also resulted in the exclusion of the citizens of the southern states from many of the economic and social developments that characterized the rest of the nation during the last half of the nineteenth century and the first three decades of the twentieth century.

There were two major societal tasks in the last part of the nineteenth century. One was the *production of goods and services for a rapidly expanding population*, a large portion of which lived in cities where households could not be self-sufficient. The other was *building communities from a population of strangers*—that is, building socially functioning local communities on the frontier where there was no established society (Smith 1966), and in the cities where thousands of people from many different cultural backgrounds were thrown together.

Several distinct organizational models emerged during this period that contributed in different ways both to the production of goods and services and to the building of communities. One was the *stock corporation*, through which thousands of investors combined their resources to create large industrial firms and to build railroads linking all corners of the nation. The stock corporation made it possible to separate the sources of capital investment from the responsibilities of organizational management. This created new opportunities for aggressive entrepreneurial business leaders who did not have inherited family wealth, and it also created a rapidly expanding class of salaried business managers.

A second model was the *organization of industrial firms as unified production systems* using unskilled and semiskilled workmen under the guidance of industrial engineers, displacing the tradition of individual skilled craftsmen prepared through long apprenticeships (Shenhav 1995). These factory workers could be readily laid off, and then replaced, during the economic boom-and-bust cycles associated with the expanding but unregulated market economy following the Civil War (Lens 1969).

A third model was the *governmental bureau* (as distinct from the legislative, or governance, elements of government). The organization of the governmental bureau reflected, in part, the experience of the military forces with a structured command hierarchy, a separation of policy formulation from day-to-day production activities, and a system of rules and regulations intended to produce consistency and predictability. This was a model that provided relatively stable and dependable employment but did not allow for an aggressive entrepreneurial manager.

A fourth model was the *philanthropic corporation*, which combined the model of the business firm with its board of directors, but without owners or stockholders, or stock dividends, with an older model of the charitable foundation or trust. The role of the philanthropic corporation as a "nonprofit" corporation became prominent after the adoption of the federal income tax in the early 1920s, with the exemption of nonprofit organizations from tax obligations together with provisions for income tax deductions for "charitable" contributions to such nonprofit organizations.*

A fifth model was the *public university* as a setting for large-scale, practical education of the occupational specialists needed in the new society, and for the application of scientific discoveries to the development of new products and technologies. The public university was distinctly different from the private liberal arts college that served as a setting for the education of elite social and political leaders. One important difference was the coeducational student body in public universities, in contrast to the almost universal division of private colleges into men's and women's colleges.

---

*The terms *nonprofit* and *not-for-profit* are used interchangeably by different authors to refer to organizations recognized under Section 501(c)(3) of the federal income tax code. The term *nonprofit* is used throughout this book.

A sixth model was the *organized profession* that brought together large numbers of occupational specialists, for example in law and medicine, to form national, mutual-benefit associations in order to develop ethical standards of practice and to advance their economic interests (Starr 1982). Professional associations also served to define, as well as to control, the process of entrance into such "professions" through accreditation control of professional schools attached to colleges and universities and the establishment of systems of governmentally sponsored professional licensing procedures (MacDonald 1995).

All of these organizational models were part of the process of "rationalizing," "standardizing," and "civilizing" a society that was expanding rapidly and incorporating large numbers of new arrivals from very diverse cultural backgrounds. The linkage of these "rational" organizations into a series of national networks was one important element in preventing the fragmentation of the society of the United States into a series of small, competitive nation-states reflecting the historical traditions of Europe. The Civil War of the 1860s had indicated that such a fragmentation was indeed a possibility. In addition to these large-scale organizational structures, the post–Civil War era was marked by the development of a dense network of local voluntary organizations and associations reflecting the cultural diversity and diversity of interests among the residents of local communities. These "mediating" organizations mediated the relationships between individual households and the larger structures of government, business, and national associations, creating a "civil society" that also provided a wide range of leadership opportunities for individual citizens (Drucker 1990b). The development of the civil society was also influenced by the tradition of locally initiated voluntary associations that were a key element in the conversion of frontier settlements into functioning "communities" (Smith 1966).

THE DEVELOPMENT OF "SOCIETAL" SERVICES

One of the significant areas to be affected by this process of rationalization was the broad range of organizationally based social, or "societal," services provided through the diverse combination of nonprofit, voluntary organizations and governmental service organizations that functioned outside of the competitive, marketplace economy, which was the most powerful force in shaping the emerging society. These services supplemented, or replaced, services previously provided within families, or extended family networks, in traditional societies. These societal services included public elementary and secondary education; day-care centers, nursery schools, and kindergartens; health-care services, primarily through hospitals; law enforcement and the courts; criminal justice services directed at law offenders; and a broad range of social welfare services involving care of orphaned and abused children, care of persons with chronic illnesses and disabilities, provision of basic necessities to destitute households, the assimilation of new arrivals into the existing American society, and the organization of self-maintaining "neighborhoods" and "communities." These services were simultaneously part of an expanding service production process and of a community building process across the United States.

The actual pattern of organizational development for these societal services was strongly influenced by the basic structure of political forces in this new society. European immigrants who flooded into the center of the cities, near the factories that provided employment, became a dominant force in urban political organizations, controlled by new political leaders, or "ward bosses." In contrast, the new entrepreneurial economic leaders were creating an elite society in the outlying areas of the city, and in the new suburbs, largely controlled by the "established," English-descended, Protestant populations (Baltzell 1964). This elite society included a tradition of voluntary philanthropy and nongovernmental "civic leadership" (Bruno 1957). These two population groups, the "newcomers" and the "establishment," were largely separated by religious identification, by language, by economic position, and by residential location.

As the leaders of the elite society lost direct control of local, and often state, political/governmental structures, they began to establish a network of "voluntary" civic organizations outside of the structure of government (Westby 1966). The objective of these civic leaders was to establish organizations that were responsive to their version of traditional values, and that were organized in a manner consistent with the new forms of rationalization in the business community rather than being controlled by political patronage systems or populist political movements.

This system of voluntary, philanthropic organizations was shaped, in part, by the traditions of the diverse and independent Protestant church organizations in the United States that, unlike those in Europe, did not receive governmental support. This system of independent, voluntary, nongovernmental organizations, created through the efforts of "nonpolitical" civic leaders, included charitable hospitals, charitable foundations, privately financed colleges and universities, and, in particular, a wide range of philanthropic social welfare organizations. This movement also included separation of the control of the public schools in many communities from local "partisan" governmental structures through the establishment of independent, nonpolitical "boards of education." The influence of the leaders of these nongovernmental philanthropic organizations was often built into the existing governmental social welfare systems through their appointment to state boards of charities that served as overseers of the custodial institutions established by state governments during the latter part of the nineteenth century (Bruno 1957; Leiby 1984).

The development of voluntary philanthropic service organizations and other civic organizations was directly influenced by the rapid growth of personal fortunes. The development of these philanthropic service organizations was also shaped by the massive influx of immigrants from Europe, by the periodic economic crises that suddenly created widespread unemployment among factory workers, by the emergence of "radical" European social philosophies (Lens 1966), and by initial efforts to organize labor unions.

In response to these pressures, the network of voluntary philanthropic organizations was expanded, in part in an effort to limit any expansion of the limited, tax-supported, governmental social welfare programs, controlled by local politicians, and in part, to blunt the appeal of more "radical" socialist proposals. This established the conceptual framework for the model of "welfare capitalism" that characterized the social welfare structure of the United States during the twentieth century (Skocpol 1994).* This model included a commitment to a competitive

---

*The term *welfare capitalism* has also been used to describe social welfare policies dealing with wage supplements, asset building, and community capitalism (Stoesz and Saunders 1999), as well as to describe the provision of supplemental and fringe benefits by corporations to their employees (Jacoby 1999).

capitalist marketplace economy and to the voluntary provision of social welfare services and other types of human services. These services were supported by contributions from persons benefitting from the marketplace economy. They were controlled at the local community level together with a minimal level of tax-supported governmental services.

As the number of local voluntary philanthropic social welfare organizations increased, the concern for organizational rationalization increased. This concern was reflected in the Charity Organization movement that began in London and was brought to the United States in the 1870s (Leiby 1984). Charity Organization Societies (COS) were initiated by business leaders to rationalize the provision of charity, or emergency assistance, to impoverished families and individuals (Lowell 1884). Such assistance was then being provided by a large number of independent charitable groups, many of them church based, that turned repeatedly to a small group of wealthy families and business leaders for financial support.

One part of the COS rationalization objectives was increased "efficiency." Another objective was to treat individuals and families impartially, independent of religious affiliation, and to offset the skill of some individuals in manipulating existing charitable resources by going from one charitable organization to another. The concern for rationalization was also reflected in the establishment of the National Conference of Charities and Correction in the 1870s, which brought together civic leaders and organizational managers, primarily from philanthropic service organizations, from across the United States (although largely from the East and Mid-west) to share information about program management (Bruno 1957).

Business leaders, and members of established professions—medicine, law, and the clergy—dominated the boards of directors of the Charity Organization Societies, and increasingly of the entire range of philanthropic organizations, together with a small number of independently wealthy women and wives of wealthy businessmen. It was the personal values of these nineteenth century business and professional leaders and their concepts of leadership and management that largely shaped the emerging network of voluntary social welfare organizations (Lowell 1884). The process of organizational rationalization and the support of "civic virtues" also impacted local governments as business leaders banded together at the beginning of the twentieth century in "good government" movements to control political corruption and to install administrative and professional technicians, rather than political appointees, as the managers of governmental "bureaucracies" (Dahlberg 1966).

Another part of the rationalization initiative was attention to the systematic education of the persons who were to work in the new service organizations in health, education, and social welfare. This initiative underlay the reorganization of medical education in the United States, primarily promoted by the General Education Fund of the Rockefeller Foundation (Flexner 1910). This rationalization initiative also supported the development of university-connected law schools (Frankfurter 1915) and that of schools of nursing, and the initiation of systematic programs of training for the emerging profession of social work (Austin 1997). The graduates from these professional education programs became the leaders of the organized professions that, in turn, became a central element in the actual operation of the system of societal service programs during the twentieth century (Starr 1982).

Developments in the Twentieth Century

By the beginning of the twentieth century, four major sectors were involved in the production and distribution of the goods and services that were central to the operation of a complex, interdependent society (Austin 1988). The largest of these sectors continued to be individual households, which, across the society, produced many of the products needed by household members and provided most of the educational, health and mental health care, and social welfare services, broadly defined, that household members required. The other three sectors included the marketplace system of private, for-profit firms, the multilevel system of governmental bureaus, and the network of voluntary nonprofit philanthropic corporations and civic associations (Weisbrod 1977). Also significant in the society of the United States at the beginning of the twentieth century were the wide variety of intermediary nonprofit corporations and associations that constituted the civil society that mediated the connections between households and individuals and the large-scale formal structures of national associations, government, and the economic marketplace (Drucker 1990b).

The societal roles of all three of the organizational sectors expanded steadily during the twentieth century. This was, in part, a response to the disruption of traditional extended family networks as new waves of immigration arrived and as family size decreased. Personal and family mobility increased, in particular the movement of individuals and families from rural and small-town communities to cities. In turn, the importance of the economic marketplace in the production of goods and services required by households increased dramatically. Economic crises like the Depression of the 1930s led to the expansion of both governmental and nongovernmental service organizations. Military mobilization during war periods was accompanied by a dramatic growth in for-profit industrial firms and in the scope of governmental authority. The scope of nonprofit organizations and voluntary associations expanded in part as a response to the growing cultural diversity of the population in the United States. The pattern of organizational services in the general community was duplicated, in many instances, by the organization of similar services within distinctive cultural communities. Parochial schools were organized in Roman Catholic parishes and orphanages were organized in both Jewish and Roman Catholic communities as well as under the auspices of different Protestant denominations.

During the twentieth century, the size and complexity of organized professions also increased. Each of the organized human service professions developed a particular set of relationships with the organizational service systems that emerged. Medicine established a general model of an arms-length relationship between individual professional practitioners and organizations—contractual, independent practitioner relationships rather than employment relationships, until the emergence of the health maintenance organization (HMO) in the 1970s (Starr 1982). Nursing followed an organizational employment model with the provision of direct health-care services to individuals in organizational settings in which nurses were not the senior administrators. Law developed a mixed pattern of individual practice, group professional practice, and organizational employment in for-profit firms, as well as organizational employment in governmental and nonprofit organizations.

The professional education curricula in these three professions did not include systematic attention to organizational theory or to the practice of organizational management. However, in the development of the teaching profession, the local public school organization was considered the normal employment setting and administration was considered an integral part of the professional practice context. Educational administration became a substantial curriculum element in professional schools of education.

Social work developed as an organized profession around a model of organizational employment in both voluntary, nonprofit organizations and governmental organizations. The professional education curriculum was focused on preparation of social work practitioners to provide direct services to individuals and households. But it also included a basic orientation for all students to the characteristics of service organizations and management tasks. Since the 1970s, the curriculum in many of the graduate schools of social work has also included a minor, but distinct, curriculum track dealing with management practice (Austin 1995, 2000).

In part, the development of a management track in the social work curriculum reflected the lack of attention to the management of nonprofit service organizations in larger management education programs—business administration, public administration, and educational administration. In part, this development in social work was also shaped by the career interests of persons who already had significant work experience in social welfare organizations and who were interested in becoming program managers and executives. And in part, this development in social work reflected the barriers facing women, throughout most of the twentieth century, in gaining access to management education and management careers in other types of employment settings.

By the end of the twentieth century, a complex system of human service organizations had been established in the United States. This included a large system of educational organizations, a large, and rapidly changing, system of health/mental health care organizations, a system of policing and juvenile and adult criminal justice organizations, and a very diverse system of social welfare programs and social service organizations. These organizations ranged in size from those that are worldwide in scope to very small organizations serving a single neighborhood or ethnic constituency. They included traditional, voluntary, nonprofit organizations, community-based or "alternative" nonprofit service organizations, governmental bureaus, quasi-governmental nonprofit organizations, and for-profit firms.

Human service organizations across different institutional sectors are very diverse. Individual service organizations are affected by broad social changes and by changes within specific service sectors. However, many aspects of management practice are also similar across differences in legal structure, differences in service programs, differences in size, differences in funding patterns. In particular, there are similarities in the management of relationships between the service organization and its operating environment. It is these areas of similarity in management practice across the diversity of human service organizations that are the focus of this book. In particular, this book deals with relationships of the human service organization with its operational environment and the political economy dynamics that shape those relationships.

INITIAL CONCEPTS

Human Service Organization

A group of core concepts that are used throughout this book are briefly identified here. Some are the focus of specific chapters. Others are recurrent themes in several chapters. *Human service organization* is one such concept. Early in the 1970s, as the number and variety of specialized service organizations increased, in part as a result of new forms of federal funding, governmental officials began to examine the concept of "services integration" (Austin 1978; Gans and Horton 1975). This was a response to the long-standing problem of fitting different types of specialized and categorical programs together within a single community, or the problem of linking such programs to serve a single household when a series of problem conditions are affecting household members.

In examining the processes of service delivery, it became apparent that there were large areas of similarity in organizational structure and management requirements that cut across traditional professional and discipline boundaries, as well as categorical funding distinctions (Agranoff and Pattaos 1970). Regardless of differences in the characteristics of specific services such as the care of patients in a hospital, the education of young children, and the adoption placement of a victim of child abuse, there was a high degree of similarity in the organizational processes and management tasks in nonprofit general hospitals, public elementary schools, family service agencies, neighborhood service centers, and public child welfare agencies. The term *human services* began to be used to describe a broad range of service programs with distinctive characteristics and a distinctive set of management requirements (Hasenfeld and English 1974; Hasenfeld 1983; Austin 1988). The characteristics of "human service programs" are set forth in more detail in chapter 2.

Traditionally, the term *human service organization* has been used to refer to voluntary nonprofit service organizations, quasi-governmental nonprofit organizations, and governmental bureaus that have similar service responsibilities (Hasenfeld 1983). However, in the era of privatization and managed care in which the provision of human services by for-profit firms is expanding rapidly, it is relevant to examine the application of the concepts of human service management to for-profit service production organizations. Although there are important distinctions among these different categories of service organizations—for example, in the structure of accountability—many human service management issues are quite similar. Similarities can be seen in the relationships between the service organization and service users, in the relationship of the service organization with professional specialists and organized professions, in the evaluation of organizational effectiveness, and in the functions of the human services executive. One critical element common to all types of human service organizations is the role of ethical standards in production of services and in policy-making and management functions (Reamer 1995).

Organization

Organization is a socially constructed concept. That is, the meaning of *organization* can vary markedly depending on the specific situation being described (Morgan 1986). However, in general, *organization* can be defined as a regular and ongoing set of structured activities involving a defined group of individuals. *Communal organizations* are those social structures that are created around personal and affective connections in which the continued existence of the social structure is the primary purpose of such activities. Communal organizations include families, friendship groups, communities, and societies (Hillary 1968). *Formal organizations* are those organizations that have an explicit productive purpose. That is, they are established to produce goods or services, or to make something happen in the larger social order within which they operate. Formal organizations use resources—"inputs"—from the larger society to create goods or services—"outputs"—that are, in turn, used within the larger society. Formal organizations also include *mutual benefit associations* that are established primarily to provide outputs, or benefits, to a defined group of members—individuals or organizations. Mutual benefit associations include, among others, credit unions, labor unions, and professional associations, as well as trade associations such as the Child Welfare League, the American Human Services Association (formerly the American Public Welfare Association), and the American Hospital Association.

Organizations are part of the larger society that constitutes the *organizational environment*. The "task environment" is the immediate social context. It includes other service organizations, service user households, other residents in the immediate community, local media, local business firms, funding sources specific to the organization, governmental policy-making bodies, and issue-oriented membership associations. The "societal environment" includes the larger political, social, and cultural context within which a particular organization is functioning (Martin 2000b).

Service Delivery Networks

Individual human service organizations participate in *service delivery networks* that develop around socially recognized problems or around the service needs of particular population groups (Austin 1991). Organizations are linked together by "boundary-spanning" exchanges involving user referrals, information exchanges, and financial transactions. The increasing complexity of service networks has led to the development of boundary-spanning "case management" support services. Case management services deal primarily with service users who have chronic conditions that require a variety of services, households with multiple service needs at one time, and multiproblem households that require multiple services on an ongoing basis. Service delivery networks are dealt with in more detail in chapter 5.

Stakeholder Constituencies

Although a human service organization can be viewed as a structured set of activities by a defined group of individuals, it can also be viewed as a field of action involving a number of different *stakeholder constituencies*, each of which has a "stake" in the performance of the organization. For-profit stock companies, or business firms, are legally defined as having a single, primary stakeholder constituency—that is, the stockholders, or "owners" of the firm. However, governmental and nonprofit service organizations have a number of different stakeholder constituencies, none of which is explicitly defined as being primary. These stakeholder constituencies, described in more detail in chapter 3, include service users, legitimators and funders, members of policy-making and advisory bodies, organizational staff members and their families, members of organized professions, and collateral service organizations, as well as advocacy organizations, the media, and members of the public.

Legitimation and Resources

Human service organizations require two types of fundamental inputs from the environment to operate—*legitimation* and *resources*, subjects that are dealt with further in chapter 8. *Legitimation* involves recognition within the larger social order that a particular organization exists and that it has a socially approved purpose. Legitimation may take such forms as legislation, incorporation, accreditation, licensing, recognition as a receiver of funding support from an established community funding source, or recognition as a receiver of other forms of support from the society such as volunteers. Legitimation is essential for the organization to receive the operational *resources* that are required for the organization to function on a regular and ongoing basis. These resources include money, personnel, service technologies, facilities, and operational supplies, as well as potential service users, either on a self-referral basis or as referrals from other sources. An initial ability to obtain such resources is a major element in establishing legitimation, and legitimation is essential to maintain a regular flow of such resources.

Private Goods and Public Goods

Both governmental and nonprofit human service organizations produce a mixture of *private goods* and *public goods* (Austin 1981; Austin 1988). *Private goods* include, among others, those benefits that are received by the immediate service user, or the household of which the service user is a part. Private goods benefits include the receipt of financial resources such as financial payments, food stamps, or subsidized housing; changes in one's own behavior or emotional responses that are valued by the service user; personal care and protection by another person; an increase in personal knowledge of a particular subject; the development of new skills; information that results in benefits for the service user; recovery from illness or injury, or improved personal health; protection from abuse; and legal defense of personal rights and possessions.

Public goods, or "collective" goods, are those benefits that accrue to other members of the community or of the whole society through the provision of private goods benefits to individuals and households. The education of individual students creates a productive labor force that results in a larger pool of goods and services that can be shared among members of the society. The vaccination of young children protects other children from contagious diseases. The provision of social services to women who are victims of violence provides a base for public education intended to reduce the level of violence in the community. The provision of economic supports in periods of high unemployment helps to maintain the economic and social structure of impacted communities. Human service organizations—in particular, nonprofit and governmental organizations—must maintain a balance between the production of private goods and that of public goods, consistent with the specific needs and expectations of service users and with the expectations of other members of the community or society who participate in the support of such an organization.

Accountability

The services that are produced by a marketplace for-profit organization are evaluated by individual service users who directly or indirectly (through insurance arrangements) pay the costs of such services, and who may continue their use of such services or change to another provider. Services that are produced through particular nonprofit and governmental human service organizations are often the only services available, particularly for individuals who cannot pay a marketplace price for such services. Moreover, such services involve a complex mixture of private benefits and public benefits. Provisions are required for establishing the accountability of such services to service users, to service funders, and to the community through systematic evaluation. These provisions are dealt with in more detail in chapter 11.

The specific products, or services, that are created by a human service organization can be evaluated using several different criteria (Martin and Kettner 1996). Among the more frequently used criteria are efficiency, effectiveness, and user satisfaction. *Efficiency* is a measure of the level, or amount, of outputs that result from a given level of inputs. Greater efficiency involves the production of more services from the same level of resource use, or the use of fewer resources to produce an existing level of services—for example, the use of group counseling procedures instead of a series of individual counseling sessions for persons recovering from substance addiction.

Effectiveness is a measure of the degree to which the services produced accomplish the purposes for which they are created—for example, the extent to which sixty days of intensive family preservation services makes it possible to maintain children in their homes who might otherwise require placement in a foster home or institution. *User satisfaction*, or "responsiveness," is a measure of the extent to which the goods or services provided through a human service organization are consistent with user expectations (Chism 1997). For example, do the parents who are seeking limited assistance that could make it possible for a child who has a developmental disability condition to remain in their home actually receive such services. Or, alternatively, do they receive a recommendation that the child should be placed in a residential institution because the organization is aware that there are specific sources of external funding for such residential care, whereas the costs for community-based services would have to come directly from the limited financial resources of the organization.

Different stakeholder constituencies may view one of these three criteria as being the most important, while recognizing the relative importance of the others. Funders may view efficient use of resources as being of central importance. Professional specialists may view technical effectiveness, whether in health care, teaching, or child welfare services for abused children, as being the most important. Service users and members of the community may view user satisfaction, or attentiveness to their immediate concerns, as most important. These differences in perspective contribute to the difficulties in assessing the contribution of specific service programs to an improved quality of life for members of the society.

Cultural Transformation

One of the most critical elements in the societal environment of human service organizations is the *cultural transformation* of the society of the United States. During the last decades of the nineteenth century and the first two decades of the twentieth century, a massive movement of European immigrants to the United States changed the cultural context of the society. What had previously been a society in which most persons lived in small towns and rural communities and in which Protestantism was the dominant religious perspective, became a city-centered society in which Roman Catholicism and Judaism also became influential elements in the social fabric. Members of both of these religious traditions became influential forces in local, state, and national political systems, in the developing system of human service programs, and in the national economy.

A second process of cultural transformation has been underway since the 1950s. Its beginnings included the movement of millions of African American citizens from the rural South to the urban North with the mechanization of cotton agriculture, the Supreme Court decisions dismantling the structure of legal segregation, and the civil rights movements of the 1960s. This was followed by attacks on traditional patterns of discrimination affecting women, and by the appearance of organized constituencies of gay, lesbian, and transsexual citizens. Changes in immigration policy, refugee populations, economic forces, and demography have resulted in a massive increase in the number of persons in the United States coming from cultural backgrounds rooted in Latin America, including Mexico, and from a wide variety of Asian nations. The model of ultimate assimilation of all newcomers into a Euro-American, English-speaking society is being replaced by a model of cultural and language diversity that links the population of the United States with every part of the world society. Economic globalization and worldwide communication through television and the Internet have contributed further to the diversity of cultural forces shaping the society of the United States.

The consequences of this cultural transformation are particularly visible among human service organizations. Increasing cultural diversity in the society affects the processes of organization formation, the selection of organizational employees (preference for multilingual employees), and the selection of members of policy-making bodies, both governmental and nongovernmental. Funding decisions and program design decisions are affected by the distinctive requirements of serving a wide variety of cultural populations, including large populations for whom English is not the language of daily conversation. The cultural traditions of diverse populations require adaptations of traditional service methods. The consequences of a governmental policy action, or a program administration directive, have to be analyzed in terms of the potential impacts on a large number of distinctive cultural communities, including American Indian tribes. The international diplomatic dilemmas dealt with by the Foreign Service establishment are duplicated by the cultural dilemmas dealt with within the United States by human service managers in education, health care, criminal justice, and social services.

THEORIES ABOUT ORGANIZATIONS

As background to an analysis of the management of human service organizations, it is useful to establish some general understandings about the analysis of formal organizations and to identify those underlying assumptions that are central to the content of this book.

Organizational Components

Formal organizations of any size or type can be viewed as having three functional subsystems. These three subsystems exist in all human service organizations but with different patterns of relationships among them— for example, in small nonprofit start-up organizations, established nonprofit organizations, governmental bureaucracies, and for-profit human service organizations.

The *institutional subsystem* involves those sets of activities that sustain the organization through exchanges with the organizational environment. These exchanges involve establishing procedures for obtaining resources of all types, or "inputs," from the environment, and establishing the organizational "policies," including service production policies, that connect the organization with the larger society and shape this flow of resources. The *management subsystem* involves those sets of activities that translate general policies into operational plans and procedures for the implementation of those policies. The *production subsystem* involves those sets of activities that translate operational plans and procedures into regular and ongoing processes of producing the services, or "outputs," that constitute the rationale for the existence of the organization. These service production activities are organized as program components, described further in chapter 4. Each program component involves a *program rationale*, or cause-and-effect theory, a *program strategy*, and specific *program intervention tactics*.

Most organizations also include support functions or auxiliary activities, such as personnel administration, accounting, public relations, clerical support services, and computer services, that facilitate the basic production processes, as well as specialized technical services, such as research, staff training, grant writing, and legislative lobbying, that directly influence the core policy-making, management, and production subsystems (Mintzberg 1979).

Open and Closed Social Systems

Using a general social system framework, organizations may be viewed as being closed social systems or open social systems in terms of the pattern of interaction with the social environment. *Closed social system* models assume that the significant elements affecting organizational performance are primarily within the boundaries of the organization. Such models assume that there are defined resource "inputs" from the environment and defined goods and services "outputs" to the environment, and that the transformation of inputs into outputs is shaped almost entirely by processes within the organization. For example, a closed system model would assume that a child protective services program can be analyzed by studying the input flow of funding resources, personnel resources, and referrals of abuse and neglect situations, with a further assumption that it is the way that organizational personnel manage the interactions of these elements that determines the pattern of services actually provided to children and to their families. Efforts to improve the efficiency, effectiveness, or responsiveness of such services would focus primarily on internal organizational processes.

Open social system models assume that there are multiple and continuous forms of interaction between an organization and its environment and that environmental forces affect all aspects of organizational performance. In the instance of a child protective services program, an open systems model would direct attention to factors other than resource inputs and internal organizational procedures that may have a substantial impact on the pattern of service outputs. These could include cultural attitudes toward child discipline, the level of media attention to child abuse situations, the state of the local economy, the role of elected officials in decisions about child abuse procedures, the availability of legal representation for parents, the impact of judicial decisions, and the curriculum content of professional education programs. In this model, efforts to improve the efficiency, effectiveness, or responsiveness of services would focus on forces in the organizational environment as well as on internal organizational processes.

It is assumed in this book that the human service organization is a "dynamic open system," meaning that the boundaries of the organization are "permeable," that all parts of the organization are regularly involved in exchanges with the environment, and that these exchanges have a continuous and variable impact on the organization and the quality of the services provided. Individuals who are part of the structure of a human service organization are involved in ongoing processes of interaction with the organizational environment. This includes individuals involved with the institutional subsystem, the management subsystem, and the production subsystem. For example, the actual pattern of services provided by a child protective services program may be affected as much by the personal reactions of front-line service workers to media criticisms of the program as by the formal statement of policies adopted by the agency board or by the program directives issued by the executive staff.

Organizational Dynamics

There are a variety of theories about the forces that shape organizational processes (Morgan 1986). Some theories assume that technological developments are the most significant factors in shaping organizational structure and performance. Scientific management theories in the early part of the twentieth century focused on the implications of new production methods for the organization of workers in industrial firms like steel plants and automobile factories (Taylor 1947). Contingency theories have emphasized the role of differences in production technologies in shaping differences in organizational structure (Lawrence and Lorsch 1967; Thompson 1967). More recently, new developments in information technology have been viewed as central to the restructuring or "reengineering" of business firms.

Some theories assume that economic factors are the most powerful forces shaping organizational performance. Current emphases on the role of marketplace competition in improving efficiency in the provision of health care rely largely on economic analyses. Population ecology theories focus on the role of economic forces in determining the growth, survival, or disappearance of individual organizations or groups of organizations (Carroll 1988). Public choice theories focus on the role of economic self-interest in motivating human behavior, including the behavior of organizational participants (Buchanan 1962).

Human relations theories give the most prominence to psychological forces related to the role of human motivation in organizational performance (Vinokur-Kaplan and Bogin 2000). Such theories are central to organizational development (OD) approaches to the improvement of organizational performance (Argyris 1962). Japanese quality circles are one recent example of the application of such psychological theories. Organic theories are biological analogies for analyzing organizational dynamics; they include theories about organizational growth and decay and organizational life cycles. Neo-Marxian theories focus on ways in which societal patterns of power and conflict affect the dynamics of growth and survival in individual organizations.

This book gives primary attention to two bodies of theory about the forces that shape organizational dynamics. One is institutional theory; the other is political economy theory. Institutional theorists such as Selznick (1957), Zucker (1988), and Powell and DiMaggio (1991) view organizational processes as being shaped by social and cultural patterns in the larger society that result in consistencies of organizational patterns in otherwise unconnected organizations. Traditions and assumptions in society about the nature of nonprofit organizations, including such concepts as the "fiduciary responsibility of boards of directors to protect and conserve organizational assets," result in a general pattern of organizational decision making among nonprofit organizations that differs from that in for-profit firms. Institutionalized patterns of ethnic and gender discrimination have consistently shaped the patterns of service delivery in many types of otherwise unconnected human service organizations in past decades. Today, the existence of society-wide efforts to dismantle such discrimination has a similar impact on organizational behavior in nonprofit organizations, governmental bureaus, and for-profit firms. Institutional theory thus emphasizes the importance of a variety of external, societal patterns on processes within individual organizations, including human service organizations.

Political economy theory assumes that it is the interplay between *"political" forces*, including, but not limited to, those forces involved in community and societal governance, and the forces that shape *economic resources* in the organizational environment that determine the processes of legitimation and the distribution of resources in the society that, in turn, create opportunities for, or constraints on, the performance of individual organizations (Zald 1970; Benson 1975; Mintzberg 1983; Austin 1988). In addition, it is the interplay between "political" forces within organizations and forces controlling economic resources that shapes the internal dynamics of the service organization.

The use of institutional theories and political economy theories reflects the emphasis in this book on the importance of understanding the external forces that shape organizational processes in human service organizations. These theories direct the attention of human service managers to the impact of persistent institutional patterns in the larger society on the individual organization and to the interaction of political and economic forces in shaping the legitimation of the organization and the flow of resources to that organization.

Theories of Organizational Management

Just as *organization* is a socially constructed concept, *organizational management* is also a socially constructed concept. As the scale and complexity of the world of organizations has increased throughout the twentieth century, a number of different conceptual frameworks have been proposed for examining the relationships between organizational functioning and management performance (Ashley and Van de Ven 1983; Kanter 1997).

Theories about the relation between organizational processes and managerial practice can be analyzed along two dimensions:

- Micro level versus macro level—that is, the degree to which a discrete individual organization is the focus of analysis or, alternatively, the degree to which the experience of a single organization is viewed in the context of a population of organizations or a network of organizations
- Deterministic versus voluntaristic—that is, the degree to which events in the organization are viewed as largely controlled by structural constraints within and outside of the organization over which individual managers have little control or, alternatively, the degree to which events are viewed as being shaped primarily by the deliberate actions of organizational managers and other organizational participants

The combination of these two dimensions provides a framework of analysis (Ashley and Van de Ven 1983); the relationship of the elements is shown in the following table:

	Deterministic	Voluntaristic
Microlevel	System-structural	Strategic choice
Macrolevel	Natural selection	Collective action

These elements can be described as follows:

- System-structural: Organizational processes within individual organizations are viewed as being largely "deterministic"—that is, determined by impersonal mechanisms that act as external constraints on organizational participants. The manager's basic role is reactive, fine-tuning the performance of the organization to deal effectively with the circumstances that confront it.
- Strategic choice: Individual organizations are constantly constructed, sustained, and changed by participants' definitions of the situation. The environment is not a set of intractable constraints; it can be changed and manipulated through negotiation processes. Managers

are regarded as performing a "voluntaristic" proactive role; their choices are viewed as autonomous; and their actions are viewed as energizing forces that can shape the organizational experience (Oliver 1988).

- Natural selection: Societal environmental resources—in particular, economic resources—are structured in the form of "niches" that are relatively intractable to manipulation by single organizations. There are definite limits as to the degree to which autonomous strategic choice is available. Primacy is ascribed to the "deterministic" environment that inhibits choice by channeling organizations in predetermined directions. Whole populations of organizations are viewed as surviving, or failing, regardless of the actions taken by single organizations. The managerial role in the growth or survival of a single organization is largely symbolic or limited to organizational maintenance, having little to do with the long-term survival or disappearance of the organization.

- Collective action: Societal conditions can be shaped by "voluntaristic" purposeful action at a collective level. Organizational survival is achieved by collaborative efforts among organizations to construct a regulated and predictable social environment. A key concept is the role of the interorganizational network as an interlocking system of exchange relationships negotiated among members of different organizations as they jointly make efforts to shape their environments. Movements toward solutions to organizational challenges are guided by norms, customs, and laws—the working rules of collective action. Managers' roles are interactive. They interact actively with others through collective bargaining, negotiation, compromise, political maneuvering, and advocacy.

This book uses a strategic choice model of managerial behavior, with a focus primarily at the level of the individual organization and with managers viewed as having a voluntaristic, proactive role in the shaping of organizational processes both within the organization and in the interactions between the organization and its environment. This book recognizes that managers may also play a proactive role in collective action involving other organizations and associations in efforts to shape the broader societal environment that impacts the organization. However, this book does not deal specifically with that aspect of the managerial role.

SUMMARY

Human service organizations emerged as societal institutions during the last half of the nineteenth century as part of the rationalization of the social order in the United States. Complex and expanding systems of human service organizations in health care, education, social services, and criminal justice developed during the twentieth century, shaped by the changes taking place in the society of the United States. These systems included voluntary nonprofit, quasi-governmental nonprofit, governmental, and for-profit organizations. An understanding of the characteristics of these organizations and of the forces that impact their development is essential for organizational managers, organizational policy makers, and the professional practitioners who participate in the provision of services to individuals, households, and communities.

This book uses an open-system perspective in examining the dynamics of human service organizations. The development of the human service organization, whether in social services, health care, education, or criminal justice, is shaped as much by forces outside the organization as by the forces within the organization. Both institutional and political economy frameworks are used to examine ways that these external forces impact management practice. The book uses a strategic choice model of managerial action, focused primarily at the level of the individual organization. Managers are viewed as having a proactive role in the shaping of organizational processes both within the organization and in the interactions between the organization and its environment.

OVERVIEW

Chapters 2 through 5 provide an overview of the human service organization and the social structures that shape the organization. Chapter 2 deals with the characteristics of human service organizations that create a distinctive setting for managerial practice. Chapter 3 deals with the general characteristics of the several stakeholder constituencies that create a diverse, and often conflictual, environment for managerial practice. Chapter 4 deals with variations in organizational structure among human service organizations and with program design—that is, the ways in which human resources are systematically organized to respond to particular types of service requirements. Chapter 5 deals with the relation of the individual service organization to multiorganization service delivery networks.

Chapters 6 through 10 deal with the system participants that shape the performance of the human service organization. Chapter 6 deals with the roles that service users play in human service organizations. Chapter 7 deals with the roles of organizational staff members—in particular, the ways in which professional specialists and organized professions participate in the production of human services. Chapter 8 deals with the role of legitimation sources and funding sources in shaping the management of human service organizations. Chapter 9 deals with the role of the executive in human service organizations. Chapter 10 deals with the roles of boards of directors, governmental policy bodies, and advisory committees in the direction of service organizations.

Chapters 11 and 12 deal with two critical processes that are particularly significant for contemporary human service organizations. Chapter 11 deals with accountability and the assessment of organizational effectiveness. Chapter 12 deals with the processes of organizational change.

TWO

HUMAN SERVICE ORGANIZATIONS

All organizations need raw material as input to produce their products. Human service organizations are distinguished by the fundamental fact that people are their "raw material." . . . I want to highlight the fact that the core activities of the organization are structured to process, sustain, or change people who come under its jurisdiction. It is this transformational process to which people are subjected . . . [that] differentiates human service organizations from other bureaucracies. . . . Inherent in people work is the fact that it is also moral work. —Hasenfeld (1992a:4–5)

D URING THE 1970s, the term *human service organization* began to appear in discussions of governmental service programs. At first, the term was applied primarily to consolidated state government administrative organizations that included some combination of social services, mental health, and health services (Demone and Harshberger 1974; Gans and Horton 1975; Austin 1978). However, by the 1980s this term was being applied to a broad spectrum of service production organizations, including voluntary nonprofit and governmental nonprofit as well as governmental bureaus in a number of different fields of service (Stein 1981; Hasenfeld 1983; Austin 1988).

The concept of human service organizations was based on similarities in organizational structures and organizational processes in social services, health and mental health services, education services, and criminal justice services, although the production technologies, technical skills, and service products were different. Moreover, it was argued, there were significant differences between this group of human service production organizations and other types of service production organizations (Austin 1983a; Hasenfeld 1983). More recently, it has become evident that the concept of human service organization also includes for-profit firms producing similar service products. Indeed, it is particularly in the area of human service organizations that traditional distinctions between for-profit, governmental, and nonprofit, third sector, or "non-owned" organizations have become the most blurred (Najam 1996; Goddeeris and Weisbrod 1997; Kramer 1998).

There are many areas of overlap between human service organizations and other types of service production organizations (Fitzsimmons and Fitzsimmons 1994). For example, there are both similarities and differences between nonprofit child welfare agencies and nonprofit theater companies. There are both similarities and differences between a county highway department and a county social service department. And there are both similarities and differences between a chain of for-profit psychiatric hospitals and a chain of for-profit hotels.

However, there is disagreement as to whether *human service organization* is a true analytic classification—that is, whether there are consistent distinctions between all human service organizations and all other types of service production organizations, or whether the differences among human service organizations are at least as important as their similarities (Stein 1981). There are also authors who intend the term *human services* to be limited to "social services" and who discuss only those organizational settings in which social workers are the dominant professional group or at least a recognized professional specialty (Haynes 1989; Weiner 1990; Edwards and Yankey 1991; Lewis, Lewis, and Souflee 1991). Although the background of this author is primarily connected with social work and social welfare organizations, and many illustrative examples are drawn from such organizations, a more inclusive definition of human services is used in this book.

In this book, *human service organization* is used as a descriptive category, not as a formal analytic category. Although the boundaries of the definition of *human service organization* are fuzzy, a set of core characteristics, when taken together, make human service organizations a distinctive context for managerial performance. One of the important consequences of these distinctive characteristics is that organizational managers in human service organizations deal continuously with a series of *unresolvable dilemmas*, dilemmas that are inherent in the nature of human service organizations. Hasenfeld (1992a) describes these as human service organization "enigmas." Both organizational structures and service production processes involve complex trade-offs among important human values and important organizational goals. There is no ultimate "correct" structure or "correct" service production process in any human service organization that completely resolves these dilemmas.

THE HUMAN SERVICES

The concept of human services can include the following (Austin 1988):

- Education and socialization of children and youth
- Prevention of illness, accident, interpersonal violence, and psychological and social distress
- Care, treatment, and rehabilitation of individuals who are ill, including those with mental illness
- Transfer of economic resources, or the direct provision of food, shelter, and medical care to individuals and households without such resources
- Care, treatment, and rehabilitation of individuals with disability conditions
- Care and protection of dependent persons
- Mutual assistance in emergencies and catastrophes
- Control of dangerous or deviant individual behavior
- Development of work skills
- Recreation and social activities
- Information and counseling for individuals with psychological difficulties
- Development of social interaction skills involved in group participation and in collective decision making
- The organization of problem solving groups
- The organization of social support groups and support networks

In addition to these areas of direct service production, the term *human service organization* may be applied to related support service organizations such as planning and coordination organizations, issue advocacy organizations, and technical service organizations.

All of these "human" services may be produced within family and friendship networks as well as by individuals for themselves. Indeed, on a worldwide basis, it is clear that families and individuals are the primary producers of such services. It is only in diverse and changing industrial and postindustrial societies, like the United States, that the production of the full range of these services takes place on a large scale through formal organizations.

CHARACTERISTICS OF HUMAN SERVICE ORGANIZATIONS

The day-to-day operation of human service organizations involves many processes that are common to all formal production organizations, including all types of service production organizations (Fitzsimmons and Fitzsimmons 1994). These include the management of financial resources, recruitment and selection of personnel, the motivation and coordination of the activities of a variety of individuals, the balancing of centralization and decentralization forces in the organization of technical production activities, protection of the continuity of the organization, the development of internal information systems, and the monitoring of organizational results. Considerable attention has been given in recent years to the transfer of organizational and administrative concepts from for-profit production firms to human service organizations on the basis of similarities in these core processes. Competence in these core management processes is a necessary, *but not sufficient*, condition for the effective management of human service organizations. It is the distinctive characteristics of human service organizations that are the most critical for the development of effective management.

This chapter deals with the distinctive characteristics of the production of human services through governmental, quasi-governmental, voluntary nonprofit, and for-profit organizations and with the organizational implications of these characteristics. These distinctive characteristics have implications for the structure of the organization and the organizational production processes as well as for the activities of the specific individuals who are part of a human service organization.

Moral Decisions

The production of human services includes critical decisions that involve complex value judgments and have moral consequences. The choices involved have crucial and often long-lasting consequences for the lives of individuals:

- The selection of an inracial or transracial adoptive family for an infant
- The decision to prolong the life of a physically handicapped premature infant
- The choice by a teacher between giving greater individual attention to the college-bound high school student or the potential dropout
- The advice of a high school counselor to a high school student regarding academic and career options
- The organizing of a neighborhood association in a deteriorating urban neighborhood to protest the efforts of a "gentrifying" developer to replace low-cost housing with expensive housing
- The choice of a family therapy procedure for use in a disrupted marriage in which divorce is being considered
- The decision between institutional placement, or respite care and support, for the parents of a multihandicapped child
- The choice between family preservation services or court-ordered removal of an abused child from her or his home
- The assignment of priorities among emergency room patients
- The decision between voluntary admission or legal commitment of an individual to a psychiatric hospital
- The choice of a disability definition that may provide essential income for an adult living in the community who has a mental retardation condition
- The choice of a recipient of a donor heart to be used in a heart transplant

These are morally important value decisions. They are not neutral, value-free decisions; the option that is selected is intended to "do good." Sometimes these decisions are made by an individual service provider, sometimes by the service user, and sometimes jointly. These decisions may also involve choices by organizational leaders among service program designs or public policies. As Hasenfeld (1992a:5) states, "Every action taken on behalf of clients represents not only some form of concrete services . . . but also a moral judgment and statement about their social worth." The importance of these decisions has been highlighted by the attention that has been given to the "ethical" decisions that families and health-care specialists must make in many hospital situations as well as by the debates over ethical issues involving transracial adoptions, the allocation of organ transplants, and affirmative action decisions in college or university admissions. The outcomes of the decisions that are made are judged in human value terms, not just in instrumental terms. The choice to use the withdrawal of social benefits, the enforcement of constraints, or other forms of individual punishment in an effort to achieve the objectives of a service program is first, and foremost, a moral decision rather than an issue of relative program efficiency.

> There is another sense in which working on people is inherently moral. Fundamental to such work are decisions about the allocation of resources to the clients. These may include money, time and expertise. Inevitably, the demand for these resources outstrips their supply, resulting in a system of rationing (e.g. first come first served, clients with the greatest perceived need, younger over older patients). Rationing resources to clients involves a moral categorization of deservingness.
>
> —Hasenfeld (2000:330)

Persons involved in the production of human services are considered to be morally accountable for the consequences of their individual actions. This applies to personnel working in for-profit human service organizations as well as those working in nonprofit, quasi-governmental, and governmental service organizations. Indeed, much of the basis for the concept of professional malpractice rests on the assumption that the professional specialist has a direct, personal, moral accountability for providing services that are "helpful," not "harmful" (Reamer 1995). Organizational personnel, however, often face conflicting definitions of what is "good," or "helpful," based on the perspectives of individual service users, organizational policy makers, the courts, professional peers, the media, or special-interest advocates.

Given the significance of value choices, normative criteria and ethical guidelines are essential elements in the organizational culture. These guidelines may be embodied in an accepted definition of the history of the organizational mission, or in normative statements set forth by policy makers and/or the organizational executive—or they may be implicit in the culture of the organization. In some areas of activity, ethical guidelines are determined entirely within the organization; in other areas of activity, these guidelines are embodied in law, such as laws dealing with ethnic and/or religious criteria in adoption decisions or those dealing with abortion. In many human service organizations, normative criteria and guidelines are based on a code of ethics that has been adopted by an organized profession (National Association of Social Workers 1996), or on positions taken by professional bodies. In individual health-care organizations, the assessment of the ethical and moral implications involved in particular treatment decisions may be assigned to an ethical review board. In organizations sponsored by religious bodies, the normative criteria may be drawn from specific religious traditions.

These normative criteria and guidelines, including the definition of worthiness, become important elements in the organizational culture through the formal, and informal, processes of orientation for new organizational personnel and as they are reinforced through ongoing training and retraining of existing personnel (Hasenfeld 2000). The recognition of normative criteria and a commitment to the use of such criteria in the work setting also become the standard, either explicit or implicit, in the selection of personnel. These normative criteria also play a role in admission decisions for the professional education programs that prepare professional specialists to work in these organizations. And these normative criteria are reinforced by the standards of professional licensing and credentialing bodies.

Regardless of the nature of the organizational culture and the existence of explicit rules and regulations, front-line personnel necessarily exercise a substantial degree of autonomy, acknowledged or unacknowledged, since any application of value-based judgments involves individual perceptions, attitudes, and beliefs (Lipsky 1980). Given the critical consequences of many of these decisions, there is often some form of organizational provision for review, or appeal, of decisions in individual situations. These provisions may include regular review of decisions by supervisors or consultants, review by professional peer bodies or ethical review boards, mandatory court review (for example, in the case of an agency decision to remove a child from a birth family), formal appeal procedures within the organization, provision for formal negotiation of service plan decisions, external complaint channels, external case advocacy organizations, ombudsmen, and individual appeals to the court system. The role of moral or normative criteria, and the procedures for enforcing them, are particularly critical issues in the production of human services by for-profit organizations—for example, in for-profit managed health-care organizations.

Mixed-Goods Benefits

Human service organizations produce services that result in both "public" benefits and "private" benefits. Governmental and voluntary nonprofit human service organizations are created through collective action—by a voluntary group of individuals or through the decision-making processes of government—to fulfill a public purpose rather than a primarily private profit or private benefit purpose (Goddeeris and Weisbrod 1997). In fulfilling this public purpose, the services that most human service organizations produce, by intent, result in "mixed-goods" benefits—that is, they are designed to produce specific "primary" benefits to individuals (private goods) and also "spill-over" or "secondary" benefits to other members of a local community or to the members of society (public goods) (Austin 1988). The distinctions between private goods and public goods, in the instance of any one organization, may be largely definitional and may shift depending on the audience.

The public-goods benefits (sometimes called "collective" goods) may be, in part, a consequence of the universal availability of the service (elementary education services, for example) or the redistributional characteristics of the service (the provision of unemployment benefits to unemployed workers so that they can stay in their home and maintain their purchasing power in the local economy). Public-goods benefits may also include the behavior change or social control results of the service—for example, changes in the public behavior of an individual with severe delusional symptoms of mental illness (Austin 1988) or the economic self-support initiatives of individuals previously receiving tax-supported benefits under the Aid for Families with Dependent Children (AFDC) program. Many traditional types of residential services, including psychiatric hospitals, juvenile criminal justice facilities, and shelters for homeless individuals, have been established both to provide care and treatment for particular individuals and to remove such persons, and their potentially disruptive behavior, from the local community.

Many voluntary nonprofit and governmental human service organizations are established with the intent of having a specific service available in a specific locality—an elementary school, a community hospital, a residential home for abused and neglected children, a neighborhood daycare center, or a psychiatric hospital to serve a particular region of a state. An important part of the public-goods benefits of such services is the financial benefit for the local economy, including the wages and salaries of employees and the local purchase of supplies. Indeed, the public-goods benefits provided through the availability of high-quality human services—a good school system—may be directly reflected in the economic valuation of local property.

The production of human services by for-profit firms may also result in mixed-goods benefits, although the production of the public-goods benefits may not be an explicit objective of the firm. However, the availability of high-quality prenatal and obstetric services in a for-profit hospital is a benefit for the community as well as being a private benefit for specific mothers and infants. Provision of remedial education services by a for-profit firm for a school-age child may benefit the school system in which the child is a student, as well as the child and the family. Indeed, for-profit human service firms, as well as other for-profit businesses, may emphasize to the local community their public-goods contributions in the form of charitable donations, sponsorship of educational activities, and participation in civic organizations. But by narrowly defining the services to be provided without any consideration of public-goods benefits, a for-profit organization may be able provide such services at a cost that is lower than comparable costs in a nonprofit or governmental human service organization.

The production of mixed-goods benefits means that the human service organization must pursue two sets of objectives simultaneously: objectives that define the benefits intended to be produced for service users, and objectives that define the benefits intended to be produced for the local community, state, or national society. This represents one of the human service "enigmas" to which Hasenfeld (1992a) refers.

In many instances, the "private" benefits to be produced for service users are, in reality, "merit goods" (Austin 1981). That is, the benefit characteristics of the private goods are defined by someone other than the service users themselves (Musgrave 1959). The private-goods benefits for the adult caretaker in the Temporary Assistance to Needy Families (TANF) programs have been defined by public policy as the preparation of, and motivation of, that person to become economically self-supporting through employment, in place of the transfer of financial resources to the household under the AFDC program. This is in contrast to Social Security Survivor's Insurance and Military Dependents Allowances, in which the objective is to make a private benefit transfer of economic resources for household support without specific behavioral requirements. Similarly, the benefits for students in the local tax-supported educational system are often defined by action of the local school board as the preparation of competent workers for the employment market rather than as the provision of a student-defined program of personal development.

Most human service organizations have several program components and produce several different service products, each involving a different part of the organization (see chapter 5). Each service product involves a different mix of private-goods objectives and public-goods objectives, requiring different adaptations to user constituencies and other external constituencies. For example, the athletic program in a high school involves a mix of private-goods benefits—good health and the development of individual athletic skills—and public-goods benefits—public entertainment—that is quite different from the mix of objectives in specialized college-oriented advance placement courses in the same school. The private-goods/public-goods characteristics of services for individuals with chronic and severe mental illness provided by a community mental health center are different from the preventive mental health education services provided by the center for a local school district.

These variations among service components in the mix of public-goods and private-goods objectives, and in the external constituencies that are concerned with the public goods, contributes to the "loose-coupling" characteristics of human service organizations (Ouchi 1978). Because there is a different mix of operational objectives and of external constituencies for each service component, there are, typically, only loose connections among the different program components and, indeed, between each program component and the central management and policy structure of the inclusive organization. The dilemmas posed by the mix of program objectives among program components are reflected in the difficulties often experienced in defining a single set of organizational objectives for the purposes of evaluating the effectiveness of the total organization.

In the human service organization, a constant tension exists between two dynamics. The first dynamic is the reinforcing of organizational structures intended to maintain consistent central control over the production of public-goods benefits by the organization as a whole. The second is the decentralizing of authority over budgetary and personnel resources in order to encourage the development of the distinctive elements of each program component that are responsive to the private-goods needs and preferences of distinctive groups of service users.

A significant aspect of organizational structure, under these conditions, is the existence of "buffering mechanisms" between different parts of the organization; these mechanisms serve to contain the conflicts over priorities, as among the different program component objectives. In particular, program supervisors often provide a buffer between direct service personnel in different program components and central administrative and policy personnel. This buffering permits direct service personnel to adapt general rules and directives to the idiosyncratic situations of distinct groups of service users, while administrators and policy makers lay claim to the public-goods benefits for the community on the basis of broad organizational objectives and official program regulations.

Co-production

There is another important source of technological indeterminacy that distinguishes human service organizations, having to do with the ability of clients to react and participate in the service technology.

—Hasenfeld (1992a:15)

Effective production of human services requires co-production—that is, person-to-person interactions between service specialists and service users and self-initiated actions on the part of the service user (see chapter 6). The production of many types of human services requires interaction between the service user and the service specialist in which both parties are active parts of the effective production process—examples include the elementary teacher with children in a single classroom where effective education requires active participation by the students in "learning," a childcare worker working with a group of children in a residential institution to develop a self-directed process of group decision making, and the social worker in an interactive verbal counseling session with a rape victim.

To be effective, other services require the initiation of action on the part of the service user—the social worker working with the parents of an abused child when the objective is for the parents to take responsibility for incorporating changes in their habitual patterns of behavior, the ward nurse in a surgical recovery ward where the rate of recovery depends heavily on the behaviors and attitudes of the patients, a family therapist interacting with a family group in which the members practice new forms of communication with each other between counseling sessions, the physician encouraging a patient with high blood pressure to make changes in personal life style, the probation officer working with a teenager to persuade him to change his pattern of personal behavior in the community. Even law enforcement and the implementation of "social control" procedures affecting persons who have committed crimes depends to a very large degree on the peaceful compliance of most arrested individuals with the verbal instructions of law enforcement personnel.

The process of establishing eligibility for the federally administered Supplemental Security Income (SSI) disability assistance program or the state-administered TANF program providing financial assistance to families requires co-production through the provision of accurate personal information by the applicant in response to the questions of the eligibility worker. Moreover, the quality of the ultimate outcomes that result from the provision of financial support payments and other services under TANF programs is highly dependent on the self-initiated behaviors of the adult recipients rather than on the actions of program staff members.

Each type of service production activity—the treatment of a mental illness, the education of a young child, or the protection of an abused spouse—involves a "service trajectory" (Strauss et al. 1985:8) or course of action in which the service user is an active participant. The "reactivity" or pattern of compliance by the service user with the expectations involved in that course of action largely determines the effectiveness of the service production process (Littell, Alexander, and Reynolds 2001). An essential element in the *effective* delivery of most types of human services is the *motivation* of the service user to become an active participant in this service co-production process. In many human service programs, the "empowerment" of the service user—that is, the motivation of the service user to take personal responsibility for initiating positive action—may become a primary objective of the service (Rapp and Poertner 1992).

The support of co-production may include a mix of supportive reinforcement and rewards as well as critical feedback, constraints, and punishments. Decisions about the mix of positive reinforcements and negative constraints that are used to encourage co-production participation are a critical program design decision. Such decisions are also made by service providers in individual situations. The use of constraints and punishments to encourage user compliance with the expectations for co-production is often affected by the extent to which participation in the service production process is voluntary or involuntary.

Services in which the service user has other options for obtaining services, or the opportunity to express objections about the quality of services—that is, the service user has "exit" options and/or "voice" options (Hirschman 1970)—are more likely to use rewards and reinforcements to support co-production participation, whereas services in which the user has neither exit options nor voice options—public psychiatric hospitals and adult criminal justice institutions—are more likely to use constraints and punishments in an effort to encourage cooperative co-production behavior.

The level of co-production motivation of the service users becomes a significant factor in analyzing the dynamics of service production. Such an analysis requires that the relevant definition of the system boundaries of the human service organization includes service users within the boundaries of the production system. It also requires organizational and program design elements that encourage and support co-production. Specific provisions may deal with program access, program characteristics that support continuance of effort on the part of the user, acknowledgment of the contributions of the service user to effective production, and provision for systematic feedback from service users about the quality of the co-production process.

Gender Structure

Human service organizations are shaped by the institutionalized gender structure of production tasks in the larger society. "Historically, the care of people has been entrusted to women, and the bureaucratization of human care resulted in the predominance of women as human service workers" (Hasenfeld 1992a:7). Traditionally, there have been gender-structured distinctions between human service workers and workers in production activities in many other aspects of society. Social workers, elementary and secondary teachers, child-care workers, and nurses have nearly all been women; factory workers, soldiers, farmers, professional athletes, stock brokers, business executives, public administrators, and elected public officials have nearly all been men.

Traditional gender distinctions have also existed within human services. Organizational executives have been men, as have university professors, physicians, lawyers, and workers in criminal justice institutions, whereas women have been the core direct-service workers in social services, nursing, day care, and elementary and secondary education. These occupational distinctions have been reflected in differences in power and authority within society, as well as in the pattern of economic rewards.

The adult users of human services are also predominately women (except in criminal justice services) either directly or acting in behalf of children or of persons who have limited ability to act for themselves because of disability or illness. Women are most often the victims of violence and exploitation. They are, in some instances, the only stable adult present in households with young children. Pregnancy and child birth are the major health-care concerns among younger adults. Women are often the hands-on caretakers of persons with disability conditions or an illness and of older adults who need assistance in the activities of daily living. Because women have longer life careers, in particular in the population over age eighty-five, they are the vast majority of persons who use social and health services of all types. Women are frequently the majority of household participants in neighborhood associations, parent–teacher associations, or "grass-roots" advocacy organizations, and they are often the leaders of such groups.

During the second half of the twentieth century, changes have occurred in traditional gender occupational patterns. Women have become a large part of the industrial work force, not only in the United States but worldwide, as well of the military establishment. Increasing numbers of women are business executives, public administrators, and public officials. Increasing numbers of women are physicians, lawyers, university faculty members, judges, and executives in human service organizations.

At the beginning of the twenty-first century, there are two significant characteristics of the gender structure of human services. First, the core direct service activities in elementary and secondary teaching, social services, day care, and nursing are still primarily provided by women. Second, human service programs are one of the crucial arenas in which changes in gender roles are taking place.

There is little agreement about the causes of the persistent gender structure of human service organizations. Similarities can be found among the "unpaid"—in terms of a formal wage or salary structure—tasks of the family homemaker, the unpaid tasks carried out by service volunteers (largely women), and the "poorly paid" care taking or "maternalistic" direct service tasks of teachers, nurses, and social workers. One similarity of all of these positions, in general, is that they have a low level of social power and authority in settings in which men generally have more power.

It has been argued that women, in general, bring a distinctively female pattern of values to "human service" tasks, a pattern that is reinforced by the gender structure of early childhood socialization of girls (Gilligan 1982). These are values that give priority to social connections and person-to-person caring relationships in contrast to primarily instrumental relationships and impersonal rule-structured organizational processes. The social values of women have also been viewed as including altruism, which Wakefield (1993), in "Is Altruism Part of Human Nature? Towards a Theoretical Foundation for the Helping Professions," argues is fundamental to human service professions.

One of the forces for institutional change in gender patterns throughout the human services is a focus on "empowerment," primarily as applied to women as service users. Empowerment can mean changes in the relation of women who are service users to service providers as well as changes in the relation of women to patterns of unequal treatment and discrimination in their social environment. The concept of empowerment is particularly relevant in human service programs that include women who are working in low-wage, exploitative industrial settings, in programs that include women who have been the victims of violence, in the relationship of women to service providers who are the caretakers of children or of persons with a disability condition. Empowerment can have specific consequences for women in dealing with "bureaucratic" service programs as well as in confronting human service organizations that have low wages and salaries for direct care workers and institutional barriers to the access of women to supervisory and management positions.

Human service programs are also being affected by changes in the roles of women in the larger society in addition to specific forces that shape the roles of women in human service occupations and human service organizations. Many of these changes were set in motion by the women's rights movement and an emphasis on affirmative action for women during the 1970s and 1980s. These include changes in the gender characteristics of legislatures and of policy-making bodies in nonprofit and governmental organizations, as well as potentially in for-profit firms, continuing changes in the gender pattern of all types of organizational executives, and in demographic patterns across human service professions, including university faculty. Women make up more than half of all college and university students and are enrolled in increasing numbers in the traditional male professional schools in law, medicine, and business administration.

Service Professionals

The production of human services depends heavily on service specialists who are members of organized professions—social workers, teachers, nurses, physicians, rehabilitation counselors, psychologists, lawyers. To varying degrees, professional practitioners in service organizations are involved in dual loyalties to the service organization and to their profession (see chapter 7). Membership in an organized profession provides professionals an alternative power base independent of the authority of the executive and the policy-making board. As Mintzberg (1979:351) points out, "The standards of the Professional Bureaucracy originate largely outside its own structure, in the self-governing associations its operators join with their colleagues from other Professional Bureaucracies." Personal career choices may be influenced more by professional status opportunities than by organizational loyalty and opportunities for internal promotion. Service production behavior of professional specialists may be shaped in significant ways by the content of professional education, by professional peers, and by exposure to new information through professional channels of communication.

The professionalized human service organization is an inherently "loosely coupled" organization (Ouchi 1978), within which authority is diffused (Mintzberg 1979). Hierarchical models of authority in which all personnel are subject to the direct authority of the executive are generally not applicable, depending on the intensity and pervasiveness of professionalization. Unlike organizational relationships with labor unions, in which the authority of the union depends largely on its formal recognition by managers and policy makers, the authority of organized professions is not dependent on formal recognition by an employing organization. Organized professions are part of the institutional environment over which any single service organization has limited control. Organizational structure and program design are directly affected by professional definitions over which administrators have little control. Job positions are frequently defined by professional titles. Professional specialists may expect to be assigned responsibilities consistent with their professional identity regardless of the actual task requirements of a particular program activity.

Relationships among professional specialists within service organizations often reflect institutionalized distinctions, and conflicts, within the larger society, such as the conflicts among social workers, psychologists, and psychiatrists over their respective roles in mental health therapy, or among social workers and nurses over their respective roles in hospital discharge planning and case management, or among school counselors, visiting teachers, and social workers in school settings. Such conflicts among professional groups, which cannot be resolved within any single service organization, are often a significant factor in internal organizational tensions.

These "professional turf" conflicts may result in rules and organizational rigidities that may control the assignment of responsibilities to particular staff members, the introduction of new technologies, and the possibilities for innovative reorganization of organizational staff components. Professional criteria, often reinforced by state licensing requirements, substantially limit executive options in the employment of individuals for particular staff positions. Moreover, transferable professional credentials become increasingly important for the individual human service professional practitioner, given the inability to depend on long-term employment in a single organization and the rate of personnel change within many human service organizations.

Professional credentialing and licensing requirements often limit the ability of entry-level employees within a single organization to achieve a greater degree of authority and a higher income through seniority and internal promotions unless they also have specialized education outside of the organization. This particularly affects individuals employed as aides, or paraprofessionals, who may come from the service community and have specialized knowledge about the backgrounds of service users.

Some "professionalized" human service organizations are essentially only a group practice setting for individual professional specialists. In the for-profit sector, this may take the form of a "professional corporation." However, in most instances, professional services are produced within the framework of a structured "service program." Examples include the curriculum structure within which the teaching activities of individual teachers are carried out not only in elementary and secondary schools but also in colleges and universities; the systematic and interrelated procedures of a hospital emergency room or surgical operating room within which medical and nursing services are provided by individual medical practitioners; and the coordinated pattern of services involving different occupational specialties required for the treatment of an individual with chronic mental illness. Even the practice of general medicine becomes part of a service program structure in managed health-care systems. The structure of such service programs involves an interface between professional specialists and administrative personnel in which the quality of individual service activities, and the consistency of those activities with the intended program design, are a constant focus of attention.

Production Variability

A substantial degree of variability and unpredictability exists in human service production processes. Variations in the individual characteristics of both service providers and service users (Littell, Alexander, and Reynolds 2001), the balance between worker autonomy and rule-controlled procedures, the volatility of personal behavior in interactional situations, the influence of other individuals related to the user, and the uncertainties of co-production processes are some of the factors that contribute to the unpredictability of most service production processes. Service production technologies such as verbal counseling of an individual in a life crisis situation (as in a rape crisis center), or the treatment of accident victims in a hospital emergency room, or a home visit to investigate a complaint of child abuse, require on-the-spot, and often complex, judgment decisions by individual service providers.

Maintaining the integrity of the service technology in intensive, customized service production activities, such as psychiatric counseling or the treatment of cancer by an individual physician, requires extensive buffering of these activities against external interference (Thompson 1967). This also results in limited control over such activities by administrative and supervisory personnel. Mintzberg (1979) identifies the professional bureaucracy as an organization in which control over production is achieved through consistency in service skills rather than through direct control of production processes. External technical and professional education, including professional continuing education, and internal staff training are used in efforts to maintain service skill consistency and dependability when direct administrative supervision is not possible (see chapter 7). The resistance of health-care professionals to efforts by administrative personnel in managed health-care firms to impose rigid treatment protocols through organizational directives is an example of the tension between the variability of actual human service production activities and organizational expectations of consistency.

Many types of human services are produced under conditions of privacy—the teacher in the closed classroom; the social worker, the doctor, or the lawyer in a private office; the nurse in the hospital room; the individual child protective services worker in a home visit. Some service production processes involve legally protected privacy, particularly for lawyers and physicians. Supervisory personnel in most human service organizations have very limited control over actual service procedures and, therefore, only limited ability to enforce standardized production procedures (Lipsky 1980). Efforts to control service variability through detailed operational guidelines and elaborate manuals and rule books often have little effect on the events in a specific service encounter.

After-the-fact supervisory evaluation and consultation procedures are largely based on information provided by the service provider without direct information from the service user. The quality of production of human services, and protection of the service user against exploitation or abuse, depends largely on the judgments and skills of individual service personnel dealing with complex, multidimensional situations. The establishment of a high degree of real consistency in service provision in highly variable service situations is a major management task.

Evaluation Limitations

Service products of human service organizations are difficult to evaluate in a precise or consistent manner. In most human service organizations, there is no clear or consistent feedback about the outcome effectiveness of the services being produced (see chapter 11). Moreover, the variable role of individual service users in co-production often contaminates efforts to evaluate the effectiveness of individual staff members. The instructional material presented by a classroom teacher to a group of twenty-five students may produce twenty-five different results, and potentially twenty-five different scores on standardized tests. Many of the desired outcomes from human services production involve complex changes in the behaviors and attitudes of individual human beings, for which there are few precise measures. And many of the measures of outcomes that are used depend on self-reports by service users.

There may be important differences between short-term evaluations of outcomes by service users, and longer-term evaluations by the same user, and these differences can create serious problems of evaluation consistency. A service user who has low expectations for a service may rate a service positively that meets those expectations, whereas the user who has high expectations may rate a better-quality service negatively because it did not meet expectations (Chism 1997). The ultimate significance of some services, such as early childhood (newborn to three years) education, may not be evident for many years. In many instances, the particular individual who is a service user (a child), and other family members directly involved, may evaluate a service in very different ways. In addition, user satisfaction measures do not take into account the "public-goods" purposes that underlie the formation, and funding, of governmental and nonprofit service organizations. The multiple purposes of service production activities may require multiple, and even contradictory, evaluation measures (Rapp and Poertner 1988).

Consistent evaluation of service results is additionally complicated by the fact that effective service provision may require services from more than one organization, and they depend, therefore, on the cumulative effects of a particular series of services. The success of a college freshman with a handicapping condition may be the combined result of participation in an early childhood developmental program, marriage counseling that the parents participated in to help deal with family conflicts related to their child's handicapping condition, an effective reading teacher in the third grade, a health-enhancing diet developed by a nutritional specialist, the linkage of educational experiences within the school system as planned by the assistant superintendent for special education, and a summer camp experience in which students met adults with handicapping conditions who had been successful college students.

The high degree of variability (and the imprecision of outcome evaluations) means that executives and policy makers have limited control over, or ability to predict, the exact effect of the service production activities for which they are accountable. Highly standardized reports of service production activities, or of service outputs, produced through management information systems (MIS) are, by themselves, of limited value in evaluating the actual consequences of policy or program design decisions. Effectiveness evaluations require periodic, carefully designed studies rather than routine collection of large amounts of detailed operational statistics.

On an ongoing basis, it is the *quality* of service production processes, rather than the quantity, that is most relevant for evaluation efforts. The development of selective quality indicators becomes more important than numerous activity measures (Brannen and Streeter 1995). A low profile organizational structure that provides opportunities for direct access by policy makers and executives to the service production processes may also be an important element in the ability to assess the quality of service production (Peters and Waterman 1982). However, the most critical elements in the organizational operation over which policy makers and executives may have a significant degree of control are the characteristics of the actual service production personnel. In the absence of dependable outcome effectiveness measures, staff selection and staff retention procedures become essential elements in controlling the quality of service production.

Environmental Dependency

Human service organizations are highly dependent on multiple sources of external financial support and on other external constituencies over which there is very limited control.

> Thus human service organizations are highly dependent on their institutional environment for legitimacy, and it is the key to garner other resources. Yet the institutional environment in a culturally pluralistic society is both heterogeneous and turbulent.
>
> —Hasenfeld (1992a:10)

Few human service organizations generate a substantial amount of direct income from service users. The actual payment of the costs of program operation generally comes from, or is authorized by, persons who are primarily concerned with the "public-goods" or "collective" benefits from the service program, rather than from persons who directly experience the "private-goods" or "primary" benefits. Even for-profit managed health-care firms are primarily dependent on payments from employer firms or governmental bodies, for which the "public good" of controlling health-care costs is more important than the health condition of any single individual.

The major external sources of funding support for any one organization may include contributions, grants, contracts, legislative allocations of tax funds and direct tax revenue, third-party payments for service, and volunteer services (see chapter 8). Although governmental, nonprofit, and for-profit organizations generally have different combinations among these several types of funding sources, they are all characterized by being dependent on a diversity of income sources over which they have limited control (Lohman 1980).

Each income source requires a different fund-raising, or "marketing," strategy. Motivating personal commitment as expressed through contributions and/or volunteer services may be more important as a support strategy than designing a particular fee-charging strategy. Efforts to increase support may involve appealing to individual, or community, conscience, or fears, as well as to various forms of "enlightened self-interest." The financial well-being of a specific service organization may depend less on efficient service production technologies than on effective marketing to funding sources.

Fund-raising strategies may also involve generating expanded demand for services—"if your teenager is out of control or your trusted employee is an alcoholic (and if you have health-care insurance), call us." Demand marketing in human service organizations, whether it is the promotion of health care or the selling of the value of college education, is seldom connected directly to a price strategy.

Human service organizations operate in unstable financial environments with few methods for protecting themselves against unpredicted changes. These changes can include a sharp drop in tax collections or the income levels of corporate contributors to the United Way, stock market changes that affect income from endowments, changes in governmental rules for service eligibility and for payment systems in entitlement programs, or the establishment of a new, competitive governmental procedure for awarding purchase-of-service contracts.

Other external, and often controlling, constituencies include the organizations that control licensing or accreditation, as well as academic institutions, particularly professional schools, that control the numbers of, and characteristics of, key professional specialists. Other service organizations may be an essential source of user referrals. Organized user groups and public interest and advocacy groups, legislative committees, and state and federal courts can be important external constituencies that force changes in organizational policies or programs.

Different types of fund-raising procedures require different staff skills and organizational structures—contract negotiation in public purchase of service programs, grant writing for foundations, lobbying for legislative appropriations, and solicitations of the general public (Grønbjerg 1993; Edwards et al. 1997). Different funding sources require different reporting and evaluation procedures. Different program components involve relationships with different personnel recruitment sources, and often with different legitimation sources. Geographically decentralized programs require distinct structures for relationships with user and community constituencies. The result of the requirements for dealing effectively with the variety of elements in the external environment is a reinforcement of the operational pattern of organizational decentralization and "loose coupling" in most human service organizations.

In the public for-profit firm, the stockholder, or "owner," constituency is defined as having first priority in determining organizational policies, although governmental regulatory bodies may have ultimate authority. However, there is no official priority order among the various external constituencies of governmental or voluntary nonprofit human service organizations. The external constituencies of these organizations often make conflicting demands. To enforce these demands, they may actually "intrude" into the organization: defining specific purposes for particular elements of funding; imposing external definitions of "quality" service production in exchange for accreditation or licensing, or as a requirement for assigning professional "trainees"; and making demands for the modification of service production processes to fit the preferences, or convenience, of particular user populations. For example, demands from the user constituency of persons with disability conditions, enforced through federal legislation, has forced nearly every human service organization to make modifications in physical facilities and in program operations.

The degree of environmental dependency affects the level of organizational resources invested in external relationships. The diversity of unpredictable external constituencies, including funding sources, requires diversified organizational structures for dealing effectively with these constituencies, as well as a substantial investment of resources in "intelligence gathering" about actual and potential changes in different parts of the organizational environment. Moreover, the potential power of key sectors of the environment to impact the organization may make it essential for any single organization to participate in a variety of coalitions in efforts to control, or influence, particular sectors, such as the legislative appropriation system (Emery and Trist 1965).

Financial Management

Human service organizations, particularly nonprofit and governmental organizations, do not fit the financial-planning, control, and analysis procedures of traditional for-profit goods production firms.

Person-to-person human service production cannot be stockpiled; it is "used" as it is produced (Fitzsimmons and Fitzsimmons 1994). Personnel costs are, therefore, relatively inelastic, remaining at much the same level when there are short-term variations in service utilization. It is also difficult to establish a true cost-of-production price for individual services that would allow for direct cost comparisons between different service providers, given the mixture of "public goods" and "private goods" in human service production, particularly in nonprofit and governmental organizations.

Moreover, service production resources in nonprofit and governmental services also involve a wide variety of unpriced elements including indirect subsidies such as exemption from various taxes (Goddeeris and Weisbrod 1997), in-kind contributions of goods and services, the use value of physical facilities that have been financed through special "capital campaigns" or governmental bond issues, and volunteer services. However, all forms of service production by nonprofit and governmental service organizations, as well as by for-profit organizations, do involve "costs"—that is, the use of limited resources—and, therefore, all forms of service production are constrained by limitations regardless of the level of the "need" for a particular service.

The service provider staff in most human service organizations includes a large number of women, as well as both men and women from diverse ethnic backgrounds, in technical and professional positions. These employees are often paid less than White men with comparable education in other employment settings. This distorts production cost comparisons with many for-profit goods production industries. In addition, the value of the co-production effort on the part of the service user is not included in any cost analysis. Given equal levels of staff costs, services that are used by highly motivated individuals will show much higher levels of cost effectiveness than services in which the users have low levels of motivation.

Given the variations in these unpriced elements, such as co-production, cost comparisons among different types of services are very difficult to make, limiting the application of many financial management analytic procedures. For example, it is difficult to compare the unit costs of educating a very bright student in first grade, who requires very little teaching time to master basic requirements and whose parents provide many forms of supplementary education, with the costs of educating a resistive junior high student with a learning disability whose family provides no educational reinforcements. The long time horizon for determining actual outcomes, the central role of self-reports in evaluating outcomes, and the imprecise nature of the production processes also make it difficult to carry out comparative cost–benefit, or cost-effectiveness, analyses (Buxbaum 1981).

"Prudent man" principles that guide nonprofit policy boards, and external audit and control procedures in governmental agencies, serve to minimize financial risk taking. Sizable capital expenditures are, in general, funded through one-time fund-raising campaigns or special governmental appropriations, rather than out of current operating budgets or through interest-bearing loans (Goddeeris and Weisbrod 1997). However, large medical facilities, colleges and universities, and governmental human service organizations that have independent taxing authority (such as local school boards) may operate more as commercial firms do, using interest-bearing bonds for expansion that are then repaid out of current income.

The financial management structure of nonprofit and governmental human service organizations is primarily designed to monitor and control expenditures within a stay-within-the-budget, break-even framework (Lohman 1980). The typical twelve-month budget/financing cycle shapes many other aspects of organizational operation. There are internal, and often also external, pressures to maintain close supervision over the level of expenditures and the consistency of expenditures with an approved budget. Fiscal controls are often more detailed, and consistent, than programmatic controls.

Voluntary nonprofit and governmental human service organizations operate financially on an annual break-even budget balancing basis rather than on a profit-and-loss, or return-to-stockholder basis. Most governmental and voluntary nonprofit organizations also operate day to day on a break-even cash flow basis (Lohman 1980), having limited provision for access to any operating line of credit. Although voluntary nonprofit organizations may, under some conditions, be able to operate at a loss (over budget on expenditures), drawing on reserve funds, endowment, or budget balancing contributions at the end of the fiscal year, governmental programs seldom have even this much flexibility.

There is limited benefit to the executive, or to the organization, from operating at a level of expenditure below the projected budget and having a year-end surplus. In governmental organizations or organizations dependent on a central fund-raising source such as the United Way, unexpended funds are often credited against the funding requirements for the next year rather than being retained by the organization as a reserve for future developmental needs. *Financial resources in nonprofit and governmental organizations, in contrast to for-profit firms, are primarily treated as a means for achieving the current purposes of the organization, not as an indicator of goal accomplishment or as a resource to be accumulated for the future.*

In most human service organizations, there is a structural separation between resource procurement activities and service production activities, except in those limited instances in which direct fee-for-service payments are a major source of income for a specific service program. The major responsibility for procurement of financial support involves different personnel from those involved directly in producing the service, whether the source of funding is tax funds, voluntary contributions, or third-party payment sources such as those that support for-profit managed-care firms. The separation between the teaching functions in elementary schools and the tax-levying functions of the school board and the office of the superintendent represents one of the more extreme examples of such separation. There is a similar separation between board members representing the nonprofit neighborhood center to the United

Way allocation committee and the staff personnel at that center involved in production of services for a neighborhood group of elderly adults.

Executive Motivation

The pattern of executive motivation in human service organizations is complex. In both governmental and voluntary nonprofit organizations, there is normally a formal separation between policy-making structures and the role of the executive. This is not limited to human service organizations. In governmental organizations, the separation is between the legislative structure, or in some instances a legislatively established intermediate governance or policy structure such as the governing board of a public authority, and the executive. In many instances, the governmental policy-making body may also have formally defined authority over some decisions within the organization (in addition to the selection of the executive), such as approval of other senior personnel appointments. In voluntary nonprofit organizations and quasi-governmental nonprofit organizations, the separation is between the board of directors and the executive, with the formal authority of the executive subject to definition by the board (see chapter 10).

The executive normally does not have a vote in policy-making decisions in governmental and voluntary nonprofit organizations, in contrast to the for-profit firm, in which the chief executive is a participating member of the board of directors and frequently the presiding officer of the board. Although the scope of responsibility is very broad, any psychological rewards or tangible "perks" for the executive in nonprofit and governmental human service organizations resulting from the direct exercise of personal power and authority are often severely limited.

Substantial financial benefits as a reward for effective management are also generally not available to executives in nonprofit and governmental human service organizations. When executives have had access to such rewards, they are often identified as "illegitimate," as in the example of the United Way of America executive as described by Glaser (1994) in *The United Way Scandal*. The break-even pattern of budgeting generally excludes any unusual financial recognition for the executive on the basis of the performance of the organization. Opportunities for entrepreneurial initiative are often limited by the separation between the executive and the policy-making process, the low-risk perspective of policy boards, and the lack of organizational control over major sources of funding.

In most governmental and nonprofit organizations, executives have limited employment security and limited provision for financial compensation if they are dismissed. In governmental organizations, employment tenure is often controlled by political officials or by policy bodies appointed by political officials. Whereas civil service procedures may protect the employment tenure of other staff members, such protections are seldom extended to executives, although multiyear contracts are used in some settings, such as for school system superintendents and collegiate athletic coaches.

Executives of nonprofit organizations generally serve at the pleasure of the board of directors (see chapter 10). Any major disagreement between the executive and the board is likely to result in termination of employment, either voluntary or involuntary. The uncertainty associated with many human service executive positions—the three-year syndrome of public school superintendents and many state agency executives— means that they must give serious attention to the relation of current activities to future employment and career options. For some executives, this leads to a modest version of the "golden parachute" of the corporate world—that is, the use of a current executive position for the development of personal connections that might lead to future employment opportunities. Recently, in the health-care field, executives of nonprofit hospitals and health insurance organizations have made agreements that have resulted in substantial personal financial benefits through stock option provisions when the hospitals have been converted to for-profit organizations (Goddeeris and Weisbrod 1997).

The satisfactions of human service executives are often defined in terms of personal commitment to the interests of service users and professional career values, rather than to organizational growth values. Visibility in community leadership positions and the opportunity to work with professional colleagues and community volunteers with similar value orientations are other forms of reward. For some executives, the challenge of the entrepreneurial opportunities involved in negotiating new sources of financing and developing new service programs provides satisfaction, although without the financial rewards of for-profit entrepreneurship (Gibelman 2000b). It is clear, however, that given the complexity of the management context and the limits on financial rewards, traditional economic self-interest models of executive motivation do not apply to most executives in human service organizations in social services, health care, criminal justice, and education.

SUMMARY

Effective management has become a central issue in the organizationally complex society of the late twentieth century. Frustration with ineffective organizational management, including the management of human service organizations, has become a widespread source of public discontent, not only with specific organizations but with the general structure of community leadership and democratic governance. One of the difficulties in improving such management has been the failure of many of the proposals to take into account the distinctive characteristics of human service organizations.

One of the most important consequences of these distinctive characteristics is that the organizational executive in human service organizations must understand, and deal with, the recurrent, and often unresolvable, dilemmas, or "enigmas," that are inherent in the nature of human service organizations. These dilemmas include the moral choices involved in service production, the mixture of public-goods and private-goods objectives, the dual loyalties of professional specialists to professional standards and to organizational purposes, and the often conflicting interests of external funders and legitimators, service users, and service personnel.

THREE

STAKEHOLDER CONSTITUENCIES

Organizational behavior is a power game in which various players, called influencers, seek to control the organization's decisions and actions. . . . Since the needs of influencers vary, each tries to use his or her own levers of power—means or systems of influence—to control decisions and actions. . . . Thus to understand the behavior of the organization, it is necessary to understand which influencers are present, what needs each seeks to fulfill in the organization, and how each is able to exercise power to fulfill them.
                                                                      —Mintzberg (1983:22)

A S SET FORTH in chapter 1, the human service organization is a socially constructed image. It may be analyzed in a number of different ways depending on the perspective being used. From one perspective, the organization can be analyzed as a production machine with human beings as the key elements in the production technology rather than gears or electronic circuits. This perspective is embodied in "scientific management" or "rational-legal" conceptual frameworks (Hasenfeld 1992a). From another perspective, the organization can be analyzed as a network of relationships among those individuals who occupy social roles in the organization. This perspective is embodied in the "human relations" conceptual framework (Hasenfeld 1992a).

Still another perspective views the organization as essentially a "political economy" arena (Zald 1970), in which individuals involved with the organization are viewed as influencers (Mintzberg 1983:23), or "stakeholders." The individuals who are participants in stakeholder constituencies are involved in a "political" process of both collaboration and competition within the framework provided by organizational goals and organizational structure (Gummer 1990). This "political" process often involves various forms of power, including financial power, legal authority, and symbolic power, as well as various forms of persuasion.

Organizational participants reflect not only their individual perspectives and interests but also the interests they share with others who are part of the same stakeholder constituency. Some of the individuals who are part of a stakeholder constituency represent only themselves, or a particular household; others may represent the interests of another organization, or an even a larger set of interests such as an organized profession. Moreover, in the case of any specific organization, there may be various coalitions among stakeholder constituencies, involving constituencies inside the organization as well as external constituencies (Mintzberg 1983). For example, in certain political environments, there may be a coalition of interests between organizational employees and employee households and persons who are part of external governmental funding sources, with the result that the protection of employment and employment benefits takes priority over organizational efficiency or effectiveness.

This book approaches the organization from the "political economy" perspective rather than from a "rational–legal" perspective or a "human relations" perspective. From this perspective, the responsibilities of the policy body, such as the board of directors of the nonprofit service organization, and the executive can be understood to include the development and maintenance of processes of collaboration among the several stakeholder constituencies in pursuit of those organizational goals that are broadly supported by the several constituencies while also dealing with the separate interests of the different constituencies that may have access to different forms of power (Martin 1988).

This chapter explores the basic framework of the stakeholder constituencies. All human service organizations involve a basic set of stakeholder constituencies, although the specific characteristics of those constituencies and the relationships among them may be quite different in voluntary nonprofit, governmental nonprofit, governmental, and for-profit service organizations. The characteristics of several of these stakeholder constituencies are examined in more detail in the chapters that follow.

Key stakeholder constituencies include the following:

- Service users, members of service user households/families and user representatives or surrogates
- Sources of legitimation and financial support, and of other essential resources including personnel and technology

- Organizational employees, including members of organized professions, and their households
- Members of policy-making boards and advisory bodies
- Other human service organizations
- The media
- Members of the community/society

The participants in these constituencies are potentially affected by what takes place within the service organization; they have a "stake" or "investment" in the organizational performance. Service users and potential service users have a stake in the quality of services produced by the organization (Chism 1997). Organizational employees have, among other concerns, a stake in the financial stability of the organization and the level of monetary support that can be attracted for the activities of the organization. Funding supporters have a stake in the effective and efficient use of the financial resources that are made available to the organization.

Persons working in other service organizations have a stake in the receptiveness of the organization to referrals from other organizations, the characteristics of referrals from the organization, and the ability of the organization to provide the services it is expected to provide. Members of the media have a stake in the level of public interest in the organization and in the characteristics of the information provided through the organization. Members of the community have a stake in the "public-goods" benefits that the organization can produce—that is, the benefits that are produced for the entire community—in addition to the benefits provided to particular individuals or households. These "public goods" benefits may include various forms of social control.

SERVICE USERS, USER HOUSEHOLDS, AND USER SURROGATES

Many different terms are used to describe the consumer or user of the services produced by human service organizations—patient, student, client, prisoner, recipient. All of these terms, except for some uses of the term *client*, reflect an asymmetrical power relationship. None are used across the full range of human service programs. The choice in this book is to use the term *service users,* a more general and more neutral term. Examinations of the effectiveness of human service programs often focus on the users of the services produced by the organization. This user constituency can include individuals, households, and entire communities. The service user role is a complex one, particularly because of the importance of the co-production processes that are characteristic of most human service programs (Hasenfeld 1992a; Fitzsimmons and Fitzsimmons 1994). From an ethical perspective, and in recognition of the importance of co-production, it is clear that service users should be the most important of the stakeholder constituencies for both voluntary and governmental human service programs (Rapp and Poertner 1992). The balance of interests between service users and stockholder owners is always one of the critical issues in for-profit human service organizations.

Some comprehensive, or universal, service organizations, such as public schools and emergency medical services, may serve a broad and inclusive user constituency. Other service organizations, such as private college preparatory academies or shelters for undocumented immigrant women and children, may be concerned with only a very specialized group of users. However, regardless of the type of organization, the service user constituency is usually diverse and fragmented. Most often it is a totally unorganized constituency.

Service user constituencies are often separated along economic lines. There are service users who are able to buy services directly and to make choices among service providers; service users with stable incomes who may have limited choices but who may have access to subsidized services from nonprofit and governmental organizations; service users who have service entitlements, such as military veterans and persons covered by Medicaid or Medicare programs or by employer-financed service programs; and potential service users with marginal incomes who have only limited assurance of access to even minimal services of any type.

Service users are often divided by ethnic backgrounds, by language differences, by gender, by sexual orientation, and by age. There are reluctant and resistant service users including parents being investigated for child abuse and persons arrested for criminal offenses. There are also potential users who need a particular service but for whom there is no available service, such as a treatment program for drug addiction.

The roles of particular service users within the service-provision process can vary widely. Some service users may have a very brief, voluntary, and nonintensive service experience, as, for example, persons who participate in a social event or a single physical fitness class at a YWCA or YMCA. Some service users may have an extended but nonintensive service experience, as in the instance of older adults receiving a regular payment from the Social Security Administration. Some individual service users may have an intense but time-limited experience, as in the instance of persons receiving emergency medical care or minor emergency out-patient services, women served by the emergency response services of a rape crisis center, or families that undergo an initial investigation resulting from a community complaint alleging possible child abuse or neglect. Still other persons may have an extended, and intensive, service experience, as in the instance of individuals with severe and chronic mental illness, children participating in a local public school system, and families who are charged with child abuse with court action being taken to terminate their legal authority as parents. Evaluative feedback from the service user constituency dealing with particular service experiences may involve a series of responses, both formal and informal, from long-term service users or a single, time-limited evaluation by short-term users.

Most individual service users are in a disadvantaged or relatively low-personal-power position among the several stakeholder constituencies (Hasenfeld 1983; Hasenfeld 1992b; Rapp and Poertner 1992). The exceptions are those individuals who may be able to pay the full cost of purchasing services through the marketplace and who have a choice among service providers. In the instance of voluntary nonprofit, governmental nonprofit, and governmental service organizations, as well as for-profit organizations providing services under a contract with a governmental "authority," users come to the service organization because they have a "need" for a service that the organization controls—a health need, an educational need, a social service need—and do not have the financial resources required to buy a total package of services in the open marketplace.

These service users include the homeless individual who needs emergency medical attention for a fractured leg, the homemaker and mother who has been deserted by her husband, the family with three school-age children who need a complete education program, the physically assaulted spouse who needs a safe shelter, and the individual with a developing cancer who is totally dependent on an employer-financed managed health-care plan for medical services. In addition, some individuals are forced to participate in a particular service as the price for receiving basic subsistence services—for example, participation in job search and job training programs as part of the Temporary Assistance for Needy Families (TANF) program in return for receiving basic financial support for young children. Other persons become subject to community social controls and are mandated, through the use of the community police powers, to participate in a service program—for example, resocialization in a juvenile criminal justice institution.

Service users in all types of human service organizations, including for-profit firms, are also usually in a low power position because the services they are seeking often require the attention of individuals with specialized training and preparation, including professional education (Hasenfeld 1992b). Widely accepted institutional patterns in the general society call for deference to the judgments of the professional specialist, whether it is the classroom teacher, the child welfare social worker, the surgeon, the university professor, or the courtroom judge.

Moreover, many service users have other disadvantages that limit their power in organizational relationships. They may be in a legally disadvantaged position, such as undocumented immigrants and individuals who have been convicted of a felony and are on parole, having served time in a state prison. They may be a member of a group of persons who have historically experienced discrimination, exploitation, and oppression such as individuals from African American, American Indian, Asian American, or Latino backgrounds, or persons whose native language is other than English. In many service settings, girls and women have historically been disadvantaged, as have individuals who are gay or lesbian.

To a very large degree, the quality of services received by service users in all types of human service programs is highly dependent on the values, ethical commitments, and motivations of the members of other stakeholder constituencies, including funders, board members, organizational staff persons, and members of the community. Only in a limited number of settings, and for particular types of service, are service users able to exercise independent power over the quality of service provision, either as a result of being able to pay the full cost of the service and having a choice among service providers, or through group pressure from an active association of service users or service user surrogates, such as an association of the parents of children with autism. One of the issues requiring attention in human service organizations is the establishment of procedures that can serve to increase the relative power of service users (see chapter 6).

In many service situations, other members of the service user household or extended family, or friends and neighbors, may be an active part of the co-production process—for example, by supporting behaviors required by a developmental or rehabilitation process as well as by being a significant force in monitoring service effectiveness. In turn, such persons may also be directly affected by the service outcomes. Parents are often actively involved in the process of elementary and secondary education, both by monitoring the quality of the educational activities involving their children and also by serving as advocates for their children in their school experience. In turn, their life experience as parents is directly affected by the effectiveness of the school services provided for their children.

A process of individual or family mental health therapy, or marriage counseling, that results ultimately in a decision to dissolve an existing household through divorce or other form of separation often has secondary consequences not only for children but for other members of extended households, such as grandparents. These persons are, in many ways, consumers of the service outcomes and are, therefore, an interested constituency, although they are not directly involved in the service production process.

In a similar way, members of an extended family are often affected by a child protective services investigation, because, in some instances, they become involved as kin foster parents or even adoptive parents. The complex issues related to the role of parents of adults with severe and chronic mental illness has led to formation of a national association—the National Alliance for the Mentally Ill (NAMI)—to advocate for the interests of parents and other members of the family of individuals receiving treatment for such illnesses.

Many service users must depend on other individuals for support and social protection. In many situations, these individuals represent the service user as a user surrogate in the service transaction. This is particularly so in the instance of children and adolescents, most of whom have limited ability to act in their own self-interest. They have limited economic resources and are limited by the institutional patterns in the larger society that define such persons as being in a dependent relationship with, and under the control of, their parents or parent surrogates. Under the concept of *in loco parentis,* adults in organizational positions, such as teachers in elementary and secondary schools, have responsibility for and formal authority over children in their classrooms, an authority similar to that of parents. They also have the power to define what children "need" in terms of educational experiences, and the services they will receive as service users. For example, educators are now defining computer skills as an essential part of every child's education without regard for the preferences of the child or of the parents.

Thus, in services for children, it is parents and parental surrogates who are the acknowledged participants in the service user stakeholder constituency when children are the actual service consumers. A similar situation may exist in the case of service organizations providing services for adults with severe disability conditions or with mental and physical limitations. However, in the instance of adults receiving such services, the parents of the service user may not be officially recognized as being a surrogate having any authority to act in behalf of such an individual unless a legal guardianship has been established. And in the instance of gay and lesbian households, a long-term partner may not be acknowledged as a surrogate with authority to make decisions in medical crisis situations.

The service user stakeholder constituency also includes persons who are designated to function as formal surrogates for the interests of service users or potential users. Formal surrogates include individuals specifically appointed to such a position, such as a lawyer serving as a guardian *ad litem* in behalf of the child who has experienced parental abuse. Other lawyers may represent the interests of the parents. Also included are lawyers, ombudsmen, and other specialized advocates who have been designated as acting in behalf of individual service users or groups of service users. Surrogates may include neighborhood residents, who, as leaders of an organized neighborhood association, act in behalf of all of the residents in a given neighborhood area. Surrogates may also include leaders or staff members of associations established to represent particular groups of service users, such as the ARC (formerly the Association for Retarded Citizens). Such user surrogates may have access to forms of influence that individual service users do not have. However, such surrogates may also have interests in a particular situation that are different from those of the immediate service user—for example, an interest in establishing a legal precedent that could affect the situation of an entire class of service users.

The service user constituency for any single organization has many diverse elements. Each subgroup within the service user constituency may have a different perception of the significance and the quality of the services provided. Particularly important is the connection of the user constituency to other stakeholder constituencies. One of the critical issues in many human service organizations is the lack of a connection between the service user constituency and other constituencies, such as funders and board members, particularly in large urban communities, so that there is little opportunity for direct, personal feedback to policy makers about the quality and effectiveness of services. This requires the development of other methods for obtaining such feedback. It is, in part, a recognition of the limitations on the opportunity for individual service users to evaluate the quality of service provision that has led to an emerging concern with user participation in comprehensive quality control procedures (Chism 1997) (see chapter 11).

LEGITIMATORS AND FUNDERS

Whereas service users may be the largest, but the most diffuse, stakeholder constituency, the legitimators and funders constituencies are perhaps the most focused in terms of expectations. And it is the legitimators and funders that have ultimate control over the ability of any single service organization to survive. Controlling actions by legitimators and funders may involve formal action by a specific policy body or actions by particular individuals who are the members of such policy bodies.

Among the sources of organizational legitimation, or public recognition, are licensing bodies, including governmental offices dealing with incorporation, and accrediting bodies. In some instances, organizational legitimacy is assumed to exist upon application unless challenged—for example, an organization applying for initial incorporation as a nonprofit, or "elemosynary," organization under state statutes or applying for tax exempt status under the Internal Revenue Code. In other instances, establishing legitimacy involves a detailed application and an external review—for example, as a condition of admission to financial participation in a local United Way or of being recognized as an "accredited" organization in a specialized field of practice, such as a child welfare agency, a hospital, a college, or a university.

Funding sources by the act of allocating monetary resources also contribute to establishing the legitimacy of the service organization. A foundation grant may provide an endorsement that is essential for recognition by other funding sources. Furthermore, the withdrawal of funding in some circumstances (for example, by a United Way organization) or cancellation of a contract by a state social services agency may be viewed as a withdrawal of legitimacy as well as of operating resources. Recognition of a professional training site—a social work practicum setting or a medical residency—also serves as a form of public recognition or legitimation. In many situations, such as incorporation, the establishment of legitimation may be a one-time event or, as in accreditation, it may require periodic reestablishment. The legitimating structure may be dominated by persons from the occupation, or "industry," as in the instance of educational accreditation, or it may be controlled by independent lay persons, such as in the admissions committee of a United Way, or by public officials, as in the instance of incorporation and taxing authorities. The formal legitimating constituencies are largely discrete and separate bodies, each of which has substantial authority, but that seldom act together as a constituency coalition (Mintzberg 1983).

Funding constituencies, which, as indicated previously, may overlap with legitimating constituencies, are a continuous part of the "political" environment of the service organization. Most nonprofit and governmental service organizations generate only a limited amount of internal funding from the sale of goods or services. As a result, such organizations are particularly dependent on external sources of financial support and are thus directly affected by conditions attached to such support. For example, for-profit and nonprofit health-care organizations that are dependent on funding from third-party sources such as corporations and governmental programs (Medicare/Medicaid) are directly affected by the conditions attached to such funding. Moreover, for-profit human service organizations are often dependent on third-party funding sources, including business firms that are funding health-care and other services for corporate employees and arc thus affected by the constraints attached to such funding.

Funding source constituencies include the decision makers who control the allocation of financial resources for service organizations. These include the following:

- Individuals or families who make a donation to a voluntary nonprofit service organization, participate in a fund-raising event, or purchase directly some type of human service

- Corporation policy bodies that control contributions to service organizations or to a community-wide combined fund-raising organization, such as the United Way
- Boards of directors of philanthropic foundations that make funding grants to service organizations
- Policy bodies in United Way organizations and other combined fund-raising organizations that allocate funds to support service organizations
- Federal and state legislatures, county commissioners, school boards, and city councils that allocate tax funds for the support of governmental service programs, or for the purchase of services from nonprofit and for-profit service organizations
- Corporate policy bodies and governmental bodies that authorize the purchase of services as part of employee benefit programs, either directly or through insurance or managed care programs

As late as the 1950s, funding patterns for nonprofit and governmental service organizations were relatively simple. Nonprofit organizations were supported through some combination of contributions from individuals and businesses, income from endowments, and grants from voluntary community-wide fund-raising activities such as the United Way, together with modest income from earnings. Philanthropic foundations often provided start-up funds for new programs in nonprofit organizations.

Governmental service organizations or quasi-governmental nonprofit organizations were funded directly through appropriations from governmental bodies, with some mixture of federal, state, county, and city funds, depending on the organization. Public schools, public hospitals, and public social service organizations were largely self-contained organizations with authority to establish program structures and a staff of governmental employees who provided the actual services.

Few for-profit corporations were involved in the competitive production of human services, given the financial advantages that accrued to both governmental and nonprofit organizations by virtue of their tax-exempt status. Individuals with sufficient income bought services of various types directly from individual professional specialists, or from nonprofit service organizations in the instance of private adoption services and private schools. Even existing health-care insurance plans—Blue Cross/Blue Shield—assumed that there was a direct fee-for-service arrangement between a specific health-care provider and the service user. The insurance plan reimbursed the service user for personal health-care expenditures after the fact, having no role in the professional decisions about what health services should be provided.

Individual organizations were particularly subject to influence from the dominant funding source among the various funding constituencies. For organizations with large endowments and/or substantial fund-raising activities organized by the board of directors, the board members and their friends were the most influential constituency, even if that influence was primarily expressed in support of the existing service programs. For organizations without wealthy supporters that were heavily dependent on community-wide fund-raising such as the United Way, an annual public budget review process, including descriptive and statistical summaries of activities, and the recommendations of the United Way budget committee, were critical. For the small number of voluntary nonprofit organizations with funding grants or purchase-of-service contracts from governmental sources, primarily for the residential care of children, the legal specifications of the purposes of such funds controlled many of the program elements. Legislative intent, and requirements for financial audits controlled the direct service program structure of tax-supported governmental service organizations.

For organizations that did generate substantial levels of service-based income, such as teaching hospitals, the ability to be responsive to well-to-do service users was important, leading many such hospitals to develop special private room sections that commanded higher payments. YMCAs and Jewish Community Centers developed adult health and exercise programs that commanded higher membership fees than those paid by the general membership.

Current funding patterns are much more complex, as are the relationships of funding bodies to service organizations (Grønbjerg 1993). Funding patterns cut across traditional organizational distinctions. Governmental sources have become major funders of voluntary nonprofit organizations through program support grants and through purchase of service contracts (Smith and Lipsky 1993; Salamon 1995). For-profit businesses of all types purchase services directly for their employees—alcoholism treatment, day care, mental health services—from nonprofit organizations, or through an intermediary for-profit Employee Assistance Program (EAP) services firm. The extension of health insurance programs to cover mental health services has expanded the possibilities of fee-for-service reimbursement for mental health–related nonprofit service organizations. Federal (Medicare) and federal–state (Medicaid) programs have become major funding sources for health care and related services provided by both governmental and nonprofit service organizations. For example, in Texas in the 1990s, 50 percent of all childbirths within the state, in both public and nonprofit hospitals, were funded through the Medicaid program.

The most dramatic change in funding patterns has been the emergence of for-profit firms in the health and mental health care areas as well as the increasing use of for-profit firms for the administration of technical functions such as the bill-paying processes in state-administered Medicaid programs. In some instances, nonprofit service organizations are part of a service network organized by a for-profit managed health-care firm with the service organization receiving payments for services under a contractual agreement. In other instances, nonprofit organizations, primarily hospitals, have been sold to for-profit firms and are being operated directly by the managed-care firm. With Medicaid programs at the state level being shifted to managed-care arrangements, existing nonprofit health and mental health service providers may be funded through a service fee contract or through a capitation agreement.

Funding sources are initiating more elaborate analyses of the efficiency and effectiveness of funded organizations and are examining their operation within a larger community, or state, context. The role of the United Way has changed, with most financially participating organizations receiving a much smaller proportion of their total operating budget from that source than during an earlier period. Many United Way organizations are also attempting to develop more elaborate, ongoing analyses of the efficiency and effectiveness of individual service organizations and the rationale for their activities within an inclusive community context. Moreover, funding from the United Way organization is now often defined as a "contract" providing support for specific service packages rather than as a budgetary support grant for the general operation of the service organization.

The United Way is one example of an intermediary body (a British term) that serves as an "agent" representing the interests of the individual funders—households and corporations—that provide the funds. In a similar way, the members of a city council, or a county board of commissioners, may represent what are perceived to be the interests of the individuals who contribute, through tax payments, to the support of local governmental service organizations. In for-profit service organizations, the board of directors is viewed as the "agent" for the stockholder investors. When the stockholders include large investment trusts, such as employee retirement plans that own large blocks of stock, the stockholder constituency may become a powerful indirect influence in the organizational operation.

One important change in the nature of the funding constituencies is the increasing number and diversity of funding sources for individual organizations (Grønbjerg 1993). Nonprofit organizations may receive funds through grant and contract arrangements with federal, state, and/or local governmental sources, contracts with business firms for services for employees, grants from foundations, and income from a variety of special fund-raising initiatives and third-party reimbursements as well as some direct fee income (Wernet 1988).

Some funding sources may provide unrestricted support that can be used flexibly to meet central administrative costs as well as direct program costs. However, many of the current funding sources provide categorical or targeted funds that are intended to be used only for a particular group of users or for a particular type of program. This often requires specific accounts and specialized statistical reports for each funding source. The funding cycle for each funding source may be different, involving reports that are due at different dates. The requirements for reporting expenditures and service activities may be different for each funding source. This funding complexity often requires computerized accounting systems and specialized accounting personnel, making it difficult for start-up, community-based, or faith-based service programs to survive.

In an effort to maintain oversight control of funding without direct administrative control, many funding sources require the establishment of an accounting paper trail that can identify the specific ways in which designated funds are used for the particular purpose for which the funding was provided. Organizational managers, on the other hand, are concerned with using a total pool of funding to maintain a stable cadre of staff members, with core administrative and organizational maintenance tasks being supported as well as specialized program components. Managers are therefore concerned with *fungability*—that is, the ability to make flexible use of funds from a particular source; funders are often concerned with enforcing constraints on the discretionary use of such funds.

Organizations providing services under contract with a governmental agency may be included in program audits that are initiated by state officials, including governors or state legislators. Legislatures, at both national and state levels, that authorize funding for service programs may impose restrictive eligibility requirements, accompanied by intense oversight of the procedures involved in applying these requirements. One example was the imposition of error-rate-monitoring procedures on the state administration of the Aid for Families with Dependent Children (AFDC) program until the termination of that program in 1997.

Although few service organizations are forced to deal with a coalition of funding sources, there may be similar emphases, or reporting requirements, across several funding sources. These requirements, currently, are likely to emphasize detailed financial accountability and evidence of program effectiveness. This may require increased expenditures for record keeping and financial management as well as for various forms of program evaluation, rather than for expanded services.

Among the several stakeholder constituencies, funding sources often have the most direct impact on the program structure of the service organization: "Nonprofit social service and community development organizations are captured by resource relationships that depend critically on the reputations they maintain" (Grønbjerg 1993:285).

The availability of a new funding source, or a change in the priorities of an existing funding source, may result in the establishment of a new program component. Direct or indirect pressures from funding sources are often a major factor in mergers and other forms of organizational consolidation. Changes in the pattern of funding health-care services for the employees of large businesses set in motion the restructuring of the entire health-care services system in the United States in the 1990s. Although policy bodies in governmental, nonprofit, and for-profit service organizations may have ultimate control over organizational program policy, in many instances they are faced with ratifying program changes that have actually been determined by the action of funding sources.

ORGANIZATIONAL EMPLOYEES

Organizational employees and their households are a significant stakeholder constituency. The influence of the employee constituency is seldom as explicit and focused as the influence of funders. On the other hand, the support of the employee constituency for the mission and objectives of the organization is a fundamental requirement for providing effective services.

Employees are the largest visible representation of the organization in the community with a crucial role in the public reputation of the organization. In the case of governmental organizations, employees may also be a significant political force among community constituencies. For example, school employees may be a political force in school board elections, or employees of a state residential facility and their families may be a political force in the election of members of the state legislature, particularly in rural communities. In some settings, it is the nonprofessional personnel with long employment careers who have the greatest political influence in the community, rather than professional specialists who may come from outside the local community and may have shorter employment careers.

Long-term employees and their families may also be a major channel of communication between the organization and the surrounding community. Information—both favorable and unfavorable—about the organization and its programs, official and unofficial, may be communicated to persons in the general community; informal advice from members of the community about what the organization should and should not do may come to the organization through members of the staff living in the community. Such community input was very significant in the 1950s, when neighborhood settlement houses and community centers and other youth-serving organizations, as well as neighborhood schools and health-care services, began to address the patterns of segregation that were characteristic of their service neighborhoods and had often characterized their service programs.

Much of the existing human service management literature deals with organizational employees as a single constituency. However, the employee constituency involves several diverse groups. These include direct service workers who are members of an organized profession, together with supervisors and managers who also identify themselves as professional specialists, direct service workers who are not members of an organized profession, those supervisors and managers who identify themselves as career organizational employees rather than as members of a profession, technical and secretarial support staff, and custodial and maintenance personnel (particularly in residential programs).

The employee constituency may or may not be an organized constituency. Union membership among direct service employees in human service organizations is the exception rather than the rule, although labor union membership among some employee groups may be significant in states with a general pattern of unionization among governmental employees and in large cities with a strong history of unionization.

Many service organizations have informal, or formal, internal associations among employees, with varying degrees of representative participation in the determination of personnel policies and in other areas of policy making. These employee associations may or may not include all employees. Indeed, in most human service organizations, there are likely to be persistent organizational and status distinctions, such as among managerial, professional, and technical and support personnel, distinctions that are reflected in the structure of internal employee associations. Such distinctions are also reflected in the degree to which the employee stakeholder constituency acts like a single organized constituency.

Among many of the organization employees of all types, and particularly among members of their households/families, continuity and predictability of employment may be more important than the organizational mission. This may result in a general bias among staff members against organizational risk taking. Continuity of employment may be particularly important for employees with young children, but it may also be very important for households with two adult workers in which continuity of employment for one person has a direct impact on continuity of employment for the other person. Fringe benefits—health insurance, retirement plans, and holiday/vacation provisions—may also be more important for many employees than pay levels, given the general constraints on sizable wage and salary increases in nonprofit and governmental service organizations and the limited opportunity for individual bonuses.

As indicated in chapter 2, human service organizations are distinctive, in part because of the central role of professional specialists. These include social workers, nurses, elementary and secondary teachers, lawyers, physicians, psychologists, and early childhood educators. Staff members who are members of an organized profession often have a special role within the organization because of their connections outside the organization (see chapter 7). Professional training is controlled by individuals and groups outside the organization. Human service organizations may also contract with professional education programs in colleges and universities to do internal staff training. Professional specialists may have access to information about program innovations through professional channels.

Professional specialists, because of their identification with ethical traditions and standards established by organized professions, are often viewed as carrying the central responsibility for defining the moral standards that guide service production—that is, as being the conscience of the organization. Indeed, professional specialists may view themselves as representing and advocating for the interests of service users within the organization. However, there may also be substantial differences between the perceptions of professional service providers as to the "needs" of service users, and the perceptions of service users, or user surrogates such as parents, as to the nature of those needs.

Professional identities may define status and authority within the organization separate from managerial responsibilities. Such identities may also define patterns of distinctive and separate subgroups within a service organization—social workers and teachers in a public school setting, doctors and nurses in a hospital. Communication may be very active within such subgroups and almost nonexistent across the boundaries of these subgroups. The ability of professional specialists to network with other members of a profession outside of organizational boundaries, both as a regular part of professional responsibilities and outside of the work setting, can strengthen their relative power within the service organization. Professional career opportunities that are not limited to a single organization may be very important for professional specialists, whereas stability and continuity of employment may be more important for staff members who are not members of an organized profession. Innovation and experimentation through time-limited funding grants for new programs may have a high value for the professional specialists involved in such programs, but they may be of much less importance to other members of the staff. Program expansion may be a higher priority for professional staff members than the initiatives of the board of directors intended to protect the financial viability of the organization.

Given the labor-intensive processes of service production in human service organizations, the employee constituency, and indirectly the employee household constituency, may be very influential in the ongoing process of policy and program decision making. Although in some instances this influence may be exercised through formal and inclusive channels, including union organizations and staff associations, the employee constituency is often fragmented by position and status distinctions, with different subgroups having different priorities.

The general body of members of an organized profession may also be a critical stakeholder constituency for many organizations (see chapter 7). Where there is a formal accreditation process, professional specialists—physicians, social workers, nurses, lawyers—may have an important role in the accreditation review process. To the extent that the organized profession also has a significant or controlling role in the accreditation of professional education programs, and in state-administered professional licensing procedures, the profession has a major role in selection and training of the professional specialists who become staff members in the service organization.

The organized profession is also an external force that may be appealed to on issues of ethical standards in program services, or on issues involving the treatment of staff members who are members of the profession. In many organizations, professional specialists who are not staff members may serve on the policy board or on a technical advisory board. Connections through professional associations may provide professional staff members access to such individuals, who may be viewed within the organization as being advocates for professional staff interests in board decision making.

POLICY-MAKING BOARDS

Although policy boards and advisory bodies are elements in the core decision-making and authority structure of the service organization, the members of such bodies also are a significant constituency in the organizational political economy (see chapter 10). The role of the board of directors differs among nonprofit, quasi-governmental nonprofit, governmental, and for-profit service organizations. In governmental programs, including quasi-governmental nonprofit organizations, boards and commissions are established by, and are ultimately accountable to, a body representing the general electorate. In publicly held for-profit businesses, the board of directors is elected by and ultimately accountable to the stockholder/owners of the business. Nonprofit boards of directors are generally accountable only to themselves or, in a more general sense, to the community. Despite these differences, there are also similarities in the position of board members as members of a policy-making constituency.

Board members are not only individual participants in decision making. They also represent a variety of interests related to the service products of the organization. Their presence is an essential element in the community legitimation of the service organization. Many board members are directly connected to sources of funding support, either because they participate in funding decisions in another organization (for example, as a corporation officer), through their service in organizing fundraising events, or through their participation in the network of political/governmental relationships. On the other hand, few board members are members of labor unions and relatively few are elected public officials or public administrators.

Board members of voluntary, nonprofit service organizations have formal legal and fiduciary responsibilities within very broad and general guidelines (Chisolm 1995) (see chapter 10). That is, they are collectively responsible to the general community for the prudent use of the funds made available to the organization, for the conformance of the organization to applicable laws and regulations involving the use of funds, and for the maintenance of the organization as an ongoing source of services in the community. There are similar board responsibilities in quasi-governmental nonprofit organizations and in governmental bodies that are governed through a formal board or commission, although the specific framework of accountability is established through legislation. In for-profit service organizations, the legal responsibility of a board of directors for the financial soundness and legal behavior of the organization and the accountability of the board to the stockholder/owners is even more explicit.

In voluntary nonprofit organizations, the fiduciary responsibility of the board is combined with the "mission" responsibility. That is, it is the board of directors that is ultimately responsible for defining the purposes and objectives of the organization and for monitoring the consistency of the organizational activity with such statements of purpose. On the other hand, in the governmental service organization, it is the legislature, or a similar governmental body, that carries the ultimate responsibility for defining the organizational mission and for holding the organization accountable. State "sunset" laws requiring the periodic review and evaluation of all state agencies is one method of enforcing such mission accountability.

Nonprofit boards of directors, in general, function as community "trustees" rather than as "representatives." And in the vast majority of these organizations, board members are selected from a limited sector of the society. Consistently, board members of nonprofit service organizations are predominantly men, between the ages of forty-five and sixty-five, with college education and from business or professional backgrounds. The other substantial group of such board members are women from similar social and economic backgrounds who either have careers in business or a profession or are married to men with such careers. Most nonprofit board members have had prior experience as officers of self-governing voluntary associations, including religious organizations and civic clubs, and bring that experience with them to the nonprofit board. Moreover, most nonprofit board members are likely to have lived in the local community for a relatively long period of time, in many instances longer than most organizational staff members, including the executive.

Nonprofit board members come predominantly from White ethnic backgrounds. Board members from other ethnic backgrounds are likely to come from similar social and economic backgrounds. The normal self-perpetuating process of nonprofit board member selection is biased in the direction of the maintenance of the social and economic characteristics of the board. Board nominating committees often recruit individuals that they are acquainted with or feel comfortable with. The increasing emphasis on the responsibility of nonprofit boards for fund raising (see chapter 10) also skews the selection process in favor of persons who have personal wealth or have connections with individuals who have access to funds.

Individuals selected to serve on the boards of quasi-governmental nonprofit organizations or commissions often come from similar backgrounds, although particular individuals may be selected by governmental appointment authorities to "represent" other sectors of the society, such as organized labor. Board members of for-profit human service organizations also have similar characteristics, although they are more likely to be selected on the basis of previous experience in business.

Board members in all types of human service organizations—nonprofit, quasi-governmental nonprofit, governmental, and for-profit—are likely to have little overlap with the service user constituency. They are likely to have little first-hand information about the quality of services provided by the organization. However, they, and other members of their families, are likely to have informal and social contacts with individuals serving on boards of directors of other service organizations, as well as with persons who are part of the funder constituency. Thus the perceptions of the organization within the board member/funder network may have more saliency in board decision making than the perceptions of the organization among service users.

OTHER SERVICE ORGANIZATIONS

Other organizations, including other human service organizations, particularly those that are part of the immediate "task environment," are another important stakeholder constituency. The most important organizations are those that are part of a common service network serving a particular community constituency (see chapter 5). Such networks include the network of services for abused and neglected children; the network of services for mothers and infants, including individual professional specialists and hospitals and clinics; the network of services for persons with severe and chronic mental illness; the network of services for individuals with cancer. In many ways, the local public school system is a network of individual educational service organizations—elementary and secondary schools—a network that functionally also includes the local community college and nearby colleges and universities as well as local employers. Each organization in this network is affected by the performance of other network organizations.

The service network includes organizations that make referrals to, or receive referrals from, a given "focal" organization (Austin 1991). This service network stakeholder constituency may include individual organizations that provide similar services and may therefore may be competitors for market share, as well as organizations that have the same funding source and who may be competitors for funding although providing an entirely different type of service. For example, at a state level, the Department of Adult Corrections may be a major competitor of public school systems for state financial support.

Organizational ecology theorists focus on the "population of organizations" and on the dynamics within such a cluster of organizations in which some organizations expand, including diversification and mergers, and others disappear (Carroll 1988). Although access to funding support may be the essential requirement for organizational survival, for many service organizations the ability to receive referrals from other organizations may be equally important—for example, particular forms of specialized medical services, or residential treatment centers. The willingness of other organizations to make referrals may be a major factor in the general community reputation of a given organization with potential consequences for funding. Community reputation among other service organizations may also have a direct bearing on the ability of an organization to recruit persons in positions of community leadership to serve on a board of directors and to recruit experienced professionals as staff members.

The willingness of other service organizations to accept referrals may also be important; for example, the ability of local school districts to access specialized mental health services for particular students may have consequences for classroom management in a particular school. Similarly, the willingness of mental health service organizations to accept referrals from jails or prisons has consequences both for individual prisoners and for the criminal justice organizations.

The willingness of other service organizations to collaborate in negotiations with a funding source, to engage in advocacy on a legislative issue that is critical for several organizations, or to participate in combined training activities may also be very important for an individual organization. Participation in the development of such a collaboration is usually a responsibility of the organizational executive (see chapter 9). Neither board members nor other organizational staff members can, by themselves, effectively represent or act for the organization, particularly when other executives are the key participants in such collaborations.

For some executives, coalition/collaboration development may be a central part of their activities, particularly when an entire segment of the community service network faces fundamental "turbulent" changes in the institutional environment (Emery and Trist 1965). For example, governmental and nonprofit health-care service organizations facing fundamental changes in the funding environment in the 1990s have been forced to create coalitions, partnerships, alliances, and mergers to survive.

In other situations, active competition may exist among service organizations in the same general service area. This can include competition for service users, particularly those with financial resources, or competition for funding and community status. There was an intense organizational competition for patients with health insurance coverage for mental illness conditions during a period in the late 1980s when there was an aggressive expansion of for-profit psychiatric hospital facilities as a result of increased coverage of psychiatric conditions by health insurance plans. This resulted in expensive and aggressive media campaigns to recruit patients, and high-visibility professional continuing education programs to enhance the reputation of individual hospitals among professionals with the potential ability to influence referrals.

In some settings, this also led to unethical and even illegal activity, such as indirect kickbacks to individual psychiatrists in return for regular referrals (Vandenberg 1996) and the forcible retention of patients until their insurance resources were exhausted. The exposure of these unethical and fraudulent practices resulted in a general collapse of the for-profit psychiatric hospital industry.

In some communities, the service organization constituency may be very diverse and fragmented. However, in such settings there may also be an informal system of linkages through personal professional connections and local professional associations. Alternatively, there may be inclusive community-wide associations of service organizations, or community planning councils that include service organizations as member organizations. Such planning councils may be linked to a central funding source such as a United Way. Leadership within such interagency associations may have important consequences for the status of the organization within the community.

The pattern of relationships between single service organizations and the network of related service organizations may be a crucial factor in the ultimate effectiveness of services for a particular service user. The maintenance of such relationships may require a substantial amount of time from the organizational executive and other staff members. It may also require some sacrifice of the autonomy and visibility of the service organization, with potential negative consequences for the fund-raising initiatives for which members of the board of directors take responsibility.

For-profit human service firms may respond to the complexities involved in interactions within the service organization environment by efforts to control these interactions through contracts, acquisitions, and mergers. This has been particularly evident in the managed health-care sector as exemplified by the pattern of acquisitions in local communities by Columbia-HCA (Health Corporation of America) and other nationwide health maintenance organizations (HMOs). When there is an aggressive pattern of acquisitions, an individual service organization may face a choice of becoming a subordinate part of a larger system or being left out of the dominant funding/referral network in the local community.

MEDIA

The media constituency and the staff members who work in newspapers, magazines, radio, and television are often a critical link between a service organization and the general public. In addition to the media outlets that cover the entire community, there are often radio, newspaper, and television firms that serve particular ethnic publics. Although the media constituency may be divided among many separate organizations, personal connections among newspaper reporters and among television and radio announcers may result in very similar treatment of specific events affecting a service organization.

The power of the media constituency is primarily symbolic power—that is, the ability to define an issue and to link positive or negative symbolic language to that issue. The identification of AFDC recipients as "welfare queens" by some media elements was a significant factor in the public support for "welfare reform." All types of human service organizations, including for-profit firms, are highly dependent on the influence of public opinion on legitimation and funding, as well as on service user self-referrals and interorganizational referrals. This makes relations with the media important for most human service organizations. In particular, positive media attention may be very important for organizations that depend heavily on voluntary contributions from the general public, either directly, such as the Salvation Army, or indirectly through the United Way or the Black United Way. Positive media attention may be equally important for organizations that depend heavily on service contracts with governmental bodies.

Creating positive media attention may require special events that are particularly designed for media coverage, the development of linkages with key members of the media, and the regular provision of information to the media about the organization and its services. The responsibilities of a public relations staff member may include development of personal connections with key members of the media as well as the preparation of specific public relations materials. Members of the board of directors may have a special role in developing and maintaining linkages with local media. Larger organizations may recruit members of the media to serve on a board of directors or may employ persons who have media experience to handle public relations. Such linkages may be particularly important when there are public policy issues that directly affect the organization or its service users.

The media may be able to highlight a general social policy issue, such as family violence, that is central to the community advocacy initiative of a battered women's shelter. Media interpretation of a community problem condition—homelessness, juvenile violence, adolescent pregnancies, school dropouts—may have a major influence on funding priorities, community mobilization, and on the program guidelines established by funding sources. Media support, including the support of specific media personalities, may also be crucial for organizational fundraising events.

Access to members of the media may be particularly important when there is an organizational crisis, whether it is an internal policy conflict, a funding problem, or a service failure, such as the death of an abused child who has been returned to the biological parents by a child protective services organization. Nonprofit and governmental service organizations are expected to be open to public examination to a greater degree than for-profit firms and are also expected to spend fewer resources on public relations than similar for-profit firms. A single newspaper story or television interview may determine the public reaction, and the reaction of other members of the media, to a complex organizational problem in such organizations. The responses to such a situation from media serving the general community and from media serving particular ethnic communities may be very different. Reporters and writers may win special honors within their profession for an investigation of problems in an organization that is expected to serve the public.

In some situations, media staff members may participate in an ad hoc and unofficial coalition that may also include organizational staff members in attempts to influence an organizational policy decision by calling public attention to the issues involved. An external interest group—for example, from a particular service neighborhood—may form a coalition with a media staff member to exert pressure on a service organization to develop a new service program, to expand an existing program, or to prevent the termination of a service.

MEMBERS OF THE GENERAL PUBLIC

Members of the general public are the ultimate constituency for all human service programs. The general public includes actual and potential service users, actual and potential financial supporters through contributions or tax payments, and actual and potential volunteers. The influence of the general public on a service organization is largely mediated by intermediate structures—elected public officials, community fundraising organizations, and public influence organizations such as churches. The perception of a service organization by the general public is largely shaped by the representation of the organization through the media. This often takes the form of endorsement of, or participation in, special fund-raising events by media personalities.

Some organizations develop service programs that are consistent with the existing community consensus on values and problem definitions and are able to establish a broad base of public support. Some organizations develop programs that deliberately depart from the existing community consensus—service programs for gay and lesbian adolescents, rape crisis centers that encourage criminal prosecution of date rapers, charter schools that highlight distinctive ethnic heritages, organizations providing elective abortion services. Such organizations may try to find a small but committed group of sympathetic supporters and volunteers from among the members of the general public and may seek to change attitudes among the general public. Here again, linkages between the board members and staff members of the service organization and the media may be of crucial importance in the effort to achieve organizational goals.

CONSTITUENCY CONFLICTS

The following discussion briefly explores potential areas of conflict among these stakeholder constituencies. One consistent area of potential conflict among stakeholder constituencies is the balance between public goods and private goods in specific human service programs as noted in chapter 2. This includes, for example, the conflict between the interests of governmental funders of child protective services programs in protecting all children from abuse, and the interests of particular parents in maintaining control over their children. In particular, social control service programs, including involuntary placement of a law violator into prison, often conflict with the preferences and interests of the individual who becomes a prisoner.

The political economy dynamics that are relevant to a particular organization take on additional complexities as a result of the broad pattern of societal changes taking place in the United States. Of particular importance for human service organizations is the process of cultural transformation that is taking place, and the resulting changes in the relative position of all of the ethnic constituencies within this society. Similar changes are taking place in the relative position of gender constituencies, sexual preference constituencies, and disability constituencies. These changes are reflected in changes within each of the stakeholder constituencies and in the relationships among the several stakeholder constituencies.

The cultural transformation changes include a steady increase in the proportion of U.S. residents who come from Latino, African American, American Indian, and Asian American backgrounds, and in the number of persons born outside the United States. These population groups have been increasingly able to heighten their influence within this society through political action, legal action, and appeals to cultural traditions of fairness. As a consequence, persons from White backgrounds have been forced to share elements of power and influence that they dominated a half century ago. Similar changes have taken place in the relative position of men and women. These changes have been accompanied by high levels of tension, political competition, and political conflict throughout the society. These conflicts have major consequences for all types of human service organizations because these organizations— health care, education, social service, and criminal justice—are central to the social fabric of the society. Such organizations can become the focus of controversy over control of the organization.

User access to services has been one of the areas of tension and conflict; such issues include ethnically and sexually discriminatory eligibility policies, physical accessibility, language accessibility, citizenship status, and geographic location. Affirmative action in access to higher education has become a major focus of conflict. Access to employment and to career opportunities is equally important. Human service organizations have been an important source of employment for individuals from traditionally excluded populations and from limited economic backgrounds. Increased access of women to professional education in law, medicine, and business administration is changing the characteristics of the body of practitioners in those fields.

Formal and informal employment affirmative action policies are often a key element of controversy, including such issues as preferences for men in elementary education or preferences for the employment of women as faculty members in traditionally male-dominated university academic departments. The recognition of alternative sexual lifestyles has also had consequences for the organization of services, accessibility to services, and access to employment in human services. The issue of creating ethnic as well as economic diversity in nonprofit boards of directors and other policy-making bodies runs counter to traditional internal nomination procedures that often result in the continuous perpetuation of existing patterns of board membership. Funders may face demands that they support new service organizations serving specialized user constituencies rather than supporting traditional community-wide service organizations.

In many service arenas, there are also conflicts affecting stakeholder constituencies that involve religious traditions and patterns of social change. These include conflicts over abortion services in health-care programs, criteria for the selection of textbooks in public education, public prayer in school, guidelines for distinctions between parental discipline and parental abuse, and conflicts over the recognition of gay or lesbian households as adoptive parents.

Because of the large and critical role of human services that are provided through organizations in education, social service, health care, and criminal justice, the organizational conflicts created by societal changes have had broad consequences for the whole society. Two examples of conflict are the conflict over maintaining neighborhood schools or using community-wide magnet schools to support desegregation, and the conflict over the official recognition of languages other than English in governmental service organizations.

Many of these conflicts have led to public policy conflicts that can affect funding patterns and program policies affecting individual service organizations. Politicized conflicts over affirmative action in higher education, the access of adolescent girls as single parents to financial assistance programs, unrestricted access of women to abortion services, and the access of immigrants to public social and health services have led to changes in the political balance of power in both federal and state governments.

Changes in the political environment have resulted in the massive expansion of both state and federal prison systems, the replacement of the AFDC federal-state financial assistance program with the TANF program, the exclusion of legal immigrants from governmental service programs, the privatization of some Medicaid health-care programs, and the authorization of public financial support for private "charter schools." These changes have far-reaching consequences for all of the stakeholder constituencies, the service user constituencies, the legitimating and funding constituencies, the employee constituencies, the media constituencies, and the public. It can be expected that these processes of societal change, including changes in the relative position of ethnic and sexual constituencies, and political responses to the conflicts resulting from such changes, will continue with consequences for all types of human service organizations.

SUMMARY

The performance of the human service organization is strongly influenced by the power and influence of the various stakeholder constituencies. These include service users; sources of legitimation and financial support; employees, including professional specialists; policy makers; other service organizations; the media; and members of the community. The interest and support of these constituencies are essential elements in the ability of the service organization to produce the services that benefit individuals, families, and the community. However, there are important differences in the interests and objectives of different constituencies that can result in internal organizational conflicts. Dealing with and resolving such conflicts is a major responsibility of organizational managers.

FOUR

ORGANIZATIONAL STRUCTURE
AND PROGRAM DESIGN

The structure of an organization can be defined simply as the sum total of the ways in which it divides its labor into distinct tasks and then achieves coordination among them. —Mintzberg (1979:2)

It is one thing to understand a need; it is quite another matter to design an intervention that will meet that need. . . . The purpose of the program design phase is to put together that service or combination of services that appears to have the best possible chance of achieving the program's objectives. —Kettner, Moroney, and Martin (1999:12)

THE CHARACTERISTICS of the services that individuals, families, and communities receive through human service organizations are directly affected by the way in which the service organization is structured and by the operational design of the service program. This chapter deals with the structure of human service organizations and with the design of service programs within such organizations.

The first section of this chapter uses a framework set forth by Mintzberg in *The Structuring of Organizations* (1979) and in *Power In and Around Organizations* (1983) to identify the most common structural characteristics of human service organizations. The second section examines the variety of auspices that exist for human service organizations. Traditionally, the world of human service organizations has been viewed as divided between voluntary nonprofit organizations and governmental bureaus. However, the crossover patterns between nonprofit and governmental organizations that have emerged recently, together with the appearance of for-profit human service organizations, have resulted in an increased diversity of organizational auspices. The third section of this chapter examines variations in governance structures among human service organizations. The fourth section explores the choices in rationale, strategy, and tactics involved in designing an operational service program.

ORGANIZATIONAL STRUCTURES

Mintzberg (1979) identifies five basic organizational patterns:

- Simple structure
- Machine bureaucracy
- Professional bureaucracy
- Divisionalized form
- Adhocracy

All these patterns exist in human service organizations. Two of these patterns—machine bureaucracy and professional bureaucracy—are the primary focus of this chapter and are discussed in some detail after brief commentaries about the other three patterns.

Adhocracy

Adhocracy (Mintzberg 1979:431–467) is the high-tech start-up business in which technical skill–sharing unifies the participants, team projects are the norm, and the organizational structure changes frequently. There are similar organizations in the broad field of human services that may have many of the characteristics of an adhocracy. These include a de-emphasis on managerial authority, the absence of status differentials among staff members, flexibility in work responsibilities and work schedules, and collective decision making (Hyde 1992). Some of the adhocracy-type organizations are nonprofit start-ups in which a small group of individuals decide to initiate a new service program, either to try out an innovative service technology or to provide services in an unserved community. Others are on-going "alternative," "community-based," or "social movement" service organizations. However, the nature of the external funding environment, including limitations on venture capital funding sources, primarily foundations, for start-up human service organizations, often makes it difficult to maintain an adhocracy social movement structure over an extended period of time (Powell 1986; Hyde 1992, 2000).

Simple Structure

Mintzberg (1979:305–313) describes the *simple structure* as a relatively small organization with a highly centralized and personalized structure of supervision and control. An executive, who may also have been the founder of the organization, is the key source of power and authority. Simple structure human services organizations may include long-standing, small- to medium-sized organizations, such as neighborhood social services and emergency assistance centers, small school districts, county child welfare organizations in rural communities, and local hospitals with a physician administrator. The management style is largely determined by the personal style of the executive. The board of directors generally defers to the executive. Staff relationships involve a mixture of personal relationships and task-oriented relationships.

Divisionalized Form

The *divisionalized form* (Mintzberg 1979:380–430) occurs in large organizations that operate in more than one geographic location or produce different products for different markets. Such organizations often take on a divisionalized form structure in which varying degrees of authority are moved from a central administrative structure to divisional administrative structures with central coordination. Organizations like the American Red Cross, the Salvation Army, multicampus "university systems," and nationwide managed-care organizations involving complex health-care service systems in a series of different communities are large-scale examples of divisionalized forms.

   Although adhocracy, simple structure, and divisionalized form organizations exist among human service organizations, *machine bureaucracy* and *professional bureaucracy* are the most widely found structural patterns.

Machine Bureaucracy

Machine bureaucracy is the traditional model of goods-producing industries or governmental service organizations such as the U.S. Postal Service. There is standardization of work processes and a closed system of action—that is, the impact of forces in the task environment on the production processes is limited (Mintzberg 1979:314–347). This model is also consistent with what Thompson describes as organizations using "long-linked technology" (1967:15). The automobile assembly line and the computer assembly line are classic examples in which each worker (or electronically controlled robot) is responsible for a limited number of standardized work tasks, even though the factory may produce a variety of products.

Only a few human service organizations are actually organized as a machine bureaucracy. One example is that part of the Social Security system that is responsible for maintaining individual records of employment and for routine payments to recipients of Social Security benefits.

However, a number of human service organizations are formally organized around the traditional structure of the machine bureaucracy. In particular, the machine bureaucracy pattern has been the formal model in many public administration settings and in many governmental human service organizations. These include the organizations that have historically administered the Aid for Families with Dependent Children (AFDC) program, food stamps, public housing programs, and veteran's benefits. Indeed, many of the writings about governmental human service programs, including those that are critical of such programs, often use the term *bureaucracy* in a way that indicates that the reference is to a machine bureaucracy structure (Lipsky 1980). Contributing to the persistence of a machine bureaucracy pattern in public administration settings is the high proportion of senior managers, primarily men, who have had previous experience as officers in the military bureaucracy.

One important rationale for the persistence of the machine bureaucracy structure in governmental human service programs is an emphasis on procedural fairness—that is, the concept that each person served by a governmental bureau, particularly those that deal with "entitlements," should be treated in exactly the same way (Montes 1997). An ethical commitment to procedural fairness in governmental service programs is often reinforced by the fear of public criticism, legislative attack, or legal assault if individual service users are served in different ways on the basis of the judgment of individual service providers. Moreover, a failure to maintain and reinforce procedural fairness has often been associated with persistent patterns of unequal treatment or discrimination by front-line workers in social service, education, health-care, and criminal justice service programs (Lipsky 1980:111–116). The question of what is meant by procedural fairness is particularly involved when the role of affirmative action in governmental service programs (including admission policies in higher education) is being debated.

The emphasis on consistency in work processes in a machine bureaucracy requires a centralized authority structure with attention given to explicit rules and regulations as well as to oversight and control procedures (Mintzberg 1979:315–316). This requires a technical staff whose major function is to devise and enforce rules and regulations. The most prominent example of the application of machine bureaucracy concepts in human services has historically been in the federal and state AFDC and food stamp financial assistance programs. Both federal and state authorities have established detailed rules governing these programs, rules that are developed by a mid-level body of technical rule writers covering eligibility, payment levels, and worker performance.

The fundamental assumptions of the machine bureaucracy include a simple, stable, and predictable environment, together with routine production activities and a work force consisting largely of semiskilled workers. A machine bureaucracy may be both efficient and effective when these conditions are met. However, when they are not met, a pattern of anomalies and inconsistencies within the service organization is likely to develop (Lipsky 1980; Richan 1984; Hasenfeld 2000). Such service organizations may have a consistently low level of service effectiveness and a high level of internal tensions although they continue to exist over extended periods of time. Two examples of service organizations that are often structured as a machine bureaucracy but that have an unpredictable environment and nonroutine service production requirements are the state- or county-administered public child protective service programs, and the state-administered Temporary Assistance to Needy Families (TANF) programs.

Societies for the protection of children were originally established in the nineteenth century as nonprofit service organizations with a child welfare, "child saving," mission and a largely decentralized structure of services together with a flexible pattern of staff activities including the mobilization of community resources in support of children at risk. This simple structure pattern was carried over into the early governmental child welfare programs established in the 1930s under Title IV-B of the Social Security Act. In many instances, these federally supported programs, largely located in rural areas, involved a single county-level social worker who responded to very diverse child abuse and neglect situations by dealing directly with the family situation as well as by mobilizing community resources.

In the 1960s, the Title IV-B programs became comprehensive child protective services programs covering an entire state. They were frequently combined administratively with the AFDC income assistance program that was increasingly being structured as a rule-controlled, hierarchical machine bureaucracy. The result was a long-standing pattern of conflict between efforts to establish consistent rules and regulations governing the procedures of child welfare workers who had very limited specialized training, and, on the other hand, efforts to individualize service responses to unique family situations. Glisson (1992) identifies this as a situation involving an incongruity between structure and technology with the organizational structure shaping the operational service technology rather than the technology shaping the structure. This is contrary to organizational contingency theories that describe organizational structures as normally being determined by production technology (Lawrence and Lorsch 1967).

One of the results of the pressure to shape the child protective services organization to the requirements of a machine bureaucracy has been an operational situation in which service supervisors serve a buffering function. This involves shielding front-line workers from excessively detailed rules and regulations and shielding the technical core and central administrators from information about the diversity and unpredictability of the individual situations with which workers are dealing. One outcome is what Victor Thompson describes as bureaupathologies (1961), which include a high degree of discontent among service workers, burnout (Schaufeli, Maslach, and Marek 1993), and high levels of staff turnover, as well as public discontent with the quality and consistency of the services provided. Similar problems existed within the AFDC program and have continued in the TANF programs.

One response to these problems has been to privatize, or contract out, specialized professional services, which establishes some additional buffering between the administrative bureaucracy and the actual front-line service providers. The implementation of child welfare family preservation services has reflected the tension between machine bureaucracy and professional bureaucracy, as seen when a professionalized, high-intensity, experienced staff model with a low caseload is used in the initial demonstration projects, but a standardized, less intensive, inexperienced staff model with a larger caseload is used in statewide replication of the original model.

Similar machine bureaucracy conditions exist in some elementary and secondary schools in which standard curriculum and testing requirements assume standardized student participants and a stable and predictable environment throughout the school system. Standardized curriculum requirements, standardized teaching plans, large-scale standardized testing, centrally selected textbooks, and highly centralized control of school schedules represent efforts to duplicate the consistency of work processes found in industrial assembly lines. The objective is to produce a standardized high school graduate who will fit local labor market requirements or college admission requirements. Massive misfits often exist between these organizational assumptions and the environmental reality in areas of rapid population change or where households do not fit standard cultural assumptions. This can result in high levels of discontent among both teachers and parents and a high level of school failure and dropout among students (Romo and Falbo 1996).

Professional Bureaucracy

Mintzberg identifies the *professional bureaucracy* (1979:349–378) as an organization in which there is an emphasis on standardization of *skills*, rather than of *work processes*. In *Power In and Around Organizations*, Mintzberg describes the professional bureaucracy as a form of *meritocracy* (1983:393). That is, organizations depend on "the skills and knowledge of their operating professionals to function; all produce standard products or services" (Mintzberg 1979:349). As Kanter states, "Professional disciplines ensure control and coherence without elaborate hierarchies of supervision" (1997:159). The general hospital, the child guidance clinic, the college preparatory high school, the residential treatment center, the adoption agency, the community mental health center, the family counseling center are all concerned with producing consistent services and consistent results through a core of practitioners who are selected on the basis of comparable work skills. Although Mintzberg refers to these specialized practitioners as "professionals," such organizational employees may include experienced individuals who are largely trained internally as well as those who have formal external professional credentials.

The professional practitioner works closely with the service user but is relatively independent of colleagues (Mintzberg 1979, 1983). Training, including on-the-job training and indoctrination, are critical elements in developing consistency in practice. Training often requires an extended period of time. Authority is based on professional expertise—the chief of the medical service in a hospital; the clinical director in a family counseling agency; the "lead teacher" in a decentralized, professionalized, public school system; the nurse practitioner in the family practice clinic; the clinical director in a community mental health center; the department chair in the university. "The work is too complex to be controlled personally by managers or bureaucratically by the simple standards of the analysts" (Mintzberg 1983:396).

Bureaucratic elements enter in through an emphasis on consistency of outcomes—for example, an emphasis on quality control and evaluation. Other bureaucratic elements enter in through professional qualification requirements, standardization of training through accreditation of professional education programs, and state level professional examinations and licensing. Although services may, in many ways, be individualized, they are also standardized through the application of consistent diagnostic or assessment procedures that categorize service users (Mintzberg 1979:352; Hasenfeld 1983:192–197). One example involves the use of the *Diagnostic and Statistical Manual of Mental Disorders* (DSM-IV) to categorize and label individuals with mental disturbances so as to define the appropriate method of treatment and then establish a basis for determining the level of payment to the professional service provider.

In some organizations structured as a machine bureaucracy, such as the child protective services programs cited, internal processes of training and staff development may be used in an effort to increase the consistency of work skills. One example is the development, under the provisions of Title IV-E of the Social Security Act, of statewide in-service training programs, supervised jointly by protective services and schools of social work, for child protective services personnel. This is an effort to achieve greater consistency of outcomes in a single-practice setting without the formalities of fully developed professional education in so-cial work. One consequence, however, is that the participants in such training are generally unable to get formal recognition for this in-service training beyond the employing organization, through either academic credit, membership in the professional association (the National Association of Social Workers), or licensing.

Professional bureaucracy service organizations may develop primarily around a single profession—the elementary and secondary school system, the university, the nonprofit adoption agency, the criminal court system. In such instances, members of the profession often "capture" the administrative structure as well as dominate the service production process (Mintzberg 1979:358; 1983:397). That is, it is assumed that only persons with the same professional background can serve as managers. In multiprofession settings, such as general hospitals, there may be several parallel vertical professional structures (see chapter 7). And managers, such as hospital managers, may be selected on the basis of management training rather than on the basis of professional identity.

Often, a substantial degree of equality of status exists among professional specialists in a professional bureaucracy, with "democratic" decision making on issues affecting professional staff members. However, there may also be a high degree of centralized control over technical support staff members and other support workers, with little participation by them in organizational decision making. Indeed, it may be a major function of central management to ensure that support personnel are consistently responsive to the expectations of the professional personnel (Mintzberg 1979:355).

Summary

Among human service organizations, examples of all five of the organizational patterns that Mintzberg identifies can be found. However, it is the professional bureaucracy, or a combination of machine bureaucracy and professional bureaucracy, that is the most frequent organizational structure in established human service organizations. In particular, it is the pattern of the professional bureaucracy, as described by Mintzberg, that provides the primary framework for the balance of this and the following chapters.

AUTHORITY STRUCTURES, OR "AUSPICES"

Diversity of Auspices

Human service organizations have traditionally been viewed as being largely divided between nonprofit and governmental service organizations. However, such a classification obscures the fact that a wide variety of auspices structures occur, some of which blend the characteristics of these two types of organizations. Examples of this diversity include the following:

- A community-based nonprofit social movement organization with collective decision making by a combination of volunteer and paid staff members (Somerset Women's Center)
- A nonprofit corporation with a board of directors that has full authority to adopt by-laws, to appoint future members of the board, to appoint an executive, and to control the resources and assets of the corporation (Jefferson County Family Service Association, Tennessee Boys Ranch)
- A religious congregation that receives funding from a governmental agency to operate a day-care center with a governance board appointed by the members of the congregation (Woodstone Faith-based Children's Program)
- A nonprofit organization that is under the programmatic control of a larger nonprofit organization, that has the power to grant or withdraw the "charter" of the local organization, and that may have ultimate authority over the disposal of the organizational assets (Smithville Salvation Army)
- A nonprofit organization established by another nonprofit organization to carry out specialized functions as defined by the parent organization, with the parent organization having the authority to appoint the board of directors, to establish the policies under which the organization functions, and to control the assets of the corporation (The Children's Home of the Southern Diocese of Texas)
- A nonprofit organization established as the corporate instrument of an unincorporated association, with the members of the association selecting the members of the corporate board and having final au-

thority over the assets of the corporation (New Homes Corporation of the Woodland Neighborhood Association)

- A quasi-governmental nonprofit corporation established under state law that has a board of directors appointed under procedures established by the legislature with the board having the power to appoint an executive director and to administer a budget, largely financed by governmental funds (South Virginia Regional Mental Health Center, City of Hawksberg Senior Citizens Center)
- A joint powers authority established by two or more governmental bodies to carry out activities on behalf of all of them with appointments to a governing board and the selection of the executive subject to approval by the participating governments (Williamson City-County Park Board, Spring Valley Area Special Education Cooperative)
- A publicly funded authority or commission with a policy board appointed directly by a governmental body or public official that can appoint an executive and administer a budget (the Board of the Texas Department of Mental Health, Jonestown Municipal Hospital Board, Orange County Public Housing Authority)
- A special-purpose authority or district with taxing authority and an independently elected nonpartisan board of directors that has the authority to appoint an executive and to administer a budget (Ridgeway Independent School District, Gallaway Hospital District)
- An administrative unit of a general-purpose government with an executive directly accountable to an elected public official or a legislative body, with one or more advisory boards or committees and with limited organizational control over the level of the budget (Silver County Child Welfare Department, Massachusetts Department of Human Services)

The functioning of these different types of nonprofit and quasi-governmental and governmental organizational structures may be directly affected by the characteristics of their funding patterns. Community-based, start-up service organizations that begin with primarily volunteer service providers develop more formal structures when there is incorporation, funding from outside sources, and employed staff while some of the social movement motivation involved in their initiation is maintained (Hyde 2000).

There are similar variations in auspices structure among for-profit human service firms. These can include the following:

- A family-owned and -operated unincorporated home health firm, or nursing home, serving a single community
- An independent, publicly owned business firm providing a limited range of services in several locations (a kidney dialysis corporation)
- A conglomerate-owned subsidiary providing specialized services, with conglomerate control of capital funding and of the definition of profitability benchmarks
- A publicly owned, centrally controlled nationwide or multinational service corporation with a divisionalized form of organizational structure

Nonprofit, Governmental, For-Profit Distinctions

The diversity of auspices patterns has increased dramatically as the human service sector in the United States has increasingly taken on the characteristics of a mixed economy (Kramer 1998). This is largely a result of the process of privatization, through which governments are contracting out functions that have traditionally been operated directly by government (Bendick 1985). Privatization includes the contracting out of both auxiliary services—computer services, food service, building maintenance—and service provision. Contracting out by governmental service organizations increasingly includes both nonprofit and for-profit contractees, depending on the field of service. In the administration of community mental health centers that include funding through state Medicaid programs, both for-profit, large-scale managed behavioral health care firms and specialized nonprofit services may be contractees. A similar pattern exists in substance abuse treatment programs.

The process of contracting out and the enforcement of even-handed, competitive contracting procedures have created a market opportunity for the entrance of for-profit human service organizations into an economic sector that has traditionally consisted largely of governmental and nonprofit service organizations. In addition, there has been an increasingly important process of converting nonprofit service organizations to for-profit organizations, particularly in the health care sector (Goddeeris and Weisbrod 1997). This raises many questions about the distinctions between for-profit firms and traditional governmental and nonprofit service organizations in the production of human services. One fundamental difference is in the nature of the governance structures, which is discussed in the third section of this chapter.

GOALS AND MISSION   The goals (or missions) are different in nonprofit service organizations, governmental service organizations, and for-profit corporations. As indicated earlier (see chapter 2), both governmental and nonprofit service organizations have the responsibility to produce both private goods and public goods (Austin 1981). The public goods may include contributions to the development of social networks and community capacity over and beyond the benefits for individual service users (Backman and Smith 2000).

Jeavons (1992) describes the essential nature of the traditional (nongovernmental) nonprofit organization as the expression of deeply held values. The service program of the nonprofit organization is an expression of those values, with an emphasis on consistency of values within the organization and a concern for the outcomes of service provision. Since the nonprofit organization is committed to expressing through its activities a particular set of values determined by organizational history and the policy board, it is not committed to a model of community control over policies as determined by a political majority.

Governmental organizations, including quasi-governmental nonprofit organizations, are ultimately subject to control by a political majority and to the determination of fundamental policies by political structures outside the service organization itself. Changes in the pattern of political power can change the definition of the organizational mission (Montes 1997). The definition of the mission of the governmental service organization often includes specific definitions of public-goods objectives—reduce juvenile delinquency, prevent disease, protect families. For the governmental organization consistency, procedural fairness and due process in personnel procedures are more important than consistency of values among staff members; consistency, procedural fairness, and due process in service procedures within the context established by the political process are more important than specific service outcomes and user satisfaction. The quasi-governmental nonprofit organization combines the authority and financial resources of government with the greater degree of independent authority and administrative flexibility associated with the nonprofit organization. The public-goods objectives of such a service organization, however, may be defined in the authorizing legislation.

The primary mission of publicly traded for-profit organizations, by law and tradition, is to produce economic benefits for the shareholders who are the legal owners of the organization. Indeed, the expanded role of equity investments in individual and corporate retirement plans and the increasing use of equity options for executive remuneration have resulted in an increase in the emphasis on the priority given to shareholder interests. Such shareholder benefits may include the payment of dividends and increases in the value of the ownership shares. One result may be a difference in the mixture of public goods and private goods produced by the service organization (Backman and Smith 2000). Public-goods production may have a less important role in the for-profit organization than in either the nonprofit service organization or the governmental service organization. However, to the extent that user satisfaction is connected with financial profitability, service user private-good preferences and satisfaction may, in fact, have a more important role in the for-profit corporation.

CHANGES IN TRADITIONAL PATTERNS Changes taking place in funding patterns are creating unanticipated consequences for traditional distinctions among the three types of auspices (Kramer 1998). Governmental organizations are increasingly using contracts with nonprofit and for-profit organizations to produce specific services (Wolch 1990). Some nonprofit organizations receive a substantial majority of their income from governmental sources (Salamon 1989, 1996) with accompanying pressures to take on the characteristics of a governmental organization. This can mean that the mission-oriented nonprofit board of directors defers to the more formal fairness and due process rules and regulations that accompany the governmental funding, rules that are primarily applicable to larger and more comprehensive programs (Montes 1997).

Other nonprofit organizations may receive a major part of their income from tax-exempt marketplace sales of goods and services with accompanying requirements for giving priority to marketing and promotional initiatives, similar to those in for-profit firms (Cordes and Weisbrod 1997). When for-profit subsidiaries are created for handling merchandising activities with resulting tax obligations, there may be an incentive to shift overhead costs to the for-profit organization, where such costs may be deducted from earnings before taxes. Some nonprofit organizations have been converted to for-profit firms, particularly in the health care area (Goddeeris and Weisbrod 1997), with complex issues regarding the future status of financial assets created under the nonprofit status. And under some circumstances, for-profit organizations may convert to nonprofit status.

A steady increase has occurred in the number and size of for-profit corporations providing human services in health and mental health, in criminal justice, and in education. One consequence of this is increased competition based on cost between for-profit and nonprofit service organizations for governmental contracts. As Backman and Smith (2000) point out, one result can be that nonprofit organizations become more like for-profit businesses, cutting back on public-goods investment in the development and maintenance of community networks and in the development of social capital. Some communities have proposed removing the tax-exempt status of entrepreneurial nonprofit hospitals (Maynard and Poole 1998).

Governmental organizations that operate through government-created nonprofit organizations, or that contract with a number of different nonprofit organizations or for-profit firms, may discover that the result is a patchwork of services with different characteristics, responsive to a variety of governing constituencies. These constituencies may successfully resist efforts to enforce the uniform rules and regulations intended to apply to all programs. Moreover, a coalition of contracting organizations may exert political pressure to expand program funding while seeking to limit budget allocations for contract enforcement.

For-profit firms that receive most of their income from governmental sources, either through program contracts or through payments for services to individuals, may come to resemble a regulated utility. Political processes expressed through the level of regulation and limitations on profit levels may determine the economic benefits for shareholders more than marketplace forces.

The effect of these changes is to blur many of the traditional distinctions that are assumed to exist among the three sectors, particularly in the production of services for the service user (Kramer 1998). Moreover, to the extent that service organizations in all three sectors have the characteristics of a professional bureaucracy, service production distinctions among the three sectors may be quite limited. That is, the nature of professional influence, or control, over the *processes* of service production, and the pattern of private goods provided for the service user, may result in broad similarities across nonprofit, governmental, and for-profit sectors. Professional specialists may move from nonprofit to governmental to for-profit firms. Professional specialists in all three sectors may come from the same, or similar, professional education programs, join the same professional association, read similar journals, attend the same professional conferences, and participate in the same, or similar, continuing education programs.

Private colleges and universities and public colleges and universities deliver similar, though not necessarily identical, educational experiences for the individual student. For-profit, nonprofit, and governmental adoption services provide similar professional services. Nonprofit child guidance clinics, governmental community-based mental health services for children, and for-profit managed behavioral care services for children employ staff members with similar professional backgrounds and may provide generally similar services in individual situations. Maternity services in governmental, nonprofit, and for-profit hospitals have many similar characteristics, as do pediatric health-care services provided by all three types of organizations.

Summary

In the United States, organizational patterns in the human services are very diverse, including traditional differences among nonprofit, governmental, and for-profit auspices and significant variations within each of these three sectors. There is also a blurring of such differences in many instances as a result of contracting relationships that cut across the three sectors. Economic dynamics in individual organizations within each sector have both similarities to and differences from those in the other sectors. To the extent that professional specialists have a key role in the provision of services, operational distinctions among the three sectors may be blurred. Indeed, there may be more variation in authority structures within each sector than there is across the three sectors. However, differences in auspices patterns, and the changes taking place in these patterns, do have important consequences for the nature of the governance systems in each sector and for the role and responsibilities of the organizational executive. Some of these consequences are briefly explored in the next section and developed more fully in chapter 9 on the executive and chapter 10 on boards.

GOVERNANCE STRUCTURES

A wide range of differences exists in governance structures across human service organizations. There are differences across the three sectors—nonprofit, government, and for-profit—and differences within each sector. Most of the discussion of governance structures focuses either on the role of a board of directors (Carver and Carver 1996) or on the role of the organizational executive (Menefee and Posner 1997). However, fundamentally the governance structure involves both a board of directors and the executive, in various combinations.

The range of governance structures includes those in which a single executive has the formal authority for both policy making and management, and those in which a collective body carries both policy-making authority and management authority. Within all of these various governance structures, the critical issue is the formal, and the operational, division of authority between the executive and the policy-making body.

Although the governance structure is often described as the policy-making component, the governance structure actually involves (1) the boundary-spanning function of structuring the framework of interaction between the organization and the task environment, particularly as such interactions deal with legitimation, with resource procurement, and with accountability for internal program and personnel policies, and (2) the function of structuring the framework of authority within the organization.

The variety of governance structures in nonprofit and governmental service organizations is illustrated by the following examples:

- *Independent executive.* A single individual has both policy-making and management authority. This primarily includes the directly elected state or local public administrator who has the authority to determine policy and to administer a governmental organization within the broad limits established by a legislative body. Depending on the state, examples can include the state attorney general, the state superintendent of education, the commissioner of agriculture, and the county sheriff. In some cities, the chief of police may have comparable authority. A similar governance structure may exist in a privately owned business in which the chief executive officer is also chairman of the board and the largest shareholder.

- *Executive-centered governance.* In states with a cabinet-style structure of department managers, human services executives may be directly appointed by the governor, subject to legislative confirmation, and have broad policy and management authority, subject only to continued support by the governor. A similar pattern may exist at the level of county government. The governance structure of individual human service departments may include one or more advisory bodies as required by state law, or by federal law when federal funds are involved. In both nonprofit service organizations and publicly held for-profit firms, there may be a similar strong executive pattern in actual practice if the organizational executive has a dominant role in the selection of members of the policy board as well as controlling the agenda of the meetings of the board and the flow of information to the board.

- *Public commission or public authority governance structure.* In these governmental organizations, an elected or appointed policy body may be established that has independent authority for selection of an executive, for establishing a budget, and, in some instances, for levying taxes. Such bodies may be directly elected, or they may be established by an elected body. Examples include school boards, water authorities, hospital districts, park districts, and housing authorities. In some board and commission states, this category includes the major state human service agencies. The executive in such human service organizations generally does not vote in decisions by the commission board but serves as the primary source for policy recommendations to be considered by the commission and participates in policy discussions. The executive may, or may not, have independent and comprehensive authority for personnel decisions as well as for operational management.

- *Quasi-governmental nonprofit corporation.* Governmental bodies also create semiautonomous nonprofit corporations that operate under general policies established by the governmental unit. In many instances, the legislation that establishes the organization also speci-fies how the governing board is to be created. The members of the board may be appointed by governmental and nongovernmental en-tities external to the service organization itself. The board of the quasi-governmental nonprofit corporation generally has the authori-ty to establish a budget and to appoint and discharge an executive. The executive does not vote in board decisions. A particular charac-teristic of the quasi-governmental nonprofit corporation is the ability to receive funds from diverse governmental sources, foundations, di-rect and third-party payments for services, and contributions, as well as to enter into contracts for the provision of services for which it has ultimate responsibility. Examples include community mental health centers and public hospitals with independent boards.

- *Voluntary nonprofit corporation.* A self-perpetuating board has broad responsibility for policy decisions, to appoint and discharge the exec-utive, and for establishing the organizational budget including funding strategies. The board is the legal representation of the service organi-zation. The executive does not vote in board decisions. Policy recom-mendations may come from the executive or from within the board. The executive is generally expected to have comprehensive authority for operational management and personnel decisions. Examples in-clude the family counseling center, the voluntary nonprofit adoption agency, the visiting nurse association, the YMCA and YWCA, and the private university.
- *Voluntary association.* The voluntary membership association has a governing board selected by the individual members that has both policy-making and management responsibilities. The association may have employed staff members, but board officers often carry admin-istrative responsibilities. Examples include the Junior League, the Oakhurst Neighborhood Association, and the National Alliance for the Mentally Ill. Large membership associations like the American As-sociation for Retired Persons may combine the governance character-istics of an association and of the voluntary nonprofit organization, including a salaried executive.

In the governance structure of the publicly traded, for-profit human service business, in comparison to the nonprofit and governmental gov-ernance structures, the chief executive officer (CEO) of the business firm is a shareholder and therefore one of the owners of the firm and also a voting member of the board of directors. In many businesses, the CEO may also serve as the board chair, although in very large businesses the board chair may be a separate position. The CEO, as a shareholder, may benefit financially from policies that result in an increase in the firm's profitability, and therefore in the value of the corporate stock, in addition to direct salary payments and benefits.

A key element in the governance structures that include a separate policy-making body is the extent to which the members of that body represent, either officially or unofficially, various stakeholder constituencies. In nearly all types of service organizations, the organizational employees are not directly represented by voting members of a policy-making body. Moreover, in most service organizations, the service user constituency is not directly represented by members of the policy-making body. On the other hand, in nonprofit organizations, external sources of legitimation and funding support are often represented in the policy-making board, either directly or unofficially. In governmental service organizations, a variety of political constituencies are likely to be represented in such a body. The board of the for-profit firm is explicitly intended to represent the shareholders of the firm, but the members of the board of directors may also represent a wide variety of other constituencies including capital funding sources and related businesses.

Each of these governance examples has a different pattern of responsibilities for dealing with the external legitimation and funding environment, for internal personnel and program policy making, and for internal organizational control. In the chapters that follow, the governmental authority, the quasi-governmental nonprofit organization, and the voluntary nonprofit organization, all of which have a policy board and a salaried, nonvoting executive, will be the primary focus of attention. Much of the content, however, may also be relevant for service organizations that have other forms of governance, including for-profit businesses.

Summary

Human service organizations include a diversity of organizational structures with a variety of governance structures. These differences have implications not only for internal organizational processes but also for the relations of the organization with its external task environment, as well as for the capacity of different organizations to collaborate with each other in providing a comprehensive array of community services.

ISSUES IN PROGRAM DESIGN

Just as there are problematic aspects in the organizational structures of human service programs, there are also problematic aspects in the program technologies being used in many human service organizations. These include the following:

- A combination of low effectiveness and low efficiency that results in a very low cost–benefit ratio
- Creaming—that is, the admission to service programs of only those persons for whom successful outcomes are most likely to occur under any circumstances
- Prescription of inappropriate treatments—for example, institutional care when noninstitutional care is more appropriate
- Use of service delivery procedures that negate program objectives—for example, stigmatizing administrative procedures that interfere with co-production in income support programs and in turn with the achievement of programmatic objectives related to economic self-support
- Uncontrolled, and often unknown, variations in the application of treatment methods within a given program
- Use of highly technical treatment methods by service workers without appropriate training
- Use of well-trained professional staff persons to carry out routine, rule-controlled tasks
- Failure to address factors that continue to generate problem conditions while concentrating on individual problems
- Failure to adapt program methods to variations in service user characteristics
- Problems in access that interfere with utilization of existing services
- Staff burnout as a consequence of inappropriate program design.

These problems indicate that the technical design of service programs is a critical administrative policy issue in human service programs (Rossi 1978).

Program technology design issues in the human services have distinct characteristics that make them different from technology design issues in other types of production organizations. Moreover, the programs in each field of service have distinctive elements of program technology. However, some program design elements are relevant to all fields of service within the human services. These include the *program rationale* (or theory of intervention), the *program strategy*, and the *program tactics* (or operational plan). An understanding of program technology design issues is essential both for the analysis of existing service programs and for the design of new service programs.

The unit of analysis for the study of program design is the *program component* (also see chapter 5). Specific service production activities take place as person-to-person transactions within program components, distinctive units of activity within an organization in which a specific group of staff members interacts with a particular group of service users to produce a specific type of human service. Most service organizations operate a number of distinct program components. For example, a county child welfare department may include an investigation unit, a foster-care unit, an adoption unit, and an emergency shelter for adolescents. In most instances, each of these program components has a distinctive subbudget within the total organization budget, a program manager, specific staff personnel, and often separate organizational space.

Each such program component may have a distinctly different combination of program rationale, program strategy, and program tactics. Functional decentralization of program organization and program management, or "loose-coupling" among program elements (Weick 1976), makes it possible to deal with potential conflicts between different rationales and different strategies within the same organization. Organizations need to have procedures in place to resolve conflicts between service components, either through administrative hierarchical channels or internal processes of mediation. In a professional bureaucracy, professional linkages may be used to coordinate across program components or to resolve conflicts between components.

The detailed design of operational technology is seldom dealt with in discussions of either social planning or organizational management.

There is often an assumption that the design of program technology in the human services is largely dictated by legislation, regulation, professional tradition, or organizational history, and that it is, therefore, a given rather than an area of strategic planning and organizational policy decision. However, decisions about program design are often the most important internal policy decisions made by policy bodies and executives, even if the decision is to accept and implement a program technology that is specified by tradition or by sources outside the organization.

The design of the program technology determines most of the other internal elements of the service organization, including the characteristics of the service personnel, the pattern of program expenditures, the nature of the expected program outputs, and the relation of service users to the organization (Thompson 1967). Program technology also determines many aspects of the relationship of the organization to its environment, including its relationship to funding sources and personnel sources, and its relation to legitimating and evaluating organizations.

The existence, or potential creation, of a service program, and therefore the need to deal with the design of program technology, assumes that there is a *demand* for such services. That is, there is recognition of a need for, or a desire for, some form of purposive action. However, the *effective demand* for the provision of services through a service organization reflects only one segment of all the persons affected by the underlying condition. For example, alcoholism may be a pervasive problem across all elements of society, but it is only a limited part of the problem population that represents an explicit demand for organizationally produced alcoholism treatment services. It is this part of the potential demand, in any given situation, rather than the totality of the persons affected by alcoholism, that is crucial in the design of the program technology of a particular alcohol services program.

The three major elements in the design of program technology are as follows:

- The *program rationale*, or theory of intervention—that is, the theory of cause-and-effect relationships that underlies the program technology
- The *program strategy*—that is, the specific program technology
- The *intervention tactics*—that is, specific operational procedures that affect utilization, effectiveness, and efficiency

Program Rationales—Theories of Intervention

Every human service program embodies a theoretical model, or an assumed cause–effect rationale. The rationale is a definition of the relationship between the condition to be dealt with, the nature of the intervention (or programmatic activities), and the expected outcomes. Major rationales used in human service programs can be broadly classified into two categories: (1) those that assume that the condition that is the object of intervention is within the individual who has the presenting symptoms and (2) those that assume that the condition that is the object of intervention is, at least in part, external to the individual with the symptoms.

Given any problematic human condition, there are choices to be made as to the rationale to be used in the design of a service program, since more than one rationale may be viewed as relevant. The selection of a rationale may be based on research that documents differences in effectiveness among programs using different rationales, or on social science theory that argues for the choice of one rationale over another. In many situations, the selection of a program rationale may be based on normative, or ideological, arguments. However, the choice of a particular rationale has extensive implications for the criteria to be used in the selection of service personnel and for the content of their educational preparation, for the level of financial resources required, for the administrative structure required, and for the role of the service user in the service co-production process.

In the discussion of program rationales that follows, it is assumed that it is *individuals* who demonstrate the symptoms of the condition that is the object of intervention. However, the same rationales may be relevant when the unit that is the object of concern is a *family*, or another primary group, or a *community*. Any of these social units can be substituted for the individual in the following discussion.

ACUTE ILLNESS OR THE MEDICAL MODEL RATIONALE The *acute illness* rationale assumes the existence of an immediate problem, pathology, or deficiency condition located in the individual who has the presenting symptoms. The delinquent child has an acute pathological condition; similarly, the neighborhood with a high rate of violent crime may be thought of as having a neighborhood pathology. The use of the acute illness rationale assumes the application of a diagnosis–prescription–treatment (or assessment–plan–intervention) sequence under the authority of a professional specialist, directed at the individual with the illness condition (the patient). Key professional functions are those of diagnosis and prescription. Making a precise diagnosis, and selection of the correct form of treatment from a number of alternative forms of treatment are essential steps for achieving a successful outcome and for preventing harm to the individual from the use of an incorrect form of treatment. Early identification of symptoms—for example, through comprehensive screening programs—and early treatment intervention are often considered essential for successful outcomes.

There is a high level of direct control by the professional specialist during an intensive, but limited, treatment period to ensure that the treatment is carried out correctly. The actual treatment may be carried out by the diagnostic professional—for example, a social work therapist, a psychiatrist, or a clinical psychologist interacting with the service user in a co-production process. However, in many instances, the patient must carry out the treatment—for example, by taking medication on a regular schedule or by changing patterns of diet and exercise or other habitual patterns of behavior. In still other instances, other professional or technical specialists may perform the actual treatment functions called for in the treatment prescription—for example, in radiation treatment of cancer.

There is an assumption that the correct application of the appropriate treatment should result, in most instances, in the patient being cured and being returned to a condition of wellness, after which the treatment activity should no longer be required. Treatment costs associated with the acute illness rationale may be very high but are expected to be time limited. The rate of cure and the return of individuals to a wellness condition are the criteria of effectiveness in using the acute illness rationale.

CHRONIC ILLNESS OR HANDICAP/DISABILITY RATIONALE The *chronic illness* rationale is similar to the acute illness rationale in that it assumes an explicit problem condition in a discrete individual. Chronic illness conditions may include the child with muscular dystrophy, an older person with mobility limitations because of arthritis, the adult who has a mental retardation condition, the young adult with schizophrenia. Similarly, the multigenerational, multiproblem family may be defined as having a chronic pattern of behavioral pathology. The chronic illness rationale also assumes a diagnostic–prescription–treatment sequence but a complete cure is not the expected outcome. Treatment intervention may extend over a long period of time with the objective of offsetting the continuing effects of an incurable illness condition or of maintaining a stable level of functioning in spite of a handicapping condition or disability.

Diagnostic tasks are the most critical professional activity, particularly since the treatment prescription may involve a number of specialists whose work over an extended period of time is shaped by the original diagnostic judgments. The diagnostic process often involves consultations with specialists or an interdisciplinary diagnostic team. A variety of treatment activities may be tried to find the most effective combination for a particular situation, and these treatments may be carried out by a variety of persons with different types of technical and professional training.

There is usually no specific limit on the period of treatment, although the intensity of treatment activities may diminish over time if a stable level of functioning is achieved. Most of the ongoing treatment or rehabilitation activities are carried out by persons other than the professional specialist who is responsible for the basic diagnosis and prescription of treatment, with only general supervision by the person with ultimate professional responsibility. In most instances, the patient/service user has a major responsibility for carrying out prescribed rehabilitation treatments or activities—for example, taking medications on a regular schedule.

Successful intervention may, in some instances, result in reduced treatment costs over time, but in other cases costs may remain high indefinitely (for example, kidney dialysis). The criteria of effectiveness in the use of a chronic illness rationale are the maintenance of stable functioning and the prevention of deterioration over an extended period of time. Total elimination of the chronic condition, or total remission of symptoms, may be an outcome, but it is not the normal expectation. Since evaluation of effectiveness involves a measurement of "what is" against "what might have been" over a long period of time, definitive evaluation of results is particularly difficult.

DEVELOPMENTAL RATIONALE The *developmental rationale* assumes that the object of intervention is a particular individual and that the objective of intervention is (1) to support "normal" development or (2) to stimulate compensating development when there has been a failure to achieve "normal" standards of development. The Boy Scout/Girl Scout/Campfire Girls/4-H Club movements support normal cognitive and social development. Special education programs are directed to the remediation of developmental deficiencies. The developmental rationale assumes that normal patterns of development reflect biological processes, or cultural and social norms, that are relatively unchangeable, and that the desirable end-state in an individual situation is achievement of an age-relevant, or life-stage, norm of cognitive, emotional, social, or physical development.

Access to specific service programs may be tied to developmental age, with participation potentially open to all persons who meet the age criteria—for example, elementary school. Diagnostic/assessment functions involve a comparison of individual development with age-related norms and a definition of the degree of difference, if any. This may be done through mass testing, as in diagnostic evaluation of reading achievement levels in a classroom, or it may include individualized testing, as in the development of an individual educational plan (IEP) for a child with a developmental disability condition.

Diagnosis, prescription, and the carrying out of intervention activities may involve completely different specialists. For example, the evaluation of hearing and sight in a young child involves one type of specialist, and the design and implementation of a developmentally oriented educational program for the hearing- or sight-limited child often involves a different specialist. Program interventions are designed to encourage and support normal development, or to overcome barriers to development when development lags behind the norm. Whereas the developmental rationale is often associated with service programs for younger persons, active socialization programs for older adults may focus on the developmental transition between "empty nest" or retirement and a new period of growth and development.

The active co-production involvement of the service user or participant is usually the most important factor in achieving the developmental objectives of intervention. Motivation of the service user becomes a key task of the professional specialists. Cost factors may be relatively low in the instance of programs supporting normal development that may include large numbers of persons and use volunteers as well as employed staff. Costs may be high in the instance of persons with severe developmental disabilities. The criterion of effectiveness in the use of a developmental rationale is the degree of success in achieving, or exceeding, developmental norms in any or all of the developmental areas with which a program is specifically concerned. In many programs in which the outcomes for most of the participants fall within a "normal range" of development, there may be little effort to determine the specific achievement level of individuals—for example, in informal education and social development activities for children, adolescents, and young adults.

DEVIANCE RATIONALE The *deviance rationale* also assumes that the condition that is the object of intervention is in a particular individual. The evidence of the condition is behavior that deviates from established behavioral norms and is therefore problematic either to the individual involved or to others, or both. The use of a deviance rationale for service programs is primarily identified with violations of legally defined norms or rules: delinquency, truancy, criminal behavior, or the use of proscribed substances. Deviance may also be defined as immorality—that is, behaviors that violate community norms or accepted moral standards that are not formalized as laws. The deviance rationale is also potentially applicable to personal behaviors defined as undesirable, such as compulsive eating or cigarette smoking, persistent family conflicts, or even to the general pattern of behavior within a single community.

An intervention sequence is followed that involves classification of a behavior as deviant, prescription for corrective action or "re-socialization," and corrective treatment with the objective of eliminating or changing the deviant behavior. Classification of the behavior as deviant often involves a judicial or administrative judgment, frequently preceded by an adversarial determination of "facts," rather than a diagnostic assessment by a professional specialist. Corrective treatment is often behaviorally focused with varying combinations of incentives and disincentives, rewards and punishments, designed to encourage and reinforce conforming behavior or to discourage or suppress deviant behavior. Professional tasks include the design of standardized treatment programs directed at particular forms of deviance. Implementation of such treatment programs within specific guidelines may not require the direct supervision of a professional specialist— for example, in the use of demerits or a "token economy" to control disapproved behavior in a residential living facility.

Active co-production engagement of the service participant is essential even though participation in treatment may be involuntary, since a permanent and stable change in the overt and habitual behavior of the service participant is the objective. Motivation of the participant by the program specialist becomes a critical issue in treatment outcomes. Corrective treatment is assumed to be time limited and is considered complete when behavior falls within a "normal range." Cost factors may be relatively low (probation supervision) or high (commitment to a maximum security penal institution). The effectiveness rate in the use of a deviance rationale is often defined by the absence of recidivism—that is, the nonrecurrence of the deviant behavior. A major complicating factor in measuring effectiveness is that "normal" growth or developmental processes may be the most powerful factor in changes in particular behaviors over time—for example, in a decrease of delinquent activity between early adolescence and late adolescence.

ENVIRONMENTAL RATIONALE The *environmental rationale* assumes that the condition that is the object of intervention exists in the social environment rather than in the individual who shows symptomatic evidence of the problem condition. It also assumes that the affected individual has little or no direct control over such environmental conditions. The problematic environment may be defined as *deficient* (that is, lacking in needed resources and supports) or as *oppressive* (that is, actively harmful). High unemployment rates among young persons from a particular ethnic background may reflect overt racial barriers to employment (oppressive), and/or a stagnant economy (deficient). Limited educational achievement among children with a cerebral palsy condition may reflect the absence of specialized resources in a school system (deficient) or the exclusion of such children from school (oppressive).

A sequence of research/analysis, planning/policy-making, and implementation is followed, focusing on the linkage between specific environmental conditions, specific changes to be brought about in those conditions, and a reduction in the symptomatic problems. An environmental rationale is generally used with conditions affecting population groups rather than with unique individual situations, but it can be applied to individuals. Since the persons involved in implementation action cannot control every aspect of the environment, the implementation/intervention action is necessarily directed to specific elements of the environment.

Emphasis in the design of an intervention is on the selection of a strategic point of impact within the total environment. The objective may be to change the current situation of particular individuals, or to prevent negative consequences for other individuals in the future (primary prevention). Those individuals whose condition serves as the justification for intervention may become active participants in the process of implementation action—for example, through participation in advocacy action such as in the civil rights marches of the 1960s or the organization of Mothers Against Drunk Driving (MADD). Or they may have no direct involvement at all, as in the instance of class action law suits filed in behalf of all young children with a developmental disability condition.

Key professional tasks include research/analysis, planning or design of an environmental intervention, and implementation. Often, different individuals, and sometimes different organizations, are involved in each set of tasks. Intervention is completed when a change in the environment is implemented and symptomatic conditions have changed. Examples include a reduction in the incidence of severe breathing problems when the level of air pollution is reduced, and a reduction in deaths from drunken driving after restrictions on the access of adolescents to alcoholic beverages are imposed. This may involve a few days, or a decade or more. However, in many instances, the initiation of implementation—for example, setting up an administrative organization after the passage of a new piece of legislation—is treated as the end of the intervention sequence.

Outcomes are often very unpredictable when intervention is initiated. Evaluation of the effectiveness of an intervention may vary widely as in the instance of affirmative action programs. In principle, the measure of effectiveness is the elimination of the problematic conditions affecting individuals, without significant negative secondary consequences. However, the variety of intervening variables that can affect outcomes in a broad environmental approach and the length of time over which action occurs often make it difficult to determine if, or when, the objective of the intervention is achieved, or if the specific intervention is the primary cause of such an achievement.

PERSON–ENVIRONMENT RATIONALE The *person–environment rationale* assumes that the condition that is the object of intervention is a characteristic of the pattern of interaction between a particular individual, or group of individuals, and a particular aspect of the social environment. It assumes that the problematic condition is a joint result of the characteristics of the environment and the pattern of responses to that environment. Limitations in the social functioning of individuals with mental retardation is an interactive consequence of individual limitations *and* institutionalized community attitudes toward individuals identified as mentally retarded. Symbolic interaction theory and labeling theory that emphasize the role of social environmental factors in defining the social reality to which individuals respond and react are examples of cause–effect theories consistent with a person–environment rationale. The person–environment rationale involves situational assessment, covering characteristics of the immediate environment and assessment of individual behaviors in interacting with that environment, followed by prescription/planning and intervention.

Intervention is directed centrally at the interactive processes between the perceptions, attitudes, and coping behaviors of the affected individuals and immediate environmental factors (Meyer 1983). For example, the problematic behavior may involve the responses of a group of individuals with a handicapping condition, such as mental retardation, to an indifferent or hostile environment. Similarly, it may involve the responses of individuals experiencing active discrimination and exploitation. The intervention may involve "consciousness raising" among the concerned individuals, leading to individual or group action to modify the environment, in turn leading to enhanced perceptions by the individuals of their ability to cope with the environment.

Enhanced effectiveness, or empowerment, in such interactions may lead to positive changes in the responses from elements in the environment. The service participant role in intervention is an active one, since the objectives of intervention include changes in the coping behaviors of individuals and the level of effectiveness of those behaviors. This is done by supporting direct involvement of the individual, or a group of individuals in common circumstances, in systematic efforts to modify detrimental factors in the environment.

Key professional tasks involve assessment of the person–environment interaction, definition of action options, and participation in the planning of an implementation process. However, these professional tasks always require active participation of the individual, or individuals, whose condition was the initial cause for initiating intervention, particularly in the selection of an action option and in the actions taken to modify environmental responses. The intervention sequence is completed when there has been an increase in the coping capability, or empowerment, of the individual and a related change in the problematic elements of the immediate environment and thus a change in the desired direction of the pattern of interaction with the environment. Outcomes may be assessed in terms of observed changes in the environment, in terms of changes in the perceptions of the environment by the individuals involved, or in terms of the observed behaviors of those individuals.

IDEOLOGICAL RATIONALE The *ideological rationale* assumes that a problem condition exists because of an incorrect, or inappropriate, set of attitudes or beliefs, either on the part of an individual who shows the symptoms of the problem condition or on the part of other persons who have the power to affect that individual. The use of an ideological rationale has often been associated with conditions involving hostile or discriminatory actions—for example, the exclusion of women from access to particular occupations, such as building construction, on the basis of traditional beliefs on the part of both employers and potential women employees about women's occupational interests. The ideological rationale assumes a sequence that includes definition of the nature of the incorrect beliefs and attitudes, specifying a more appropriate set of beliefs, and initiation of action through education and persuasion to change beliefs and attitudes in the desired direction (Mayer 1976). The definition of the incorrect beliefs may occur as a result of an initiative by an outside "change agent," or by the direct exposure of the individuals holding the beliefs to cultural settings involving different belief systems.

The object of intervention may be individuals in a power position—to change their beliefs and in turn to reduce or eliminate negative actions by such persons. On the other hand, the object of intervention may also be the persons who are oppressed by such negative actions—to change their beliefs about their relation to discriminatory conditions (consciousness raising). Key professional tasks may include efforts to increase awareness of the problem condition, but these are primarily the implementation tasks of education and persuasion.

The role of the individuals who experience the effects of the problem condition may be relatively passive if the intervention is directed by a third party toward persons in power positions holding incorrect atti-

tudes. On the other hand, these individuals may be very active participants, either in the effort to change the belief systems of others or in
changing their own belief systems. The intervention sequence is completed when the process of change in a belief system leads to consistently maintained behavior changes on the part of those who are the object
of action. The outcome effectiveness criterion, however, requires evidence of changes in behavior rather than being limited solely to indirect
evidence of changes in beliefs.

The Choice Among Alternative Rationales

The rationale that is being used in an existing service program may
have been developed under different circumstances in the past. It may
persist primarily because it is built into the organizational structure
and the pattern of existing staff personnel rather than because it is the
most appropriate rationale. The ability to change program rationales
when new knowledge becomes available, or when environmental conditions change, may be directly related to the ability of a particular organization to survive in the competitive ecological processes of multi-
organizational environments (Weick 1981).

The choice of a program rationale may reflect the outcome of political processes, since particular rationales are often viewed as having ideological implications that are significant beyond a particular service program. For example, the choice between an *acute illness rationale* and a
deviance rationale as the intervention structure for a government-funded
alcoholism service program may be influenced by the political commitments of legislators either to medically oriented treatment programs or
to Alcoholics Anonymous programs. Arguments over the choice of an ill-
ness/deficiency rationale or an environmental rationale for programs
dealing with household poverty are often linked with conflicts between
political conservatives and liberals (Wilson 1985).

The design of a particular program may include a deliberate decision
to use a combination of two or more rationales. One example is the establishment of alternative schools within public school systems, combining developmental and deviance rationales for children who have
had behavioral problems in regular "developmental" classrooms. However, the use of more than one program rationale within a single service

organization, where the differences in the operational implications of the different rationales are not made explicit, often results in staff conflict over program policies, financial allocations, the selection of new personnel, and the criteria for the evaluation of outcomes.

Differences in rationales used in different service organizations involved in a service delivery network can result in difficulties in communications between organizations. Service workers operating within one rationale often cannot "hear" what workers operating with a different rationale in another organization are telling them about a particular case situation. Because there are differences in the outcome evaluation criteria among the different rationales, the implications of a program rationale for the definition of outcome criteria for a particular program is a critical factor in the design of a program evaluation.

Particular program rationales are often associated with the treatment of particular conditions. Cancer and a number of other severe organic conditions are increasingly being treated under an acute illness rationale. This is a change from an earlier period when the treatment of such conditions was primarily carried out under a chronic illness rationale. Mental retardation traditionally has been dealt with using a chronic illness rationale, but today it is often dealt with by using a developmental rationale. Problems of limited cognitive development among young children in low-income households have been dealt with through a developmental rationale—for example, through a Head Start program. However, there are relevant arguments that an environmental rationale, focusing on harmful factors in low-income residential neighborhoods, including high levels of lead pollution, would be more appropriate. Still others suggest that an ideological rationale, focusing on changing the beliefs of such children about their own capabilities for achievement, is a more appropriate framework for intervention.

Over time, the chronic illness/handicap rationale, the environmental rationale, the developmental rationale, the deviance rationale, and the ideological rationale have all served as theoretical frameworks for interventions directed at the problems of poverty among single-parent households with young children. Problems of delinquency among juveniles have been addressed through an acute illness rationale (child guidance clinics), a deviance rationale (criminal justice institutions), an environmental rationale (opportunity theory), a person–environment rationale (labeling theory), and a developmental rationale (training schools).

There is no body of empirical data that conclusively demonstrates that a particular rationale, and only that rationale, is relevant for a specific problem condition. The choice of rationale in the process of program design may be affected by many factors, including the tradition of using a particular rationale in a given program area reinforced through the content of professional education, individual beliefs among policy makers about the cause–effect assumptions underlying each rationale, beliefs about the probable consequences for the individuals being served and the consequences for the larger society of using a particular rationale on a large-scale basis, and the relative power position of individuals and interest groups advocating different rationales as a framework for intervention. However, it is also possible to make analytic comparisons of alternative combinations of program rationale, program strategy, program tactics, and service user role that may assist in establishing a rational base for choice in a given situation.

Program Strategies

Each human service program uses a particular type of program strategy for the application of technology to service production in addition to the underlying rationale that serves as a theoretical framework. The program strategy controls the manner in which service tasks are assigned to service personnel or to the service user, the methods through which specialized knowledge and technical skill are applied within the service delivery process, and the procedures used for accountability and quality control. The program strategy chosen for a particular program component, within a particular organization, is often the result of historical precedents; it is frequently taken for granted without systematic consideration of alternatives.

There are some consistent patterns of association between particular program rationales and particular program strategies, such as the association of the professional strategy with an acute illness rationale, or the public health strategy with an environmental rationale. However, any specific problematic condition can be addressed by a number of different combinations of program rationale and program strategy. Each program strategy has specific implications for the pattern of program costs, for the administrative support structure required, and for the use of service workers with varying levels of technical and professional preparation and experience. The identification of program strategy is a distinct and separate step in either the analysis of existing programs or the process of design for new programs.

PROFESSIONAL STRATEGY The *professional strategy* involves the organization of service production around the central role of the specialized professional as diagnostician, treatment prescriber, and frequently as the direct service treatment specialist and treatment outcome evaluator. This strategy assumes a direct professional–client/patient relationship, a recognition of the authority of the professional specialist in dealing with the individual case, and accountability of the responsible professional for the quality of service outputs (Mills et al. 1983).

There is usually an administrative assignment of the service user to a particular practitioner in organizational programs using the professional strategy. In the provision of professional services through the marketplace, there is an individual choice of a professional practitioner. Managed health care often involves a mixed model, with individual choice of the service provider within a limited pool of professionals. However, when the professional strategy is used, there is an emphasis on establishing a personalized "professional" relationship between the practitioner and the service user, even if for a limited period of time.

The administrative and technical functions associated with a specific service program are defined as supports to, and subordinate to, the authority of the professional practitioners. In the professional strategy, the degree of autonomy—that is, the independent authority of practitioners in their area of competence—is perceived as an important criterion of the technical quality of the service program. In turn, autonomous practitioners are responsible for managing the use of their time to meet the needs of the individuals in their service caseload. Service records are maintained by the professional primarily for professional purposes and are under the control of the professional. Resource mobilization on behalf of an individual patient or client is the responsibility of the professional practitioner.

When the professional strategy is used, the major element of organizational cost consists of the salaries of professional specialists, together with the costs of the technical equipment and assistants required for professional practice. Quality control is assumed to be primarily a responsibility of professional peers. The quality of a program using the professional strategy is often assessed in terms of the academic and professional qualifications of the service staff. Effectiveness, rather than efficiency, is the primary criterion for evaluating the service production process.

The professional strategy is frequently associated with an acute illness rationale—for example, in the instance of medical practice, or private law practice (a personal injury is an "illness" that is cured by a successful legal suit for damages). However, the professional strategy is also found in association with the developmental rationale (the professional teacher in the self-contained classroom), or in association with the environmental rationale (the architect designing a supportive residential complex for older adults), or in association with the person–environment rationale (the professional protective services social worker dealing with the pattern of interaction between a neglectful parent in a single-parent household and other residents in an indifferent or hostile neighborhood).

SYSTEMS STRATEGY The *systems strategy* involves the organization of service production around a structured and coordinated service delivery system or "client pathway" through which the client or service user is involved sequentially with a number of different service specialists around such service delivery functions as outreach, intake, diagnosis/assessment, service planning, service provision, case management and service monitoring, and service outcome evaluation (Rosenberg and Brody 1974). The service user may have an opportunity to make specific choices about service production arrangements at several different points in the service sequence, including the right to appeal decisions made by service personnel.

Program component administrators have overall responsibility for development and maintenance of the service delivery system and for the quality of service within the system, and they have ultimate authority over program management decisions. Professional practitioner specialists provide specific services as needed within the system, but professional responsibilities in an individual situation are defined narrowly. The concept of professional autonomy applies only within the boundaries of the specific responsibilities assigned to the professional practitioner within the system. An individualized relationship between a professional specialist and a service user may be established, but this is not the norm.

The systems strategy often includes a staff role that carries responsibility for planning, coordinating, and monitoring the process by which various specialized resources in the system are utilized in an individual situation. This may be an internist in a general medical clinic, the primary care physician in the health management organization, the rehabilitation counselor in a rehabilitation clinic, the academic advisor in an undergraduate academic program, or a case manager social worker in a social services support program for adults who are mentally retarded and who are living in the community (Weil and Karls 1985).

Individual user records are under the control of the organization rather than being controlled by individual professionals. Service records are used to guide program policy decisions within the system as well as decisions involving particular individuals. The service organization, rather than any single service specialist, is ultimately accountable for service outcomes. The management of the organizational workload is the responsibility of managers rather than of individual specialists. Program monitoring through computerized management information systems and formal service outcome evaluation procedures may be used both to measure efficiency and to maintain quality control (Weirich 1985). Resource mobilization is primarily an organizational responsibility rather than the responsibility of individual service professionals.

Primary cost factors include both professional services and administrative technical services. Total program costs using a system strategy may be relatively high, but service unit costs may be low given intensive utilization of the program. The quality of the program in an organization using a systems strategy is assessed in terms of both the efficiency and the effectiveness of the total program operation and also by the degree to which the specialized elements are integrated into a smoothly operating system. User response is likely to be defined in terms of the total experience rather than in terms of a response to any single person in the service delivery process.

The systems strategy may be found in the treatment programs carried out within institutional settings—for example, psychiatric hospitals. However, it is also found in a number of other settings—for example, comprehensive rehabilitation centers, comprehensive service programs for older adults, undergraduate educational programs, and specialized medical diagnostic clinics, as well as public health clinics. The emergence of health-care organizations (HCOs) in managed health care and managed behavioral health care represents a large-scale combination of *professional* strategies with *system* strategies in both general health care and mental health care. The balance between these two strategy models is frequently a subject of contention between individual professional specialists and system managers.

AD HOC SERVICE STRATEGY The *ad hoc service strategy* involves immediate, limited, short-term assistance by organizational staff personnel. Information and referral services, Travelers Aid, rape crisis centers, telephone hot lines, financial assistance provided only on an emergency basis (general assistance, in some states), disaster assistance including short-term counseling, runaway shelters, and intake and referral services in multiservice centers are some examples of service components utilizing an ad hoc service strategy. Similarly, hospital emergency rooms, emergency medical services, and minor emergency centers utilize an ad hoc service strategy, although with different requirements for technical competence. Academic admissions interviewing and career counseling are examples of the use of an ad hoc strategy in higher education.

The form of the services in an ad hoc strategy is defined by the function of, and specific resources available to, the service organization. The provision of ad hoc assistance does not assume a personalized relationship between the service user and the service worker. The service delivery structure is primarily arranged around staff work schedules on a work-flow basis. That is, service is provided as needed during those specific times when service personnel are on duty, usually on a first-come, first-served basis. In some instances, there may be coverage twenty-four hours a day, seven days a week. Staff training is often on-the-job training within the organization, and service workers may not be required to have any specific form of prior technical or professional education, although supervisory and administrative personnel may have had professional education. Volunteers and employed service workers may have similar responsibilities. High turnover among direct service workers may be characteristic.

Rapid diagnostic or assessment judgments, prompt decisions on action recommendations, and immediate implementation, all by the same service worker, are often characteristic of the ad hoc strategy. Explicit rules, organizational reporting forms, and direct administrative supervision are used to ensure quality control. Autonomy for direct service workers is limited. Service records are brief and are controlled by the organization. Service situations requiring specialized services or long-term assistance are referred, or transferred, to other organizations. Information about such alternative resources is often an important element of the service worker competence.

Cost factors for any single service episode may be relatively low, but overall costs are largely determined by the level of the service demand, the fit between service demand and the costs of maintaining the availability of service personnel, and the extent to which unpaid volunteers, or a telephone response system, can provide the service. Quality of performance may be judged primarily by the promptness of response, accuracy of problem assessment, and the intensity of attention given to an individual situation during the short period of direct service activity.

SOCIAL CARE STRATEGY The *social care strategy* involves the organization of services around substitute arrangements for personal care that might otherwise be provided through a primary group relationship (family, household, friends, or neighbors) (Morris 1977). The social care strategy is used both within residential settings and in nonresidential settings. Social care may be designed to be supportive of specific developmental and socialization processes, as well as providing the basic elements of regular personal care—for example, in a child-care institution. Social care personnel may include both professional specialists and direct care workers. Direct care workers in the social care strategy include foster parents, homemakers, ward attendants or mental health aides, prison guards, chore service providers, home health aides, child-care workers, and house parents, as well as volunteers—as in Big Brothers/Big Sisters, and Foster Grandparents. Direct service workers, among whom there is often a high level of employment turnover, receive only limited training and generally receive low wages. Basic nurturing and care skills that are acquired as a part of adult socialization are often assumed to be the core skills required.

In a social care strategy, administrators and professional specialists in the service organization carry the responsibility for the development of individual service plans, for supervision and training of direct service personnel, and for case management, rather than responsibility for direct service, except as they may function as a backup resource in crisis situations. Depending on the setting, administrators and professional specialists may or may not have personal contact with the service users. Other professional specialists may serve as consultants or as providers of direct services on an as-needed basis—for example, in the provision of routine medical care for a particular individual in a residential treatment center.

The organization that employs direct service workers is primarily accountable for the quality of service outcomes. A system of direct administrative supervision is normally used to maintain quality control. In the instance of foster parents or volunteers, who are not direct employees, supervision is often very limited. Limited records of service provision are kept, primarily for accountability purposes, and are maintained under the control of the service organization. Social care providers normally have limited autonomy, operating within explicitly defined limits on responsibilities. Quality of care is generally assessed in terms of the dependability and humaneness of service provision rather than in terms of a fixed set of technical criteria.

Social care is frequently associated with a chronic illness rationale, involving programs in both residential settings (state schools or Intermediate Care Facilities—Mental Retardation for persons who have a mental retardation condition) and nonresidential settings (homemaker programs for older adults with functional limitations). Cost factors vary markedly depending on the intensity of the social care services required, ranging from volunteer friendly visiting and occasional chore services to twenty-four-hours-a-day personal supervision and care in residential settings such as nursing homes.

NATURAL CARE STRATEGY The *natural care strategy* involves the provision of organizational assistance in support of personal services that are provided through "natural" or primary relationship systems including households, neighborhoods, and friendship groups (Silverman 1978; Froland et al. 1981). Assistance may be provided through funding arrangements (payments to a relative to provide homemaker care for an older individual); through arrangements for providing respite and relief services (for example, to support family care of a child with a severe developmental disability condition); through professional consultation to primary caregivers as in home-based hospice services; through the development of, and ongoing support of, peer support groups, such as Parents Anonymous or Alcoholics Anonymous or mental health peer support groups (Onken 2000); or through mobilization and coordination of specialized community resources (diagnostic and testing services, for example) that can be used by natural care providers if needed.

The primary functions of organizational service staff include outreach to groups of primary care providers; the organizing of primary care resources, if such resources do not already exist (for example, the development of a peer organization of ex-addicts); developing the support resources needed by primary caregivers; providing consultation to primary care providers; and monitoring the general quality of care being given. Organizational functions are often structured around administrative program units, which are, in some instances, defined on a geographic, or neighborhood, basis. Employed staff personnel often do not have a direct service relationship with the ultimate beneficiary of service, but there may be an active support relationship with a primary caregiver. Service staff members may also assist the primary care provider in an advocacy role, obtaining specialized services for the ultimate service user.

Primary caregivers, including the members of peer support groups, function with a high degree of autonomy (Onken 2000). The organizational staff involved in providing support also function with substantial discretionary authority and flexibility. Service records consist primarily of information about service activities. They may or may not include detailed individual information about the ultimate beneficiary of the primary care provision. Cost factors may vary widely, depending on the nature of the resources required to support existing natural care providers. The costs may be very minimal if natural care resources already exist. On the other hand, developing such a natural care provision where it does not already exist—for example, a network of cooperative family day-care homes in an urban neighborhood—may require a relatively high initial expenditure.

PUBLIC HEALTH STRATEGY The *public health strategy* involves the organization of technical and professional resources to discover and identify environmental conditions and causative agents that result in problem conditions in a general population group, and to design interventions that will modify the environment or control the causative agents. Particular emphasis is placed on laboratory studies, field research, and epidemiological studies to identify the sources of problem causation, and on potential points of intervention for effective preventive action. Experimental research may be used to test the level of effectiveness of particular forms of preventive intervention.

Program activities are often structured on a project basis, although one outcome of a project may be the establishment of an ongoing service activity. Professional roles are primarily linked to research and the design and development of new forms of intervention. The actual implementation of an intervention may be by technical specialists, or by technicians with limited training—for example, in the spraying of ponds to prevent mosquito-transmitted diseases or in the provision of free breakfasts and luncheons in a nutrition support program.

Preventive interventions in the public health strategy may take many different forms: a public education program, regulatory legislation, a professional service program, an application of engineering technology, or a modification of the living environment. One form of intervention is the organization or mobilization of constituency groups or special-interest associations to (1) bring about specific changes in environmental conditions or prevent the occurrence of harmful conditions, or (2) bring about changes in the economic, social, or political power structure that controls specific aspects of the social environment. One example of the use of the public health strategy involves the establishment of programs to promote safe sex and needle exchange to prevent the spread of human immunodeficiency virus (HIV) and acquired immunodeficiency syndrome (AIDS).

Program documentation generally consists of research reports, professional papers, monographs, and program summaries. Widespread dissemination of such research information is often a major program objective. Program quality is often defined, in the short run, by the technical competence of the research and analysis reports and the intervention proposals as judged by peers. Ultimately, the program is judged by changes in intermediate conditions and a decline in problem occurrence. Cost factors vary widely depending on the nature of the research technology involved and the unit costs and extensiveness of the proposed interventions.

A major difficulty in the use of a public health program strategy is the time lapse that frequently occurs between the initiation of research and the beginning of an intervention, and then the time between the initiation of the intervention and the point when the outcomes can be analyzed to determine the effectiveness of the intervention. During these time periods, some type of short-range intervention is often required to deal with existing problem conditions. The attractiveness of a public health strategy is the possibility of large-scale reductions in the occurrence of problem conditions if an effective intervention can be designed—for example, the development of a vaccine for poliomyelitis, the potential development of such a vaccine for HIV infections, or the organization of comprehensive programs for the early identification of breast cancer, colon cancer, and prostate cancer.

Choosing Among Alternative Program Strategies

Each of these program strategies may be relevant for application in any human service program area. For example, while the social care strategy predominates in the temporary care for young children outside the home through day-care programs, the professional strategy (developmental disability programs for preschool children with severe handicaps), the natural care strategy (family day care), and the ad hoc strategy (leave-your-child-while-shopping service) are also used. Program objectives, the preferences and needs of service users, the state of available technology, the level and type of resources available, and the preferences of policy makers affect the choice of program strategy.

Many human service programs involve a combination of program strategies. However, differences in staff requirements and in the nature of the administrative structures and procedures involved can make such combinations difficult (Paulson 1984). For example, a combination in the same program of a professional service strategy with professional practitioners providing direct services to households with an immediate problem, and a public health strategy with social science researchers gathering information about underlying factors that may affect the nature of presenting problems in the future, can result in administrative problems and staff conflicts over budget priorities.

Similar problems exist when there is a difference between the official program strategy and the actual operational strategy—for example, when a service that is defined as using a professional strategy is in reality using an ad hoc strategy. At a minimum, such situations require explicit recognition of the differences between the several program strategies and the consequences for staff roles and administrative procedures. Proposals in child protective services for the separation of investigative services (ad hoc strategy) from ongoing services for a child removed from the biological parents (social care or natural care strategies) is a recognition of the organizational stresses that may result from combining very different strategies in a single program structure.

Program Tactics—Operational Procedures

Program rationales and program strategies are translated into an operational program through program tactics, or a plan of operational procedures. The program tactics also involve a series of choices. Some of the choices are defined by the nature of the funding and accompanying regulations. Others represent organizational choices. Specific aspects of the operational procedures may be changed without changes in program rationale or program strategy, but there may be feedback consequences from certain tactics choices. Many of the operational procedure choices potentially involve conflicts between the interests and preferences of service users and those of organizational staff members and of policy makers—for example, in decisions about facility locations and work schedules.

One example of a critical program tactics issue, the allocation of program access, will be analyzed in this chapter. This issue is illustrative of the variety of choices involved in the tactics design of a specific program. Other examples of program tactics issues include the centralization or decentralization of facilities, the definition of the role of the service user (see chapter 6), and program and personnel scheduling.

ALLOCATION OF ACCESS Access arrangements are an important tactical element in program design. To a substantial degree, they determine who, out of a total pool of potential users, will actually use a service. They may also determine the quality of co-production that results, as well as the evaluation of the service by the service users. Access arrangements include information and outreach activities, intake procedures, receptionist and waiting room provisions, transportation, service hours, facility location and accessibility, and availability of translators (Austin 1979). Although each of these involves specific design choices, the overall pattern of access services is often determined by the pattern of *access allocation* established for a particular service.

In most human service program areas, there is, and will always be, some gap between available service resources and all possible requests for service, particularly if there are no costs, or very low costs, to the user. In any given situation, the choice made by an individual with a problem or a service need (for example, a choice between relying on personal or primary group resources, seeking services directly through the marketplace, or utilizing a human service program) is determined in part by knowledge of the access allocation rules used by the service program. The visible demand for a particular service program is in part determined by the restrictions on access and the extent to which those restrictions are generally known.

The allocation of access to services may be determined by specific provisions in legislation or regulation, or they may be a consequence of unplanned, and often unacknowledged, informal decisions such as the selection of unattractive service facilities in an inaccessible location. Explicit decisions on access allocation at a program policy level are often essential to avoid inequities that result from unintended access constraints. In some instances, in the absence of an explicit allocation system, direct service workers establish unofficial allocation procedures to control their own workload (Lipsky 1980). Access allocation policies may be defined in either *inclusive* terms—that is, by defining the characteristics of individual situations that are eligible for service—or in *exclusive* terms—that is, by defining the characteristics of individual situations that are not eligible.

Social policy analysis as applied to human service programs often emphasizes a distinction between *residual* and *universal* services. This is an important conceptual distinction when analyzing the role of a particular service within a society. There are important differences between very limited, residual provision of publicly funded day-care services, based on household economic criteria, and universal provision of publicly funded day care. However, there is no totally universal service under any real-world conditions. Those services that are established to serve a broad and inclusive user constituency still operate under resource limitations at any given moment and must use some access allocation procedures to fit service demand with available resources.

The access allocation rules used in any given program that is supported by community contributions or governmental funding determine the degree of economic benefits redistribution that may result from the operation of the program. Broadly inclusive programs, approaching universality, are less redistributive than categorical, targeted programs; residual categorical programs that are highly redistributive cannot be universal. Universality and strong redistribution objectives represent values that cannot be maximized simultaneously.

Access allocation rules can affect the nature of the public support base for a given program. A broadly inclusive program may have a broader support base than a highly targeted program, but there may be limited willingness on the part of funders (contributors and taxpayers) to provide the resources for a completely nontargeted program, particularly if they themselves are not likely to use the program. For example, there may be limited willingness on the part of older taxpayers to support through taxes universal access to day care for all families with young children.

Access allocation rules determine to a substantial degree the characteristics of the user population. The user characteristics affect the effectiveness measures of staff performance and the viability of particular program rationales and program strategies. Allocation access rules can be a significant factor in determining, in advance, a high level of probable program effectiveness for a program with an acute illness rationale and a professional service strategy by limiting access to only acute, treatable conditions, excluding chronic conditions that are highly resistant to change. For example, alcoholism treatment programs that accept only those individuals who have made an explicit, personal decision to seek treatment will have greater effectiveness than programs that also serve persons who are mandated to seek service by a court. Alternatively, access allocation rules that result in a service population with predominately chronic problem conditions in a program that uses an acute illness rationale and a professional service strategy may create a high cost service with limited achievement of service objectives (Perlman 1975). One example is a short-term, acute illness, professional strategy, intensive mental health verbal counseling service in which the service population consists primarily of persons with severe and chronic mental illness because of the priority eligibility criteria imposed by the funding source.

A variety of alternative methods of allocating service resources can be used when the effective demand exceeds availability. Some are imposed explicitly, some affect access indirectly. These include the following:

- Allocation by fee, using either a fixed fee schedule or a sliding fee schedule, thereby limiting utilization by persons unable or unwilling to pay a fee. Allocation by fee may or may not include a provision for some situations in which all fee charges may be waived.
- Allocation by income/asset eligibility limits (means test)
- Allocation by order of application for service (first come, first served), often accompanied by a waiting list
- Allocation by diagnosis or problem assessment, using either severity and urgency, or treatability as the eligibility criterion

- Allocation by establishing inclusive definitions of service eligibility on the basis of such factors as residential location, age, gender, or household status
- Allocation by establishing exclusive definitions of service eligibility, for example, by exclusion of noncitizens
- Allocation by imposing indirect access costs on the user—that is, by creating difficulties or barriers (travel costs, inconvenient hours, unattractive facilities in a low-status neighborhood, long waits in a crowded waiting room)
- Allocation by imposing collateral procedures on service users (requirements for documents such as birth certificates, naturalization papers, pay stubs, or evidence of employment placement registration, or requiring prior approval from a primary health-care provider)
- Allocation by imposing collateral actions on service users (identifying sexual contacts to receive treatment for venereal disease; requirements for identification of the biological father to receive TANF benefits, participation in a community work program to receive food stamps)

Some of the allocation procedures mentioned may be used because of physical limitations on resources—for example, limits on the number of residents permitted in a group home facility. Some may be used because of limits on financial resources in a specific program. However, some of these access allocation procedures may also be used to limit the scope of a service that was established primarily with the intent to prove that such a service is available in the community. One example is the provision of a small number of winter shelters for homeless individuals without any intention of serving all the persons who urgently need such a service.

A decision not to use any of the aforementioned allocation procedures for services does not mean that there will be no limitation on service availability. The absence of an explicit allocation procedure when the effective demand exceeds the available resources results in allocation by *rationing*—that is, a reduction in the amount of service provided or the quality of services for all users. This may be accomplished through cutbacks in the duration of service, increased caseloads or larger numbers of students in each classroom, elimination of facilitative services (transportation), overcrowding in sleeping areas in residential institutions, reduction of maintenance and safety inspections in residential facilities, reduction of service monitoring (fewer follow-up visits to foster homes).

Service rationing may lead over time to an unintended change in program strategy. A family counseling service organized around a professional strategy becomes an ad hoc strategy brief information and referral service. Or a residential psychiatric treatment program becomes a custodial social care program.

Summary

The technical design of a service program involves a series of choices that involve the underlying rationale, the operational strategy, and the tactical decisions shaping the provision of services. These choices affect the administrative structure of the service organization, the personnel requirements, and the criteria for assessing effectiveness. These design elements can also provide a framework for analyzing and comparing existing service programs.

CONCLUSIONS

The analysis of an existing human service program or the design of a proposed program involves a number of complex design elements. These include the basic organizational structure, the nonprofit, governmental, for-profit auspices structure, the governance structure, and the program design. These analytic design elements apply to a wide range of human service programs including health care, personal social services, and education and criminal justice programs. Although the choices involved in any single program are often shaped by organizational or professional traditions, an almost infinite variety of governance and funding structures and program design alternatives can be used to deal with a particular type of problem condition or service need. Each combination of design elements has specific implications for the definition of program objectives, administrative functions, personnel requirements, cost allocations, and evaluation criteria. This framework of design elements also provides a context for the comparative analysis of existing service programs, making it possible to determine if comparisons are being made between similar programs or between distinctively different programs.

FIVE

SERVICE DELIVERY NETWORKS

The forces that most influence organizations come from outside the organization, not from within.   —Drucker (1998:174)

Alliances that both partners ultimately deem successful involve collaboration (creating new values together) rather than mere exchange (getting something back for what you put in). Partners value the skills each brings to the alliance.   —Rosabeth Moss Kanter (1997:225)

THE MANAGEMENT of any organization involves dealing with the external environment as well as with internal organizational processes. For human service organizations, a significant element in the external environment is the human service delivery network (hereafter referred as a service delivery network)—that is, that set of organizations that are involved in providing a particular type of service within a given community (Hage 1986; Austin 1991; Reitan 1998). To a large degree, the way in which any single service organization develops over time is shaped by the characteristics of the service delivery networks that the organization is a part of. The literature dealing with human service programs emphasizes the importance of "coordination" or "integration" of service providers (Reitan 1998) to improve the outcomes for service users, particularly for those with complex, multiple, or long-term service requirements. Nugent and Glisson, in a study of children in the juvenile justice system who have mental health problems, point out, "Characteristics of service systems clearly impact the outcomes of services" (1999:57). This chapter provides a framework for understanding the characteristics and dynamics of the service delivery networks with which organizational managers and other staff members are involved.

Businesses are involved in supplier chains, or networks, and marketing networks. They are also likely to be involved in technology networks, personnel networks, stock ownership networks, and political influence networks. Some of the connections in these networks are based on regular exchanges—the consistent purchase of office supplies from a single dealer, or between a "just-in-time" automotive component producer and the automobile factory that assembles the car for delivery to a local dealer. Some of the connections take the form of alliances, as Kanter notes, including partnerships that may be loosely defined by personal connections or that are formally structured through contracts or written agreements. Connections among businesses may include memberships in a common trade association, as well as the connections that are mandated by law and regulations between publicly held corporations and the Securities and Exchange Commission. As Drucker notes, attention by corporate executives to these external relationships may be one of the most important responsibilities of contemporary business chief executive officers (CEOs). Similarly, attention to the service delivery systems that the organization is involved in is one of the most important responsibilities of human service executives.

Networks of human service organizations develop around a socially recognized problem—child abuse or the human immunodeficiency virus (HIV)/acquired immunodeficiency syndrome (AIDS) epidemic—or around the service needs of particular population groups—the education and socialization of children, the development of health and social care services for older adults who are no longer able to maintain themselves in their own home, or the support of single adolescent mothers without economic resources. Such networks may also include a variety of membership associations that bring together individuals who have a stake in the effective functioning of the network. These stakeholder associations may include parents' groups and issue advocacy groups as well as trade unions and professional associations that include staff personnel in the service organizations.

The characteristics of these service delivery networks are an important element in the provision of essential community services such as mental health services (Scott and Black 1986). For example, an individual with a severe psychotic episode may be taken from the family home by mental health deputies from the sheriff's department to a state-administered acute-treatment psychiatric hospital for initial assessment and the prescription of medication, referred to a half-way house run by a community mental health center, and further helped by a community case management program through which he or she may be involved in an assisted housing program, a job-training program, and continued medical supervision through an out-patient psychiatric clinic. Related membership associations that are part of such a network may include the local units of the National Alliance for the Mentally Ill, the National Mental Health Association, the National Alliance of Mental Patients, and a state employees labor union. Similar service delivery networks are involved in juvenile justice programs, programs for pregnant adolescents, and programs for victims of intrafamily abuse.

The effectiveness of the service provision in a community depends on the effectiveness of the working relationships among the organizational participants in service delivery networks as much as on the quality of service provision by individual service organizations. For example, the effectiveness of specialized services for pregnant adolescents may be determined, in large part, not so much by the skills and motivations of the staff members in individual specialized service organizations but by the quality of the relationships of those organizations with the public schools.

Service delivery networks are found in some form in every community. Sometimes they involve only a few organizations and relationships among a few individuals. In large cities, large and complex networks often depend on written agreements among organizations covering collaboration and referral procedures as well as formal contracts for the funding of specialized services. There are also "latent" networks, specifically disaster-related networks, that become operational only under unusual circumstances—earthquake (Streeter and Gillespie 1992), an airplane crash, a tornado—or as part of a disaster-response rehearsal.

The functional characteristics of service networks in a given field of service, such as child welfare or mental health, that are located in different communities are often quite similar, representing the influence of institutional forces in the larger society (Powell and DiMaggio 1991). However, one systematic source of difference among service delivery networks is the structure of governmental services in each of the states. States differ in the extent to which tax-supported human service programs in a given field of service are primarily administered through statewide organizational structures or decentralized and administered through county and city governments. The basic characteristics of a single service delivery network in a given community are likely to persist over time even as the characteristics of individual service organizations change, as new organizations are created or disappear, or as existing organizations become components of larger organizational structures through mergers and acquisitions.

As Hage (1986) and Reitan (1998) point out, organizational networks are largely symbolic—that is, they are understood differentially depending on the frame of reference being used to describe the network. The perceptions of networks also take on different forms depending on whether they are being described by an organizational manager, an individual case manager, a service user, or a governmental policy maker. Reitan identifies a series of different theoretical perspectives that are potentially applicable to interorganizational networks as well as to individual service organizations:

- Client-need perspective—bottom up perspective (Hasenfeld and Steinmetz 1981)
- Professional perspective—professional linkages and conflicts (Hall 1986; Oliver 1997)
- Leadership perspective—an executive view (Austin 1989)
- Resource-dependence/political economy perspective—processes for the allocation of financial and legitimation resources among participating organizations (Zald 1970; Benson 1975; Walmsley and Zald 1976; Pfeffer and Zalancik 1978)
- Economic perspective—principal-agent theory—costs of interorganizational transactions (Williamson 1996)
- Network governance perspective—networks as a framework for the implementation of public policy (Woodard 1994)
- Institutional perspective—organizations and networks as molded by broader societal patterns (Powell and DiMaggio 1991)
- Marxist/sociology-of-knowledge perspective—organizations and networks as expressions of economic power relationships in the larger society (Abercrombie 1980)
- Postmodern perspective—organizations and networks as symbolic creations (Boje, Gephart, and Thatchenkery 1996)

This chapter is developed primarily around a combination of the leadership perspective and the resource-dependence/political economy perspective. It includes the following:

- A framework for analyzing the structure of interorganizational service delivery networks
- An analysis of the political economy of the service network
- A description of critical network stakeholders

- An analysis of interorganizational network processes
- An identification of critical elements in a fully developed service delivery network

THE STRUCTURE OF THE INTERORGANIZATIONAL SERVICE DELIVERY NETWORK

Hjern and Porter (1981) set forth a framework for the analysis of service delivery networks. This framework was developed to emphasize that the implementation of a public policy initiative—for example, job training for young adults—is not limited to the operations of individual service organizations. The analysis of policy implementation requires an understanding of the "program implementation structure" (Hjern and Porter 1981), or the interorganizational service delivery network, composed of a set of "program components" that must work together if the objectives of the public policy are to be accomplished.

Nearly all contemporary human service organizations are, in a limited sense, conglomerates. That is, they administer several different program components, each of which involves a distinct service technology or serves a distinct service population (also see chapter 4). These program components are often "loosely coupled"—that is, they function as semiautonomous units within an inclusive administrative structure (Weick 1976; Hasenfeld 1986). In many analyses of service delivery networks, reference is made to "the service organization" when it is a specific program component that is primarily involved in a specific network. Program components within a human service organization generally have (1) an identifiable subbudget within the financial structure of the administrative organization, (2) a component manager, (3) direct service personnel assigned specifically to that component, and, in most cases, (4) a distinct physical location as the base of operations, ranging from a single office to a separate building(s).

Examples of a single service organization with several different program components include the following:

- A family service agency that may have a preventive mental health/family life educational program, an individual and family counseling service, and one or more contract employee assistance programs with local business firms

- A community mental health center that may include psychiatric assessment and prescription services, half-way houses, an individual psychological/social work counseling service, community-based case management services, and a short-term hospitalization facility
- A county social services department that may include a protective service investigation unit, a foster care service, a program of services for home-bound older adults and an assisted-living program for individuals with physical disabilities

Large public school districts combine an administrative structure and a service delivery network structure that includes geographically decentralized components—individual schools serving a particular part of the community; a vertical, age-graded system of interrelated educational components; and community-wide specialized service components (the special education component, or the school social work component). Many aspects of educational administration resemble network processes as much as traditional internal management processes (Weick 1976). Shanley and Lounsbury (1996) illustrate how a network model of analysis as applied to a state child welfare organization provides a better explanation of organizational dynamics in a nonmarket bureaucracy than an economic efficiency model.

Hjern and Porter's analysis of the actual structure of service delivery leads to a "community matrix" model. In this matrix model, the service production "components" in individual service organizations are viewed as being linked together vertically by the structure of the inclusive administrative organization of which they are a part. The administrative organization also includes such organization-centered functions as personnel administration, financial management, and organizational accountability processes (figure 5.1).

However, individual service production components are also linked horizontally at the community level across separate administrative organizations through interorganizational exchanges and patterns of collaboration that constitute the "program implementation structures," or the term used in this chapter, *service delivery networks* (figure 5.2). These horizontal service delivery networks are linked together by a variety of boundary-spanning interactions through which staff members in

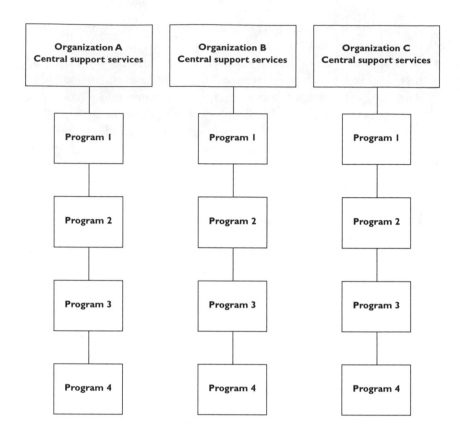

FIGURE 5.1. Administrative organizations.

one component deal regularly with staff members in other relevant components in other administrative organizations. A service organization with several program components may be involved in several different service delivery networks. Indeed, a single program component in one organization may be involved in more than one service delivery network. A service delivery network may also include more than one program component in a single administrative organization.

The system framework for analyzing an interorganizational service delivery network involves four system elements:

- *System element 1* is the community "suprastructure," which includes political, governmental, organizational, and association elements that

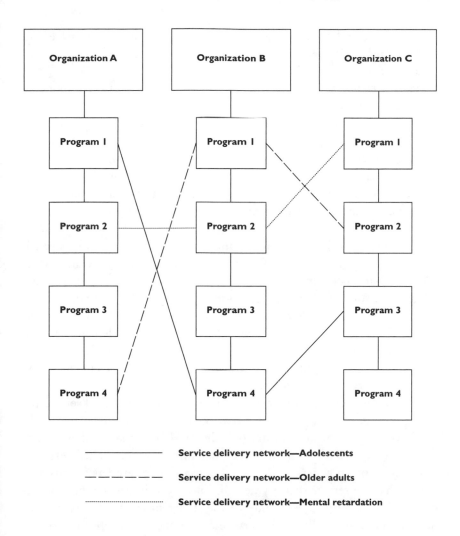

FIGURE 5.2. Service delivery networks.

together constitute the day-to-day operational framework, or task environment, for the service delivery networks in a given geographic
area, as well as for the individual human service organizations that
participate in such networks.
• *System element 2* includes the vertically structured, individual administrative organizations: governmental, quasi-governmental, voluntary

nonprofit, and for-profit service organizations, as well as state and sometimes federal service organizations that are providing services in a given community.

- *System element 3* includes specific specialized program components within individual administrative service organizations.
- *System element 4* includes the horizontally structured service delivery networks, or "implementation structures," that include the particular program components in service organizations through which a particular type of service becomes available to the residents in a given locality. System element 4 is the primary focus for this chapter, although attention is given to system elements 2 and 3.

At the level of the community suprastructure (element 1), it is possible to identify an inventory of vertically structured administrative service organizations (element 2) that are the primary channels for funding allocations, for organizational decision making, and for formal accountability. It is also possible to identify an inventory of interdependent, exchange-linked, specialized service delivery networks (element 4). The vertical administrative organizations (element 2) establish and maintain the program components (element 3) that are the active elements in the service delivery networks (element 4).

One of the most important distinctions between individual service organizations and service delivery networks is that networks generally do not have a hierarchical structure (Chisholm 1989)—that is, they do not have a clearly defined locus of power and authority. Service delivery networks are not, in general, "managed" on a day-to-day basis. This also means that the service delivery network itself can in no way be held accountable by a service user. Indeed, the recurrent cry for better coordination among network-linked service components is a reflection of the limited level of control and authority, and accountability, that typically exists within a service delivery network.

In fact, there is a continuum of network structures, largely reflecting differences in the extent to which there is some degree of centralized network management and control. A service delivery network may fit one of the following descriptions:

- A set of occasionally interacting organizations in a general field of service, with personal connections among individual staff members involving referrals and information sharing, but with little public recognition that it is a service delivery network. An example is social/health services for older adults.

- A set of frequently interacting organizations that is recognized as a service delivery network but that does not include any formal referral agreements or any single dominant organization. Much of the networking is by individuals who are familiar with each other, have much of the useful information in their heads, and trust the information they receive from those they have worked with in the past. An example is an AIDS services network.

- A set of frequently interacting organizations with some formal arrangements (referral agreements, purchase-of-service agreements, funding contracts, and some joint activities), shared training opportunities, and at least one major funding source that can influence developments within the network. An example is a county child welfare/protective services system.

- A set of interacting organizations that have some network-level activities (for example, an information and referral service), and that includes at least one organization with a major funding role that performs network coordination functions, including eligibility determination, case management, collaborative training, and community education. An example is a publicly funded community mental health network of services for children.

- A "managed" network that is partially controlled by a dominant organization through central control of funding, with some mix of ownership, alliances, contracts, case managers, and a common computerized information system. Operational components are loosely coupled with significant operational autonomy but not policy autonomy. Examples are managed health-care organizations and Veterans Administration health services. Large public school systems are similar (Weick 1976) but without as much diversity of functions as in the managed health-care systems.

Whereas individual administrative organizations have relatively explicit organizational boundaries and identifiable core functional elements (personnel offices, financial management offices, public relations/marketing offices), most service delivery networks have open, only loosely defined, network boundaries. And service delivery networks do not have

comprehensive core functional elements such as personnel/human relations, financial management, or marketing—although the managed networks have begun to develop such functions.

Internal Structure of the Service Delivery Network

A service delivery network includes a pool of organizations, organizational subgroups, core organizations, and network maintenance structures.

POOL OF ORGANIZATIONS The pool of organizations for a specific
service delivery network includes all the organizations with one or more
program components that are involved in the provision of services relevant to a particular problem condition (mental illness) or a particular
service population (older adults). In most communities, the total pool, or
inventory, of organizations involved in any single service network is likely to be quite large. This pool of organizations, in addition to the actual
service-providing organizations, may include funding organizations,
rule-setting and regulating bodies, monitoring and advocacy organizations, associations of service users, providers of technical and support
services to service organizations, specialized personnel training organizations, and so on. The pool of organizations may also include a number
of peripheral organizations that are on the outer edges of the service delivery network, involved only occasionally or around a very limited form
of service provision. The size of the pool of organizations is one indication of the significance of a particular service delivery network in the
community system, and an indication of the potential impact of any
changes in the characteristics of the network.

NETWORK SUBGROUPS Within the total pool of organizations there are
clusters of organizations in which the relevant program components
have more intensive and regular interactions with each other than with
the components in other organizations within the network. Thus, within the network of services for older adults, organizations that include
health-related service components are likely to have more interaction
with each other than such organizations have with social service organizations that include such program components as Meals on Wheels, senior luncheon programs, and a senior center (Chung 1996). Using a basic

set of information from each organization in the network about interactions with other organizations in the network, these network subgroups can be identified by the application of blockmodel and cluster analysis procedures (Streeter and Gillespie 1992).

CORE ORGANIZATIONS Within the total pool of organizations there are a limited number of central (Streeter and Gillespie 1992) or "core" organizations. The characteristics of the working relationships among the relevant components within these core organizations are particularly critical in determining the effectiveness of a service delivery network.

Core organizations may include those organizations that deal with the largest group of network service users, that are involved most frequently in relevant exchanges with other service organizations, that have several program components involved in the network, that control major sources of funding, or that have a formal coordinating or leadership role within the network. Interviews with key informants involved in a specific service delivery network usually result in agreement as to the three to five organizations that are commonly viewed as core organizations. Examples of core organizations include the public child protective services agency in the child welfare services network, the community mental health center in the mental health services network, the general hospital in the child and maternal health services network, and the public school system in the adolescent services network. In a managed health-care network, a for-profit general hospital is often one of the core organizations.

NETWORK MAINTENANCE STRUCTURES Many, but not all, networks include organizational components that are involved with the maintenance and development of the network rather than in the direct provision of services. In some instances, a single individual may fulfill the function of network maintenance, either as a specific responsibility or as part of management responsibilities in one of the core organizations.

Organizational maintenance structures may also include informal interorganizational committees, formally structured interorganizational councils, system planning organizations, and/or jointly created organizations that provide technical and support services for direct service organizations. The latter may include a central information and referral service for the general public, joint purchasing arrangements, joint training programs, and joint data processing, data analysis, and information technology services as well as collaborative public policy analysis and legislative representation. In some networks, the network maintenance functions may be carried out for the entire network by a component of one of the core organizations, as when the public mental-health-services-for-children component of a community mental health center carries out network maintenance functions for the children's mental health services network. Connor, Kadel-Taras, and Vinokur-Kaplan (1999) identify management support organizations as a form of secondary-level consultant organization that may provide collaboration development and network maintenance services.

THE POLITICAL ECONOMY OF
THE SERVICE DELIVERY NETWORK

The External Political Economy

The political economy involves the impact of political power or influence on the distribution of economic resources, and, in turn, the impact of the pattern of economic power on the exercise of political power. An analysis of the political economy of the service delivery network involves two related and overlapping frameworks. These two political economy frameworks shape the development and operation of the service delivery network. One framework is the *external political economy* of the network task environment, the "social context within which network relations are negotiated" (Benson 1975:238). The second framework is the *internal political economy* within the service delivery network.

Political, in the external political economy, refers to all forms of local governance, authority, control, and decision making and includes official governmental processes (primarily at city and county levels—including local school boards—and decision making at the state level for many governmental services) and decision-making processes in a variety of temporary special purpose task forces and study commissions. Also included are decision-making processes in the voluntary nonprofit service sector. Examples of the latter are the process for admission to membership and the process for funding allocation decisions in the local United Way organization. *Political* also includes all the informal power-related interactions among key individuals in the community, or "politics," that shape the formal decisions.

The external political economy of the network includes community systems involved in governance, authority, and control, and in the allocation of economic resources. For example, concentrated economic power may impact the local political processes that determine the allocation of funding support for service organizations, not only from city and county governments but also from the United Way. Similarly, political power may create funding opportunities that, in turn, may shape the development of individual organizations within a service network. The external political economy also includes the distribution pattern of economic resources, including the level of resources available to local governmental bodies and to the nonprofit service sector, the degree of concentration of economic resources in the business community, and the distribution of economic resources among individual households.

For example, in a community with a single, dominant employer, the attitude of the officers of that business about local tax levels and about the most important service sectors—health, education, or criminal justice—can shape the balance between governmental support and voluntary support and the actual allocation of resources among service sectors. Similarly, the existence of a large number of households with incomes below the poverty level may result in the dependence of local human service organizations and service networks on political decision processes at state and federal levels and on federal and state funding streams.

Recognized community leaders, representatives of important economic power centers, local mass media, and specialized advocacy organizations all have important roles in the politics of the external political economy. In the United States, the community-level political economy also includes the locally relevant effects of decisions at federal and state levels and, in some instances, of decisions by national nonprofit and for-profit organizations. With the establishment of inclusive managed health-care organizations, decision making within large, for-profit health-care systems outside the local community has become an important element in the local political economy of human services.

As Benson points out, the political economy is "concerned with the distribution of two scarce resources, money and authority" (1975:229). The distribution of money resources, or, more broadly, economic resources, may involve various forms of financial support for individual service organizations and, in some instances, access to land and building space. The distribution of "authority" resources, as Benson (1975) describes them, or "legitimation resources," involves the right and responsibility to carry out programs of a certain kind. Local authority processes may include designation of service organizations as exempt from local property taxes, as having the right to solicit contributions or to receive particular forms of funding, as having the right to be used for referrals from other community health and safety services, or as complying with local health department, fire safety, or zoning regulations.

The interactive processes between political power and economic power within the external political economy that shape the distribution of authority/legitimation and economic resources are critically important for service delivery networks. Both authority/legitimation resources and economic resources are essential for the survival of specific organizations, as well as for the ability of the organizational components within the service delivery network to produce the services needed by service users. Reduced funding by a legislature for an initial access service in a network, such as the investigative function of child protective services, may reduce the timeliness and accuracy of such investigations, with consequences for every other organizational component that is part of the local child welfare service delivery system.

As Benson (1975:239–240) points out, the pattern of the political economy of the external network task environment in any one community may have many different characteristics:

- Resources within the task environment may be concentrated (resource disbursements reside in one or a few sources) or dispersed (resources flow through multiple channels).
- Networks may be highly dependent on local environmental forces or have a high degree of autonomy—"social service networks tend to be subservient and dependent" (Benson 1975:240).
- Power within the task environment (the ability to influence or dominate) may be concentrated or dispersed.
- Power within the task environment may be concentrated in bureaucracies, or in "publics" such as ethnic groups, social movements, clientele groups.
- Resources in the task environment may be abundant or scarce, and the level of resources may vary over time.

- Control mechanisms based in the task environment may be authoritative (involving the delegation of authority to act) or incentive (based on the potential provision of resources).

The external political economy may be affected by crosscutting community-level political disagreements and conflicts such as the trade-offs between property tax levels and the quality and quantity of publicly funded human services, conflicts between development-oriented business leaders and environmental advocates, conflicts over the role of service organizations sponsored by religious congregations, conflicts about the relative position of African American, Latino, and White populations among the community service constituencies, and disagreements over specific service policy issues such as whether health-care services for sexually active adolescents should include information about abortion services.

Specific political party alignments are likely to be of less significance in the external political economy in most local communities than at state and federal levels, although political ideologies may influence the positions taken by leadership individuals on local decision issues. As in all political economy arenas, organized interest groups are likely to have a greater influence on policy and decisions about the allocation of resources than larger unorganized constituencies, such as service user constituencies or community residents. Such unorganized constituencies may become influential, however, around highly visible and contentious issues, such as the location of a half-way house in a residential neighborhood, or around the involvement of a service delivery issue in local electoral processes. News media—local newspapers, radio, and television—may play a decisive role in ad hoc mobilizations of such unorganized forces.

The Internal Political Economy

According to Benson, the participants in the internal network political economy are primarily concerned with the pursuit of "an adequate supply of money and authority" (1975:232). The ability of the leadership of a service organization to advance its interests—that is, to develop and protect the organizational power base—is based on (1) the position of the organizationally based network program components within the network—that is, the degree of centrality of the organization and its components; and (2) the linkages of the organization to sources of influence and resources outside the network, including the support of important publics. The power base of a service organization may be used to defend the organizational domain, and it may be used in processes of negotiation among network organizations that influence the distribution of influence power and economic resources within the network.

Individual organizations may use a variety of different strategies to advance their interests in gaining access to, or protecting, resources (Benson 1975:232–233):

- Establishing a claim to a supply of resources based on the adequacy and effectiveness of established programs
- Maintaining a clear-cut, uncluttered claim to a service domain of high social importance
- Maintaining an orderly, reliable pattern of resources so that the organization can anticipate an adequate and certain flow of resources
- Defending and extending the organization's way of doing things—its own definition of problems and its own techniques of intervention

In addition to the forces within the external and internal political economies of service delivery networks, networks are also shaped by institutional patterns in major sectors of the society, such as health care or adult criminal justice. Networks are also shaped by leadership initiatives (or the absence of such initiatives) by specific individuals, particularly in core, or dominant, network organizations. However, the pattern of authority and economic resource distribution to, and among, the organizations in the network is a major, and constant, force in shaping the development of a service delivery network, and, in turn, the characteristics of the services available through the network to service users.

NETWORK STAKEHOLDERS

The task environment of a service delivery network includes a number of key stakeholder groups, similar to the stakeholders related to individual human service organizations (see chapter 3). These include funding sources; referral sources that are part of other service networks (for example, criminal justice programs that make referrals to the mental health system); professional education programs that are likely to be more concerned with training opportunities and employment patterns within a network of services, or a field of services, than within a single organization; and service users, particularly those who are involved for an extended period of time with several service organizations within a single service delivery network. Some of the network stakeholders are organized and focused consciously on network characteristics. Other network stakeholder groups may be largely unorganized. This is particularly likely to be characteristic of service user populations.

The objectives of different network stakeholders are often in conflict. Service users often want expanded and more responsive services, funders seek tighter fiscal controls, and service personnel argue for more financial flexibility, increased financial support for service personnel, and a reduction in redundant paperwork. In the case of a single service organization, a key individual—the executive or a board president—may negotiate with organized stakeholders to resolve conflicting demands on the organization. However, in the case of the service delivery network, there is seldom any single individual who can negotiate on behalf of the entire network. This means that the network may be particularly vulnerable to external pressures from various stakeholders and to conflicts among stakeholders. In some instances, these conflicts may result in one of the core organizations serving as an unofficial advocate and negotiator on behalf of all the organizations in the network.

Service Users

The power imbalance between service users and individual human service organizations (see chapter 6) is even more pronounced in the relationship between service users and the set of organizations that constitute a service delivery network. This is particularly true when the problems that a user experiences are a function of network deficiencies rather than of the limitations of a particular service organization. Negotiating the service pathways in a network of organizations is usually much more difficult than dealing with a single organization. In extreme situations, service users can file a lawsuit against an individual service provider or a specific service organization. But it is not possible to file a lawsuit against a service delivery network that has no formal, or legal, existence, in contrast to the "incorporated" service organization. One critical aspect of the development of health management organizations (HMOs) is the creation of a formal service delivery system that can be sued for service delivery errors. Moreover, users of most nonprofit and governmental human service programs that are part of a service delivery network include disproportionate numbers of low-income individuals and households, persons from disadvantaged ethnic populations, and women and children, many of whom occupy positions of limited power in the society.

In some service delivery networks, there are network-level associations of service users or households that have more influence than an association at the level of an individual service organization. For example, mental health advocacy organizations such as the local units of the National Mental Health Association and the National Alliance for the Mentally Ill are concerned with the effectiveness and responsiveness of mental health services networks as much as with the effectiveness of individual mental health service organizations. Similarly, the parents of individuals with mental retardation are active at a service network level through ARC (originally, the Association for Retarded Citizens). And older adults who are actual or potential service users have created the American Association of Retired Persons (AARP) and the Gray Panthers as advocacy organizations concerned with network-level service provision arrangements. The existence of such organized user initiatives at the network level may result in the formal inclusion of service user representatives at a network planning and policy level.

However, the development of user advocacy organizations requires intensive efforts sustained over time on the part of service users and/or surrogates. Thus, it is most likely to occur when user involvement with the network is maintained over an extended period of time. It is also most likely to occur when service users, or user surrogates, include individuals with organizational experience and with access to sources of power and influence within the community. Service users who have only a short-term involvement with a single service organization, or who are largely unknown to each other, such as the participants in the Temporary Assistance to Needy Families (TANF) program or the recipients of food stamps, are unlikely to create such a formal advocacy, or user support structure. One alternative is the publicly funded, state-level, protection and advocacy organizations in the fields of disabilities, mental illness, and mental retardation that can provide a network-level resource for individuals and households concerned with the adequacy and appropriateness of network service provision.

Service Personnel

Professional networks, including professional associations and more informal networks of personal relationships among professional specialists, overlap the interorganizational structures of service delivery networks. In some instances, personal connections within a network of professional specialists may be the most important force for tying a service network together (Hall 1986). Doctor-to-doctor referrals may be more important for health-care users in gaining access to specialized medical services than formal referral procedures established by a managed health-care organization. Information sharing within a network may follow professional linkage lines faster than more formal methods of information dissemination. However, professional linkages within service networks may be as important for who is left out as for who is included. Specialized training programs within networks limited to physicians, or nurses, or social workers, such as educational programs dealing with managed health care, may reinforce boundary-spanning network linkages within those professional groups across organizational boundaries. But profession-specific network linkages may also be limited in effectiveness by omitting other personnel who are also directly involved in service provision.

Gender may play a larger role in linkages among service personnel within service delivery systems than in individual organizations, where personal relationships often cross gender boundaries. Distinct and separate informal communication systems within service delivery networks may develop along gender lines to the extent that gender characteristics and occupational categories overlap—for example, in the instance of secretarial and technical support staff (who tend to be female) or in the instance of senior managers (who, as a group, tend to be male). These communication systems may serve to share information that is not official or publicly acknowledged about developments within individual organizations. This may include information about organizational changes that create new career opportunities for other personnel in the network.

Professional personnel in human service organizations have traditionally operated as individual practitioners; they are often members of professional associations that do not deal directly with the organizational working conditions of individual association members. However, this has been changing. Professional associations are increasingly concerned with the characteristics of service delivery networks on a nationwide basis. These concerns include definitions of personnel requirements, patterns of financial arrangements with professional personnel, and requirements for professional education and licensing. These national developments can become an important factor in defining the role of professional specialists within a local service delivery network.

As public education networks and local school districts have become larger, elementary and secondary educators have become members of associations that function either as an official labor union—the American Federation of Teachers—or as a professional association that serves a similar function—the National Education Association. Nurses, particularly in large hospitals or large health service networks, have also become union members. The National Federation of Clinical Societies, whose social work members consist largely of private practitioners, many of whom are part of managed health-care systems, has formed an affiliate relationship with the American Federation of Labor–Congress of Industrial Organizations (AFL-CIO). In 1999, the American Medical Association endorsed the concept of union organization among individual physicians who are associated with managed health-care associations. And in January 2000, the executive director of the National Association of Social Workers raised the issue of collective bargaining for social workers (Nieves 2000).

In general, the principle of parallel levels of organizational development seems to apply. That is, when service organizations and service networks become larger, more complex, and more bureaucratic, employees and contract personnel, including professional specialists, are more likely to become organized. Economies of scale may be as relevant in negotiations about conditions of employment as they are in the production of goods and services.

Staff support personnel in governmental network organizations, as well as some professional specialists, may also join a public-employee labor union, particularly in states that have a strong tradition of union organizing. Large human service networks, such as managed health-care networks, may well be the focus of intensified union organizing in the future, particularly as the labor movement gives increased attention to organizing women in the labor force.

Policy Stakeholders

Policy making for a service delivery network is usually diffuse, with responsibility shared among a variety of power centers. A number of different organizations and/or individuals may have some degree of policy-making authority or influence within a network. Even when a formal network coordinating body has been established, policy-level decisions of the coordinating body may need to be approved either formally or informally by other relevant power centers.

In most contemporary service delivery networks, one or more governmental bodies are likely to have a significant, although not exclusive, policy-making role through control of major funding sources. In some instances, network policy making may be a function of an administrative position in a core organization that controls major funding flows or that serves large groups of service users. Senior officials in a state child-welfare system have an important policy-making role in the child welfare service network that includes referral sources, contract agencies, and judicial authorities. Senior officials in a state mental health department or department of criminal justice have a similar network policy-making role. However, governors, or their designates, or appointed boards may also have important network policy-making roles, either directly or through the secondary consequences of policy decisions that affect the operation of a core state agency.

Large network components that provide front-line services, or an association of several organizations, may also have a significant policy-shaping role. For example, a statewide trade association of community mental health centers that are created as quasi-governmental nonprofit corporations under state law and that are largely state funded may be a significant force in policy making for mental health service delivery networks. Representatives of such an association may deal directly with state officials and legislators on potential changes in the service network.

Suppliers and contractors that sell into a network (for example, textbook publishers in relation to public education networks, or medical supply providers in relation to managed health-care networks) are another potentially important policy-relevant stakeholder constituency. Providers of specialized equipment, including computers and computer services, may promote competitive perspectives among network organizations to promote sales of expensive products to several network members.

External systems of network monitoring and oversight may expand as service delivery networks become larger. Examples include state health departments and state insurance regulators that monitor managed health-care systems, state finance offices that monitor the performance of contract agencies providing child welfare services, and state boards of education. In some instances, one or more governmental bodies may establish a formal oversight or coordinating body to monitor the performance of a service delivery network or to investigate network problems. State legislative "sunset" provisions, calling for periodic legislative review of each state administrative organization, provide an opportunity to examine the effectiveness of service networks as well as the performance of a single organization. Official advocacy or ombudsman organizations, primarily at a state level, may also have a service delivery network oversight function.

External system monitors may be primarily concerned with system-level efficiency and cost controls. They may also be concerned with representing unorganized constituencies, including service users and related family members. In some instances, federal courts have instituted delivery system monitors because of major deficiencies in service delivery networks—for example, in the state-level service delivery networks in mental health, mental retardation, and criminal justice in Texas in the 1980s and 1990s.

To a limited degree, a local United Way organization may have an influence on service delivery network policy making through its budgetary review of individual organizations or through the appointment of an independent citizens committee to examine problems in service provision in a particular field. Similarly, a mayor, city council, or county commissioners' court may appoint a task force, or a study committee, to examine problems associated with a particular service delivery network.

Network policy making may also be substantially influenced by individual actors, such as a senior member of the state legislature who operates as a self-appointed policy maker by virtue of power in the state budgetary process. On occasion, individual members of the news media may take an investigative interest in the functioning of a particular service delivery network, with the result that policies and procedures within the network are changed.

INTERORGANIZATIONAL EXCHANGES

Service delivery networks function through processes of horizontal, or lateral, linkages and person-to-person interactions rather than through the exercise of hierarchical authority and control. In the words of Kanter, alliances "cannot be controlled by formal systems but require a dense web of interpersonal connections and internal infrastructures that enhance learning" (1997:225). The individual organizational components that participate in a service delivery network are linked together by a variety of exchange relationships. Some of these exchanges involve only specific program components within the organizations that are linked. In other situations, the organization as a whole is either directly or indirectly involved in the exchange. The literature on networks and on the exchanges that link networks together generally deals with organizations rather than with program components. The following discussion uses interorganizational exchange as the unit of analysis rather than the level of exchanges among program components.

Exchange Content

The examination of interorganizational exchanges involves both the content of the exchanges and the characteristics of the exchange relationship (Streeter and Gillespie 1992). The content of exchanges among network organizations may include referrals of service users, purchase of goods or services by one organization from another, provision of information from one organization to another, shared use of facilities or equipment, cooperation in interagency case conferences around a specific service situation, cooperative exchanges involved in interorganizational planning and problem-solving processes, joint purchasing, cooperation in public education and public advocacy, and a wide variety of other exchanges.

An analysis of the specific content of a single interorganizational exchange among two or more network organizations can involve a wide variety of factors including the following:

- The specific elements in the exchange

  Resources
  Information
  Influence
  Support

- The frequency of the exchange
- The size or scale of the exchange
- Who initiates the exchange
- The benefits each organization receives from an exchange

Interorganizational Relationships

Interorganizational exchange relationships may take several different forms including the following:

- *One-way transactions.* One organization provides a resource or benefit to another organization, such as a service referral, without receiving a specific resource or benefit in return.
- *Two-way exchanges.* Each organization receives something of value from the transaction, such as a service contract between a child protective services agency and a residential treatment center.
- *Cooperative exchanges.* Several organizations contribute jointly to an activity that benefits all the organizations, such as a joint staff training program or a joint volunteer recruitment campaign.

One-way transactions between organizations have some of the same characteristics that such transactions between individuals have. Some one-way transactions, or "grants" (Boulding 1973), may be an outgrowth of "love" or may evolve from cooperative or integrative commitments; other one-way transactions may be the outgrowth of "fear" or a result of threats or anticipated threats (Boulding 1973).

The analysis of interorganizational two-way exchanges was described initially by Levine and White (1961). Hall et al. (1977) analyzed the nature of such exchanges under three conditions. These include voluntary two-way exchanges, contract exchanges, and mandated exchanges.

VOLUNTARY TWO-WAY EXCHANGES Individual organizations participate in voluntary exchanges because of perceived mutual advantage (the win-win situation). The use of resources by each organization involved in the exchange results in some form of return benefit. The referral of a child under the custody of a state child welfare agency to a group home results in a receipt of financial reimbursement by the group home and the release of the state agency from immediate responsibility for the care of that child. The group home receives information about the child, which contributes to the development of the individual service plan. The state agency receives reports on the child and the services provided that become part of a report to the governor and the legislature in support of the agency budget request. In a voluntary exchange, each organization is free to withdraw from the exchange if the exchange is deemed to have, on balance, negative consequences for the organization, including the use of resources that could be used more effectively in other activities.

O'Brien and Bushnell (1980) note that "managed" voluntary exchanges may take place within the context of a coordinating council that provides leadership and overall planning for the development of the service network without directly controlling any of the participating organizations. Voluntary exchanges may also include cooperation among several organizations in a joint activity—staff recruitment, public relations, joint purchasing—in which the collective provision of resources results in benefits for each of the several organizations. Participation by voluntary nonprofit organizations in the United Way through the provision of required budgetary and service information and the recruitment of volunteers for the annual fund-raising campaign is exchanged for funding support. However, an organization is free to leave and to initiate its own independent fund-raising activities if the reporting expectations of the United Way and constraints placed by the United Way on other forms of fund-raising are viewed as not being consistent with the level of funding support received.

CONTRACT EXCHANGE   Contract exchanges are transactions in which individual organizations agree to participate in an exchange relationship for a specified period of time under specified conditions (Woodard 1994). Such contract-based exchanges may take place between a public child welfare organization and a specialized nonprofit adoption agency, between a community mental health center and a for-profit managed behavioral health-care organization, or between a central day-care funding organization and individual day-care centers. Many local United Way organizations have shifted from a voluntary exchange relationship involving general support for service organization budgets to a pattern of support contracts through which United Way financial support is tied to support of specific program components within the organization and evidence of the effectiveness of those components.

A contract exchange may, in fact, result in unequal benefits to the contracting organizations—the adoption agency discovers that there are unusually high costs associated with placement of the older children referred by the public child welfare organization, or the behavioral managed-care organization discovers that the individual situations being referred require more, and more costly, services than had been anticipated. A day-care center is required to reserve a specific number of "day-care slots" for referrals from the state TANF organization even though other parents would be willing to pay higher fees for day-care services than the contract provides for. But the contracted organizations are not free to refuse referrals from the contract funding sources until the end of the contract period because of potential financial penalties. Moreover, the contracts may guarantee a stable level of funding for an extended period of time, whereas other funding sources, such as contributions or fee payments from individual households, are unpredictable.

MANDATED EXCHANGES   Mandated exchanges are exchanges in which legislation or administrative directives mandate that one organization must participate in exchanges with another organization even though it is clear that the benefits for each organization are unequal. The power of state or county judges to mandate the placement of individuals with severe mental illness in a state psychiatric hospital, regardless of overcrowding or budgetary limitations, is one example of a mandated exchange, as is the power of juvenile judges to send individuals to a state juvenile justice authority without prior approval by the authority. The legal requirement that a public school system must accept a child who has been evaluated as having severe learning disabilities, and must pay the costs of providing specialized educational services, is another example of a mandated exchange. One financial advantage for new, publicly supported "charter schools" (which change the nature of the elementary/secondary educational service delivery network) is that they are not likely to be subject to such disability mandates if there is a traditional public school system available.

O'Brien and Bushnell (1980) indicate that mandated exchange relationships may be "unmanaged"—that is, without clear guidelines governing the content of the exchanges or any mechanism for resolving disputes. Mandated exchanges may also be "managed" (O'Brien and Bushnell 1980) through an inclusive planning council, or through a central funding organization such as a state department of mental health with rules for formal exchange procedures, such as patient referrals. Such managed mandates may also involve hierarchical authorities with the power to resolve interorganizational conflicts. Woodard (1995) describes the use of interorganizational agreements (IAs), in which there is a mandate by a public funding source that a written IA [also known as a memorandum of understanding (MOU)] be established between organizations serving the same population groups with state-level, or local, service organizations having the responsibility for negotiating the details of such an agreement.

Analysis of Interorganizational Exchange Relationships

The analysis of the pattern of interorganizational exchanges within a service delivery network may use any of three different structural frameworks:

- *Focal organization* exchange analysis involves the use of a single organization as a point of departure for the analysis of the pattern of exchanges between that organization and one other organization (figure 5.3).
- *Organizational set* exchange analysis involves an analysis of the pattern of all the exchanges between a focal organization and the "set" of all the other organizations and associations with which it has exchanges (Evan 1966; O'Brien and Bushnell 1980). Such an analysis may also include an examination of reasons for the absence of exchanges with

FIGURE 5.3. Focal organization exchange analysis.

particular organizations that might be considered as important organizational elements in the service delivery network (figure 5.4).

- *Network* exchange analysis involves the analysis of the pattern of exchanges among all the organizations within a service network. This would include, in particular, exchanges, or the absence of such exchanges, among core organizations (figure 5.5).

The Dynamics of Interorganizational Exchanges

Interorganizational exchange relationships involve four properties:

- Power—the relative ability of each organization to achieve organizational objectives vis-à-vis other organizations
- Level of commitment—willingness of separate organizations to work together, or collaborate, for mutual benefit
- Level of conflict—competition for access to, and control over, resources required to achieve organizational objectives, potentially resulting in hostile exchange relationships
- Economic utility—the calculation (by each organization) of relative costs and benefits of participation in a cooperative exchange

Jacobs (1974) explored the effects of power differentials between organizations on the pattern of interorganizational exchanges. When the benefits of a voluntary exchange involving two organizations are more critical for one organization than for the other organization, and there is no other source for obtaining those benefits, the more "dependent" organization may have to pay a higher "price" for participating in the exchange. For example, a residential treatment center may be forced to ac-

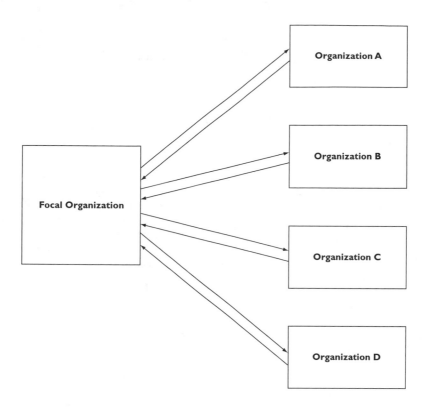

FIGURE 5.4. Organizational set exchange analysis.

cept a substantial number of referrals of difficult, and costly, service situations from the state child welfare agency in return for continuing to receive a dependable flow of the less difficult referrals that are essential for
the financial survival of the center. The state child welfare agency, on the
other hand, may be able to choose among several residential treatment
centers in making the less difficult referrals. A similar pattern of unequal
power may exist between a service organization and its largest funding
source (Oliver 1990).

Interorganizational exchanges may involve varying levels of, or intensity of, commitment. Mattessich and Monsey (1992) make a distinction
between cooperation, coordination, and collaboration. *Cooperation* is

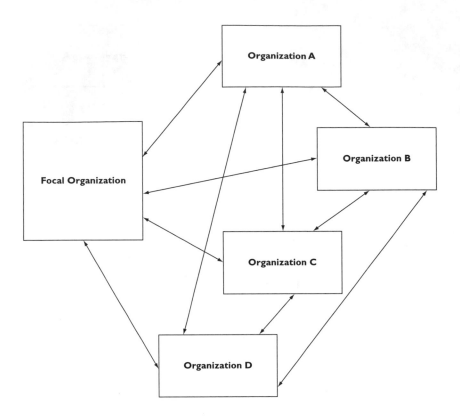

FIGURE 5.5. Network exchange analysis.

characterized as involving informal relationships without formal structure, with control of the relationship retained by each participating organization. *Coordination* is characterized by more formal relationships
with shared understandings of objectives but with authority retained by
each organization. *Collaboration* brings separated organizations into a
new structure with commitment to a shared purpose; authority rests with
the collaborative structure, and resources are pooled or jointly secured.

Interorganizational exchanges may involve elements of conflict, and
even hostility, as well as cooperation, particularly when there are power
imbalances and when the relative costs and benefits are unequal for the
organizational participants in the exchange. For example, the acceptance

of a new service organization, supported by prominent individuals in the community, by other long-standing service organizations may be an important element in creating public support for that organization, even though key individuals in the other organizations resent the increased competition for community funding.

Each interorganizational exchange involves some mixture of costs and benefits for each organization. One of the barriers to interorganizational exchanges is the difficulty for any one organization to determine the relative costs and benefits of any particular exchange. The costs include primarily the use of staff time and/or financial expenditures. The benefits of an interorganizational exchange may be in part financial, but they may also involve noneconomic factors, such as the reputation of the organization, the professional status of staff members, or a belief by board members and staff members that the exchange contributes to the achievement of the organizational mission. In the instance of the submission of a grant proposal to a foundation, or the submission of a proposal for a purchase-of-service contract to a public funding authority, the major costs involved in the exchange—the preparation of a proposal and the negotiation of its consideration—are incurred at the beginning; the benefits in the form of increased financial resources and program expansion come later.

Although it is possible to identify potential categories of costs and benefits, it is nearly impossible to determine the actual financial trade-offs between the present costs, including the level of risk that a grant proposal or a contract proposal may be turned down, and potential future organizational benefits. A decision to proceed with an interorganizational exchange generally depends on a political calculation, involving an assessment of the interests of various stakeholder groups, including potential service users, funders, staff members, board members, and the executive. The uncertainties inherent in such calculations may deter action on what may otherwise appear to be a highly desirable exchange transaction between two or more organizations in a service network.

Aiken and Hage (1968) point out that the analysis of interorganizational exchanges also involves examination of the consequences of such transactions for the internal structure of the organizations involved in the transactions. Perceptions about the organizational consequences of an interorganizational exchange at the organizational policy-making level and at the executive level may differ from those perceptions at the level of a program component directly involved in a particular service delivery network. An interorganizational exchange that may increase the relative power position of a particular program component within its own organization may be viewed at the policy and executive levels as having negative consequences for the organization as a whole. For example, a specialized program component that has an important power position within the network with which it is most actively involved may propose initiating a request to a foundation for an interorganizational collaborative demonstration service project that will include funding for additional professional personnel for the service component. However, this project may be viewed as potentially having negative financial consequences at the organizational level because of the foundation requirement for an organizational commitment to provide future financial support to replace the foundation grant.

MANAGEMENT OF NETWORK PROCESSES

Boundary Spanning

Interorganizational exchanges that tie program components and service organizations together within a service delivery network are shaped by the fundamental political economy dynamics of the network. But networks are also shaped by the interpersonal connections that cross organizational boundaries, generally described as boundary-spanning connections.

Boundary-spanning activities include letters and telephone calls to personnel in other organizations, face-to-face negotiations, and now Internet communications. Such boundary-spanning activities often involve the executive but may also involve other personnel throughout the organization. The objectives of boundary-spanning activities may be to make a referral for a service user who needs a specialized service, to obtain information about the eligibility requirements of a service in another organization, to arrange a purchase-of-service contract between a funding "authority" and a specialized "service provider," to plan for a collaborative staff development program, or to develop a common strategy for legislative advocacy.

Organ (1971) and Aldrich and Hecker (1977) were among the early authors to examine the forces that affect boundary-spanning roles, drawing on initial work by Kahn et al. (1964) dealing with "system boundaries" and "boundary personnel." "There is evidence that these roles are qualitatively different from those that are largely internal to the organization" (Organ 1971:74).

Among the special characteristics of boundary-spanning roles that Organ (1971:74–76) identifies are the following:

- *Role conflict.* Boundary spanners have to maintain loyalty to, and interaction with, other persons within the organization and also with representatives of the other organizations involved in the exchanges. One result is often conflicting expectations.
- *Lack of authority.* Boundary spanners often operate in situations in which they do not have formal authority but must rely, instead, on trust and negotiation.
- *Agent of change.* Boundary spanners become brokers between the perceptions of persons in other organizations and perceptions of other persons within their own organization, often attempting to reconcile the differences in these perceptions.

Case Management

Efforts were made in the 1970s to improve the effectiveness of federally supported human service programs in responding to service situations in which more than one type of service was involved. These efforts included demonstration projects that focused on policy coordination, primarily at the interdepartmental level of state government (interdepartmental efforts at the federal level to achieve policy coordination had largely failed); projects that focused on coordination at the program management level; and projects that focused on coordination at the individual service case level. Only service-level case coordination—case management—appeared to achieve any actual improvement in service effectiveness. These initiatives were often described as "service integration projects" following an effort by Elliot Richardson, Secretary of the U.S. Department of Health, Education, and Welfare in 1971, to achieve a greater degree of coordination among federal human service programs at the service delivery level (Kagan and Neville 1993). A more recent report on five federally funded services integration pilot projects stated, "The central mechanism for services integration was case management" (Bell and Associates 1994:19).

Case management, as a specialized form of boundary spanning, has received increased attention during the 1980s and 1990s (Weil and Karls 1985; Rose 1992; Raiff and Shore 1993; Frankel and Gelman 1998). Although *case management* can be defined in a variety of ways, it primarily involves gaining access to, negotiating, and overseeing a series of service arrangements involving organizational and nonorganizational sources in behalf of a household or individual.

In most personal situations, access to and coordination of services is handled directly by the individual involved (in the instance of adults) or by an adult in behalf of a minor child or a functionally dependent adult. Examples include adults with a physical injury who handle the arrangements for rehabilitation services for themselves, and parents who handle the arrangements for intensive care for a child with leukemia. Indeed, current developments in communication technology, including the Internet, may make it easier for many individuals to obtain access to and handle the coordination of specialized services for themselves or another household member.

However, as governmental service organizations shift from direct provision of comprehensive services to contract arrangements with a mixture of governmental, quasi-governmental, nonprofit, and for-profit organizations, each with different funding arrangements and eligibility requirements, it becomes increasingly difficult for many service users to negotiate service delivery networks. The case manager boundary-spanning processes become important elements in such complex service delivery networks.

The growth of case management services reflects the impact of several types of special service situations. One of these is the individual who is affected by a chronic and persistent problem condition or disability. Such an individual may require a variety of services over an extended period of time, as well as assistance in negotiating access to such services, in making financial arrangements for the payment for such services, and in maintaining a pattern of regular use of such services where that is necessary. In the past, many individuals with such conditions have been cared for in long-term residential institutions, such as state psychiatric hospitals and state schools for the mentally retarded, and nursing homes, in which the coordination of access to specialized services has been handled by internal institutional personnel.

Currently, many individuals who would have been cared for in such residential institutions are living in the community, and they are also living longer. The coordination functions of the residential institution have been shifted to the community-based service delivery network. Case management and coordination of access to services have become essential elements in the organization of effective service delivery networks (Schwartz, Goldman, and Churgin 1982; Rothman 1994). This has happened dramatically in the public mental health system as psychotropic medications have made it possible to discharge large numbers of persons with severe and chronic mental illness from state psychiatric hospitals. It is also happening as community-based alternatives to nursing home placement are created for persons who have limitations on their ability to carry out the tasks of daily living.

A second service situation for which case management services may be required involves the household in which multiple services are required simultaneously. A school referral to a child protective services organization indicating the possibility of child abuse or neglect may identify a family that is homeless (or living under substandard housing conditions) and without a regular source of income, a family that includes children without regular preventive health care, an adolescent son who is on probation from the juvenile court, and an adolescent daughter who is pregnant but not receiving prenatal health services. The family may require intensive direct person-to-person assistance—family preservation service—together with the simultaneous mobilization of other service resources. In this instance, a family preservation worker may serve both as a clinical social worker and as a resource-mobilizing case manager.

A third situation involves the "chronic problem," multiproblem, and sometimes multigenerational household in which both adults and children have repeated difficulties that lead to encounters with school officials, juvenile justice and adult criminal courts, public health officials, child protective services, and income assistance services (Austin 1958). Advice or mandates to the household from one service organization may directly conflict with the requirements of another service organization. Indeed, senior household members may ignore directives and suggestions from all the community service organizations that are involved. Although only a few households fit this description in any one community, such households are often large-scale consumers of community-supported services over time, both governmental and nonprofit. A 1950s study in St. Paul, Minnesota, found that while such families were a small proportion of all families in the community, they absorbed 50 percent of the available services (Buell 1952).

Such households are often the focus of extended community discussions about coordination of services, with recommendations that one service organization be designated as a lead service agency with comprehensive case management and service coordination responsibility. Such procedures are difficult to implement, however, since no single agency is likely to be eager to take on such a responsibility. Indeed, the legal mandates, or stated objectives, of the several service organizations are unlikely to include such a comprehensive responsibility. Such situations may require an interagency coordination group such as the legislatively mandated Community Resource Coordination Groups in Texas (Springer, Sharp, and Foy 2000) for a case manager to be effective.

Case management services can include a broad spectrum of intensity. At one end of the spectrum is the case management service that provides referral to, or arranges access to, a limited number of specialized services selected from a panel of approved services for which contract funding arrangements have already been established. Case management responsibilities may include establishing a service plan and assisting in initial connections to one or more specialized services, followed by periodic reviews to determine whether the services being provided are consistent with the original plan. In this instance, there may be limited direct contact between the case manager and the individual receiving the services. With the establishment of the TANF program, the meaning of the term *case management* has been modified in some administrative settings to mean primarily "managing the case"—that is, forcing the service user to comply with rules and regulations, often through the use of sanctions (Weaver 2000).

At the other end of the spectrum, the case manager may have broad responsibility for making arrangements for a broad group of "wraparound" services in individual situations, as well as working directly with the service user around underlying psychological difficulties with the objective of maximizing the level of individual responsibility and initiative in managing the tasks of daily living (Lamb 1980; Rapp and Wintersteen 1989). The services involved may include those for which an individual is directly eligible on an entitlement basis, those that may be paid for by insurance or other third-party arrangements, those that are provided free, and those provided voluntarily by a friend, neighbor, or family member. Case management services are also emerging to assist individuals with intense health problems, including cancer, in negotiating the complexities of contemporary health-care systems (Vourlekis, Ell, and Padgett 2001).

Some programs of case management have provided the case manager with discretionary access to a funding account to be used to pay directly for relevant services ranging from assistance with the tasks of daily living by a family member or neighbor, to the purchase of special equipment, or to participation in a specialized training or educational program. Budgetary limits are established in such a program, either on an individual case basis or on a service caseload basis, at a level that is lower than the direct costs associated with institutional care.

Geriatric care management services have emerged as a form of fee-for-service case management, most often paid for directly by members of a family when older adults are living alone in a distant location (Parker and Secord 1988). The services that are arranged may vary widely depending on individual circumstances. In some instances, they may be associated with financial counseling or protective management of financial resources. Such individualized care management services have, to date, generally not been included in existing public or nonprofit service programs and have thus been available only to individuals whose families are able to pay the full cost.

Case management functions are affected by the characteristics of the service delivery network. Moore (1992:418–421) describes four types of service delivery systems that have different implications for the function of the case manager:

- *Rationing.* System integration is high and resources are low. Case managers have responsibility for efficient allocation of resources.
- *Marketing.* System integration is high and resources are high. Case managers have responsibility for connecting the service user to the most relevant resource.

- *Brokering.* System integration is low but resources are high. Case managers have responsibility for actively developing a package of services from diverse sources as needed by the service user.
- *Developing.* Integration is low and resources are low. Case managers have responsibility for developing resources and coordinating them in response to the needs of service users.

Several different criteria may be used to evaluate the effectiveness of case management services, such as the prevention of institutionalization in a psychiatric hospital or a nursing home, or the prevention of the removal of children from a problematic family situation, which would result in foster care or placement in an institution. These criteria may emphasize cost savings in avoiding institutional care. However, service objectives may also include improvements in effectiveness in achieving individualized service outcomes, improvements in the quality of living for the service user, and an increase in the ability of service users to manage essential service relationships by themselves.

NETWORK PLANNING AND COORDINATION

Coordination within a service delivery network is carried out primarily at the individual service case level—for example, through the primary care physician in managed-care networks or by case managers in other types of service networks, as noted. However, many service delivery networks have serious functional problems that severely limit the effectiveness of service coordination and case management services as well as the responsiveness of the service network to the requirements of services users and, indeed, to the expectations of the community. Compher (1987:105–106) has described three types of dysfunctional service delivery networks:

> The "blind" service network is composed of dispersed service entities that deal with the client in a manner that demonstrates little or no knowledge of the involvement of other organizations. . . . Some important, or monitoring, parties will have very little contact with the client because they feel overwhelmed by large caseloads. The more active service-providing par-

ticipants will feel impotent and wonder why their well-intended work is not favorably influencing the client.

The "conflicted" service network is characterized by overt, often intransigent, ideological battles, and by battles among service agencies in relation to the client.

[The "rejecting" service network] is first and foremost responsive to its own operational needs and unresponsive to a client's specific concerns. . . . The service system may be overwhelmed with too high a volume of work . . . it may be anxious about the possibility of not being paid. . . . Case turnover—for example, movement of a case from intake to a series of other specialized services, or from worker to worker—does not allow sufficient opportunity for meaningful relationships to develop between the counselor and client. . . . Gaps in services may also exist during transfers of staff.

Network problems may include the diffuse characteristics of service delivery networks, gaps in the repertoire of available services, ineffective referral procedures, complaints about uneven responsibilities for the most severe and demanding service situations among various service organizations, and unilateral changes in policies in one organization that affect other organizations in the network. Sandfort (1999) describes how these problems can limit collaboration between two core service organizations in the service delivery system for implementing the TANF program in one state. Meyers (1993) identifies a range of organizational barriers that inhibit the effective integration of services for children.

Such problems often result in proposals for creating network-coordinating procedures or structures (Glisson and James 1992; Wallis 1994). Such proposals reflect the frequent absence of any one central authority that has the power, and responsibility, for defining and enforcing the terms of interorganizational exchanges and to monitor such exchanges. One critical factor is the general lack of mechanisms to resolve conflicts among participating organizations. The effects of such conflicts—which may reflect fundamental disagreements in the underlying assumptions about the nature of the conditions being dealt with, the appropriate treatment intervention (McManus and Leslie 2000), or personality conflicts—may disrupt network effectiveness over extended periods of time.

Initiatives to strengthen interorganizational coordination often follow changes in the task environment that require organizational adaptations, or external criticisms about the effectiveness and responsiveness of the service programs involved in the network. Rivard and coworkers report on one such project involving two service delivery systems (child welfare and juvenile justice), in which "a general pattern of increasing resource exchanges over time is characterized as relatively modest but important in demonstrating fundamental growth in cooperative interorganizational relationships" (1999:62).

No universal model for managing the coordination and development planning processes exists for a service network; problems within such networks are, in general, addressed as unique issues within each service network within each community. Both internal coordination and network-level planning require a high degree of consensus except when external authorities or power centers mandate such action—and follow through on monitoring the implementation of plans. Ad hoc, time-limited planning efforts in the form of task forces, study commissions, or even intensive conference/retreat events are most frequent, together with small-scale demonstration projects.

However, the results of such ad hoc planning initiatives often lack any systematic mechanism for long-term implementation of the proposals that emerge, so that the outcome may be no action at all, or only partial implementation by individual service organizations. The creation of a strong implementing authority would threaten the organizational autonomy of the service organizations in the network so that such a move is often resisted even when organizational leaders have called attention to the need for planning and coordination.

Thus, adaptation of service delivery networks to changing conditions, or to external criticisms is often erratic and unpredictable. One consequence may be the imposition of drastic changes in the structure of the service delivery network by external authorities or power centers. Examples include the changes imposed by managed health-care firms on the primary health-care system in many local communities, the imposition of a uniform system for state reimbursement of residential treatment centers based on an externally controlled procedure for rating the treatment requirements of individual boys and girls, a similar nationwide system dealing with the treatment requirements of older adults imposed by state Medicaid authorities on nursing homes, and the permanency planning requirements imposed by the federal government on state child welfare programs.

CRITICAL ELEMENTS IN AN EFFECTIVE
SERVICE DELIVERY NETWORK

One of the limitations in improving the effectiveness of service delivery networks is the absence of a model for assessing the developmental status of an existing network. The following is a list of critical network elements that can be used to assess the level of development within an existing network.

Access

The most critical element in any service delivery network is accessibility to potential service users. Network access may involve a highly visible single point of entry for the general public, such as a child abuse hot line, or multiple points of access such as individual physician offices and public health clinics for primary health care. Problems in ready access to nonprofit and governmental services are a frequent source of user complaints. Indeed, limitations in access may be a deliberate tactic for rationing services (see chapter 4). Alternatively, access to for-profit service organizations may be highly promoted through television advertising and web sites.

One important element in access is the existence of highly visible telephone information and referral services, either on a comprehensive community-wide basis or for specialized service networks such as services for older adults. Such telephone systems will be increasingly supplemented in many communities by universal access Internet web sites that may include for-profit services as well as nonprofit and governmental services. Other critical elements in access are service locations, accessibility by public transportation, hours of service, and inclusion of language competencies other than English.

Conflict Resolution Procedures

As already noted, one of the important differences between a network and a single-service-providing organization is the absence of any formal system of accountability and authority that can be used to resolve network-level conflicts among organizational units, or between service users and service providers. Interorganizational conflicts may result from financial uncertainties, incompatible regulations or traditions, personality conflicts, or errors in judgment in service provision. Unresolved conflicts can disrupt interagency relationships for long periods or end up in the civil courts. An effective network requires provisions for conflict resolution both among organizations and between service users and the service providers. Public hearings at which the problems of service users are presented, mediation and arbitration services to resolve conflicts, and appointment of an ombudsman to represent service user concerns are among possible alternatives.

Linkage Agreements

Linkage agreements among network components can include written agreements such as financial contracts and referral agreements, as well as informal verbal agreements among program administrators. Critical areas for such agreements include provisions for collaborative case assessment, case planning, case management, and cost reimbursement. The development of such agreements requires critical decisions about the confidentiality of records and about the rights of service users to participate in service decisions.

Common Program Information Data

One of the most important problems in network coordination is an inability to share program information among service organizations or to compile information at a network level, particularly as computer-based communication among service components becomes widely available. Critical data elements in a common information system include definitions of service activities and units of service, common diagnostic and assessment definitions, and a common vocabulary for the characteristics of service users. The lack of common data specifications across program components within different administrative organizations creates problems in communication between program components that may be dealing with a single household or a particular group of households. The absence of common data specifications also makes it difficult to prepare reports describing the composite activities of the entire network. Both deficiencies contribute to the problem of generating funding for critical network elements that may not have high public visibility. Public school service delivery networks and managed health-care networks are examples of complex networks that have found it necessary to establish common computer-based program data systems.

Strengthened Connections Among Network Personnel

One critical element in improving network performance is increasing the understanding of network functioning among network participants. Such understanding can be strengthened through activities that promote information sharing across organizational boundaries among staff and volunteers in participating program components, and through activities that create public visibility for the personnel in network organizations. These activities can include newsletters and a web site for sharing programmatic information, interagency task forces dealing with particular service operations, interorganizational staff associations in program areas, and shared training activities for staff and volunteers, including policy-level volunteers. Public visibility events can include jointly sponsored community-education conferences, information about the service network prepared for service users, annual network conferences at which outstanding volunteers and staff members are recognized, and special media events that focus on the service network as well as on individual service organizations.

Public Accountability

For many individuals who have difficulty finding the services they require, difficulty with the procedures involved in interorganizational referrals, or problems with the quality and appropriateness of services, the problems are in the network arrangements rather than in any single service organization. It is important to have clearly visible and accessible procedures for registering user complaints and for obtaining assistance in resolving network-level problems. The absence of a system-level complaint (or feedback) system is one reason that problems in service networks often persist indefinitely even though they may be well known among service providers. There is also a need for regular procedures that can be used to obtain suggestions, and criticisms, from the general public, as well as from employees and volunteers working in the network. Public hearings, focus groups, issue-oriented conferences, media call-in shows, web sites, and formal surveys are all potential channels for obtaining such information.

Responsibility for Network Maintenance, Development, and Evaluation

Responsibility for maintenance, development, and evaluation functions may be assigned to a single core organization, or to several core organizations, through a general consensus or on the basis of legislation or regulation. Such responsibility may also rest with an interagency council or commission. These functions include monitoring and preparing summaries of the network performance; evaluating the performance of specific program components and of the network as a whole; environmental scanning for information about changes in the demand for services, in the availability of resources, and in legislation and technology; and strategic network planning. Although it has not generally been possible to do a comparative evaluation of the performance effectiveness of the several different organizations within a network, Nyhan and Martin (1999) have reported the use of data envelopment analysis for such comparative evaluations among a set of human service organizations.

SUMMARY

The provision of human services often involves not just one organization but a service delivery network. The effectiveness of any single service program is often dependent on the characteristics of the network that it is part of. Service delivery networks consist of vertical administrative organizations, and specialized program components within those organizations that are linked together in horizontal networks by boundary-spanning exchanges. The characteristics of a service delivery system are shaped by the dynamics of the external political economy of the task environment, and the internal political economy involving the organizations and program components that make up the service delivery system. A service delivery network includes all the organizations and associations involved in exchange relationships, subsets of organizations that have the most frequent exchanges, core organizations, and network maintenance structures. Network analysis may include analysis of the exchanges between a focal organization and one other organization, between one organization and all other organizations that the first organization is involved with, or all exchanges among all organizations in the network.

Interorganizational exchanges are shaped by the degree of voluntariness in the exchange and by the relative power position of the participating organizations. Case management has become a major form of interorganizational boundary-spanning activity through which network resources are shaped to meet the needs of particular service users.

Service delivery networks are low-profile, nonhierarchical structures without a central authority to define and enforce interorganizational exchange agreements or to resolve conflicts. One of the major complaints about service networks is the lack of effective coordination, which often results in poor-quality service outcomes and unnecessary costs, both for users and for individual service organizations. Procedures for functional coordination, network oversight, and strategic planning are critical for improving the quality of services provided through a network. Although no two networks are identical, a set of critical network elements can be used to assess the developmental status of individual service delivery networks.

SIX

THE USER/CONSUMER CONSTITUENCY

> *With the help of computer technology, customers are* entering the internal
> business process *[emphasis added] in unprecedented ways. Customer
> choices direct production. Customer feedback drives product develop-
> ment. Customer communication creates membership groups.*
>
> —Rosabeth Moss Kanter (1997:122)

THE SERVICE USER/CONSUMER IN
THE HUMAN SERVICE ORGANIZATION

Theoretical analyses of formal organizations traditionally define the consumer or user constituency as being part of the task environment—that is,
as being outside the formal organization and, therefore, outside the
boundary of an internal organizational analysis. It is interesting to note
that Mary Parker Follett (Graham 1995) does not refer to the users or
consumers of the products of industrial production in her discussions of
the principles of effective business management. In for-profit goods production organizations, it has been assumed that the relationship with the
consumer is mediated by a marketplace exchange process that separates
the production organization from any interactive involvement with an individual consumer. Thus the purchaser of an automobile is not directly
involved in the production process of the automobile, and the producing
organization has no involvement in the uses that the buyer makes of the
automobile. It is also assumed, in a competitive free market situation, that
consumers of such goods have a variety of choices available. Consumers
can decide not to purchase a particular product if previous experience
with the product, or the procedures through which it is made available,
are unsatisfactory, or they may decide not to make *any* purchase.

However, the definition of the consumer constituency as being outside
the organizational boundaries is now changing dramatically in business
and industry. Competitive marketplace forces and the pressure to in-

crease sales have resulted in redefinitions of the role of the consumer. Prospective car buyers may be able to select in advance from among many options for the custom assembling of a specific vehicle. Automobile manufacturers also include after-purchase service options, including free road service and satellite-based emergency communication systems. In the computer/high-tech industry, ongoing support and problem-solving services extend system boundaries to include consumers around the world, who, in turn, become part of the process of designing the next generation of products. Total quality management (TQM) explicitly defines the product user as part of the quality control process (Deming 1986) (see chapter 11).

The service user constituency, both in goods production and in human services, can also be thought of as including not only the direct user of the end product but also other individuals and organizations that are involved in exchange relationships with the organization (Chism 1997). These include other service providers who make referrals to the service organization or who receive referrals from the organization, and organizations that provide services or materials to the organization or that receive services or materials from the organization (such as blood testing services that receive blood samples from a hospital). The quality of the service involved in such interactions and the level of satisfaction of the persons involved in such interactions may have direct consequences for the efficiency and effectiveness of service production. However, this chapter focuses specifically on the user of the end product—that is, the user of the service that is the central purpose for which the organization exists.

In the human service organization, like other service organizations, the users are part of a triadic relationship involving the service organization, the specific service providers (or contact personnel), and the users (Fitzsimmons and Fitzsimmons 1994). The characteristics of the service user role vary widely depending on the type of service being provided. Some service users may have a brief contact with the service organization, such as the user of emergency medical services or the information and referral telephone caller. Other users, such as the individual with chronic schizophrenia who receives social support services through a community mental health center, may have a long, continuing relationship with a single service organization.

Some users may have an intensive, personal relationship with service providers, such as the adolescent in a residential treatment center. Some users, such as the participants in specific program activities at a YMCA or Jewish Community Center, may have an ongoing but nonintensive relationship with service providers. Some service users have only an indirect relationship with a key service provider, such as when there is an indirect relationship between a child in a long-term, stable foster home and the child welfare caseworker who has contact primarily with the foster parents.

Some individual service users may have a relatively equal social status relationship with service providers, as in the instance of upper-middle-income parents paying full fees for services at a child guidance clinic. Other service users have a highly dependent and unequal relationship with individual service providers—for example, the older adult with Alzheimer's disease in a nursing home who is dependent on Medicaid funding for continued care, or the seventeen-year-old single parent applying for benefits under the Temporary Assistance to Needy Families (TANF) program. Children in an elementary school, as well as college students, may have an extended relationship with a particular service institution but relatively limited personal connection with many, or most, of the individual teachers.

Similar variations in the role of the service user exist in for-profit human service organizations, including the individual who has a single contact with a private practice physician or dentist, and the individual with a brain-injury condition who may spend years in an ongoing relationship with the personnel in a for-profit rehabilitation center. Although most users of human services are voluntary participants, some are involuntary service users, including inmates of jails and prisons and legally committed patients in public psychiatric hospitals. Adults with severe disabling health conditions may not be free to leave a nursing home on their own initiative. Children are compelled by truancy laws, and the actions of their parents, to participate in educational programs. Any analysis of the role of service users must recognize that each type of service program involves a distinctive pattern of user roles that shapes many of the transactions between service users and service providers.

The relationships among the service organization, the service providers, and the service users are the most critical element in human service production. The production of services in nearly all human service organizations involves a co-production process (see chapter 2), through which service users become an essential element in the production component of the organization (Fitzsimmons and Fitzsimmons

1994). Functionally, the service user must be regarded as being within the system boundaries of the organization. The service product cannot be produced without the interactive participation of the service user. Indeed, the quality of the service is highly dependent on the quality of the co-production participation by the service user, including involuntary service users.

Family preservation services provided by a child protective services agency cannot be effective unless there is active participation by adult members of the household. Addiction treatment services cannot be effective unless there is active participation in rehabilitation services by the person with a chemical addiction. The provision of educational services cannot be completed unless there is active participation by students. In the Head Start program, parents as service users are explicitly defined as co-producers, official members of the service production staff. The characteristics of service users and their co-production participation are as significant for effectiveness and efficiency as the characteristics of those staff persons who are defined as the direct service producers. However, the pattern of participation of service users in human service co-production is directly affected by their relative power, as among the several stakeholder constituencies.

THE POWER POSITION OF THE SERVICE USER

The normative framework for human services calls for service users to be considered the most important of the several stakeholder constituencies, as Rapp and Poertner assert in *Social Administration: A Client-Centered Approach* (1992). Increased attention to quality management in the for-profit sector of society has brought attention to the issue of service user satisfaction in human service organizations (Moore and Kelly 1996). Moreover, the concept of service user, or client, *self-determination* has long been identified as a fundamental ethical and practice principle in social work practice (Levy 1983).

However, in most human service programs, the service user constituency, including user surrogates, has, in reality, a weak power base, as among the several stakeholder constituencies (Hasenfeld 1983, 1992b). In nonprofit service organizations, funding sources are the dominant power constituency, a constituency that may be represented, in part, through membership on the board of directors. In governmental service organizations, legislative bodies as funding sources and rule makers are the ultimate power constituency, although organizational employees as a group may also constitute a significant political/power constituency.

As indicated earlier, in for-profit production organizations, the owners, or stockholders, a constituency that may include many of the senior managers of the organization, are the dominant power constituency. In for-profit organizations, service users are seldom organized. As an unorganized constituency, they only have real power when they have significant economic resources and when there are real marketplace choices. However, if the payment for services from a for-profit service organization is made by a third party, as in the instance of employer-funded managed health-care programs, individual users may have few marketplace choices in accessing health care and a weak power position even if they are relatively well-to-do.

Most individual human service users do not have the economic resources required to pay the full, marketplace-equivalent cost of the services provided by nonprofit and governmental human service programs, whether in social services, education, or health care, and least of all in criminal justice. Therefore, the choices available to service users are limited by the availability of funding from other sources to defray some part of the costs of providing the services. This is true of the neighborhood community center, the mental health counseling center, the general hospital, the public school, and the university.

Service users are likely to have limited knowledge about the processes involved in providing particular services, limited knowledge of their legal rights in a service relationship, limited social status and social networking connections, and limited political power. Moreover, the monopoly characteristics of most nonprofit and governmental human service programs result in a high level of organizational power in the relationship between the service organization and the service user (Hasenfeld 1983, 1992b) when the service need of the user is not a deferrable need and cannot be met satisfactorily through primary relationships (household or friends).

For example, few parents, except for those with substantial incomes, can choose which elementary school their child will attend or the classroom teacher to whom their child is assigned. And they have limited power to make the choice of not sending their child to any school. The development of managed health-care systems with monopoly character-istics—an employer has a health-care contract agreement with only one provider, or users are limited in their ability to change from one plan to another—has substantially restricted the ability of a health-care user to choose among physicians and hospitals. Particularly affected are users with a health-care need that cannot be postponed, such as a woman with a late-term pregnancy or an individual having a heart attack. For persons dependent on services from a child guidance clinic, a rape crisis center, a community mental health clinic, or a public health clinic, there is usual-ly only one service provider available and usually no choice as to the in-dividuals who directly provide the services. Even the option of not using any service is unavailable when the service user is an involuntary user, as in the criminal justice system.

Fundamentally, the service user is in a subordinate power position in relationships with most nonprofit or governmental service organizations (Hasenfeld 1983, 1992b) and with many for-profit service organizations, such as for-profit nursing homes. The power of the service organization is expressed through the enforcement of administrative regulations and through unilateral service provision decisions made by organizational personnel in individual service situations. The service user does not have either the implicit authority, or sufficient power vis-à-vis the organiza-tion, to determine the nature of the service provision by bargaining, ex-ecuting an enforceable contract, or withholding payment if not satisfied. Moreover, the service user, or service user surrogate, may have limited access to information about characteristics of the service that directly af-fect the quality of the service being provided. Comparing nonprofit and for-profit child-care programs, Gelles (2000) found significant differ-ences in program characteristics that could affect service quality, and he found that parents had limited information about these differences. For-profit centers were more likely to follow detailed policies focused on re-ducing costs, with two thirds of the for-profit directors also being dis-satisfied with the financial position of their center. Pearl and Bryant (2000), in a study of parent participation in the governing boards of state-sponsored early childhood intervention programs, found that par-ents were very aware of their limited power in the program decision-making process.

In a setting in which the user has a real choice to use or not to use a service, and when the organization needs users, as in youth-serving or-ganizations such as the YMCA and the Girl Scouts, the organization is forced to be directly responsive to the preferences of users. The other set-ting in which service users may have a significant degree of power is the "cooperative," in which service users are also the funders and owners, as in credit unions, many private elementary and secondary schools, and country clubs. A similar situation may exist when the service organiza-tion provides services for a narrowly defined user population that also controls program policies—for example, a service program controlled by tribal officials that serves residents on an American Indian reservation.

The power of the service user is also affected by the pattern of control within the service organization—that is, the extent to which the actions of individual service providers are limited by rules and regulations or, al-ternatively, by the level of discretion that can be exercised by the imme-diate service provider. Three potential patterns of organizational con-straint are described by Perrow (1986): (1) obtrusive direct control, (2) bureaucratic control, and (3) control through shared decision-making premises. *Obtrusive control* is represented by the early structure of many public welfare offices, in which the direct service workers functioned in large, open warehouse-like areas under the direct observation of supervi-sors whose offices were placed around outer edges of the area. *Bureau-cratic control* is represented by the public child-protective service organi-zations, or the state-administered Medicaid programs, that have detailed, frequently updated, manuals covering service decision making. *Shared de-cision-making premises* are represented by the professionalized nonprofit adoption agency, in which individual service workers are guided by a set of commonly agreed upon decision principles, shaped, in part, by the con-tent of their professional education and the professional code of ethics.

Among human service programs, there are few obtrusive direct con-trol organizations, whereas many service organizations are bureaucrati-cally controlled or controlled by "shared premises" or "professional standards" (Weaver 2000). However, some service organizations involve an uneasy mix of bureaucratic controls and shared premises, and in these organizations, individual service providers may differ in their assump-tions about which form of control is actually dominant. There are also service organizations in which individual service providers in practice have a large amount of individual discretion without a common profes-sional background *or* any internal agreement on the principles of deci-sion making. These ambiguities may provide an opportunity for highly flexible responses to variations in individual user situations. However, they may also allow unequal and discriminatory treatment of some service users as well as a high degree of special arrangements in the treatment of others (Lipsky 1980; Handler 1992; Brodkin 1997).

As an example of special arrangements, during the activist 1960s, in a state that used individualized family budgets to determine the level of the Aid for Families with Dependent Children (AFDC) payment, AFDC caseworkers in an economically depressed central city district were able to get physician friends to certify that all of the children in an AFDC household were malnourished and required supplemental food allowances. Workers with an unsympathetic "bureaucratic" supervisor would wait until the supervisor was absent for a day and then take the approval forms to a more sympathetic supervisor, whose values about maximizing assistance were felt to be consistent with those of the worker.

Differences in the patterns of internal organizational control represent significant differences in the extent to which individual service workers have discretion in responding directly to the individual service situation, or in the extent to which service users may be able to negotiate directly with the service worker. However, there is no assurance that increased discretion for service workers always results in increased power for the service user in the service transaction. A pattern of collegial, shared premises control, rather than administrative control, over the curriculum content in elementary schools or in university departments may also be associated with authoritarian control by individual teachers within their classrooms. A professionally staffed mental health center with collegial governance may also treat service recipients as "dependent patients."

The low-power position of individual service users may be reinforced by cultural and community patterns of unequal treatment, discrimination, and oppression that affect particular groups of people (Iglehart and Becerra 1995). Many of these patterns of unequal treatment are rooted in historical traditions such as the former, legally supported, patterns of discrimination against African Americans and the governmental programs of oppression experienced by American Indians. Other sources of unequal treatment include language differences, skin color, citizenship status, and the presence of a disability or illness. Age may be the basis of unequal treatment—for example, of very young or very old persons. The historically unequal status of women within the household may be reflected in unequal treatment in human service organizations. Gay and lesbian individuals may experience explicit discrimination in some service settings.

Individuals may have the most intense experiences of discrimination and unequal treatment when they are service users with social service, educational, criminal justice, and health-care organizations (Morton 1998). In addition, many individual conditions associated with the use of particular human services involve varying degrees of public stigma that may further depress the relative power of the service user in the service transaction. These stigmatizing conditions may include mental illness, mental retardation, adolescent pregnancy, terminal illnesses, physical disabilities, old age, and involvement with the police and the criminal justice system.

The power–dependency imbalance between the organization and the service user may have specific negative consequences for the service user (Hasenfeld 1983, 1992b). This power imbalance may also lead to two types of organizational problems in service program operation. First, the experience of the individual service user may be so negative that the co-production participation of the user is inhibited and the effectiveness of the program is reduced. As Hasenfeld points out, "The effectiveness of client–worker relations hinges on their ability to generate client cooperation. From both the perspectives of the organization and the clients, the best form of cooperation is that which is based on *trust*" (Hasenfeld 1992b:18). Elaborate, extended, and invasive application and intake procedures and unattractive service facilities may result in a buildup of anger and hostility on the part of potential service users that severely inhibits co-production participation.

Second, the preferences of an entire category of potential service users may be substantially ignored by the service organization, to the extent that the public-good objectives that are expected to be achieved through the service program are not realized, and the legitimacy of the program is impaired. Public health clinic prenatal services may be scheduled at times when they are not accessible to adolescent students, effectively excluding potentially high-risk pregnant teenagers from critical health-care resources. A mental health center may offer only verbal psychotherapy to individuals with chronic schizophrenia who are struggling with basic survival problems, including housing and routine health care. Without appropriate assistance, they may become homeless "street people" (Onken 2000).

One approach that has been advocated in some service areas for modifying inherent power imbalances so that service users may protect or support their own interests is the provision of potential service users with the necessary financial resources, either directly or through a voucher, to deal with service organizations on a marketplace purchaser basis. Such an approach does exist in the food stamp program under which food stamp recipients receive the equivalent of a "debit card" that can be used to purchase food items selected by the service user, as long as they are consistent with the purchase limitations that are part of the food stamp program. A similar voucher approach is involved in Section 8 of the Housing and Community Development Act of 1974 public housing program, although the housing choices are limited to a particular segment of the housing market. The use of vouchers has been advocated as a user "choice" alternative to the present structures for funding public education and publicly funded day care. But such vouchers do not significantly increase the power of the service user unless the user has a real choice between at least two different service organizations with available service capacity that are prepared to accept the payment level represented by the vouchers.

Although the provision of purchasing power directly to the potential service user might be applicable in some situations, it does not deal with the problem of single organization monopolies, or with the power–authority imbalance in the relationships between service specialists and service users. The deliberate structuring of the role of the service user in human service programs becomes a critical element in program design. Two design elements are involved: (1) the role of the service user in the actual process of service production, and (2) the representation of the interests of groups of service users, or service user constituencies, in the process of program policy making and policy implementation.

The following sections deal with the dynamics of the power relationships between the individual service user and the service organization and between user constituencies and service organizations, and alternative strategies for modifying such power relationships. Although the necessity for "consumer rights" or "user empowerment" provisions in human service programs is often argued for on the basis of the principles of social justice and equality, it is dealt with here primarily as an essential element in the design of programs that depend on effective service co-production (Littell, Alexander, and Reynolds 2001).

SERVICE USER ROLES IN SERVICE PRODUCTION

The production of most durable or consumable *goods* takes place prior to the existence of a specific request for such goods from a particular consumer, although examples can be found of products that are created only in response to a specific requirement. In theory, goods consumers, at the point of need, survey a variety of already existing products or detailed descriptions of potentially available products, and they select the product that is most attractive at a price that fits their price preference. *Services*, however, can be produced only after a potential consumer has demonstrated a need for, or has requested, such services, since the actual service co-production process must be designed to fit the interactive circumstances of the individual situation (Fitzsimmons and Fitzsimmons 1994).

Although different types of services exhibit some variation in the extent to which some elements of the service can be prepackaged (a standard arithmetic curriculum or a table of food stamp allotments) or can be designed only on a case-by-case basis (psychological counseling or a design for neighborhood renewal), the service production process does not begin until the service user begins participation. Teaching, regardless of the amount of preparation, does not begin until there is an interaction between the teacher and a student. The production of services for a single mother as part of the TANF program does not begin until there is a service application from such a mother.

Service users differ in their capacity to use the resources of specialized service organizations or to negotiate complex service delivery networks. A study of the experience of the Roxbury Multi-Service Center (Perlman 1975) indicated that, on the basis of the number of problems reported by service users in their first visit to the service organization, they fell into three groups:

- The "resource seekers" presented only one or two problems and had only a few contacts with the Center. These resource seekers indicated limited satisfaction with the Center in a follow-up evaluation study because it was not able to provide the services that they were seeking, primarily help with housing and employment.
- The "problem solvers" presented more problems and had more contacts with the Center. They demonstrated a coping capacity that enabled them to use information and the resources of the Center to find

solutions to their problems. They expressed satisfaction with the services that they had received.

- The "buffeted" people presented multiple problems and came to the Center repeatedly. They received the greatest amount of attention from the Center staff. In the evaluation study, they indicated the greatest satisfaction with the services of the Center. However, the evaluation study also indicated that they had limited coping capacity and were not able to use existing community resources effectively. The problems that they originally brought to the Center had not really changed even after they received extended service attention from Center staff members.

Such differences in user capacity require adaptations in the role of the service provider and often in the structure of the service arrangements. A demonstration project involving an active outreach to women who had not responded to the availability of cancer screening services distinguished between level I and level II service users who received case management telephone-support services from a peer counselor, and level III users who received brief focused telephone counseling by a counselor with a master's degree in social work and referral to specialized services (Vourlekis, Ell, and Padgett 2001).

There are five primary roles for the service user in the production of human services: service applicant, information provider, co-producer of services, service coordinator, and program evaluator. These roles require that the user be defined as being within the organizational system and that program design deal explicitly with the relation of the user to the service production procedures.

The Service User as Service Applicant

The first element in the service user role is that of *service applicant*. (It is recognized that some human service activities are mandated in situations in which the service request has not been initiated by the potential service user; in such situations, however, a third party—a neighbor, a police officer, a parent—must initiate the service request.) Without the request for initiation of service, there will be no service production activity (Fitzsimmons and Fitzsimmons 1994).

In a number of service programs in which the potential public benefits constitute a major justification for the establishment of the service (such as prenatal medical supervision through a public health clinic, the immunization of young children, or a "gang control" diversion program for street-corner adolescents), an outreach activity may be carried out to ensure an appropriate level of service requests. Under these conditions, the potential service user may be the object of active recruitment. This may make it possible for potential users to demand certain benefits as a condition of participation—for example, a convenient location and schedule, provision of child-care services or sports equipment. Such bargaining outcomes are equivalent to reducing the costs to the user of applying for and using the service.

The processes through which an applicant is admitted to a service program are shaped by variations in the degree of control, or power, that both the applicant and the organization have over the admission process, as indicated in the following table (Hasenfeld 1983:185):

Organizational Control	Client Control	
	High	Low
High	Private practice	Benevolent
Low	Public access	Domesticated

The variations in the admission process establish the context for the interaction between service users and the service providers, and, in turn, the context for co-production processes. In the *private practice pattern*, both the organization (or individual service practitioners) *and* the service users have a significant degree of control over admission. Private practitioners are free to admit or not admit an individual to the service; users are free to choose one provider over another. This is the traditional private practice model in medical practice, as well as in private practices of social work, clinical psychology, and other forms of psychological counseling.

In the *benevolent pattern*, the organization has high control over the admission process but service-use applicants who are being referred for services by a third party have little control. For-profit residential treatment centers, for-profit psychiatric hospitals, and for-profit nursing homes fit this pattern. They can exercise a high degree of control over the admission process through the physician-controlled diagnostic process. Admission to nursing homes is also largely controlled by organizational capacity limitations and organizational decisions about acceptable funding sources. On the other hand, the potential service users may be compelled to enter these service institutions by family members or other persons in a position of authority. Juvenile courts exercise control over whether to follow informal or formal procedures in a court hearing, and they exercise control over whether to assign a juvenile offender, who has little control over the decision, to probation services or to a juvenile justice institution.

In the *public access pattern*, organizations have limited control over admissions, but potential service users are presumed to have assured access. However, public access service organizations may engage in efforts to attract desirable service users, while discouraging or "cooling out" persons who are viewed as undesirable users. Emergency rooms develop procedures to exclude persons with minor health problems who are chronic users while giving priority to accident victims and victims of heart attacks. By establishing a reputation for rigorous and time-consuming eligibility screening procedures, public assistance programs, such as state-administered TANF programs, may seek to discourage applications for an "entitlement benefit" from what are felt to be undeserving, marginal household situations while admitting a limited number of "deserving" individuals (Hasenfeld 2000).

In the *domesticated pattern*, neither the service organizations nor the applicants for service have high control. Users are forced to use the services, and the organization has limited power to exclude. Public schools are required to serve all children in their service area and children are legally required to attend school. Public psychiatric hospitals are required to take committed patients and committed patients have no choice but to enter the hospital. Prisons are required to take those persons sentenced by criminal courts and convicted felons are required to enter the prison.

The Service User as Information Provider

A second component of the service user role is that of *information provider*. Since the nature of the service provided is largely determined by the characteristics of the individual situation, one of the essential inputs in the service production process is information provided by the service applicant. The accuracy of this information becomes a major element in the correctness of the diagnosis or assessment, and therefore of the prescription or plan that is based on such an assessment. In some service programs, there may be an independent check on the information provided—laboratory tests in the instance of illness, placement examinations in determining academic grade placement, and the direct check of collateral sources of financial information in the instance of a financial eligibility determination, whether the eligibility is for financial assistance under the TANF program or for financial support through academic fellowship programs.

The power imbalance between service providers and the service user may mean that there are compelling reasons for the service applicant to provide any information requested, regardless of personal preferences. On the other hand, incomplete and inaccurate information may be provided as a response to oppressive interviewing procedures that reflect the power imbalance between the service organization and the service user. A lack of truthfulness and completeness in the information provided under conditions of oppressive organizational power may be a major factor in limiting the effectiveness and efficiency of the service program.

Forceful, bureaucratic demands for information from an unmarried mother about the location of the biological father of her child who is making informal cash "child support" payments can result in misleading information that is useless. This may frustrate the state's effort to force child support payments that are then often used for repayment of the state funds used for prior AFDC/TANF support payments rather than being sent to the mother. Such information distortions resulting from negative reactions to organizational power may occur not only in information provided for individual diagnosis or assessment in an individual service situation but also in information provided through organizational surveys of community residents as part of a community-needs assessment process.

There are important elements of program design that can be used to enhance the user information-provider role and its contribution to effective service provision. These include procedures to assure the applicant of the confidentiality of private information; the interview skills of the individuals with responsibility for obtaining information, particularly where in-depth interviews are required; the choice between office location or personal residence as the primary location for initial information gathering; the choice between brief, structured interviews and open-ended interview procedures; and the degree to which interview probing is used. The choice of information gathering procedures is specific to a particular program, since there is no single pattern that is appropriate for every service program.

The extent to which the setting serves to encourage and support an appropriate level of trust between the person requesting the service and the service worker is important (Hasenfeld 1983). Also important is the extent to which the role of the applicant is defined as only that of a passive information giver or as a participant in a two-way information exchange. Another important element of program design may be the specification of limits on the type of personal information that is required, consistent with the program requirements. For example, including inquiries about citizenship status in making a determination of eligibility for receiving public health services may make a substantial difference in the utilization of services such as the immunization of children, particularly if it is assumed that negative information will be reported to the Immigration and Naturalization Service.

The Service User as Co-producer

A third important component in the role of the service user is that of *co-producer of service outcomes*. As was pointed out, nearly all human service programs require the participation of the service user in the actual production of the service (see chapter 2). The production of educational services outputs requires the active participation of students. The products of student effort, whether in the form of test results, in the form of results of competitions with other schools, or in the form of completed assignments and other academic products, are the most visible evidence of educational service outputs. The movement of a household from economic dependency to economic self-support under the TANF program depends primarily on the decisions and initiatives of the adults in the household, a process that the TANF worker can strongly encourage, even with the use of sanctions, but cannot force.

Treatment outcomes in psychotherapy require the active involvement of the patient in verbal communication with the therapist. As Littell, Alexander, and Reynolds point out, "Client participation is an important, underinvestigated part of the treatment process. Better understanding of participation phenomena may lead to the development of more effective strategies for engaging clients in treatment and, if the treatment is effective, enhance outcomes" (2001:2). The outcomes of physical rehabilitation programs depend largely on the effort made by the patient to carry out rehabilitative exercises on a regular basis. In some instances, participants in a service program must explicitly and consciously change their behaviors if the objectives of the program are to be accomplished, as in the instance of a program directed to the parents of an abused child. Current attention being given to diet modification and other lifestyle changes in programs to prevent heart disease and cancer highlights the increased recognition being given to co-production in healthcare services.

Many persons among potential service users are members of population groups that have experienced discrimination and institutionalized oppression, particularly in the instance of governmental and nonprofit service organizations (Geller 1988; Morton 1998). These persons may face a number of barriers to effective co-production, including an absence of cultural sensitivity in program procedures and among organizational staff members, inconvenient service locations, absence of persons with relevant language skills, and the use of what are perceived as inappropriate service technologies (Pinderhughes 1989; Iglehart and Becerra 1995).

Given the importance of co-production, the motivation of service participants often becomes as important a factor in the effectiveness of a human service program as the skills of the service staff. The definition of the role of the service user in ways that either inhibit or encourage active involvement in the co-production process may be the single most important aspect of program design. Schorr, in her book dealing with successful innovative programs (1997:13), quotes Handler (1996), in his report on efforts to debureaucratize a special education program, as stating that the most profound change occurred in professional norms: "The professional task was redefined. . . . Parents were seen as part of the solution rather than the problem. Everyone . . . could comfortably concede to the views of the other, confident that the matter was still open for renegotiation." Even in domesticated programs such as prisons, co-production participation by the residents is an essential element in routinely maintaining an orderly community. Indeed, the existence of either very high or very low levels of co-production motivation among service users may be one of the most important confounding factors in evaluation research studies that seek to distinguish relative effectiveness among alternative program strategies.

The potential factors affecting the motivation of service participants are numerous and not well understood (Littell, Alexander, and Reynolds 2001). These include the role of stress in supporting or inhibiting personal involvement in difficult processes of behavior change, the role of the personality characteristics of service providers rather than technical skill as a factor in effectiveness, the importance of cognitive understanding of the service production procedures in user motivation, and the role of rewards and sanctions (Hasenfeld and Weaver 1996) in encouraging co-production effort. Theories of service user motivation based on participation in contracting, goal setting, and decision making in the service production process are largely carried over from studies of motivation among organizational employees, but these theories are largely untested.

The use of professional authority to enforce cooperation and, on the other hand, the use of self-directed treatment with minimal professional involvement are each argued for as methods of achieving effective co-production. Peer group self-treatment is advocated for individuals with chronic mental illness conditions (Chamberlin 1978; Segal, Silverman, and Temkin 1993; Onken 2000) and other conditions (Powell 1995). However, the role of ideology and belief systems that have powerful effects in other areas of social life (for example, belief, or nonbelief, in the power of scientific medicine) in effecting outcomes in service programs is largely unknown.

One key issue in the discussion of user motivation in co-production involves the processes of identification and modeling—that is, whether similarity of personal characteristics between the service provider and the service user (similarity in ethnic background, religion, age, gender, or life experience) is important (Ewing 1974). Emphasis on similarity of personal characteristics as an important factor in successful co-production, however, runs sharply counter to the concept of impersonal technical competence that underlies the concepts of both professionalism and bureaucracy. Indeed, there are relevant arguments that too great a degree of identification between the service provider and the service user may have negative consequences for service effectiveness. That is, does such identification result in the involvement of the service provider on an emotional level and in a response to the situation of the service user primarily based on emotions attached to the personal life experiences of the service provider? Although there is little agreement on the definitive dynamics of co-production, an essential element of program design is identifying those assumptions in the design that pertain to the co-production process and the role of user motivation in achieving effective service outcomes.

The Service User as Service Coordinator or Case Manager

In most service transactions, individual service users, or service user surrogates such as parents or foster parents acting in behalf of young children, are expected to serve as their own coordinator and self-advocate, or "case manager." The initiation of service, the scheduling of appointments, the implementation of referral recommendations, arrangements for service payments or establishing eligibility for cost subsidy, transportation to service locations, the purchase or rental of special equipment if needed, ongoing arrangements for basic food and shelter, and the effective advocacy of self-interests may all be essential elements in effective service provision. Moreover, in many service situations, there is an automatic assumption that either the individual service user or a family member or friend will have both essential information and the resources necessary to handle these coordination/case manager tasks—tasks for which there is no reimbursement from third party sources.

The sharply reduced use of institutional care (in which coordination takes place within a closed institution, managed by a single authority) for the care of persons with long-term illnesses or disabilities has highlighted the critical importance of such service coordination (Rose 1992; Rothman 1994; Frankel and Gelman 1998). Community-based service delivery systems are often fragmented into a series of specialized service programs supported by categorical funding streams and specialized referral and access procedures. In some situations, the service user, or a surrogate, may lack necessary information or be ineffective in negotiating the service network, requiring organization-based case management. In other situations, a parent, a friend, or a member of an extended family takes on the task of service coordination, often in combination with the tasks of daily caregiving. In some situations, an overload of caretaking responsibility can result in burnout or an illness affecting the caregiver.

The Service User as Program Evaluator

The service user also has a key role as *program evaluator*. The absence of systematic evaluations of program effectiveness in most human service programs is one of the most important factors in limiting the power position of service users, particularly when users do not have a choice among service providers (see chapter 11). Systematic determinations of program effectiveness may depend largely on the perceptions of the service users or user surrogates, particularly when independent measures of program outcomes are not available (Selber and Streeter 2000).

Perceptions of service quality may involve two related but distinct elements. One is the specific effect of the service on the life situation of the service user; the other is the quality of the service production relationship. A service that may, in reality, result in positive outcomes for the service user may be negatively evaluated on the basis of limitations in the human relationships involved in the service experience. Alternatively, a service that actually has little specific impact in a given service situation may be evaluated as helpful because of the positive personal relationship between the service user and the service provider (Selber and Streeter 2000). Among the examples of both types of difficulties are the distortions that can occur in student evaluations of classroom teachers. There may also be systematic differences between the evaluation made by the service user, such as a child, and the evaluation made by a user surrogate, either a parent or a son or daughter (in the instance of services for an older adult).

SERVICE USERS AND PROFESSIONAL SPECIALISTS

Although the legal and organizational structure of an administrative bureaucracy often results in a subordinate role for the service user, the process of service provision by professional specialists may also be oppressive (Pinderhughes 1989). Both the actual knowledge base of the professional specialist and the social status of the professional role result in a persistent power imbalance between the professional and the layperson service user, even in situations in which the user is paying directly for the service. Indeed, such an imbalance may exist even when a professional specialist is the service user, as, for example, when a parent who is also a professional specialist participates in a teacher–parent conference in an elementary school, or when a professional specialist is a hospital patient.

Often, an assumption is made that one of the responsibilities of the professional practitioner is to represent and protect the interests of the service user (client, patient) if these interests conflict with organizational interests represented by managers and policy makers (Reamer 1995). However, professional practitioners are often economically dependent on an employing organization for short-run economic support and for long-run career opportunities. Individual professionals may be unable to represent service user interests effectively in situations of conflict between user preferences and organizational priorities. Moreover, the perception and definition of service user interests may be systematically distorted by the conceptual frameworks used by professionals to define the needs of service users (Hasenfeld 1983; Pinderhughes 1989).

The use of professional power to control the diagnosis and to define the appropriate service is particularly likely to occur if a distinctive program structure is being used, primarily because it supports the domain of a particular professional group. For example, the prescription of psychotropic medications to control the public behavior of the individual with schizophrenia, even though the service user complains of the side effects of the medications, may increase the power of the psychiatrist as the professional who is legitimated to write prescriptions. This model of treatment also makes the pharmacist an important mental health professional. An increased emphasis on time-limited permanency planning in child protective services, partially as a result of federal legislation, may expand the role of adoption workers and curtail the organizational investment in family preservation services, regardless of the preferences of the birth family and of the child.

The professional–service user relationship becomes particularly complex when the professional responsibility includes assessing the status of the service user for the benefit of a third party. This is characteristic of *mediative* professional practice in which third parties exercise control over how services are produced and distributed (Abbott 1988). Teachers are expected to provide an independent assessment of the educational development of a child for parents, as well as for potential employers or in connection with the admission process of other academic institutions. A social worker, after a period of providing family support services to birth parents, is expected to provide a judge with an assessment of the level of risk that exists for a child who is in foster care because of an earlier incident of abuse. Similar assessments are made for employers of the health condition or rehabilitation progress of persons who have been users of health services. Typically, there is no full disclosure of these assessment and reporting responsibilities at the beginning of service provision, nor is there shared participation between the professional service provider and the service user in preparing such assessments.

ENHANCING USER POWER

Given the assumption that a power imbalance in the relationships between the service user and other participants in service production may have detrimental consequences on the quality of the service user participation in co-production, specific procedures may be followed to enhance the power of the service user at crucial points in the service provision process. Mary Parker Follett discusses the same concept as applied to labor-management conflicts: "It seems to me that whereas power usually means power-over, the power of some person or group over some other person or group, it is possible to develop the conception of power-with, a jointly developed power, a co-active, not a coercive power" (Graham 1995:103).

The most crucial element in the power position of the service user is the actual exchange between the service user and the frontline service provider. Even when there are official program policies intended to reduce any potentially negative consequences from the discretionary use of authority by the direct service provider, there may be discriminatory and oppressive actions (Lipsky 1980). Alternatively, the immediate relationship between the service user and the service provider may be deliberately structured by the professional practitioner in ways that empower or strengthen the position of the service user (Solomon 1976; Pinderhughes 1983).

Empowerment practice in the human services has emerged from efforts to develop more effective and responsive services for women, people of color, and other oppressed groups. The goal of this method of practice is to address the role powerlessness plays in creating and perpetuating personal and social problems. It can be distinguished by its focus on developing critical awareness, increasing feelings of collective and self-efficacy, and developing skills for personal, interpersonal, or social change.

Gutiérrez, GlenMaye, and DeLois (1995:249)

Kemp, Whittaker, and Tracy (1997) identify the key elements of "client and consumer" empowerment as including participation, education, critical reflection, transformation of perspectives, competence building in clients and communities, and social environment action. In some service situations, empowerment of the family, acting as surrogate and advocate for the service user, may be the critical element (Dunst, Trivette, and Deal 1988). Fundamental to empowerment is changing the power relationship in the service encounter from power domination by the service provider to "power-with" or "power sharing" (Pinderhughes 1989).

Specific program design provisions may be used to enhance the relative power of service users in transactions with the service organization and with service providers, with the objective of increasing co-production effectiveness. These include the following:

- Written guarantees of the confidentiality of private information provided by the service user, with release only with the written approval of the service user
- Provision for written agreement of the service user to an explicit service plan, or "contract"
- Provision for the exercise of choice by the service user, including a choice of service provider
- Provision of procedures through which service applicants and service users can appeal administrative decisions
- Provision for formal, confidential evaluation of the quality of service by the service user at the completion of service, or at a defined time following the completion of service
- Provision of an advocacy service for service applicants and users through a separate structure (Legal Services) or within the service organization (veterans' organization representatives in Veterans Administration facilities);
- Provision of an independent complaint and investigation process available to service users (nursing home ombudsman)

Onken (2000) advocates the active inclusion of service users in the design and administration of program planning research. The Internet provides a new option for service users through the sharing of information with other service users about personal experiences. Such information sharing about classroom faculty does occur among college students. A limitation of the Internet information exchange is that there is no procedure for independent verification of any of the information exchanged.

SURROGATES AND ADVOCATES

The implementation of user-empowering provisions in some service situations may involve assigning, to either a service user surrogate or to an advocate, specific authority to act on behalf of the interests of the service user. *Surrogates* act directly for service users in instances when they are unable to represent themselves because of age, disability, or absence. Surrogates are most frequently family members or friends. In many instances, the surrogate is presumed to be acting as the official agent of the service user with authority to make binding decisions—for example, when a parent authorizes medical treatment for a child or a court-appointed guardian controls the financial affairs of an older adult with Alzheimer's disease.

The definition of the boundaries of the surrogate role, however, become complex as children become older, with consequences for the surrogate and for the service organization. In some jurisdictions, parents can be held legally accountable for the actions of their older children that they may have no control over—for example, persistent school truancy. On the other hand, there are lively debates about whether parents have a right to be informed directly by a college administration about the academic status of their child who is a college student or about student behavior that violates campus rules. Even more complex is the status of parents of an adult child who has been legally committed to a state psychiatric hospital, although these parents were the primary caretakers for that individual prior to hospitalization. Under procedures dealing with medical confidentiality, such parents have no right to receive information, even about a pending discharge of the patient, except from the patient. Similarly, there may be conflicts between the decision of a severely ill older adult to request termination of extraordinary life supports and the preferences of an adult child who has been serving as the primary caretaker and surrogate in making medical care arrangements.

The *advocate* is an individual who acts to assert the right of the service user to receive services, or to protect the rights of the service user during the service provision process. Third-party advocates, sometimes in the form of a guardian *ad litem*, may be provided when there is a potential conflict of interests—for example, between the interests of parents and the interests of a child in a child abuse situation. The advocate, unlike the surrogate, cannot actually make decisions for the service user. If the advocate is supported by and accountable to an organized service user constituency, the position of the advocate vis-à-vis the service organization may be strengthened.

CONFLICTS OVER USER POWER

The positive consequences of enhanced power and the exercise of self-determination by the service user may be primarily experienced by the direct service provider, particularly when there is congruence between the preferences of the service user and the objectives of the service provider. However, if the relative power of the service user in the service production process is strengthened (Gutiérrez, GlenMaye, and DeLois 1995), there may be an increase in tensions within an organization between the attention given to the provision of private benefits for the service user and the attention given to the production of public-good benefits for the community. This tension may result in increased pressure on managers from funders, community groups, and service personnel to give more attention to their priorities.

A substantial conflict may arise between program design provisions that are intended to increase the relative power of the service user, and the enforcement of legal mandates in those service programs in which participation in the service program is legally compelled, as in the instance of elementary and secondary education, or juvenile and adult probation. For example, a wider range of discretion for high school students in selecting classes may conflict with legal requirements for passing standardized examinations in reading and mathematics in order to graduate. In other situations, *self-determination* can mean that the service users are likely to be exposed to some level of risk of injury or death, or that other individuals are likely to be exposed to such risks (Hartman 1993). The balance between service user self-determination and the use of professional or organizational authority is one example of the discretionary judgments that characterize professional practice (see chapter 7).

However, to the extent that there is compulsory participation in the use of services, and the design of the program results in a very weak power position for the service user, participation motivation may be so distorted that the level of program effectiveness is seriously limited. Additional service resources may be required to overcome the initial negative effects of the power imbalance. Such a dilemma is faced in programs that involve court-mandated participation in group counseling sessions by persons found guilty of spousal abuse, or programs that force the service user to take medications that control behavior but also produce unpleasant side effects.

SERVICE USER CONSTITUENCIES
AND THE SERVICE ORGANIZATION

Service user constituencies include those individuals or households who have used, or are using, a particular service, as well as those who may be potentially eligible for such a service at some future time. In the instance of services for children and for very elderly individuals, other family members serving as surrogates may be the significant members of the user constituency. In some service situations, residents of a particular geographic neighborhood may constitute the relevant user constituency.

Although the particular characteristics of individual service users for a single service organization may vary widely, there may also be enough shared characteristics that a user constituency can be identified that consists of one or more distinctive user clusters. For some service organizations—a neighborhood service center, a police precinct headquarters, or an elementary school—the most important characteristic may be a common residential location. This may also be combined with other characteristics—ethnic identity and income level, for example.

For other service organizations, the users may be widely dispersed geographically but have similar age or gender characteristics—the maternity service of a teaching hospital, a children's psychiatric center, or a community college. Some user constituencies are defined primarily by being users of a specialized service—the participants in a kidney dialysis center, accident victims using an emergency medical service, families investigated by the local child protective services agency. Still other service organizations have a widely dispersed user constituency with a very wide variety of personal characteristics—a central city library.

Each of these user clusters has a different collective relationship with the relevant service organization. Elementary parent—teacher associations (PTAs) are often more actively involved with the local teaching staff than are high school PTAs, and much more than the parents of community college students. Participants in TANF programs are more actively involved with service personnel than participants in the food stamp program or in a state-administered children's health insurance plan (CHIP).

The shared interests of the members of a user constituency may be quite different from those of other stakeholder groups who are part of the program policy determination process—public officials, financial contributors and taxpayers, administrators, members of an organized profession (Martin 1985a). Given the relatively low power of individual service users in most service transactions, service user constituencies may also have a low-power position relative to that of other policy-impacting stakeholder groups. The absence of an effective organizational framework through which constituency interests can be expressed is often a significant factor in this low-power position.

The formal channel for acting in the interest of service users as a constituency, in the instance of governmental programs, is traditionally defined as the use of the political process—that is, through the election of, or defeat of, particular elected public officials or through efforts to influence their policy decisions. However, this is an extremely complex and relatively ineffective method of affecting program policy decisions within any single program, given the indirect relationship of any one elected public official to the administration of any one governmental program. This is particularly true when the authority/funding organization and the provider/direct service organization are separate (Felty and Jones 1998) (see chapter 8). The length of time involved in effecting a change in political representation also works against the use of this approach to address the concerns of an individual service user.

Even when such a process of enforcing accountability is potentially feasible, it is seldom open to constituencies that are not identified with majority political interests or that represent unpopular political issues, as, for example, adolescent mothers receiving financial assistance under the TANF program. However, the Americans with Disabilities Act (ADA) of 1990 (Orlin 1995) and Title IX of the Civil Rights Act of 1965 are examples of the sweeping changes that a single piece of legislation can make in the relative power of a service user constituency without dominant political power—in one instance, individuals with a disability, and in the other, women who are students in higher education.

An alternative approach for expressing the concerns of low-power service users that has been gaining increased attention is the class action lawsuit. Such lawsuits have been used on behalf of the residents in state prisons, state psychiatric hospitals, and state schools. They have resulted in specific changes and increases in the relative power of service users and their advocates. Moreover, the combination of legislation (such as ADA) and legal action can have even more powerful consequences in particular situations. On the other hand, the repeated finding of the Supreme Court that establishing the level of specific benefits in the provision of financial assistance by states, such as general assistance or TANF grants, is a discretionary legislative action, essentially labeling the assistance a form of governmental charity, rather than a constitutionally protected right of eligible individuals, has reinforced the powerlessness of the applicants for such assistance.

In the instance of voluntary nonprofit service organizations, user constituencies face even greater barriers in any effort to force change in organizational policies. The nonprofit image creates a presumption of public service that can serve to protect the organization from public criticism. Members of the board of directors are selected by the other members of the board, not through public elections. The proceedings of the board and the records of such proceedings are not normally open to the public. And class action suits generally cannot be used since the service organization has few if any assets that could be attached to pay the costs of such a legal action if it were successful. The most effective resource for an organized user constituency in the instance of a nonprofit service organization is often the support of key individuals in the media.

Program design may provide opportunities for the representation of user constituency interests at the program policy level, including the appointment of a service user as a member of a relevant policy-making body. The effectiveness and relevance of such an appointment, however, is directly affected by the extent to which any single individual can represent the interests of a user constituency. There can be true representation only when there is an organized body of service users and the participant in the policy body is accountable to such an organization (Alexander 1976). Moreover, the influence of a single representative of service users appointed to a policy body is generally limited by the token constraints experienced by any single representative of a particular set of interests in such a body (Kanter 1977; Martin 1985b).

The expression of the collective interests of a service user constituency, moreover, may not be consistent with the individual interests of a particular service user. The provision of policy representation cannot be treated as equivalent to the empowerment of the individual service user in the service production process. And the empowerment of individual service users cannot be treated as equivalent to responding to the interests of an entire user constituency.

Formal user representation in an official policy-making body by itself may also not provide significant representation of service user constituency interests if the policy body has limited impact on the actual policies controlling the service program. For example, constituency representation on the policy board of a nonprofit service organization may have limited impact on program policies in a program governed by the provisions of a funding contract with a governmental organization.

Realistic provision for service constituency involvement in substantive policy decisions may, in fact, require multiple forms of participation, including the following:

- Provision for the participation of representatives selected by service user constituencies on formal policy-making bodies
- Provision for periodic public hearings on program policies, plans, and procedures
- Provision for an advisory body composed entirely of members of the service user constituency, or composed jointly of service users and other members of the general public
- Periodic selection of a group of service users—either randomly selected or as a small, deliberately diversified sample—to participate as a "focus group" in an intensive analysis of the service experience, or as a "panel" for feedback over time regarding the service experience or the service outcomes

Even stronger representation of the interests of service user constituencies may be provided by assigning majority control of policy-making bodies to service user constituencies, or by providing for a policy body selected by, and accountable to, service constituency interests. One example has been the creation of specialized service programs for individuals with human immunodeficiency virus (HIV) or acquired immunodeficiency syndrome (AIDS), in which the majority of the members of the policy board have that medical condition or are friends and family members of such persons. Health-care programs for American Indians living on a reservation in which the management of the program is controlled by the tribal council are another example.

The strength of service user interests in the policy-making process depends not only on formal provisions for participation but also on the degree of organizational development within the constituency. Provision for formal participation of a single individual service user on a policy-making body, if there is no service user constituency organization, may be of considerably less significance than a provision for public hearings that consistently result in a large attendance by individual service users.

Onken (2000), in a study of user input into mental health planning, points out that the representatives of user constituencies who are included in advisory or policy bodies are often from middle income backgrounds and may have less severe mental health problems. The study also reported that the priority concerns of user representatives who are active within an official user organization may be distinctly different from the concerns of individuals who are not part of any organized group.

The initiative to develop a constituency organization may come from service users, or members of their families, without outside assistance. Support for such a development may also be provided by the service organization if service users are widely scattered, have few resources to use in organizational development, or are reluctant to identify themselves as service users. In some situations, an inclusive citizens' action organization may adopt the cause of a service user constituency—for example, when a central city neighborhood association takes up issues related to the services provided by a municipal hospital.

Constituency organizations may combine self-help—that is, assistance that group members provide for each other, and advocacy to change laws and organizational rules that are viewed as harmful. Such organizations may help to empower individuals as they deal with service organizations and also establish a power base for attacking barriers and discrimination in the larger society (Segal, Silverman, and Temkin 1993; Mondros and Wilson 1994). One of the larger service user advocacy movements has been the mental health self-help movement (Zinman, Harp, and Budd 1987; Onken 2000). Other major service user movements include the "independent living" movement among persons with disabilities (Berkowitz 1987) and action organizations among individuals with HIV/AIDS.

In other situations, service user interests may become part of the action agenda of larger political interest groups. The interests of TANF recipients may be supported by an African American political action group, or the interests of participants in a senior citizens center may be supported by the Gray Panthers. The identification of both political parties with the service user interests of veterans has consistently enhanced the status of the Veterans Administration as an independent medical services provider. And the American Association of Retired Persons is widely recognized as a powerful advocacy organization when it acts in behalf of the inclusive constituency of Social Security recipients.

SUMMARY

Although the quality and effectiveness of services provided to individual service users is the most important outcome criteria for nonprofit and governmental human service organizations, most individual service users have very limited power to enforce a demand for such quality in their relationship with service organizations. The parents of students in central city high schools have very limited power to force a local school board to take the actions necessary to make the education in that school comparable to a college preparatory program in a upper-middle-income suburban community. The limited power of the service user can affect the motivation of the service user to participate actively in the process of coproduction. Specific program design features may serve to strengthen the power position of the individual service user. The power of the individual service user may also be strengthened by increasing the power of the service user constituency.

The strengthening of service user participation through constituency organization, or through strengthening the role of the individual service user, imposes costs on the service organization. These may be direct financial costs or time costs related to the involvement of direct service staff in additional tasks. A major cost, however, is the potential for increased environmental uncertainty and increased pressure on the executive and other managers.

Another consequence of increased power for the service user may be an increased demand for individualized service decisions, rather than rule-controlled decisions and, in turn, for recognized professional qualifications for direct service personnel. The justification for program design provisions that result in these costs is not based primarily on theories of political *rights* applied to the organization. Instead, the justification, which will vary in degree according to the program rationale and program strategy, is based on the central, and critical, importance of the service user role in achieving effective and efficient service co-production.

SEVEN

ORGANIZED PROFESSIONS AND
HUMAN SERVICE ORGANIZATIONS

A professional association is an association with one object above all others. . . . They [the members of the association] have joined in order better to perform their function. They meet: To establish standards; To maintain standards; To improve standards; To keep members up to standards; To educate the public to appreciate standards; To protect the public from those individuals who have not attained standards or willfully do not follow them; To protect individual members of the profession from each other.

—Mary Parker Follett, 1925 (Graham 1995:271)

Self-interest alone does not produce effective organizations even when it is balanced by self-restraint. . . . Organizations must also solve the control problem: how to get guidance and coherence in light of complex activities, diverse people and the need for speed and innovation. One solution is to encourage professionalism at every level by teaching common disciplines. Professionals . . . share a knowledge base, methodology, and standards of excellence that characterize a community of practitioners. . . . Professionals generally advance in their careers by adding knowledge, not by climbing a job ladder. Professional disciplines ensure control and coherence without elaborate hierarchies of supervision.

—Rosabeth Moss Kanter (1997:159)

THE RELATIONSHIPS between human service organizations of all types and specialized occupations take many diverse forms. *Bureaucratic* public administration settings have hierarchical structures in which primary service tasks are performed by individuals who are identified only as organizational employees. These employees are unlikely to be members of any specialized occupational association (although they may be members of a labor union or an internal association of organizational employees in which occupational specialization is not a criterion for membership). Such settings include the eligibility offices of food stamp programs, state and local general assistance programs, Temporary Assistance to Needy Families (TANF) programs, state employment service offices, correctional institutions, and Social Security offices. They often resemble "machine bureaucracies" (Mintzberg 1979), although they are involved in the production of services rather than goods.

In *professionalized* organizations, professional specialists generally fill the primary service positions and most administrative positions. Such settings include colleges and universities, elementary and secondary schools, private adoption agencies and child guidance clinics, and social policy research institutes. There are also professionalized human service components within many for-profit firms, including medical services and employee assistance programs. In bureaucratic public administration settings, administrative rules and directives control work activities; in the professionalized settings, professional standards and judgments control most work activities, including administrative procedures.

Many human service organizations involve more complex relationships than either of these two patterns, with both management specialists and professional specialists having distinctive areas of authority. Collaboration between both types of specialists is required for effective service production. A key organizational design issue in what Mintzberg (1979) describes as the professional bureaucracy involves the development of structures and procedures to deal with conflicts between the imperatives of professional expertise and the imperatives of management expertise (Etzioni 1964; Mintzberg 1983). This can also be an issue in larger systems of organizations, such as managed health-care systems in which there are direct confrontations between physicians and other health-care professional practitioners and the health-care administrative organizations over the definition of priorities in medical practice (McArthur and Moore 1997).

The role of professional specialists in human service programs also incorporates the tension in a democratic society between the political model of the equality of individual status within the polity, or body of citizens, and the technological model of specialized knowledge and expertise and unequal individual status, within the organizational structures of society. The role of professional specialists is expanding as contemporary society moves further away from traditional family/clan/village social structures to individualized social structures, and as science and technology transform the nature of service production. This tension is particularly acute in the case of the human service professions that are based on ethical principles that assert the equal moral value of each individual while also asserting the importance of specialized training and preparation, and distinctive status, for those individuals who are responsible for dealing with judgmental decisions under conditions of uncertainty that critically affect the lives of other individuals (see chapter 2).

ORGANIZED HUMAN SERVICE PROFESSIONS

The organizational issues involved in the interface between management and profession are affected by the characteristics of the *organized professions* that are central to the production of human services. This chapter deals with the place of organized professions in human service organizations.

The development of nontribal forms of social organization early in the social history of mankind led to the development of specialized occupations responsible for particular functions in the society of local communities. Some of these occupations ultimately became identified as callings, or professions. An extensive social science literature developed around the study of occupations during the twentieth century, in particular around the identification of, and analysis of, "professions" (Macdonald 1995). This literature deals with similarities among professions and with distinctions between professions and other occupations.

Two historic professions have been identified by most writers: law and medicine [some authors include a number of other occupations in their lists of historic professions (Austin 1983b)]. In particular, lawyers and physicians most clearly represent the model of "professionals" in the popular culture. These two professions developed over a long period of time, each around a crucial but distinctly different aspect of society. As historic, or "established," professions, they are identified in the social science literature as having certain common characteristics that are considered important to the concept of profession: high social prestige, a presumption of expertise based on mastery of a body of knowledge that is applied to "practical" tasks, the presence of a code of ethics that guides the practitioner behaviors of individual professionals, and a commitment to public service (Greenwood 1957). In much of the social science literature, these characteristics, or traits, are attributed to a combination of role positions and particular individuals who are considered to constitute the structure of the profession.

It has also been characteristic of law and medicine that there was, by the beginning of the twentieth century, a network of organized intraprofession activities that had come to be recognized as the institutional form of the profession. Starr (1982), in *The Social Transformation of American Medicine*, describes how the institutional structure of the organized profession of medicine developed, resulting in a dramatic increase in the control of medicine over professional boundaries and professional education and, in turn, over the number of physicians. It is these intraprofession activities that have become the distinctive element in the *organized professions*, including not only the historic professions but other specialized occupations that have gained recognition as organized professions during the twentieth century. A large proportion of the currently recognized organized professions are identified with human service programs, and one of the distinctive characteristics of human service programs is the central role of organized professions (see chapter 2).

In an organized profession, the network of intraprofession activities includes collegial professional associations; entrance-level professional education programs controlled by, or accredited by, professional bodies; professional doctoral programs through which future professional educators are recruited and prepared; alumni associations of professional schools; codes of professional ethics (Reamer 1995); licensing and certifying bodies with procedures for legitimating professional status and for disciplining members of the profession; continuing professional education programs; political action groups; and a variety of channels for recognizing and disseminating specialized professional information including conferences and journals, as well as books, television programs, videotapes, and the Internet.

These intraprofession activities play a major role in structuring relationships between members of the profession and other elements of the society—for example, between the profession and governmental regulatory activities, or between the profession and sources of funding for professional services. Moreover, these intraprofession activities, in addition to their explicit functions, provide a framework for a network of personal relationships among those members of the profession who are in leadership positions, and for informal friendship relationships among many of the individual members of the profession.

The network of individuals who occupy leadership and staff support positions in these intraprofessional activities becomes a critical element of the organized profession. The overlapping roles of some individuals (for example, in professional education, in professional associations, as consultants to government bodies, and as members of editorial review panels for professional journals) result in an informal coordination system within the profession that is at least as important as any single element of formal structure. When particular individuals occupy such overlapping roles for extended periods of time, in some instances for several decades, they may perform a particularly critical function in the institutional development of the profession (Macdonald 1995), or what Larson (1977) has described as the "professional project."

The system of intraprofession activities also has a major impact on the management of human service programs, first through the impact of these activities on individual members of the profession working in service organizations (including those who are not themselves formal members of a professional association), and, second, through the impact of these activities on the environment within which the service organization functions. For example, legislative lobbying by professional associations may directly affect the level of public funding for human service programs and also the definition of the criteria to be used in the employment of professional service personnel.

"ESTABLISHED" AND "ASPIRING" PROFESSIONS

There is a substantial degree of similarity in the pattern of intraprofession activities across many human service professions, even when there are marked differences in the content of key professional tasks. However, before examining these similarities, it is important to examine some of the traditional distinctions that have been made among professions.

Social science literature has placed emphasis on the distinctions between "established" professions and "aspiring" professions (or "semi-professions") (Greenwood 1957; Etzioni 1969). One of the earliest efforts to establish a framework for such distinctions, and one that had a particular impact on the development of social work as an organized profession, was the paper presented by Abraham Flexner at the 1915 National Conference of Charities and Correction, under the title "Is Social Work a Profession?"

In this paper, Flexner identified six criteria, or traits, for an established profession, primarily on the basis of his model of the medical profession: "Professions: involve essentially intellectual operations with large individual responsibility, derive their raw material from science and learning, this material they work up to a practical and definite end, possess an educationally communicable technique, tend to self-organization, and are increasingly altruistic" (1915:581). Using these criteria, Flexner declared that social work, although a worthwhile social activity, was not an established profession and was unlikely ever to be so.

A more recent analysis dealing with similar issues is presented in *The Semi-Professions*, edited by Amitai Etzioni (1969), which includes chapters dealing with social work, nursing, elementary teaching, and library science. This analysis comes to a similar conclusion, that none of the occupations analyzed are fully established professions. It is asserted that in these "semi-professions," the majority of the members of the profession are women and that these women are not fully committed to the concept of a life-long professional career.

> A woman's primary attachment is to the family role; women are therefore less intrinsically committed to work than men and less likely to maintain a high level of specialized knowledge. . . . Women at all achievement levels were considerably less likely than men to be motivated towards work careers.
>
> Simpson and Simpson (1969:199, 203–204)

However, both of these analyses, and indeed much of the social science literature dealing with professions, are flawed by a number of weaknesses. Each writer dealing with the sociology of professions has a different list of professions considered to be "established," with general agreement only on medicine and law. Various authors, including Flexner (1915) and Goode (1969) who between them identify a total of fourteen diverse occupations as established professions, include such occupations as the clergy, university faculty, dentistry, architecture, military officers, researchers, authors, artists, and artistic performers.

In addition to the lack of agreement as to which occupations are established professions, there is also little agreement among social science writers as to the basic conceptual framework to be used in defining an established profession. At least three different approaches are used: trait, process, and power (Popple 1985). The *trait* approach, the oldest and most widely used, is marked by the wide variety of traits cited by various authors as being essential to the definition of an established profession, ranging from two, "a basic body of knowledge" and "an ideal of service" (Goode 1969:277), to as many as twenty-one as identified in a comparative analysis of sociological definitions of professions by Roth (1974). The traits that are cited include an unsystematic mix of task characteristics (dealing with issues of life and death), individual attitudes (public service commitment), organizational activities (asserting monopoly control over a unique skill competence), and characteristics of public response (high social prestige). Closely related to the trait approach is the *functional* approach, based on the comprehensive functional model of society set forth by Talcott Parsons (1954), which identifies each profession as performing a single explicit and unique function within a comprehensive social system.

Other authors have proposed a model of a "natural history" developmental *process* in the professional institutionalization of an occupation, placing various professions at different points in this process of development (Caplow 1954; Wilensky 1964). Goode (1969), however, pointed out that a number of recognized professions do not fit either the trait or the process model.

Still other authors define professions in terms of *power*—that is, the ability of an organized group of practitioners to establish control over the access of individuals to a valued role with status and economic benefits (Freidson 1970; Larson 1977; Cullen 1978; Macdonald 1995). However, neither the clergy nor the faculty of a university, which are widely accepted as professions, fits this model. Neither profession has comprehensive control over the number of persons admitted to professional status, nor any system of licensing that limits professional practice to recognized practitioners. Furthermore, neither of these two groups of professionals provides procedures for the discipline of incompetent practitioners.

An examination of the entire history of the sociology of professions suggests that the major function of the analytic models used, particularly the *trait* and *process* models, has not been to study all occupations systematically but rather to demonstrate that particular occupations should *not* be acknowledged to be a profession. The sociological literature on professions suggests two arguments as to why neither semi-professions nor aspiring professions should be accepted as established professions. The first argument, as noted previously, is that the members of these "almost" professions are primarily women, and that the personal attributes and employment career patterns of women, as described by the authors, are not consistent with their model of the true professional.

The second argument is that occupations such as nursing and social work, which Abbott and Wallace (1990) identify as "caring" professions, are too involved with holistic or nurturing activities (Simpson and Simpson 1969:234) to have the functional specificity, or limited task focus, that Talcott Parsons (1954) identified as a crucial element of profession. Both of these arguments, developed in detail by Etzioni (1969), are quite similar to the arguments that Flexner used to deny the professional status of social work in 1915. There is also an argument that an organizationally based occupation, such as social work, cannot be a profession because of the authority controls within the employing organization. "[This approach] would begin with the assumption that social workers . . . are simply organizational functionaries . . . whose work-related attitudes and behaviors are similar to . . . bureaucrats or any other organizational employees" (Epstein and Conrad 1978:178).

The rationalizations that have dominated the social science analysis of established professions, and the distinctions between such professions and aspiring professions, have two important uses. First, they serve to legitimate the ultimate authority of members of established professions in all aspects of the relationship with the service user/client/patient. Some authors, in fact, assert that the power of the professional to impose professional judgments on patients or clients is an essential criterion for an established profession (Goode 1969). The concept of professional authority is also used to support the claims of professional specialists that they have the right to override the judgments of nonprofessional administrators and lay public policy makers on public policy issues relevant to professional practice, and to impose professional criteria on the design of service programs (Roth 1974).

Second, the preferred status of established professions can be used to protect the domains of such professions against encroachment by aspiring professions. Key examples include the contests among psychiatrists, psychologists, and social workers for domain control over mental health services, and those between physicians and nurses over such health-care services as childbirth. As Macdonald states, "Professions operate in a 'competitive marketplace' rather than as an established 'system'" (1995:33). The concept of established profession appears to be, in part, a rationalization of traditional authority relationships, including traditional patriarchal relationships between men and women (Macdonald 1995), rather than being a formal, rational model based on principles established through consistent social science research. These traditional assumptions about authority relationships among professions have specific consequences for the design of human service programs and for the management of such programs.

PROFESSIONAL TASKS

The fundamental context for any single profession is the occupational sector of which it is a part. Each professional specialty is interrelated with other occupations in the same sector (Akers and Quinney 1968). The general pattern of occupations within a sector can be viewed as a division of labor, since at an earlier point in time all the tasks in a particular sector were performed by single individuals. The teacher in a one-room school performed all the teaching, administrative, pupil counseling, and building maintenance tasks now provided through an elaborate system of administrative, professional, and technical specialists.

The pattern of institutional development in any one profession is shaped by the characteristics of the key tasks around which the profession has developed. These are the tasks that serve to define the image of the profession to the individual members within the profession and to the general public. This "doing" image, together with the social values that are identified with the historic image of the profession, attract particular individuals who identify with the image, and the values, of that profession. Such a career choice involves substantial front-end costs, including the actual costs of specialized education as well as forgone earnings during the period of professional preparation.

The relative status and structure of a profession ultimately depends on the relationship of these key professional tasks to the larger occupational sector in which they are embedded.

> The actual tasks of professions are human problems that are amenable to expert service—individual problems like illness or neurosis, social problems like vandalism, group problems like fund raising or auditing. But to turn them into problems that fall within its jurisdiction, a particular profession must engage in "cultural work" that will ensure that clients, competitors, the state, and the public will acknowledge that the qualities of the problem warrant granting that jurisdiction.
>
> Macdonald (1995:163)

Within each occupational sector, there are both standardized and nonstandardized tasks. The core concept of a profession emerges around *nonstandardized tasks* in which the knowledge and skill of particular individuals making judgment decisions are perceived as having a relationship to the effectiveness with which the task is accomplished. "The greater the element of judgment required in the exercise of professional knowledge, the less likely it is that the professional tasks will be open to routinization and inspection; such a situation will tend to enhance the power of the occupation" (Macdonald 1995:135).

These nonstandardized tasks, and the decisions involved in them, take on increased importance to the extent that they, in turn, control the lives of other persons and the activities associated with other occupational tasks. The design plans of the architect and the engineer control the activities of contractors and construction workers. The decision of a lawyer serving in the capacity of a judge on a point of law changes the ownership of property or dissolves a marriage. A medical diagnosis by a doctor may shape the activities of the members of a surgical team, the hospital nurse, and the pharmacist, and change the lives of the patient and other members of the patient's family. An initial judgment by a social worker about the occurrence of child abuse sets in motion events that shape the work of lawyers and judges and may change forever the life of a child and the child's parents.

In the pattern of daily work activities, professional specialists usually perform both standardized and nonstandardized tasks. However, it is the nonstandardized judgment tasks that constitute professional practice. In human service programs, these critical nonstandardized tasks have the following characteristics.

Discretionary Judgment

The professional tasks include individual non-rule-controlled judgments on a case-by-case basis. These discretionary judgments include both diagnostic judgments and judgments involved in the actual provision of services. They require simultaneous consideration of multiple variables and their interaction. Examples include the diagnosis of illness, assessment of the degree of risk of serious harm to a child in a child-abuse investigation, the development of a new course syllabus in a college, the presentation of a legal case in a courtroom, the preparation of a social and economic development plan for a central city neighborhood, the handling of an angry marital confrontation in family counseling, and the nursing care of a postoperative critical-care patient.

Critical Consequences

The performance of the professional tasks has critical consequences for particular individuals, families, or communities, although not all of them involve life-and-death consequences. The lawyer's client may be found not guilty or may go to prison. Information provided by a vocational counselor may shape the occupational career of a college student. Emergency room counseling by a rape counselor may affect the long-term mental health of a rape victim. A psychosocial assessment carried out by a social worker may shape the choice between community care, assisted living, and nursing home care for an older adult. A judgment by an adoption worker may determine the future family identity of an infant. The effectiveness of decisions by a teacher as to teaching methods—for example, in helping a child develop reading skills— may determine whether a child ultimately completes high school or becomes a dropout.

Ambiguous Outcomes

Professional tasks have outcomes that are difficult to evaluate, or that cannot be evaluated immediately, either by the service user or by a third party. This may be because (1) the cause-and-effect relationship between the performance of the service task and the outcome is uncertain (psychological counseling and the remission of an episode of depression), (2) the criterion for evaluating the outcome is ambiguous (marital satisfaction), or (3) a substantial time-lag occurs between performance of the task and the outcome (group counseling with early adolescent girls and the avoidance of teen pregnancy).

Dependency on Knowledge

The consistent performance of the professional tasks requires mastery of a body of background information and abstract principles based on this information (Abbott 1988), rather than learning detailed information about only one operational setting or type of problem, or a single set of explicit rules. The body of information and the principles based on it—that is, the "expert systems" of the profession (Mullen and Schuerman 1990)—are assumed to be relatively stable over time so that the time involved in gaining mastery of them can be commensurate with the time period during which this knowledge is likely to be useful. Although the background information, and the principles related to it, are available to any member of the public, the concept of recognized professional status is intended to assure service users that the professional practitioner has, in fact, mastered this particular body of knowledge.

Members of the clergy use a body of biblical and theological knowledge that changes very slowly, and that is more inclusive than the traditions of a single denomination. Lawyers master a body of legal principles that is broader than the single specialized field in which they may practice, and the principles are based on the assumption that past legal precedents are indefinitely applicable to the future, except as they are changed incrementally by individual court decisions or legislative acts. Psychologists master a body of information about human developmental processes that is more extensive than what is required in any single practice setting, and the information, in general, changes only incrementally over time.

Privacy Setting

In the human service professions in particular, the performance of key professional tasks often takes place in settings where there is not direct and consistent oversight of task performance by personnel with supervisory authority or by third parties not directly involved in service production. The physician performs many of the crucial diagnostic tasks within a private office. The classroom teacher functions in the closed classroom. The social worker carries out interviews in a private office or within a home. The nurse provides nursing care in the private hospital room. The privileged conversations between a lawyer and a client normally take place in a private office. The hearing of religious confessions takes place in private.

A human service profession initially develops around nonstandardized tasks with these characteristics. Service users, having sought assistance outside the family or other primary relationships, are necessarily dependent on the judgments of the individuals involved in these nonstandardized tasks. In seeking to reduce the uncertainty involved in seeking such assistance, individuals turn to those persons who are identified as having some combination of specialized knowledge *and* specialized skill: "This is a matter on which Weber was quite explicit; the knowledge in question is that which is *certified and credentialled*" (Macdonald 1995:161). It is because of the individualized skill in applying this knowledge to the carrying out of the nonstandardized professional tasks that professional practice is asserted to be primarily "an art" rather than just a technology (England 1986; Siporin 1988).

Although the beginnings of a distinctive organized profession emerge around nonstandardized judgmental tasks, the definition of the tasks that may be carried out by members of an organized profession is seldom limited to these key tasks. The operational definition of professional tasks becomes expanded in two ways. First, it often includes related standardized activities that are consistently associated with the key judgmental tasks, although they do not have the same basic characteristics. A single professional practitioner is often involved in a mixture of professional tasks and related technical activities. Not only do physicians diagnose childhood illnesses and prescribe medicines but they also may administer the injections of the medicine. Such standardized technical activities may be assigned to individuals with more limited training when the scale of operations justifies it. Examples include the teacher's aide in the classroom, the legal assistant in the law office, the practical nurse in the nursing home.

Second, the definition of professional tasks is often expanded by members of the organized profession as part of an effort to define, and to expand, the occupational domain claimed by the organized profession. The activities of an x-ray technician becomes redefined as part of medical practice, requiring the services of a physician radiologist, although these tasks lack some of the characteristics of the key medical practice tasks, including the doctor–patient relationship. The profession of nursing defines hospital discharge planning as a part of professional nursing in a domain contest with medical social work, although the tasks involved in discharge planning are different from the key tasks around which nursing originally developed. Psychologists seek authority to prescribe psychotropic medications. The inclusion of related technical tasks or domain-expanding tasks may have important consequences for public perceptions of the identity of a profession and also for the relative position of each profession within the occupational marketplace.

DIFFERENCES AMONG ORGANIZED PROFESSIONS

The analysis of differences among organized human service professions involves a consideration of (1) differences in the patterns of production tasks involved in different occupational sectors and (2) differences in the division of labor within particular sectors. These differences can be examined in terms of several dimensions: (1) the extent to which any single organized profession exercises control over the diagnostic or assessment function and over the connections among diagnostic, prescription, treatment, evaluation, and management tasks; (2) the nature of the knowledge base used by each profession; (3) characteristics of the benefits that result from professional activity; (4) the pattern of horizontal and vertical differentiation within the occupational sector and within particular professions; (5) the pattern of social mobility

within a particular profession; and (6) characteristics of organizational settings through which professional services are produced, and the
relation of the profession to the management of those settings.

The Role of Diagnosis/Assessment in Professional Practice

The relationship of a profession to a particular occupational sector can
be analyzed in terms of its relation to five major functions: (1) *diagnosis,
assessment,* or *classification,* the process through which the distinctive
characteristics of individual situations, ranging from individuals to communities, are identified and described in ways that are relevant to a particular type of human service; (2) *prescription* or *planning,* the process
through which a program of action is identified or designed that is consistent with the diagnostic, assessment, classification process; (3) *treatment, intervention,* or *implementation,* the process through which the
prescription or plan is translated into action; (4) *evaluation,* the process
through which the effects of action are observed; and (5) in the instance
of the provision of professional services through an organization, the
pattern of *management,* the process through which resources are organized to carry out the first four functions.

The relative authority and power of a profession vis-à-vis other occupational specializations within any given occupational sector depend
substantially on the degree to which members of the profession have responsibility for, and control over, these specific production functions.
Abbott (1988) defines the first three of these functions—diagnosis, infer-
ence (prescription), and treatment—as the *professional* functions.
Human service professions vary in the relative attention given in the
model of professional practice to diagnosis/assessment and prescrip-
tion/planning tasks as compared to the attention given to treatment/in-
tervention tasks. For example, as Macdonald suggests, "In caring professions there is a considerable body of opinion that holds that practice
[treatment] is the more important aspect" (1995:134).

In general, the power of a particular profession vis-à-vis other professions in the same occupational sector, and the managers in service organizations, reflects the extent to which that profession controls diagno-
sis/assessment functions. The development by the medical profession of
a highly complex pattern of individualized diagnostic activities, which

now includes the use of complex technical equipment, contributes to the control by physicians of the activities of other occupational specialties in hospitals and within health maintenance organizations (HMOs). The establishment of a common system of diagnostic classifications and the authority to assign a diagnosis and to prescribe medications have also contributed to legitimating the key role of the physician in defining third-party reimbursements for medical care. However, the incorporation of medical practice into managed health-care systems has led to major confrontations over the relative roles of physicians and of nonphysician organizational employees in defining a controlling diagnosis, using standard diagnostic classifications.

In using the acute illness rationale in medical practice (see chapter 4), the physician carries out a specific diagnostic process in each individual situation that leads to the selection of one diagnostic definition from among a number of possible diagnoses, and, in turn, to a prescription that is explicitly targeted to that diagnosis. That prescription is intended to control the treatment, which in turn is expected to result in a cure. On the other hand, physicians (with the exception of surgeons and psychoanalytic psychiatrists) are, in general, not directly involved in implementation of the treatment activities called for in the prescription. The patient, a family member, or the nurse in the hospital, administers medication, follows a diet plan or a plan of exercise, or monitors progress following an injection.

Both nursing and pharmacy are primarily involved in treatment rather than diagnosis, and this is reflected in their power position relative to medicine. The initiatives by nursing to expand the diagnostic role of nurse practitioners in primary health care, and by pharmacists to establish an independent authority to prescribe some forms of medication, involve efforts to increase the role of diagnostic activities in those professions, even if only to the extent of distinguishing between persons who have a severe illness condition and those who do not.

The explicit diagnosis/assessment process has received limited attention in professional education in social work, although Mary Richmond, who launched social work education, emphasized the role of "social diagnosis" in individual situations. The emphasis on therapeutic counseling in the current professional practice model of clinical social work is primarily directed to methods of treatment/implementation, rather than to a distinctive model of diagnosis/assessment, except to the extent that an ongoing process of problem assessment is considered to be a part of the individualized treatment relationship between the social worker and a service user (Meyer 1993). However, such a process of treatment-enmeshed assessment does not lead to control over the activities of other persons, or over managerial decisions.

The only diagnostic system taught consistently in schools of social work that may control the activities of other practitioners is that set forth in the *Diagnostic and Statistical Manual of Mental Disorders* (DSM-IV), which has been developed by psychiatrists (Kirk and Kutchins 1992). Moreover, where control of activities beyond the immediate treatment relationship is needed, or third-party reimbursement is being sought, legitimation by a physician/psychiatrist of the diagnosis made by a social worker using DSM-IV classifications is often required.

Legitimation of a deviance classification made by a social worker—abusive parent or delinquent child—requires confirming action by a judge. On the other hand, in family-centered practice, there is no single, widely accepted diagnostic system (Hartman and Laird 1983). The limited emphasis on a systematic diagnosis/assessment model in social work practice is reflected in the relatively weak power position of social work practitioners in relation to other organized professions that do place greater emphasis on the role of individual diagnosis and assessment in professional practice.

The Knowledge Base—Science and/or Practice Wisdom?

A profession that has control over diagnosis/assessment tasks within an occupational sector must have a defined body of knowledge and practice principles that serve as a framework for diagnosis/assessment judgments. This body of knowledge and practice principles provides the foundation for professional education and, in turn, defines the boundaries of recognized professional practice. The specific content of this body of knowledge and principles is distinctive for each human service profession. However, there are also important differences among the professions in the general characteristics of this body of knowledge and principles.

The social science literature dealing with the nature of professions places emphasis on the role of science in the core body of knowledge for a profession (Macdonald 1995), going back as far as the paper presented by Flexner in 1915. According to Halliday (1987:37), professions divide into classes depending on whether the cognitive base is primarily descriptive or proscriptive. That is, whether the profession is a *scientific* profession, identified with the natural and biological sciences, or a *normative* profession, identified with matters of value or with questions of how individuals or groups ought to behave toward one another (Macdonald 1995). Halliday (1987) also identifies professions that have a **syncretic** foundation that straddles the scientific/normative divide. Thus, whereas the clergy is primarily a normative profession, social work, as a syncretic profession, is simultaneously concerned with professional practice addressed to normative issues of social justice (Gil 1998) and with the development of scientific, research-tested methods of professional intervention (Task Force on Social Work Research 1991).

Only a limited number of the human service professions are, in fact, based primarily on a systematic body of scientific theory and empirical research, with practice principles derived from scientific studies. Public health, architecture, pharmacy, and medicine are among those professions that do have a knowledge base that is largely derived from science. On the other hand, the profession of law is built exclusively on a practice wisdom base of judicial precedents, none of which are determined by scientific testing of the consequences of particular legal decisions. However, many professions are syncretic, based on an organized body of practice wisdom, or professional tradition, supplemented to varying degrees by knowledge derived from research. The practice wisdom base includes the normative values that distinguish appropriate and inappropriate forms of professional practice when there is not a scientific basis for such distinctions.

The traditional pattern for any profession has been to depend primarily on practice wisdom for its knowledge base and to seek to maintain exclusive professional control over that knowledge base. However, professions like medicine and pharmacy have, over time, developed a knowledge base largely derived from scientific research and have increasingly come to share control of that knowledge base with research scientists (Friedman and Purcell 1983). Questions have been raised as to whether a disproportionate share of the current medical practice curriculum is, in fact, in the hands of highly specialized research scientists (Bok 1984), rather than in the hands of faculty who have had the experience of being practicing physicians.

The primary factors resulting in an expanded role for science in the knowledge base of a profession, which means relinquishing a significant degree of professional control over that knowledge base, are the extent to which science provides information that is (1) more useful than practice wisdom and (2) essential. For science to be viewed as *useful* and for it to become a significant element in the knowledge base, there must be evidence that is convincing to members of the profession that scientific findings can be applied to the decisions involved in diagnosis, prescription, or treatment, and that the use of such scientific findings reduces uncertainty and leads to more consistent results.

For scientific findings and theory to be *essential*, there must be evidence that decisions and actions that are contrary to the scientific findings lead to negative results. There is limited incentive for professional practitioners in any field to invest heavily in learning to use information from a collateral scientific discipline without evidence of negative outcomes when science is ignored. There is also little incentive for the organized profession to share control of the professional body of knowledge with an outside discipline unless there is evidence of such negative consequences. It was the prevalence of postsurgery deaths that forced physicians in the nineteenth century to pay attention to scientific discoveries about the role of bacteria in infections and to change the principles of medical practice by requiring hand washing and sterile conditions in the operating room.

Diagnosis, prescription, and treatment decisions are directly affected by research findings in professions that do have a knowledge base largely derived from science. If the physiological consequences of particular prescription drugs are known as the result of systematic research, then the general conditions under which such drugs should or should not be used have been established independently of the judgment of individual physicians or pharmacists. The scope of discretionary judgment by the professional practitioner is reduced to the extent that research defines the decision rules in the prescription of medicine in particular cases.

However, even in areas of knowledge in which there is extensive research, any single situation may require simultaneous consideration of possible interactions among multiple variables, interactions that may not have been dealt with conclusively by existing research. Moreover, research findings are often stated in terms of *probabilities*, whereas decisions in individual situations must often be made in terms of *absolutes*.

Thus, there are large areas of decision making that require professional judgments—that is, judgments based on practice wisdom, even in science-based professions.

Differences among professions also involve the extent to which a profession has exclusive control over the definition of the content in the knowledge base, or whether that control is shared with other professions or academic disciplines. Evidence of control of the knowledge base by a profession includes the extent to which faculty members who are also recognized as professional practitioners control the core curriculum content of professional education, the degree to which professional practitioners read only professional journals that have editorial review boards that include only members of their profession, or, on the other hand, the extent to which specialists from other professions, or disciplines, are regularly included in programs of professional conferences and published in professional journals.

In professions in which the knowledge base and practice principles are largely derived from practice wisdom, control of the knowledge base is largely in the hands of recognized professionals. It is the writings of such professionals that become the textbooks for professional education. In such professions, such as law, seniority and credibility as a practitioner become important criteria for assessing the qualifications of a faculty member in the professional school, or the qualifications of a textbook author. This is in contrast to the science-based profession in which the quality of research methodology used in research studies becomes the basis of credibility. Indeed, young scientists, using the most contemporary techniques, may have more credibility than more senior scientists.

A practice wisdom knowledge base may be highly codified, as it is in the organization of precedents in law, or in the library classification systems used in library science. On the other hand, it may be only loosely organized and may include a variety of theories and fundamental assumptions, as in the instance of social work. However, since practice wisdom is seldom as precise as science, individual practitioners in those professions using a knowledge base largely derived from practice wisdom always have a particularly broad range of discretion in the judgments required in day-to-day practice.

A knowledge base derived from science increases the status and relative power of professional practitioners within a service organization (Macdonald 1995:134). The ability of such a profession to define what is "accepted" science and to interpret the significance of science for professional practice increases the authority of the professional vis-à-vis both nonprofessional managers and policy makers. Professions with a highly codified, or esoteric, body of practice wisdom, such as law, have a stronger power position than managers and policy makers, since only the professional practitioners can readily, and consistently, identify the particular principles that apply in a specific situation.

However, in a profession with only a loosely codified body of practice wisdom knowledge, such as elementary education or social work, professional authority is reduced by the variety of available interpretations about the implications of practice wisdom. Moreover, when professional practitioners in a practice wisdom profession serve as managers, as in these two professions, the authority of direct service practitioners vis-à-vis management is further reduced since the professional manager may be viewed as having equal status with the direct service practitioner in defining the implications of particular practice wisdom principles.

Characteristics of Service Benefits

The services produced by members of human service professions may result in both public goods (that is, indivisible benefits for the community or society as a whole) and private goods (that is, benefits primarily for individual service users) (see chapter 2). Some human service professions, such as public administration, primarily produce public goods. Some professions, such as medicine and dentistry, primarily produce private goods. And some professions, such as elementary and secondary education and civil law practice primarily produce mixed goods (that is, a combination of benefits to individuals and to the community as a whole).

Differences in the pattern of benefits produced by professional practitioners are reflected in differences in the code of ethics adopted by particular professions. An analysis of professional codes of ethics by Howe (1980) makes a distinction between those professions that deal with "the common good," and those dealing with the "etiquette" of relationships with other professionals, and with users, in connection with the provision of services to individual patients or clients (including corporations). The most "public" profession by this analysis is public administration, in which it is not possible to make a separation between private goods and public goods; the most "private" profession is medicine.

Changes taking place in characteristics of social work as a profession are reflected in the shift (Howe 1980) from an emphasis on "common good" statements in the first code of ethics adopted in 1967 to a primary emphasis on professional–client "etiquette" statements in the current code adopted in 1996 (National Association of Social Workers 1996). In spite of the normative, social justice concerns of the social work profession, the code of ethics has shifted toward a stronger emphasis on the ethics involved in the production of private benefits (Reamer 1995). In part, this reflects the fact that issues of unethical behavior and professional malpractice are more likely to emerge around the provision of private goods than around the provision of public goods (Reamer 1994). In particular, there is limited reference in the current social work code of ethics to the responsibility of the professional employed by a service organization when the public benefit objectives of the organization conflict with the private benefits being sought by the service user.

Profession–Organization Dynamics

Human service professions differ in the extent to which, during the twentieth century, they developed primarily around a structure of service organizations, voluntary and governmental, or around a structure of private practice and private practice partnerships. One consequence is that the relationship of the profession to organizational management is a more important issue in professional education in organizationally based professions than in private practice professions (Pruger 1973). Organizational managers and policy makers carry the primary responsibility in the relationship between organized professions and service organizations for the quality of the public benefits that are produced. This introduces a potential area of tension between the objectives of individual professional practitioners and the policy objectives of the service organization. Elementary and secondary teachers carry a primary responsibility for the educational development of individual students, whereas the school system, through the superintendent and the school board, carries a primary responsibility for preparing students who meet the requirements of the labor market. Child welfare social workers have a primary responsibility to respond to the unique needs of an individual child; the child welfare organization has a mandate to reduce the number of children in foster care being supported by the state, either by returning the child to biological parents or by making an adoption placement within a specific time period.

Law and medicine represent two versions of organized professions that have developed around private practice models with high levels of professional authority when they are involved with an organizational setting. Law and medicine both have centralized professional structures. Both professions have established a substantial degree of monopoly over a specialized knowledge base that can be converted into private practice income through the marketplace. There is a national, dominant collegial association in each profession. There is centralized control of the accreditation of professional education and, through this, ultimate control over the number of such programs. There is universal governmental licensing of members of the profession and, in turn, a definitive list of official members of the profession. There are explicit provisions for collegial discipline and for the removal of professional recognition, even if these are applied in a very limited number of situations.

However, with the commercialization of health care, the most important interface between profession and organization is that between physicians, other health-care providers, and for-profit managed health-care organizations (McArthur and Moore 1997). Managed health-care organizations have the dominant economic position and are more highly organized than physicians. The pressure from commercial managed-care organizations is on physicians to become more like internal, salaried organizational professionals; the response from organized medicine is to seek to protect the status of physicians as independent, autonomous practitioners working within a system of contractual relationships.

Social work and nursing, two of the "caring" professions (Abbott 1988), have developed around employment in organizational settings— settings where, in general, the profession does not have control over the actual tasks assigned to the practitioner. Moreover, social work and nursing developed around tasks that were largely defined, and limited, by the larger society. Macdonald says, "One of the main areas in which women were able to enter the market and, indeed, to professionalize, was that of health, caring and childbirth, but only into the residual activities left by the male professions with their claims to a scientific, or esoteric knowledge base" (1995:137). Abbott defines these professions as "mediative," in that they largely operate in a situation where third parties (funding sources, both governmental and nongovernmental) exercise control over both producers and consumers (for example, defining how services are produced and distributed).

In most service settings in which individuals with social work and nursing professional credentials are organizational managers, there is a clear distinction between being a practitioner and being a manager, so that the organization does not function like a practitioner-controlled or "professionalized" organization. Organizational employment settings for social workers and nurses are also numerous and diverse and generally not linked into comprehensive systems (the recently created, nationwide for-profit managed-care organizations being one exception). With the exception of those professional practitioners who do have a full-time "private practice," social workers and nurses deal with a "marketplace" of organizational employers, rather than with a marketplace of individual consumers of professional services. There is also increasingly limited provision for long-term career employment in a single organizational system, in contrast to the tenure provisions in higher education.

A steady increase in the relative size of the social work organizational employment domain has followed the expansion of community mental health services under public auspices and the establishment of third-party payments to service organizations for mental health services under health insurance plans. Particularly significant has been the change from long-term care for persons with chronic mental illness conditions in institutional settings in which nurses held the largest number of professional positions, to community-based care with social workers as the largest group of professionals. Moreover, as the treatment of mental illness has primarily involved the prescription of psychotropic medication, the role of the psychiatrist in mental health service organizations has become increasingly limited to diagnosis and prescription, and the treatment responsibilities have increased for social workers and other mental health professionals for ongoing services. The shift from institutional incarceration for first-time drug-use offenders to community-based treatment represents another potential domain enlargement for social work and other psychological treatment professions.

On the other hand, the conversion of financial assistance staff positions in the Aid for Families with Dependent Children (AFDC) program, beginning in the 1970s, from positions involving individual worker judgments to technical positions involving rule-controlled eligibility determinations eliminated the professional characteristics of those positions. The professionalized bureaucracy became a machine bureaucracy (Mintzberg 1979). The position of "social worker" became an occupational designation for organizational employees rather than a professional title (Epstein and Conrad 1978; Street, Martin, and Gordon 1979). The process of de-professionalization in financial assistance programs has been accelerated in the state-designed TANF programs established in the late 1990s. A similar process has taken place in many of the public child welfare service organizations. The result has been a steady shift of experienced social work practitioners from employment in governmental social service organizations in financial assistance and child welfare to organizational employment in community mental health, and into contract and private practice arrangements in the field of mental health services.

To the extent that key occupational tasks in nursing and social work have professional characteristics and are becoming increasingly complex, quality control, practitioner protection, and status enhancement functions within these professions are increasingly important. However, the fragmentation of the employment sectors for social work and nursing and the relatively small size of most employment settings mean that no single employment setting is likely to absorb any significant part of the costs of professional education, competency certification, and practitioner protection. Moreover, practitioners in these fields may frequently move from one organizational setting to another, further reducing the long-term benefit to any single organization that participates substantially in the costs of training and competency certification. Only a few large statewide agencies, large medical complexes, or federal organizations like the Veterans Administration provide systematic organizational or financial support for practitioner training, either at an entry level or at a career-advancement, knowledge-updating level.

Although the employment base for social workers and nurses continues to be heavily organizational, the incentives for individual practitioners to reduce their dependence on any one organizational setting and instead to support a system of strong professional associations, in part to protect and defend the economic interests of practitioners, is nearly as strong as they are for medicine and law.

Patterns of Internal Differentiation Within Professions

HORIZONTAL AND VERTICAL DIFFERENTIATION There is a steady division of labor process, or *differentiation*, within a human services occupational sector as the sector expands, both in the scope and scale of occupational activities and through elaboration of the body of information available to persons working within that sector. This includes horizontal differentiation, or *specialization*, which is the development of professional practice specialties dealing with particular population groups or problem conditions, and *vertical differentiation*, the dividing of complex tasks into separate components with less complex elements assigned to one occupational group, or role, and more complex elements assigned to another (Macdonald 1995:129–133). In industrial production, the division of tasks in an assembly line process is a pattern of horizontal differentiation, or specialization; the creation of an elaborate system of workers, inspectors, foremen, shift managers, plant managers, and corporate executives represents the process of vertical differentiation.

All human service occupational sectors have patterns of both horizontal and vertical differentiation. There is a difference between occupational sectors, however, in the extent to which horizontal and vertical differentiations are included in a single inclusive professional structure or are represented by a series of separate, but related, professions or technical occupations. For example, in the field of elementary and secondary education, professional definitions are generally inclusive. Educators at the high school level who have different teaching specializations are still defined as members in a single profession. Similarly, classroom teachers, principals, and superintendents are all perceived as members of the teaching profession and nearly always have their professional education base in colleges of education.

Even in elementary and secondary education, however, certain specialized aspects of educational services production are increasingly being handled by psychologists and social workers rather than by teachers. And separate professional associations have been established for educational administrators, separated from classroom teachers (Mosher 1977), particularly as the classroom teacher associations have moved in the direction of becoming labor unions and negotiating contracts, rather than being traditional professional associations.

Health care is a highly differentiated occupational sector. It includes a wide range of clearly defined and highly organized specializations within medicine—pediatrics, geriatrics, oncology, psychiatry, neurology, orthopedics, family practice, public health, and many others, as well as the separate professions of osteopathic medicine, social work, nursing, dentistry, and occupational therapy. Health care also includes an elaborate vertical pattern of differentiation, including a variety of aides and assistants, practical nurses, technicians, three educational levels of registered nurses, medical residents, physicians, board-certified specialty physicians, hospital administrators, and health program administrators. No single organized profession encompasses the full range of this differentiation either horizontally or vertically; health care is clearly a multiprofession occupational sector.

The organized profession of medicine does include a wide horizontal range of human health specializations but only a limited portion of vertical differentiation. The medical profession does not include anyone with less than graduate professional education, although it does, through specialty boards, give formal recognition to an advanced practice status. It also does not include medical managers, except as physicians who have incidentally become managers. And management is not part of the basic curriculum of medical education.

Nursing, on the other hand, as one of the health-care professions, includes not only most of the horizontal specializations recognized by physicians but also a more inclusive vertical differentiation. It explicitly includes the diploma nurse, who may not be a college graduate, as well as baccalaureate-level nurses, specialty nurses with graduate professional education, nursing educators with a Ph.D., and nursing managers.

The formal structure of an organized profession may lag behind the actual process of differentiation taking place in an occupational sector. Social work has had a strong historic and ideological commitment to the model of an inclusive unitary profession (Bartlett 1958). However, a pattern of *horizontal differentiation* involving practice specializations has existed since the beginning of the profession, reflecting the involvement of social work in a number of distinctive occupational settings (Gordon and Schutz 1977). Particularly important have been those specializations that are practiced within a host organization controlled by another profession, such as school social work, psychiatric social work, and medical social work, as distinguished from social work practice in social service organizations.

A significant degree of *vertical differentiation* in social work appeared in the 1970s with the recognition of graduates of baccalaureate professional education programs as full members of the profession, as well as master's degree graduates, the beginnings of doctoral education for clinical practitioners, the establishment of the diplomate (a form of advanced private practice certification), the establishment of licensing of Advanced Clinical Practitioner (ACP) in some states, and the inclusion of management practice in the professional education curriculum.

This expanded vertical definition of the social work profession represented efforts to prevent the development of separate professional structures around the several levels of vertical differentiation taking place in those fields in which social workers were employed. Such vertical differentiation in social work positions has particularly taken place within the mental health care occupational sector. This occupational sector overlaps health care, but it has an occupational division of labor that is quite different from general health care.

GENERALISTS AND SPECIALISTS One important element in the relation of human service professions to the process of horizontal differentiation, and the development of separate practice specializations, involves the concept of the *generalist practitioner*. The term may be used in two different ways (Minahan and Pincus 1977). First, the term may be applied to an individual with *entry-level competence* in a range of treatment/intervention/implementation skills (Gibbs, Locke, and Lohmann 1990) but without sufficient preparation for taking on independent, or autonomous, responsibility for complex diagnostic, prescription, or treatment tasks. Such an individual is presumed to be prepared to work in a number of different organizational settings, using a core set of practice skills, but under the supervision of, or administrative authority of, a more experienced practitioner. In nursing, the diploma nurse or the baccalaureate nurse serving as a general ward nurse is an example of an entry-level generalist. In social work, the baccalaureate graduate employed in an entry-level position in a public child protective services organization is an example of an entry-level generalist. In elementary and secondary education, the baccalaureate graduate teaching in an elementary classroom is an entry-level generalist.

Such entry-level generalists are often exposed to a wide range of job performance expectations, including those in activities that are only indirectly related to the core tasks of the profession, at a comparatively low salary level. Organizational managers in social work often express a preference for generalist graduates, indicating that such generalists may be more adaptable to a variety of organizational job requirements than graduates who have a self-definition as a specialist.

The second use of the term *generalist* is as a description of an advanced *comprehensive* practitioner who combines the practice competencies identified with the use of several methods of direct practice intervention or treatment in independent or professionally autonomous practice. Because of the difficulties created for service users by the increasingly complex process of specialization in many occupational sectors, there is a potential demand for the *advanced generalist*, particularly in the private practice context. The board-certified family medicine practitioner represents one example of such a comprehensive generalist, including competence in, at a minimum, pediatrics and internal medicine. In nursing, the primary health-care nurse practitioner reflects an advanced generalist model.

In social work, the model of the advanced, graduate-level, "treatment," "direct services," or "clinical" practitioner has been that of a comprehensive direct services practitioner (Minahan and Pincus 1977; Gibbs, Locke, and Lohmann 1990). That role is now recognized in state licensing provisions for the ACP. Loyalty to this model of advanced practice generalist in social work has resulted in substantial resistance to the concept of explicit field-of-practice specializations in the graduate professional education program (Schatz, Jenkins, and Sheaford 1990).

One significant difficulty in establishing the concept of the *advanced, comprehensive generalist* in social work is the expectation that such a practitioner would carry responsibility for diagnosis/assessment tasks across several areas of specialized clinical practice, often in fields with rapid increases in new knowledge (Minahan 1976). The wide variety of organizational settings that employ social work practitioners, and the development of specialized certifications in fields such as alcohol or substance abuse represent an alternative professional development pattern involving specialization identification (Gibelman 1995).

A current issue in human service organizations is whether the position of case manager, primarily used in organizationally sponsored, community-based social care programs for individuals with long-term or chronic conditions (Morris 1977) (see chapter 5), should be conceived of as an entry-level generalist position or as an advanced, comprehensive generalist position (Johnson and Rubin 1983). There is also a question as to whether case management is a practice specialization within social work, or a parallel occupational development that overlaps professional practice in social work (Rose 1992). Many governmental service organizations in actual practice have defined case management as an entry-level, minimal-pay, generalist organizational employee.

Social Mobility Structure

Organized professions, in addition to providing various forms of technical expertise as part of the process of producing human services, also provide a major channel for upward occupational mobility for individuals, and for upward social and economic mobility. Given the numbers of employment positions involved, the human service professions are a major element in the individual opportunity system in American society. The extent to which any single profession serves this function is primarily a consequence of the requirements for initial access to membership in the profession and of the range of vertical inclusiveness within the structure of the profession.

The range of vertical inclusiveness reflects both the range of authority and responsibility available to members of the profession and the range of economic opportunity. One of the differences between human service professions in the pattern of vertical differentiation is the inclusion of a private practice component, or positions in for-profit organizations, that may provide economic opportunities that are greater than any of the available nonprofit or governmental positions.

Within a profession with an extended vertical range, there is, in principle, opportunity for individuals who begin a career at the entry level, with the smallest economic returns, to change professional practice positions during a lifetime career with increasing responsibility, authority, and economic return, without a change in basic professional identification. Thus individuals with the minimum qualifications for, and economic resources barely sufficient for, educational preparation for an entry-level position can, through various combinations of organizational promotion, additional education, and individual initiative, achieve a high level of status and recognition within that profession. Such achievements by individual members of such a profession may, in many instances, be relatively independent of the economic or social status of the individual's family of origin, given the financial subsidies that may be available for the costs of professional education.

Those professions in which the professional structure supports upward mobility have entry-level positions at the baccalaureate level, or below, and have a broadly inclusive range of professional positions. Such a professional structure is relatively accessible to individuals from lower-income or educationally deprived backgrounds. Professions with such a structure have been a significant channel of mobility for immigrants and for persons from ethnic groups that have experienced social and economic discrimination. Some of the human service professions have also provided, until recently, the only readily available occupational upward mobility channel for women. However, many of the positions that have the highest status and the greatest economic opportunities in professions in which women are the majority of practitioners have continued to be occupied by men (Chernesky 1998). This pattern has been changing during the past decade.

The organized profession of medicine has very restrictive access, requiring a postbaccalaureate professional degree for admission. It does include a limited range of professional opportunities within nonprofit and governmental health-care organizations that might be available on a job promotion basis. However, the private practice option offers a wide range of economic opportunities for the physician. Moreover, the senior health-care leadership positions that are available within the profession and in government are most often filled by physicians with private practice experience.

Nursing has a professional structure that supports upward mobility with some entry-level positions—for example, diploma nurse—that require less than a baccalaureate degree. However, the vertical range of opportunity is restricted by the fact that the positions in health care with the greatest authority and status, and economic returns, have been legally defined as being exclusively within the domain of the profession of medicine. They are unavailable to nurses except through a professional career shift—that is, by entering medical school and becoming a physician. Efforts to gain legal recognition of the independent professional status of the nurse practitioner represents an effort by nursing to extend the upper limits of the vertical mobility pattern within the profession. Although private practice in nursing does exist, the economic returns are not significantly different from those available in organizational settings. More recently, home health care has emerged as a potential area of entrepreneurial (for-profit) initiatives in nursing.

The organized profession of social work at the end the 1950s had a very limited mobility structure with a restrictive form of access to professional status—a requirement for a two-year master's degree in social work—that, given existing patterns of discrimination in education, excluded most persons who did not come from a White background, as well as most persons from limited educational backgrounds. Social work also had a limited range of vertical mobility tied to poorly paid positions in nonprofit and governmental organizations, and it had no private practice component. Women, who were the majority of the members of the profession, had very limited access to senior management positions in those settings that employed social workers (Chernesky 1998). Moreover, the profession did not have exclusive control over any significant sector of job opportunities in the occupational sectors in which social workers were employed.

During the 1960s and 1970s, the access requirements for social work were changed. The access requirement for entry-level professional membership was redefined to include graduates of baccalaureate professional education programs. The vertical range of positions included within the profession was also substantially expanded. A private practice component was recognized by the organized profession (Barker 1992), and specific recognition of advanced practitioner status was established, including the Clinical Register, the Social Work Diplomate, and ACP state licensing (Timberlake, Sabatino, and Martin 1997). Attention also began to be given to the formal educational preparation of professional practitioners for management positions through the inclusion of management concentrations in graduate professional education programs (Austin 1993).

Explicit action was taken within the organized profession of social work to support job access and upward mobility, both of women and of individuals from ethnic groups that had historically experienced institutionalized discrimination. In the 1980s, significant professional employment opportunities also began to develop in the for-profit sector, either directly in employee assistance programs in corporations or in businesses that provide employee assistance professional services and managed health/mental health care through contracts. In the 1990s, the access of women to senior executive positions expanded in nonprofit service organizations and in governmental service programs, including both state and federal departments.

Particular types of organizational tensions exist within professions that have a vertically inclusive, mobility-facilitating structure. Within a broadly inclusive profession, there is a strong tendency for those individuals who are already members of the profession and who come from middle- and upper-middle-income family backgrounds to emphasize organizational options that might serve to enhance the social and economic status of the profession vis-à-vis other professions. This results in pressure to make the access requirements more restrictive and to increase the costs of maintaining professional status, as well as to create exclusive forms of recognition that identify those practitioners who have advanced education and extended professional practice experience.

Some members of the profession may advocate increasing the entry-level criteria for membership in the profession to limit initial access to the profession. Other members of the profession may support measures that make entry-level access easier and that reduce the costs to the individual of achieving advanced professional positions. These members may give higher priority to enhancing mobility opportunities within the profession than to competitive status with other professions. Professional education programs may reflect these tensions, especially in conflicts between undergraduate and graduate programs over educational priorities for the profession, in conflicts among faculty members over priorities in a given professional education program and in conflicts between faculty objectives and student objectives within any one program (Cohen 1981).

In broadly inclusive professions, the issue of access requirements and of requirements for professional status advancement may be a continuously agitated issue. It is difficult to maximize simultaneously the strategies that create a high degree of openness at entrance levels and that facilitate upward mobility within the profession and those strategies that create a high level of economic benefits and social status for those professional positions that carry high levels of authority and responsibility. This is a critical issue in a society that places importance on achieved social and economic status as an element of personal identity but that also tolerates a variety of institutionalized discriminatory procedures that selectively limit access to high-status positions.

One strategy open to inclusive professions, however, is to use the political power base created by an expanded definition of membership to take action to reduce discriminatory procedures in employment and thus expand the opportunities for professional advancement. This is the strategy that has been used by organized social work to expand private practice opportunities for members of the profession, first through state legislation establishing licensing procedures, more recently through legal recognition of vendorship provisions, and currently through efforts to protect the independent, fee-charging status of private practice social workers under managed health/behavioral health care and Medicare.

Professions with an inclusive vertical structure may have a significant degree of internal competition for available employment opportunities when employment is limited. This may take two forms: the substitution of persons with higher levels of professional credentials for persons with lesser credentials at a given salary level (for example, the employment of teachers with Ph.D. degrees at the high school level without a change in the salary range) or the substitution of persons with more limited credentials at a lower salary level in place of professional specialists with advanced credentials (for example, the employment of social workers with a Bachelor of Social Work degree in child protective services positions formerly filled by persons with an Master of Social Work degree, together with a cut-back in the salary range). The fiscal consequences for the employing organization may be improved by using the latter approach; the consequences for service users, however, may be negative. Such competition within a profession may increase the relative degree of discretion available to an employing organization in personnel selection, and reduce the relative power of the profession to impose the profession's preferred definition of employment criteria.

Such internal competition within an organized profession may also result in competition among different groups of practitioners divided along lines of ethnicity, economic position, and gender. Such group competition may spill over into the internal political processes within the profession, with the potential of long-range consequences for the structure of the profession. Among these consequences could be the shift of some portions of the professional association membership into a labor union structure, or the organization of a new and more exclusive professional association that asserts a claim to recognition as speaking for the profession. One example is the organization of social work "clinical societies," in which membership is limited to individuals with graduate, clinical professional education.

In the case of those professions that have a more limited mobility structure, including restrictive access requirements, the tensions that exist within the inclusive profession may take the form of domain contests with other closely related professional and occupational groups over issues of professional control of particular forms of economic opportunity, or "turf" (Macdonald 1995). Optometrists challenge the profession of medicine over control of the administration of eyedrops, and nurses challenge medicine over control of childbirth services.

THE DYNAMICS OF INSTITUTIONAL DEVELOPMENT IN ORGANIZED PROFESSIONS

An organized profession includes four major elements: (1) individuals with professional credentials who regularly perform professional tasks but are not members of any professional association and may not identify themselves publicly as members of the profession; (2) individuals with only a nominal professional affiliation, primarily through membership in a major professional association and use of membership fringe benefits; (3) active members who read professional journals, attend conferences, and participate in organized professional membership activities; and (4) a professional leadership network. The focus of the following analysis is on the developmental pattern of intraprofessional activities within organized professions, in particular those activities that involve the active members and the leadership network.

These intraprofessional activities are part of the "professional project" (Larson 1977). That is, the objective of these activities is to establish a power base that makes it possible to assert a claim for societal recognition of the occupation as a profession, to assert and maintain the occupational domain of the profession, and to negotiate relationships between the profession and other social institutions (Macdonald 1995). Abbott (1995) also describes these activities as the development of linkages among clusters of service providers in various work settings, using a variety of professional practice skills, resulting, at any one time, in an operational definition of professional boundaries. The position of an organized profession in the larger society is never a fixed and completed "project." It is always a work in progress, changing as the society changes and shaped by the internal dynamics within the profession.

The elaboration of organized professions in the twentieth century has gone far beyond the pattern of personal association among individuals in a specialized occupation. Three of the major dynamics in the internal organizational development of particular professions have been: (1) the need for *quality control* as the complexity of the tasks dealt with by the practitioners increases; (2) a practitioner need for various forms of *protection against attack* when there are unfavorable outcomes for a service user; and (3) efforts to *protect/improve the social status of the profession and the economic status of members of the profession*. Hall points out, "The process of professionalization probably is based much more on what the occupation does in trying to professionalize itself" (1969:90).

Larson (1977) introduced the concept of the professional project. The objectives of the professional project include both advancing the economic interests of the members of the occupational "interest group," through the development of a monopoly in the marketplace, and enhancing their social status. This is particularly important when the members of the occupational interest group have a specialized knowledge base that can be converted to income through the marketplace (Macdonald 1995). Macdonald states, "The occupational group is seen not just as a fact of social life but as an entity whose members have to work at bringing it into existence and who then have to keep up a continual effort to maintain and if possible enhance the position of the group. In other words the group has to pursue a **project**" (1995:188).

The dynamics of the professional project also connects the profession to the university, which is the source of the knowledge base and also a source of the credentialing that is essential for establishment of a functional monopoly of expertise.

> In modern society "knowledge" is a separate and distinctive element in society not tied directly to other institutions (church, state). . . . Once these changes in the nature of cognition had occurred it became possible for individuals to develop an area of learning and expertise and become repositories of knowledge in their own right and to form groups of specialists,

although there were few societies even in the industrial world where this could occur. Such groups were then able to take advantage of the other salient characteristic of such a society, the free market, to sell the services they could offer based on their knowledge.

Macdonald (1995:159)

In an essay entitled "The Next Society," Drucker asserts that "knowledge workers [including professionals] are the new capitalists" (2001:8).

HUMAN SERVICE PROFESSIONS AND QUALITY CONTROL IN ORGANIZATIONAL SETTINGS

One of the dynamics that has shaped the elaborated development of organized professions is the increase in the number and variety of tasks involving discretionary judgments as the scope of services provided by human service organizations and private professional practitioners has increased. The complexity of the discretionary judgments that must be made has increased as the complexity of culture and technology has increased. In turn, the requirements for quality control have increased.

Decisions involved when a newborn infant from White biological parents is being adopted by another White family become more complex when the adoption of a school-age child born to ethnically diverse parents potentially involves a single adult, or a couple from ethnically diverse backgrounds. In older cultures, such judgments were shaped by traditions within a relatively stable society that changed slowly. Moreover, in such cultures, societal institutions such as government and organized religion controlled these judgment tasks rather than particular individuals with specialized knowledge (Macdonald 1995).

In the twentieth century, more medicines have become available for prescription, more alternatives in living patterns have become available to individuals, more career choices face young people, more treatment approaches are available for use with a child with developmental disabilities. The choices among these alternatives are increasingly knowledge dependent rather than being controlled by rules established by societal institutions; they cannot be fully programmed. Not only do they involve interactions among multiple factors in individual situations, but also there is no simple and straightforward method of evaluating outcomes promptly and therefore no way of constructing a feedback loop that is consistently self-correcting when ineffective decisions are made.

When judgmental decisions are being made in the production of services by human service organizations or by independent professional practitioners rather than within the private context of a family, it is assumed by service users that there is a systematic body of knowledge that can be used to guide the diagnosis of problem conditions, the choice among prescription options, and the application of a treatment method. The assumption that there is such a body of knowledge is why professionals, rather than lay persons using common sense, are looked to, either to make a decision or to provide specialized information to an individual or family who must make a decision.

Outcomes may begin to vary erratically when there is an increase in the scope and complexity of judgmental tasks being dealt with by direct service practitioners. The degree of consistency and dependability in the performance of such tasks is likely to decline, both on the part of any one practitioner and across a group of service practitioners. This is particularly likely if the judgments are guided only by prior personal experience, or by the experience of staff members in a single organization. Some method of achieving an improved degree of consistency in service provision is required.

The first approach often tried in a service organization is an attempt to increase consistency through increased bureaucratization—that is, through extending and strengthening administrative controls and through an elaboration of rules applied to service situations, together with increased monitoring/auditing. Such an effort to reduce the "loose coupling" that is characteristic of the administrative structure of human service organizations is intended to limit the range of discretion that can be used by the direct service worker to improve service quality and to avoid the negative results of errors in judgment. Indeed, if the level of erratic outcomes is perceived as being pervasive throughout an entire field of services, both state governments and even the federal government may attempt to impose standardized procedures. Examples include the Adoption and Safe Families Act of 1977 and the federal mandates for educational testing in elementary schools enacted in 2001.

However, the process of increased bureaucratization, proliferation of regulations, and intensive monitoring is ultimately self-limiting when complex judgmental decisions are required. The organizational distance between the direct service worker and that level of the bureaucratic organization that can make, or modify, decision rules results in a substantial time lag in the transmittal of information from the service level to the decision-making level. More importantly, this distance increases the likelihood of either random or systematic distortion of the information before it reaches the decision-making level. A similar process of delay and distortion may take place in the process of transmitting a policy decision or a new rule to the service level.

In a relatively large organization, the variety of service situations involving judgmental decisions means that the information being dealt with at the policy decision level is more complex than the information from any single service situation. The more complex the information, the more time is required to make a decision or to prepare a rule, and the more likely it is that the rule will fit all cases to some degree but no single case exactly. Therefore, the individual worker, or immediate supervisor, will have to modify the rule to fit the individual situation, or the organization will be perceived as being unresponsive to the requirements of individual situations. This reintroduces the possibility of erratic and inconsistent decisions.

This situation is applicable to efforts by a service organization to define the rules for the appropriate treatment of specific disease conditions, given new forms of medication; to define the curriculum for high school courses on a statewide basis, given new scientific discoveries; or to establish guidelines for all types of child abuse situations or for all possible forms of foster care placement. A large, centrally administered service organization cannot, by organizational action alone, guarantee the public both *consistency* and *individualized judgments* in dealing with situations that are inherently judgmental (Aldrich 1978).

Efforts to intensify the control characteristics of the organization and, in effect, make all judgment decisions at a level substantially removed from the direct service level often make the problem worse (Wasserman 1971). More experienced staff members are driven out of the organization by intensified efforts to standardize decision making. They are then replaced by less experienced personnel, often with less educational preparation, intensifying the effort to control decision making centrally.

The problem is even more complex if a central funding agency that has contracts with a large number of service organizations attempts to

control detailed aspects of practice through contract-monitoring procedures. Similar problems exist in efforts by a third-party funding organization, such as a for-profit managed-care firm, to control the judgment
decisions of individuals in private medical practice through very detailed
regulatory codes.

Limitations on the effectiveness of organizational control mechanisms
in achieving consistency in practice methods as well as individualized responses in key service tasks may lead to the consideration of other approaches to dealing with the issue of quality control—that is, increasing
both consistency and individualization in judgmental decisions. One
method is to require potential staff members to undergo a substantial period of formal, or "professional," training prior to employment that includes (1) mastery of a general body of technical knowledge that is expected to guide discretionary judgments; (2) rehearsal of the application
of this knowledge to concrete situations; (3) learning and rehearsing of
specific occupational skills, such as interviewing a hostile or depressed
service user, basic surgical skills, or the use of verbal and nonverbal cues
to motivate student participation in classroom discussion; and (4) socialization in a code of ethics intended to protect service users against
malpractice. Such preemployment professional training may be followed
by a program of competency development on a continuing basis within
the organization, or the establishment of continuing education requirements for maintaining professional licensure.

A second method for increasing judgment consistency, in place of
more rules and regulations, is to provide for an initial period as a practitioner during which there is supervision by more experienced practitioners: practice teaching, social work field practicum, medical residency, or, in the university, the position of assistant professor prior to
tenure. A third method is to establish an examination and certification
process separate from any professional training program, intended to
test mastery of the content in those areas with which the professional education program has dealt. This includes licensing examinations in social
work and nursing and bar examinations in the legal profession.

A fourth method is to provide for an ongoing process of professional
review of discretionary judgments: the review of surgical actions by a
pathologist, professional supervision of social workers or nurses by a senior practitioner, the review of an elementary teacher's lesson plans by the
principal. This form of oversight has been most highly developed in the

Professional Standards Review Organization (PSRO) and the Ethics Review Board in medical settings (Csikai and Sales 1998). The testing of the professional competence of lawyers takes place in a public arena through adversarial processes in civil and criminal courts and, therefore, there has been no pressure for a standardized peer review process in law similar to the PSRO in medicine.

The organization of an extended training program, provisions for certifying initial competency, and the development of peer control procedures require an agreed upon definition of the knowledge base used in making discretionary judgments and of the skill competencies required for the successful performance of occupational tasks. Procedures are also required for testing the relevance of new information in the cognitive areas included in the knowledge base, for developing consensus about the "correctness" and "safeness" of occupational procedures, and for disseminating all this information to existing practitioners and to professional education programs.

The establishment of professional organizations and structures is required when these quality control activities apply to occupational specialists, not in a single organization, but to those working in many different organizations or as private practitioners. For example, in military organizations, quality control procedures are handled within the military organization, rather than through a separate, parallel "professional" system for military officers. However, in the instance of hospitals, these quality control procedures are handled through a variety of structures created by the organized professions of medicine, nursing, and social work, separate from the administrative structures of the hospitals.

In the instance of state child protective service organizations, these quality control procedures are handled in part within the organization and in part through professional structures, including specialized in-service training programs currently being provided through schools of social work. Moreover, ongoing quality control in a field of service in which there are large numbers of private practitioners, particularly when there are continuous changes in the knowledge base for professional practice, requires a system of professional connections and communication. One approach involves the development of "practice guidelines," "protocols," and "quality indicators" that define best practice procedures representing intraprofessional consensus (Vourlekis, Ell, and Padgett 2001).

Organized Professions and Professional Protection

In the performance of professional tasks that involve discretionary judgments, there is also a need to protect the position of the individual professional practitioner when rules and regulations, and accepted standards of judgment, were used and there were negative outcomes. For example, a child who has been abused, after careful review of all available information, is left in his or her own home and then dies from new injuries; a teacher gives a failing grade on a final examination and a high school student runs away from home; a child has an unexpected negative reaction to an immunization. Protection involves both an assurance that professional practitioners have the knowledge and competency essential to make sound judgments, and the existence of procedures to protect the service worker by legal defense or as otherwise required. Without provision for protection, professional practitioners may make the "safest" decision in all instances, regardless of the facts in the individual situation: the child welfare worker recommends removal of the child in all instances in which there has been any suggestion of abuse, the teacher gives a passing grade to all students.

If individual service organizations are unable to provide such protection for professional practitioners because of legal or organizational maintenance considerations, a variety of other provisions may be needed to protect practitioners against the threat of personal attacks—physical, legal, and financial. These provisions may take the form of collegial support through a professional association, through public acceptance of and deference to the authority of the professional specialist that the association promotes, through specific forms of assistance such as malpractice insurance and legal defense funds, and through the provision of channels for resolving complaints from service users. The viability of these provisions for protecting members of the profession in private practice as well as in organizational settings also depends, in part, on the existence of professional structures for disciplining unethical, incompetent, or incapacitated practitioners, quite apart from any procedures within an individual service organization.

There are important variations among professions in the characteristics of key professional tasks, and therefore in the type of protection needed by practitioners, as they deal with the legal and organizational environment in which they practice. The principle of privileged communication is a critical element in the service relationship of doctors and lawyers. Protection of that principle is an important concern of the organized profession. It is also a principle that the profession of social work is seeking to establish for social work practitioners (Alexander 1997).

Organized Professions and Status Enhancement

A third major function of the organized profession is to protect and improve the public recognition that is given to the knowledge base that individual professional practitioners have mastered and the skills that they have developed in the application of that knowledge base in making judgmental decisions. The economic position of professional practitioners, including those in organizational positions and those in private practice, is affected by perceptions of the public status of the profession in comparison to other professions and technical occupations. Economic recognition of the value of professional identity is a critical issue, since the process of achieving mastery of the professional body of knowledge and of developing the related skills involves substantial personal costs, both direct costs and the indirect costs of forgone earnings during professional education.

Organized professions undertake a wide variety of activities directed at increasing the public recognition of the distinctive role of the profession, the contributions of the profession as a whole to improving the quality of life in society, and the achievements of individual members of the profession. These initiatives are directed, in part, at the general public, but even more importantly at significant centers of public influence, including public officials, the media, foundation leaders, corporate leaders, and the leadership of other organized professions. For example, the organized profession of law has established for itself public recognition of being the primary source for recommendations dealing with nominees for appointments to the federal judiciary.

Status enhancement also includes status protection. The organized profession of law resists any proposal that would allow consideration of any individual who is not a lawyer for a judicial appointment. The organized profession of medicine resists recognition of any other occupational group as having the competence to perform any of the tasks traditionally considered part of the practice domain of medicine, such as overseeing normal childbirth. Social work resists efforts by the federal government to define social workers working in skilled nursing facilities (SNF) as organizational employees for purposes of reimbursement under the Medicare program rather than as independent professionals.

Social workers, nurses, and elementary and secondary teachers struggle with long-standing status, and economic, differentials between those professions in which most of the practitioners are women and those in which most of the members are men. However, the limited economic benefits generally available in each of these professions also limit the willingness of practitioners to invest their resources in efforts by the organized profession to improve the relative status of the profession.

The competitive pressure for professional status enhancement often conflicts with equally important pressures for interprofessional collaboration (Abramson and Mizrahi 1996). The need for such collaboration occurs at the level of the interprofessional treatment team within a single organization and at the level of national advocacy in support of increased governmental funding support for such service programs as mental health services, improved elementary and secondary education, and treatment of patients with human immunodeficiency virus (HIV) or acquired immunodeficiency syndrome (AIDS).

Growth Dynamics in Organized Professions

The operational dynamics of professional associations are connected to the basic functions of quality control, practitioner protection, and status enhancement. However, once the professional project process begins, the dynamics of *organizational growth* become a significant factor in shaping the development of the professional association.

The core activities that are characteristic of an organized profession and, in particular, of the professional membership association are primarily supported by membership dues. These activities develop only to the extent that they can generate and maintain support, both financial and participation, from members of the professional constituency. Among the complexities in developing such support is the fact that professions are composed of a cluster of subgroups consisting of individual practitioners working in different settings. Practitioners in particular settings who may identify themselves as social workers may also have very distinctive sub-group self-interests. Since participation in intraprofessional activities, including the payment of membership dues to the central professional association, is ultimately voluntary, association activities are necessarily shaped by the perceived self-interests of those members of the profession who choose to be active participants. Two sets of dynamics shape these association activities, particularly in professions with a private practice component, including social work.

First, the pattern of activities in the professional association tends to be significantly influenced by the interests of that group of practitioners who are in private practice, whose services are for sale in the marketplace, or who are in a setting that most resembles private practice—for example, the private consulting firm in city planning or the professional practice group in mental health services. Individuals in private practice, or whose income is otherwise related to fee-for-service payments or other forms of third-party reimbursement for individual services, have the most to gain, both directly and indirectly, from a highly developed and highly visible structure of professional activities. They are, therefore, the individuals most likely to invest the personal time and financial resources needed to support such activities. The ability to deduct costs of such activities from private practice income for tax purposes reduces the economic impact of the participation in such activities.

This disproportionate investment of effort by private practitioners has the effect of putting emphasis, within the total range of activities in the association, on those elements of professional practice that (1) lend themselves to a private practice, or fee-for-service third-party reimbursement arrangement, and (2) that particularly justify a system of professional oversight and control, including certification and licensing of practitioners and provisions for the discipline of practitioners guilty of unethical behavior. In addition to providing protection to the service users, certification and licensing can serve an important economic function for the private practitioner by limiting the number of practitioners who are competing for users who are covered by fee-for-service arrangements or other forms of third-party payment.

Second, organized activities of the profession tend to develop around advocacy support for program funding for those settings in which the largest groups of professionally active practitioners are employed, as well as for support of the status of the profession in those settings. This includes legislative lobbying for governmental funding for particular types of service programs, defense of professional domain definitions against competitive pressures from other occupations/professions, lobbying for, or against, regulations that would affect the scope of responsibility and status of practitioners in a particular setting, and defense of individual practitioners who are involved in conflicts with an employing organization. In the association network of professional social work, this has meant advocacy support for publicly funded mental health programs and child welfare programs and support of the role of social workers in such settings; in elementary and secondary education it has meant defense of the public school system by the organized teaching profession.

The professional association must develop an effective power base to be effective in these two core areas of organizational activity—the advancement of the interests of those in a fee-for-service/third-party reimbursement context, and protection/advancement of the profession in key organizational settings. The power base of an organized profession may include several elements: (1) the number of dues-paying members; (2) the level of membership dues, which is a proxy for the income level of association members as well as a measure of the level of their commitment to the organized profession; (3) the economic and social status of those persons who use the services of professional specialists and who therefore have an immediate stake in the quality of professional practice; and (4) the economic and social status of individual members of the profession or of their family of origin.

Law and medicine are powerful professions on all of these criteria. Organized activities in other human service professions are driven, in part, by an effort to develop a similar power base by drawing on one or more of these elements. Such a power base may be used to compete directly with medicine or law on specific issues of professional domain (Goode 1969), or in efforts to exercise significant power in relation to administrative authorities in service settings not dominated by law or medicine.

In the absence of several of the power base elements found in medicine and law, the development of a professional power base for social work and for similar human service professions such as nursing and elementary and secondary education is likely to be driven by the dynamics of professional association growth and visibility. This requires a steady expansion of association activities. In turn, this requires an expanded membership base, or an increase in dues, or both. There is also pressure on professions such as social work or nursing that have a large organization employment base to expand the membership of the profession to meet the personnel requirements of key organizational settings and thus protect the domain boundaries of the profession.

The power-through-organizational-growth dynamics may result in conflicts between the growth objectives of organizational leaders within the organized profession and the objectives of individual practitioners who have an interest in increased visibility of the profession but also in limiting increases in association dues. Practitioners in private practice, in particular, may also have an interest in limiting, rather than expanding, the numbers of professional practitioners.

The effort to strengthen the power base of the organized profession requires the development of a centralized and unified membership association in order to consolidate financial and membership resources, increase visibility, and increase interest group lobbying leverage. Efforts to strengthen the central professional association can also mean pressures to consolidate separate special-interest associations, as reflected in the process involved in the formation of the National Association of Social Workers (NASW) in 1956 from seven separate professional associations.

However, the national professional association may be required to adopt a less centralized internal organizational structure if it is to accommodate diverse interest groups with different priorities, representing the different clusters of practitioners who are linked together in the identity of social worker (Abbott 1995). A current example is the development of specialty "sections" within the NASW, a development that had been resisted for some thirty years following its original formation. Efforts to strengthen the national professional association can also mean giving priority to efforts by the officers and staff of the association to retain support from those subgroups within the membership that pose the most active threat of splitting off into a separate association.

Separate special-interest associations may be organized when an accommodation of diverse interests is not achieved within the inclusive national association. In social work, these special-interest associations include, among others, the National Federation of Clinical Societies, the National Association of Black Social Workers, the Association for the Advancement of Social Work with Groups, and the Network of Social Work Managers. Professional associations in the United States also face competing pressures—for example, to establish a strong power base at the national level versus to establish one within each state, since legislation and executive decisions at both federal and state levels can affect the societal position of the profession.

Tangible fringe benefits of membership, such as group insurance, including malpractice insurance, become a significant factor in attracting and maintaining membership in the professional association, particularly as the costs of membership increase. This, in turn, increases the self-interest element in association membership. Protection of, or advancement of, the status and prestige of the profession, and the status and income level of the economic opportunities available to members of the profession, become high priorities of the professional association as the effort to attract and hold dues-paying members intensifies. These priorities also include advocating for a strong distinction between the functions of member professionals and the functions of members of other professions, nonprofessional organizational employees, and volunteers. In the hospital setting, for example, this is reflected in distinctions between professionals and between professionals and other employees and volunteers that are reinforced by an elaborate code of uniforms and symbolic identifications. The professional association has a stake in emphasizing the distinctive domain of the profession and the distinctive role of practitioners, even though these boundary distinctions may be very blurred in the work settings (Abbott 1995).

Efforts to build internal support are an important element in the growth dynamics of the professional membership association, since the organizational activities of a profession have inherently strong elements of instability. The voluntary nature of participation, the uneasy balance between the costs of professional affiliation and perceptions of personal benefit, and the pressures to respond to the particular interests of subgroups within the profession contribute to this instability. The turbulence of the external environment, including pressures from other professional groups, educational institutions, governmental bodies, and service user constituencies, also contributes to the pattern of instability.

The power base of a profession may be strengthened through an expansion of the domain boundaries of the profession. Such an expansion of professional domain can take several forms. Substantial numbers of professionals may move into administrative positions and technical specialties—for example, physicians in medical research expanding professional authority within a particular setting. This is most likely to occur when there are more practitioners than there is an active demand for service positions. In other instances, the career interests of experienced practitioners may take them into new areas of occupational activity, such as the move of social workers into corporate "employee assistance programs."

When a sufficient number of individuals go into the same practice area, they are likely to form a specialty subgroup tied to their primary professional identity and then lobby for recognition (by the central professional membership association) of a change in traditional domain definitions. Such a domain expansion may be recognized by adding a new program area to the traditional areas included in national professional conferences. In other instances, a professional domain may be expanded by a direct attack on the domain of another profession. Examples include the initiatives by psychologists to be recognized as having the authority to prescribe medications used in mental health treatment, the initiatives by pharmacists to be allowed to prescribe routine medications for common ailments, and the initiative by hospital nurses to replace social workers in handling the tasks of hospital discharge planning.

An organized profession is both a collegial community of interest and an organizing framework for a special-interest action system that is involved in the political and economic processes that shape the social order. The interests of individual members of the profession include varying mixtures of moral and altruistic service motivations and personal economic and career motivations. The pressure to expand the power and influence of the profession, growing out of the role of the national professional association as a competitive trade association, often run counter to the imperatives of logical coherence required by efforts to become a rationalized occupational specialization. Efforts to maintain institutional inclusiveness even as occupational diversity increases, and the endorsement of theoretical and organizational compromises to prevent the development of splinter or competing professional associations are often essential to maintaining political power.

There are two arenas for self-interest advocacy by organized professions. One is the governmental legislative/regulatory arena, both federal and state, in which service programs and funding mechanisms are established and legitimated, regulations are written, and budgets established, together with similar activities in the voluntary, philanthropic area. The second is the arena of program implementation and organizational administration. Organized professions are a major factor in the environment of most governmental and nonprofit human service organizations. In addition to supporting the expansion of those services that may require professional skills, the organized profession may also seek to affect program structure and staff patterns in ways that reflect the self-interest of the members of the profession. In many instances, there may be a clear-cut relationship between the self-interests of professional specialists and the interests of those being served by a service organization. But the actions of the organized profession are seldom based on the expressed concerns of service users, and the interests advocated for are as likely to be related to professional domain issues as they are to service user satisfaction.

The pressure to function as a special-interest advocate on behalf of the dues-paying members of the professional association can shift the pattern of activities within an organized profession so that the professional association begins to resemble a labor union, as has happened in elementary and secondary education. The dominant characteristics may become occupational inclusiveness (regardless of technical competence), advocacy as the dominant style of organizational behavior, pressure on members for organizational loyalty, and the use of the organizational structure primarily for issue mobilization rather than for professional development and quality control.

In a political economy environment of unlimited need for helping services and limited economic resources, there are intense pressures on every organized profession to function as a special-interest advocacy group. Each profession embodies a particular view of the good society and how to achieve it, a view that also includes a central role for a particular set of professional specialists and the expert knowledge and skills that they possess. Each organized profession must seek to protect existing definitions of professional domain, definitions that are often tied to access to particular forms of funding for professional services.

Moreover, each profession must assert expanded definitions of professional domain, particularly in those areas of social activity that are not clearly controlled by other professional groups, if it is to maintain a consistent level of voluntary support by the dues-paying members of the professional association. This may include asserting domain control over activities that may not, in fact, meet the criteria of professional tasks.

The public policy positions that an organized profession supports include those that strengthen the relative position of the profession, as well as those that reflect the normative stance of the profession on public policy issues. The selection of public policy issues will also reflect the perceptions of the leadership network about those issues that will generate the most internal support among the active professional membership, as well as bringing support from other groups in the society with similar interests.

However, public policy advocacy may also be a major source of dissent within a profession, both over the substantive issues involved and over the question of the risk to the public status of the profession of being strongly identified with an unpopular policy position (Gilbert and Specht 1976). Internal support for advocacy may be sought through an emphasis on professional tradition. In social work, for example, there is frequent emphasis on the social reform leadership of Jane Addams (Specht and Courtney 1994) as justifying public policy advocacy, as well as repeated appeals to professional loyalty and an emphasis on the social value/social justice traditions of the profession.

Economic Dynamics in Organized Professions

The quality control, status enhancement, and practitioner protection activities associated with organized professions involve substantial costs. Part of these are direct costs to the professional practitioner. The extended period of preemployment professional training involves direct costs for the student, some part of which may be met by the student's family. The total costs are increased by the amount of forgone earnings during the period of professional preparation, costs that are sometimes met by a spouse or other personal partner. The structure of professional education may require some individuals to move from one part of the country to another to begin professional education, and then may require them to move again to begin a professional career.

There are also other operational costs for these professional preparation activities over and above the personal costs to the individual student. The way in which these costs are met varies markedly among professions, with specific consequences for the pattern of organizational development within the profession. In the instance of professions such as law and medicine, which are organized around a private practice or partnership model rather than an organizational employment model, the initial costs, both direct and indirect, for the individual professional student may be very high even though there is substantial public subsidy of the educational costs. There are also costs to the individual practitioner to be certified as competent to practice. Some of these costs may be directly reflected in student loans, as well as in loans used to establish or buy a practice.

These costs become, in effect, a front-end capital investment by the beginning practitioner, to be recovered largely through fee-for-service income. Moreover, as private practitioners, lawyers and doctors are more likely than organizational employees to be attacked personally on issues of professional judgment and must therefore carry expensive malpractice insurance.

In both law and medicine, the social status of the profession and of the professional practitioner, the protection of professional domain boundaries, and control of the number of new entrants into the profession have immediate implications for the economic position of the individual fee-for-service practitioner. A "surplus" of qualified practitioners can have a direct impact on the income of even the most senior practitioner. In medicine, expanded federal support for medical education in the past has contributed to an increase in the current number of practitioners, which has increased the ability of managed-care organizations and federal programs such as Medicare to force reductions in the level of payments for professional services.

In both medicine and law, there is a dominant, broadly inclusive professional association, as well as a variety of specialty-interest associations with similar functions. The professional associations have a dominant role in defining the official boundaries of the profession by defining the essential knowledge base and skill training required for professional practice, and in turn, in accrediting professional education programs. Moreover, professional education programs in medicine and law are, in general, substantially buffered, both structurally and financially, against control by university-level administrators, or by faculty bodies that include representatives of other academic departments. For example, within the University of Texas system, health science centers, which include medical schools and other health-related professional schools, are independent institutions, not affiliated with any of the general academic campuses.

The costs for maintaining this complex network of professional association activities become a significant factor for individual fee-for-service practitioners in law and medicine, and thus a significant part of their established fee structure. Efforts by fee-for-service practitioners to control the level of competition among members of the profession are, therefore, in part, efforts to protect a fee structure that includes such costs. Similar efforts are made to maximize the extent to which costs related to maintaining professional status, including continuing education, can be written off as income tax deductions and thus shifted from the individual to the society as a whole.

Legal staff positions in corporations, or physician contracts with health maintenance organizations, through which professional costs, such as malpractice insurance premiums, can be shared with an employing organization, may become attractive alternatives to solo private practice. This is particularly so when the costs of professional association services, and protection services like malpractice insurance, increase more rapidly than fee income. In accepting employment in an organizational setting, however, the lawyer or physician also accepts the trade-off of limits on the potential level of professional income in return for at least some degree of income security and stability.

The economic dynamics of professional practice in nursing and social work are reflected in the mixed status of these two professions. One tradition is that altruism is a significant factor in the decision to become a member of one of the "caring" professions, professions in which the majority of practitioners are women (Wakefield 1993). This tradition assumes that economic benefits are not the primary motivation for women in choosing a career of service in social work, nursing, or teaching. However, the assumption of altruism also serves as a justification for organizational employers not to provide market-rate economic benefits for "caring" professionals. Few service organizations currently offer social workers or nurses the degree of long-term income security that would be equivalent to academic tenure, even with civil service protections in governmental organizations. Employment insecurity may be affected by sharp fluctuations in the level of appropriations for public programs, and/or changes in the organizational structure of major employers as a consequence of managed-care developments, or as a result of mergers and acquisitions.

A general pattern of change is emerging in the society, in which employers of all types are shifting the costs of employee-related risks, partially or entirely, from the organization to the employee. These risks include the risks of unemployment, risks of illness, and risks of old age (Jacoby 1999). Long-term career commitments are being dropped, employee share of health insurance is being increased, and fixed-benefit retirement plans are being substituted for open-ended retirement benefit plans. The economic value of professional organization membership is increased by offering the professional practitioner an alternative form of insurance protection against these risks and by the role of professional connections in facilitating employment reconnections.

Even when there is a degree of job protection through organizational employment, individual practitioners have only limited control over job assignment or job location. Private fee-for-service practice does provide an opportunity for greater autonomy and control over working conditions, but it introduces the risks involved in private practice (Barker 1992). Moreover, the range of earned incomes in social work and nursing, including practitioners in private practice, is more similar to members of the clergy and college and university faculty than to lawyers and doctors.

In social work and nursing, the organized profession and the professional membership association provide a framework for the development of quality control, status enhancement, and practitioner protection functions; however, the level of earned incomes constrains the level of costs that practitioners are willing to absorb. Moreover, those persons whose income comes solely from organizational settings are limited in the extent to which professional costs can be shifted to the society as a whole through the income tax process. They, therefore, have less of a financial incentive to pay the costs associated with membership in the professional membership association. Moreover, there are few negative consequences for the organizational employee for not being a dues-paying member of the professional membership association.

Given limits on the willingness of current professional practitioners to pay higher individual membership dues, leaders in the professional associations in social work and nursing face strong pressures to expand the membership base by supporting actions that result in an increase in the number of practitioners. This may result in an increase in the potential financial base of the profession—for example, by endorsing an expanded number of professional education programs. On the other hand, such actions may be viewed as working to the disadvantage of those in private practice, thus reducing their incentive to pay larger membership dues.

An increase in the number of practitioners may strengthen the influence of the association in key organizational settings in which the ability of the organized profession to ensure the availability of sufficient professional specialists to fill existing personnel requirements is a critical factor in the relative power of the organized profession vis-à-vis administrators and policy makers. For example, the inability of the organized profession of elementary and secondary teachers to ensure sufficient practitioners to fill the employment positions in public school systems has strengthened the political position of advocates for eliminating undergraduate schools of education and substituting short-term orientation training in classroom teaching for university graduates with academic majors in arts and sciences disciplines. Similarly, the lack of sufficient professionally educated social workers to fill direct service positions in governmental child protective services programs has contributed to the process of de-professionalization in such service organizations.

Leadership Networks

Over time, control of the cluster of organized intraprofessional activities, including the professional associations, the accreditation of professional education, the association of professional schools, professional journal publication, and professional conferences, comes to rest in the hands of a relatively small proportion of the active members of the profession who serve as the officers, or key staff persons, in these activities. There is often a significant overlap in role positions among the individuals in leadership positions. For example, professional school deans and senior professional school faculty members often hold multiple leadership positions. This may, in part, be a function of the ability of these individuals to shift both the time and money costs of such responsibilities onto the university.

The leadership network is not a cross-sectional representation of the professional constituency. For example, the leadership network is likely to reflect seniority since senior members are more likely to be widely known within the profession and to have been actively involved for a longer period of time. These senior members are also more likely to be recognized outside the profession and to have linkages to critical decision centers that are of importance to the profession, such as the U.S. Congress. The leadership network is also likely to reflect constituencies within the profession that have the most to gain through the prestige associated with leadership positions, or through exercising control over association policies and decisions. This includes professional school faculty and deans who are often involved in complex power relationships with other professional education constituencies within the university, relationships that are affected, in part, by the public status of a particular profession.

The official policy positions on internal professional issues advocated by many of the individuals in the leadership network often reflect the persistence of traditional beliefs, knowledge assumptions, and professional practices. The leadership network is, by definition, a "conserving" system, particularly in areas dealing with professional practice. Both the active members and the leadership group in any profession have personal identity interests in maintaining the legitimacy and authority of the body of knowledge and the practice competencies that were part of their own professional education.

Professional education for both the majority of the active members and the participants in the leadership network is likely to have taken place at least ten to twenty years in the past. New information and practice innovations may be viewed skeptically. The risk of potential damage to the status of the profession, and to individual practitioners, of endorsing what turns out to be an incorrect procedure for diagnosis or assessment, or a harmful treatment method, is viewed as being more critical than any potential damage to individual service users that might be created by a delay in approval for an innovative technique that might, in fact, turn out to be useful.

THE IMPACT OF ORGANIZED PROFESSIONS ON SERVICE ORGANIZATIONS

The network of intraprofessional activities, including not only professional associations but also the informal collegial linkages that are characteristic of an organized profession, has both direct and indirect impacts on the management of human service organizations (Zald 1972). *Direct impacts* are those that affect individual practitioners within the service organization. The general effect of these impacts is to increase the "openness" of the service organization and to restrain the authority of both policy bodies and administrators (Mintzberg 1983). The significance of these impacts varies among service organizations depending on (1) the proportion of the direct service personnel who are members of a profession; (2) the range of positions within the organization that are occupied by members of a profession; (3) the intensity of involvement of individual practitioners in professional activities; and (4) the degree of commitment by individual practitioners to professional principles and standards. *Indirect impacts* are those that affect the external environment of the service organization. These indirect impacts, in a given field of service, may be relatively independent of the degree of involvement of individual professional staff members in intraprofessional activities.

Direct Impacts

PROFESSIONAL IDENTITY Professional networks, including informal collegial linkages, can provide reinforcement for personal identity as a professional specialist, thereby lessening the extent to which the occupational identity of an individual is linked to a single employing organization. This may serve to reduce the degree of loyalty or commitment that the professional practitioner has as an employee in any single service organization. Moreover, professional practitioner identity may include strong worker autonomy, antibureaucracy, and antiadministration orientations (Munson 1976). These may result from the pattern of both formal and informal socialization in professional education programs, reinforced by professional journals and other forms of intraprofessional communication.

CAREER ADVANCEMENT Linkages among professional practitioners may be an important factor in determining career advancement patterns within a particular organization, especially in an organization that includes several different professions or a mixture of professionals and persons without a professional identification. Initial employment may be the result of recommendations from professional school faculty members to managers who are alumni of the same school. Contacts through professional meetings may bring beginning practitioners to the attention of managers who are also members of the profession. A mentor relationship between a supervisor and a supervisee may be facilitated by common professional identification. Such a relationship may result in a pattern of rapid career advancement in spite of merit system or seniority provisions.

In some instances, a professional association may intervene directly to assert, or to defend, a definition of professional domain as it applies to staff positions within the organization. Professional qualifications may be given extra weight by a manager who is a member of the profession, both in original employment and in promotion decisions, particularly in situations in which such qualifications are not an explicit job requirement.

EMPLOYMENT MOBILITY The organized profession can facilitate employment mobility for individual practitioners. Formal and informal communication channels within the profession may provide information about other employment options. Linkages to colleagues in other settings may make it possible for individuals to plan an employment change before notifying a current employer, or over the objections of a current employer. Even without changing employment, the identification of other available employment opportunities may make it possible to bargain for better terms in a current position.

The availability of professional fringe benefits through professional channels, such as group insurance, as an alternative to organization-specific benefits, can be an additional factor supporting employment mobility. These professionally linked benefits also serve to increase the relative power of the professional specialist vis-à-vis an employing organization. This is one reason that some organizations may prefer not to employ professional specialists. Mobility-facilitating professional benefits, together with a general availability of employment options, may also be a significant factor in limiting union organizing in specific human service organizations.

PROFESSIONAL PROTECTION Professional associations, and professional colleagues, may provide direct support to an individual practitioner in conflict with an employing organization. This may range from informal support, both within and outside the employing organization, to financial support for lawsuits and the possibility of formal censure of the organization by the professional association. Professional schools may participate, in a variety of ways, in the enforcement of such censure. The possibility of censure by the professional association for unethical professional behavior may also be used by a practitioner as justification for refusing to comply with administrative directives that are perceived to be unprofessional. These could include directives dealing with the handling of confidential information involving individual service users, or the implementation of service procedures that result in ethnic, gender, or sexual preference discrimination.

COORDINATION Professional associations and collegial linkages can serve to support nonhierarchical linkages among service personnel within a service organization and across organizational boundaries. These linkages may facilitate case coordination and program coordination, bypassing administrative and procedural barriers, either within a single organization or among organizations. Such linkages may also provide access to information that is not available through formal communication channels. These linkages may benefit some service users and not others because they are informal and personalized and tend to develop among members of a particular profession. Information may be shared with some service users but not with others. Resources may become available to some service users and not others.

Informal linkages among professionals within a given organization are generally viewed as legitimate, regardless of organizational position. These professional subgroups may develop a professional "subculture" within the organizational culture of the inclusive organization (Trice 1993). Such subgroups can also lead to the formation of "claques, cliques, factions and cabals" (Polsky 1978) within the organization, or to the formation of similar groups that include individuals both inside and outside the organization. The communication channels within such collegial subgroups may be used to share restricted information within the organization, or to share information critical of the organization with sources outside the organization. A professional cabal may, in some situations, be the basis for organizing a coup d'état in an attempt to oust a manager or to force a change in a policy decision.

Indirect Impacts

Organized professions also affect the task environment of individual service organizations. The extent of these impacts on any one organization depends largely on the extent to which professional practitioners occupy key service production and administrative positions within the organization, regardless of the level of professional participation by such individuals. These sector-wide activities may result in potential benefits for individual service organizations, and they may serve as constraints on both program policy and managerial decision making.

PROFESSIONAL TRAINING The organized profession provides significant benefits by supporting the development of systematic training programs for professional personnel without direct costs to service organizations. The costs of training are carried by individual students, as well as by external funding sources such as state and federal governments and higher education systems. In some instances, the funding for professional training comes ultimately from the same funding sources as funds for program operation—for example, appropriations by state legislatures. But the service organization is exempted from the need to earmark funds within a service-oriented budget for long-term basic training for personnel, who may, in reality, not turn out to be long-term employees in that organization. However, the consequence of this arrangement is that it is the organized profession working through the academic procedures of colleges and universities, rather than employing organizations, that controls the selection of students, the content of the curriculum, and the standards used to determine if a student has successfully completed professional education.

Moreover, to the extent that direct service positions in any single service organization are primarily filled by professional practitioners, it is the professional network through the professional schools that essentially controls the gender and the ethnic, intellectual, and normative characteristics of the pool of professional school graduates from which the organization selects new employees. For example, service organizations may find it difficult to achieve their own staffing diversity objectives if professional schools are unsuccessful in recruiting a culturally diverse student body.

DEFINITION OF THE BODY OF KNOWLEDGE UNDERLYING PRACTICE
In effect, the professional leadership network, particularly through the linkages between professional association, professional education, and the publication and conferencing channels, defines the body of knowledge to be used by members of a profession. Control mechanisms include collective control by faculty over the definition of the curriculum in each professional education program; control by faculty members over the specific content in individual courses; the influence of senior faculty on the selection of new faculty members and on the tenure process, and also on the classroom materials used by junior faculty by defining the acceptability of new knowledge and theories; control by leadership persons over professional publications through peer review processes; and control by experienced practitioners who serve on conference program committees over the content of conferences.

Professional specialists on the faculties of professional schools write the textbooks on professional practice. They are often the reviewers of texts written by other individuals—both before and after publication. They control the selection of texts for the courses that they themselves teach. The development of Ph.D. programs in professional schools further extends the control of the leadership network of the organized profession over the definition of the essential body of knowledge through their influence on the next generation of professional school faculty members. Thus the organized profession and, in particular, members of the leadership network, including faculty members in professional schools, effectively define the boundaries of the body of professional knowledge and of accepted practice theories.

The knowledge boundaries for the profession define the information with which the beginning professional is most likely to be acquainted. Of equal importance, it defines those bodies of knowledge that the beginning professional is not likely to have mastery of. For example, the definition of the basic body of knowledge for social work practice does include substantial content about normal psychological development and psychopathology, and some content on the dynamics of community life. It does not include content on economics or medical biochemistry. The basic body of knowledge for physicians includes substantial content in biochemistry but limited content on human nutrition and no content on the financial management of health-care organizations.

This control over the definition of the basic body of knowledge by elements of the organized profession, in particular by faculty members in professional schools, is often viewed as a strongly conservative force. However, such control may also function to exclude elements of traditional practice wisdom that are widely accepted within the practicing profession but that are no longer accepted in professional schools as having intellectual respectability (Rubin et al. 1998). Control over the professional body of knowledge may be a modernizing force as well as a conserving force. In professions with strong fee-for-service practice components, this may lead to criticisms of the professional school faculty from older practitioners. In organizationally based professions, this can lead to open conflict between employing organizations that endorse traditional wisdom about practice principles and professional education programs that no longer include particular forms of traditional wisdom about professional practice in the curriculum content (Witkin 1998).

INFORMATION ACCESS AND INFLUENCE CHANNELS The network of activities within the organized profession can provide access through informal channels to resources that may be important for the service organization. Collegial linkages, including professional school alumni linkages with personnel in funding organizations ranging from the local United Way to national foundations and federal departments, may provide an opportunity for informal access to insider information about funding opportunities well within the boundaries of official regulations. Information about application procedures, funding priorities, and review procedures may make it possible to make efficient use of grant-writing personnel, ensure timely grant preparation, and improve the grant application.

Similar linkages may assist in locating other organizations with pertinent information on research results and program technology, and in locating potential applicants for key positions in research studies and demonstration projects. Members of the profession in key positions in grant review processes may exclude grant applications proposing service programs that are not consistent with accepted professional principles, while highlighting applications that are consistent with such principles and that come from individuals and institutions that have high status within the professional network. Although these information and influence linkages may develop along lines other than professional identity, professional identity and the "old school tie" network of professional school alumni often facilitate such linkages within local communities, within states, and at the national level.

RULES AND REGULATIONS The organized profession is often able to impact the content of program implementation regulations at federal and state levels, sometimes through direct lobbying. At other times, influence is exerted by providing informal or even formal consultation to regulatory staff, or through the role of professional leaders as members of task force groups or advisory bodies dealing with regulations. Such regulations can have specific consequences for the development of the profession. The explicit identification of four clinical professions in the original National Institute of Mental Health legislation—psychiatry, psychology, social work, and psychiatric nursing—assured the access of these four professions to substantial federal support for professional education for at least five decades. Provisions for physician oversight of professional services under Medicare and Medicaid programs strongly reinforce the dominant power position of organized medicine in healthcare settings, and they protect the economic interests of physicians even when nurses and social workers are the primarily care providers.

DOMAIN PROTECTION AND ADVANCEMENT Members of organized professions are highly involved in priority setting and fund allocation processes in both governmental and voluntary nonprofit settings at all levels. Particular professions traditionally dominate such processes in particular practice areas—educators in areas touching on public education, including the United States Department of Education, physicians in any area dealing with medical care, lawyers in the criminal justice system, social workers in child welfare.

Funding requests for new service programs (at local, state, and federal levels) that do not fit traditional professional assumptions about professional domains, or that are not sponsored by recognized professionals, are likely to get a critical and skeptical review, even if some are ultimately funded. An organized profession can also be an effective lobbying force for appropriations for service programs that fit within the domain definitions of a particular profession.

Individual service organizations may be affected by domain contests among organized professions. Contests between the nursing profession and the medical profession over the definition of the boundaries between medical practice and nursing practice largely determine the opportunities and constraints faced by groups seeking to develop rural health programs. Legislation governing vendorship—that is, the right to be directly reimbursed for mental health services without physician supervision—is an issue that affects the position of psychiatrists, psychologists, and social workers in community mental health programs.

ORGANIZATIONAL LEGITIMATION Organized professions are often represented in external procedures that are involved in the examination and evaluation of the performance of service organizations. In those fields in which service organizations are formally accredited, members of dominant professions are likely to control the majority of positions on accrediting bodies. Ad hoc review panels appointed to study specific organizations are likely to include professional practitioners, most of whom have been appointed because of public visibility resulting from their activity in professional bodies. Although such accreditation and review procedures are primarily viewed as a protection for service users, they also enforce conformance with accepted professional principles and traditions. These principles and traditions can be expected to include a strong emphasis on the use of professional criteria in the selection of key staff members and on the desirability of the professionalization of service programs generally.

NORMATIVE CRITICISM The organized profession can be a major source of both public and private criticism and support for a particular set of services or a particular service organization. Although such action may be based on specific professional standards, it may also reflect normative, or ideological, orientations within the profession. Social work practitioners and associations are frequently critical of service programs that serve middle- and upper-income households on a fee-for-service basis because of social justice concerns, regardless of the quality of service provided to individual service users.

Associations in the teaching profession often oppose any policy that gives public recognition to elementary and secondary education programs under private auspices, regardless of the quality of education in a particular private educational program, on the grounds that the existence of such programs undercuts public support for an inclusive, universal system of public education. Such sweeping criticisms, whether or not they are supported by individual case examples, may constitute a significant constraint on the policy options available to funding sources and organizational managers.

SUMMARY

Human service professions are an essential element in human service programs. Professional specializations emerged to deal with nonstandardized judgments involved in the occupational sectors that are involved in human service programs. The institutional development of organized professions has been shaped by the distinctive characteristics of professional tasks in the production of human services. There are critical differences among human service professions in the degree of professional control over diagnosis/assessment, in the role of science in the knowledge base, in the mixture of public goods and private goods in the service benefits, and in the relationship of the organized profession to human service organizations.

The development of organized professions has been shaped, in part, by the growth dynamics of professional associations, associated with the necessity in each organized profession to establish a base of power and influence to advance the interests of the members of the profession. These growth dynamics are influenced by the characteristics of the core leadership network, in which a limited number of individuals occupy a number of overlapping leadership positions within the institutional structure of the profession.

Organized professions have both direct and indirect impacts on individual human service organizations and on the management of such organizations. The direct impacts come from the influence of the profession on organizational personnel. The indirect impacts come from the influence of the organized profession on the economic, political, and social environment of the service organization.

EIGHT

LEGITIMATORS AND FUNDERS

*Money should never be separated from mission. It is an instrument, not
an end. Detached from values, it may indeed be the root of all evil. Linked
to social purpose, it can be the root of opportunity.*

—Rosabeth Moss Kanter (1997:279)

MOST ORGANIZATIONAL constituencies are primarily concerned with the nature of the services produced by a service organization and with the persons who receive those
services. Legitimators and funders are particularly connected to issues
that involve conformance to standard expectations for organizational
behavior and appropriate and efficient/effective use of financial resources. Each legitimating source or funding source/funding stream imposes important constraints on the human service organization (Grønbjerg 1993). Some of these constraints can directly effect the future
existence of the service organization. Human service start-ups, community-based organizations, and cause-oriented organizations often face a
choice between protecting their autonomy and their mission commitment, and accepting the constraints that may come with the additional
funding that would support an expansion of services (Hyde 1992).

Although service personnel have a personal and professional concern with the availability and quality of the services they provide to
service users, they also have a very immediate concern with the continued existence of the service organization and their own continued employment. Organizational employees as a constituency are thus directly affected by the requirements and expectations of both legitimating
and funding sources.

Fulfilling the expectations of legitimating sources and funding sources
becomes a critical element in the ongoing operation of the organization.
Conditions attached to funding—for example, state or federal funding—
may have a direct impact on administrative procedures, the nature of the

services provided, and the characteristics of the service users. For example, the 1996 welfare reform legislation, including Temporary Assistance to Needy Families (TANF) with its limitations on the access of immigrant noncitizens to governmental services, requires organizations administering such services to make a determination of citizenship for all service recipients. The federal Adoption and Safe Families Act of 1997 imposes procedural time limits on the handling of all children under state custody when funds provided by Title IV-B of the Social Security Act are being used. Funding restrictions on federal funds for the prevention of adolescent pregnancies limits program options to the promotion of sexual abstinence. Federal child support legislation providing for a New Hires national data base imposes universal reporting mandates to track noncustodial parents who are not paying child support.

LEGITIMATORS

Legitimating sources include a variety of organized constituencies that become important elements in the continued operation of every service agency. Local school districts must be certified by a state education agency to receive state funding; medical facilities must be accredited by the Joint Commission for the Accreditation of Healthcare Organizations (JCAHO), a college or university must be accredited by one of the regional accreditation boards in higher education, a child welfare organization may choose to seek accreditation from the Child Welfare League of America, and a new service organization may apply to be admitted as a member of the local United Way federated fund-raising campaign. These program-legitimating sources are primarily concerned with whether a particular organization conforms to a set of established requirements for public recognition rather than with the specific services provided by the organization. They function as part of the institution-maintaining structure of the society.

Other critical forms of legitimation include state charters for non-profit corporations and Internal Revenue Service certification of a non-profit service organization as a Section 501(c)(3) organization. In many instances, legitimating recognition is directly tied to the ability of an organization to receive funding from a particular source. Indeed, legitimation and funding often overlap, as in the instance of a recently established nonprofit service organization admitted for financial participation in the United Way that can then use such membership participation as evidence of legitimation in approaching a local foundation.

Legitimating sources can be identified as legal, regulatory, and professional. *Legal legitimation* involves the formal recognition of the corporate existence of the organization. For nonprofit organizations, this involves having a state charter as a nonprofit corporation (except for a limited number of national organizations chartered by Congress such as the Boy Scouts of America and the American Red Cross). This provides legal continuity of the organization as well as a substantial degree of protection for members of the policy board against personal liability for debts of the organization or for acts of omission or commission by organizational personnel.

Recognition by the Internal Revenue Service (IRS) as a 501(c)(3) organization allows individuals and corporations to claim tax deduction status for contributions. It also exempts income earned from organizational activities from business income taxes, and may exempt organizational property from local sales and property taxes. Such IRS recognition also imposes limitations on certain types of organizational activities—in particular, partisan political advocacy. Suspension of the organizational charter by a state official or of the 501(c)(3) status by the IRS is often equivalent to shutting down the organization.

For governmental service organizations, legitimation is based on the action of a federal, state, or local governmental body to establish the organization. In many instances, this involves a specific legislative act or ordinance that constitutes the "charter" for the organization. Repeal of the law, or in the instance of some state "sunset" laws, the failure of a legislature to act to reapprove the organization, may also lead to the elimination of the organization.

For most for-profit firms, a corporate charter is the basic form of legitimation, although solo providers and partnerships may also have legal recognition. Business corporations also require formal recognition by federal, state, and local taxing authorities. More elaborate legitimation requirements apply to "public" for-profit firms that sell ownership "shares" to members of the general public.

Regulatory legitimation involves the rules and regulations—local, state, and federal—that deal with public health and safety and the treatment of employed personnel: food preparation, fire protection, working conditions (accessible work areas consistent with the requirements of the Americans with Disabilities Act), building and zoning code requirements of local communities, wage and hour requirements, equal employment requirements, and so forth. The authority to delegitimate, or close down, organizational activities is implicit in these regulatory requirements, although violations of most of the operational rules and regulations may involve, at the most, financial penalties.

Professional legitimation involves accreditation by professional, or organizational, peers; it acknowledges that the organizational operation is at least consistent with minimum standards. But in fields with organizational competition, peer accreditation recognition may involve compliance with exceptional standards. Thus membership in the American Association of Universities is a recognition of an academic program that includes a major emphasis on graduate studies and research. Although accrediting bodies may include representatives of legal and regulatory bodies, most of the members are drawn from relevant professional constituencies. Gaining or renewing legitimating recognition by major accrediting bodies—for example, in health care or higher education—may involve very substantial organizational costs in both personnel and financial resources.

Even though the justification of accreditation may be the assurance of quality service for service users, being accredited may be a critical factor in the recruitment of personnel and in obtaining funding. Funding sources, including foundations and governmental agencies, may expect or require status as an accredited organization as a precondition for making a grant of funds, even though most accrediting bodies are not based on either state or federal legislation. Professional legitimation through accreditation may thus have an ultimate "life-or-death" connection with the continued existence of the service organization.

FUNDERS AND INCOME STREAMS

Traditionally, most human service organizations had a single source of funding or perhaps two or three. However, as the human service sector in contemporary society has become more complex, the organizational funding environment has also become more complex. Most human service organizations are currently operating in a *competitive funding marketplace* in which organizations compete for contributions (directly from individuals and through special fund-raising events), for contracts with federated fund-raising bodies such as the United Way, for foundation grants, and for purchase-of-service contracts (POSCs) with governmental service organizations. In the instance of POSCs, the competition may include for-profit service organizations. And many organizations also raise money through the direct sale of goods, and many collect some level of fees for the provision of services, either directly or from third parties.

As a result of this funding complexity, most human service organizations have a number of different revenue sources, or revenue streams (Wernet 1988). Each of these revenue streams involves a particular constituency, including, for example, the highly dispersed constituency of fee payers and the highly concentrated constituencies of foundation boards and legislative bodies.

In for-profit human service organizations, the most important revenue stream involves organizationally generated income, or payments for services, that come either directly from the service user or indirectly from a third party, such as an insurance organization. Almost all nonprofit and governmental service organizations, however, require external support beyond any income generated directly from services. Even organizations that may generate substantial income from service payments, such as nonprofit or public general hospitals, regularly undertake substantial fund-raising events or campaigns, draw on income from endowments created by past contributions, receive grants from foundations, or receive subsidies from governmental or charitable sources.

Funding streams can be classified into a limited number of revenue groups. These include (1) reimbursement for goods and services—fees and sales, (2) contributions, (3) grants, (4) contracts, (5) direct income from taxes, (6) legislative appropriations, and (7) investment earnings (Wernet 1988; Grønbjerg 1993). Each of these revenue groups includes a number of more narrowly defined specific income sources for that organization, represented by individual revenue centers in the organizational accounting system.

One important way of comparing human service organizations is by examining the relative size of any one revenue group in the total pattern of funding. This is important not only in terms of the characteristics of the revenue group, as noted later, but because different revenue groups involve different funding constituencies. For example, public school districts generally receive the largest share of their revenue directly from taxes levied by the school district, or from taxes levied by another governmental unit—state, county, or municipal. Health-care organizations of all types are largely funded through payments for services either directly or from a third-party source. Many social service organizations are funded primarily through grants and contracts, together with contributions. Long-standing social service organizations may also have substantial revenue from earnings on endowments.

Each service organization may have a number of individual funding streams within these revenue groups. These can include several funding allocations from a single source, each of which is designated for a particular purpose—for example, the legislative appropriation to a major state service organization in which different types of services are linked to different sources of tax revenue. These multiple funding streams require a complex accounting system, largely managed today through the use of computer software programs that can track, and classify, the expenditure of funds by funding source, by program activity, and by expenditure category.

The maintenance of such an accounting system becomes a high priority for managers. Service organizations are more likely to have serious problems, either internally or with external constituencies or both, when financial accountability fails than when there are problems in the actual provision of services. "The problems of obtaining, allocating, and controlling scarce resources are the *sine qua non* of human service administration—the crucible in which the success or failure of managers is tested" (Lohmann 1980:8).

Every funding stream involves contingencies and constraints (Grønbjerg 1993). For example, with individual contributions, the constraints may include the necessity of continuing to educate past contributors about the organization and its services, with an expectation of future contributions, and of continuing to invest resources in systematic fundraising initiatives. With program operation contracts, the constraints may include a restrictive definition of eligibility for services, specifications of the type of service to be provided, and definitions of the information to be included in service reports (Green 1998). With foundation grants, there are requirements for investing staff resources in grant proposal preparation, often without a certainty of funding.

Service organizations whose operating revenue comes primarily from earmarked, or "categorical" funding, or special-purpose grants, often face the problem of supporting administrative and operational overhead costs that may be excluded from the terms of such funding. Funding streams that can be used flexibly within the organization are very important, although the total amount of funds may be relatively small in relation to the funds that are assigned to particular programs or services. Moreover, service organizations are concerned with protecting, or expanding, whatever flexibility does exist in the use of all funds in order to maintain organizational and program stability and continuity. For example, a key staff member may be supported by a time-limited funding grant. A delay in the renewal of that grant, or in the starting date of a new grant, may result in a lack of funds to cover a two-month gap in funding for that position.

The service organization, therefore, is often interested in expanding the *fungability* of the funding stream—that is, the extent to which the funds involved can be used flexibly to meet a variety of ongoing organizational costs. Funding sources are generally interested in limiting fungability so that it can be demonstrated that a particular revenue stream was used specifically for a designated purpose. Financial accountability may require the establishment of a detailed paper trail that can be used to accurately trace the use of the funds from a particular funding source.

Differences in the sources of income also involve differences in the pattern of constituency approvals required by each source. For example, school districts are usually required to obtain approval and support from a significant majority of community members, whether their tax support comes directly from their own tax levies or from taxes collected by another governmental body. Health-care organizations must respond to the requirements of third-party funders for detailed information about service users and the services provided. Social service agencies that receive funds through a United Way campaign are constrained by the community perceptions of the potential impact of their activities on the success of the annual community-wide United Way campaign.

Earned Income/Payments for Service

DIRECT PAYMENTS FOR SERVICES Some types of programs, including both for-profit and nonprofit service organizations, derive substantial income from direct payments from service users—for example, the commercial physical fitness firm and the adult health centers of YMCAs and similar membership organizations. Nonprofit counseling and psychotherapy services, intensive educational services, adoption services, and geriatric-care management services that target middle- and upper-income users are other examples of fee-dependent services. Competitive pricing, aggressive marketing, systematic collection procedures, and cost controls become important elements of organizational procedures (Fitzsimmons and Fitzsimmons 1994) in both for-profit firms and nonprofit organizations that provide such services.

Organizations providing a core service for a standard fee, such as nonprofit and for-profit day-care centers, may seek to increase income by making supplemental or specialized services available for an additional fee. The issue of market competition between nonprofit programs and for-profit firms providing similar services is increasingly an arena of legal combat, with for-profit firms claiming unfair competition because of the tax benefits accruing to the nonprofit organization, including lower or nonexistent business and property taxes (Goddeeris and Weisbrod 1997).

However, many for-profit firms that provide human services are similar to nonprofit and governmental services in that direct individual payments for services are not the dominant source of funding. In all such organizations, the fee-paying constituency is a constituency that often has limited influence on financial planning decisions because it is highly dispersed and unorganized and represents only a modest revenue stream.

Generally, direct payments by most of the immediate service users are substantially subsidized by the service organization or through payments made by a third party, as in the instance of payments from the Medicaid program or from for-profit managed health-care firms and health insurance firms. In the instance of services that are directly subsidized by the service organization, the decision about the level of subsidy, up to 100 percent, is determined within the organization.

The level of organizational subsidy depends on the linkage between a desired level of service utilization and the ability of the organization to obtain funds from other sources. For example, an organization providing services without cost to women who have been the victims of family violence, when there is also a high level of requests for such services, is likely to generate much more financial support in the form of contributions and grants than it could earn from any level of fee payments that might be established. In such a situation, the level of fee payments from such users is not likely to be a major revenue stream in the income budget of the service, even though there may be aggressive program marketing to reach service users and even some limited form of voluntary, sliding-scale fees. The income flow for such a service organization is largely determined by negotiation with funding sources, on the basis of the perceived level of expressed need for such services, rather than being determined by the collection of fee-for-service payments.

SALES Some nonprofit organizations use the direct sale of products, as well as of services, as a source of income, particularly where the organization serves middle- and upper-income households. Among such organizations are youth membership organizations that may sell a variety of clothing items, camping equipment, and other materials with organizational logos. Colleges and universities operate book stores as well as selling, for example, clothing with official campus logos and computers. Other nonprofit organizations may sell a variety of educational and training services to the general public, including books and videos. Hospital gift shops may become a significant source of supplementary income.

As Weisbrod (1998) points out in *The Commercial Transformation of the Nonprofit Sector*, the sale of such goods may become an important income source with the investment of personnel resources in marketing. Marketing through the Internet may increase the incentives for large nonprofit organizations, such as major museums, to develop such sales activities. Questions have been raised as to whether such commercial activities are likely to have negative consequences for fund-raising through contributions (Kingman 1995; Segal and Weisbrod 1997). Moreover, such commercial activities may also be attacked as unfair competition by for-profit firms selling similar products.

THIRD-PARTY PAYMENTS Third-party payments for services to individuals and families has emerged during the past decade as a large and powerful source of funding for human service organizations—nonprofit, governmental, and for-profit. Third-party payment sources, unlike direct fee–paying individuals, represent highly structured, and often highly concentrated, constituencies that are increasingly important across a wide spectrum of human service programs. Although the most dramatic developments have been in the area of managed health care and managed behavioral health care, this pattern of third-party funding is not limited to these areas.

Essentially, third-party payments are either cost reimbursement, fixed fee, or capitated. A core issue in the selection of a payment method is the distribution of risk. "Risk management" has become a key dynamic in third-party funding arrangements. The most important issue is whether it is the funding source or the service provider that is "at risk" if the costs of providing services are greater than the funds they are budgeted for.

Cost reimbursement payment involves third-party payment for individual services provided, on a case-by-case basis, as in an indemnity, or fee-for-service, health insurance plan. The reimbursement rate is either determined by current marketplace prices, or by negotiated prices for individual services based on information about the actual costs for providing the services. In this reimbursement pattern, any risk for increased costs is largely borne by the funding source. This was the situation for the federal government under the Medicare program prior to the establishment of diagnosis-related groups (DRGs) as the guide for fixed fee reimbursement of hospital costs.

Fixed fee payment involves third-party payment based on an established and standardized reimbursement schedule per unit of service or per person actually served. Public payments to residential facilities for children, or to nursing homes, based on level-of-care plans that establish a fixed daily payment rate for each category of residents, are a form of fixed fee payment, as are the DRG payments to hospitals under Medicare and other health insurance plans. State funding for education, based on a fixed amount per child in attendance, is a form of fixed fee funding support, as are fixed payment levels to families for foster care services. In all these instances, if the cost of providing the service is *lower* than the reimbursement rate, the service provider realizes a profit. Alternatively, if the cost of providing the services is *higher* than the fixed fee payment, then the third-party payments must be supplemented by the service organization from other sources. However, since the number of individuals receiving services is not specifically limited, the risk of unanticipated costs may be shared by the funding source as well as the service provider.

Capitated payment plans involve a total payment based on a fixed amount per person made by a third party to a service organization in behalf of all the members of a defined, and limited, service population. The service population is expected to include some persons who will require services in a given period and some persons who will not need or use those services. Capitated payment plans are now being used primarily in the provision of health and mental health services where the health-care funder, such as an employer, pays a total amount to cover the health-care costs of a total group of employees. However, capitation may be used for other types of services, such as legal services and social services, where it can be anticipated that some, but not all, members of a potential service population will actually use such services in a given period of time.

Capitated service reimbursement plans shift the risk of unanticipated costs to the service provider. This may provide an incentive to use preventive strategies that reduce the likelihood that there will need to be a high level of utilization of more costly individual treatment services. The effective use of preventive strategies is most likely to occur when the service population is stable and there is a long-term relationship between the service population and a given service provider. However, such plans, as currently being implemented by some managed health-care plans, may also result in financial incentives for denying access to services, or for downgrading the quality of service provided, thus discouraging service utilization and reducing costs.

Third-party payment systems require strict cost controls and computer systems that can provide careful cost accounting to satisfy the payment criteria of reimbursing organizations. Cost accounting is also important for service organizations in order to avoid severe cost overruns in particular programs that drain financial resources from other aspects of the organizational operation. For example, for-profit managed health-care programs that have offered individual health-care options to persons sixty-five years and older as an alternative to Medicare have discovered that the additional costs of the marketing that are required, together with higher utilization of medical services, threatens the level of profits that they are receiving through existing contracts with major employers covering large groups of adults in good health. Several health maintenance organizations have dropped Medicare alternative programs initiated several years earlier because of this excessive cost issue.

Contributions

DIRECT CONTRIBUTIONS The direct receipt of contributions or donations is a distinctive characteristic of the private, voluntary, charitable, nonprofit service organization (Grønbjerg 1993). Most such organizations initially receive support through individual and corporate contributions. The solicitation of contributions also provides opportunities to develop a support base of interested individuals, to bring the work of the organization to the attention of a sizable group of potential contributors, and to educate the public on issues that are important to the service mission of the organization.

The presence of a systematic public relations and fund-raising program is one of the distinctions between voluntary nonprofit human service organizations and most governmental service programs. However, some governmental service programs have also developed auxiliaries and external foundations that actively solicit contributions to support activities not funded by governmental appropriations. These range from the fund-raising activities of the elementary school parent–teachers association to the medical research foundation of a publicly funded teaching hospital.

Individual contributions can be particularly important for the financial health of the nonprofit organization because they are likely to involve few expenditure constraints. Except for large contributions that may be earmarked for a particular purpose, contributions generally can be used flexibly for core operating expenses of the organization, expenses that may not be provided for through other forms of funding. However, contribution funding is also problematic because it may vary markedly from one fiscal year to the next.

The use of contributions as a regular funding stream—that is, as an anticipated source of funding for the future—requires the development of a contribution strategy (Edwards et al. 1997). A first step in such a strategy is the identification of potential donation sources and a plan for reaching each of those sources. One of the most important sources is the body of current contributors, and a plan is required for maintaining their interest and potentially persuading them to increase their support. The social networks of current supporters, including not only individuals but also groups such as church congregations and service clubs, are also a potential source of contributions. In many voluntary nonprofit organizations, members of the board of directors are a key element in contribution fund-raising through their own contributions and through their support for the organization within their own social networks. However, a strong emphasis on financial contributions from members of the board of directors may also limit the range of persons who are prepared to serve on such a board.

Organizations can also identify constituencies that may be potentially interested in supporting particular types of services in the community. For example, organizations providing services for school-age children may target the parents of children attending local schools. Another potential source involves business firms. In many small or medium-sized corporations, contribution decisions are made by the owner, or president, of the corporation. In larger firms, there may be an internal review and decision process involving corporate officers, or a cross-section of employees, particularly in firms where employees are encouraged to contribute to a central fund for community service.

The solicitation of contributions often involves substantial costs, affecting the extent to which such efforts are actually cost-effective (Grønbjerg 1993). The employment of a full-time fund-raiser, or contracting with a fund-raising firm, involves a sizable front-end financial commitment. The direct solicitation of wealthy individuals may require an extended period of cultivation and education and a willingness to be responsive to the specific interests of those individuals (Ostrower 1995). In some instances, mailing lists may be purchased or staff and volunteers may participate in creating a mailing list from local sources. The preparation and distribution of a large-scale mail request for contributions can involve substantial front-end costs with modest results, although in some instances the public education benefits may also be considered to be important. Moreover, Okten and Weisbrod (1999) found that increasing fund-raising expenditures by nonprofit organizations did produce an increased level of contributions. They also found that increased program funding from other sources did not depress the level of contribution funding. Organizations with an active and visible program of services funded through contracts and other external sources of funding also attracted substantial contribution income.

For capital campaigns, service organizations may turn to a professional fund-raising corporation that will plan, organize, and carry out a fund-raising campaign in return for a specific percentage of the campaign results, using board members and other organizational supporters to make the requests for contributions. Such campaigns usually involve a pre-campaign period, during which a limited number of large donations are solicited so that 50 percent or more of the campaign goal has been pledged before the public campaign period. Personnel in such fund-raising organizations often receive higher salaries than the staff members in the service organization, in part because of the very tangible criterion of success.

National health-cause fund-raising campaigns often report modest fund-raising expenses, allocating important parts of the total costs involved to public education about disease conditions and preventive strategies. Such an effort to disguise the relationship of fund-raising costs to the results is one example of ethical issues that emerge around fund-raising efforts (Anderson 1996). The use of successful individual service situations to dramatize the mission of the service organization, even though such successes are not typical, is another ethical issue, as is the presentation of service activities as though they are supported by donations when they are actually funded through a Purchase of Service Contract (POSC).

FUND-RAISING EVENTS There has been a revival of emphasis on the role of boards of directors in fund-raising, with a general reduction of federal tax-supported funding for human services since the early 1980s. Attention often turns to the organization of a limited number of fund-raising events (Grønbjerg 1993) given the unpredictability and volatility of direct solicitation of contributions. Such events may be a special project of the board of directors, handled independently of the ongoing service-providing activities of the agency. Fund-raising events have existed as long as there have been charitable organizations. The most traditional event is the charity ball. In large cities like New York, the organization and management of charity balls, and other special events targeted at a small group of wealthy contributors, is itself an industry.

Special events can provide high visibility for board members and can provide a framework for solicitation of their network of friends that may be more appealing than direct requests for donations. For organizations that do not have access to a wealthy group of contributors who might be willing to contribute through the purchase of tickets to a style show at Nieman Marcus, a broader appeal is necessary. Some organizations successfully institutionalize particular events—a citywide garage sale, for example—so that members of the general public anticipate the annual occurrence of the event and associate it with the sponsoring organization.

Special fund-raising events also involve serious risks (Grønbjerg 1993). Weather and competing events may result in a financial loss on the event. Such events also require a complex organizational plan that depends on volunteer participation if there is to be any significant financial benefit. The absence of a key volunteer, or failure to complete a volunteer assignment, may require organizational staff persons to pick up the pieces if the success of the event is not to be jeopardized. However, a successful fund-raising event under the leadership of the board of directors can also result in an increase in flexible funding as well as an increase in the relative importance of the board as a funding constituency among the several sources of organizational funding.

FEDERATED FUND-RAISING For nearly three quarters of a century, many nonprofit social service organizations and some health-related service organizations have received a portion of their financial support through federated fund-raising bodies, such as the United Way. In some communities, there are separate fund-raising federations within religious and ethnic communities, such as Catholic Charities and the Black United Way. These organizations include three types of functional activities: (1) fund-raising; (2) budget review and fund allocation; and (3) quality control and system level planning. The volunteer leadership in such organizations, drawn heavily from the business community, and the United Way staff members, are an important funder constituency even though the proportion of total funding for individual service organizations from federated fund-raising organizations has decreased in recent years (Brilliant 1990; Grønbjerg 1993). For example, in 1993, United Way funding accounted for only 7 percent of the budgets of United Way affiliated service organizations in the city of Chicago (Grønbjerg et al. 1995). Designation as a United Way participating organization, however, continues to be an important form of legitimation. The United Way volunteer leaders and executive staff members, as "community influentials," can directly affect the public evaluation of individual service organizations and, in turn, affect financial support from other sources.

Collective fund-raising began in the period around World War I (Cutlip 1965). Fund-raising drives were organized as part of the home-front war effort to support overseas services for men in the military, such as the services of the Red Cross and Salvation Army, as well as local assistance to the families of servicemen. The success of these drives led local community leaders to consider the continuation of such efforts to raise funds for nonprofit service organizations in the local community.

Two YMCA executives who had been involved in fund-raising developed a fund-raising pattern that was soon adopted by local Community

Chest organizations (Cutlip 1965). This fund-raising pattern included establishing a fund-raising goal, concentrating fund-raising activities in a limited time period, building a largely volunteer fund-raising campaign structure, and using highly visible events to celebrate progress toward, and the achievement of, the fund-raising goal.

Leadership in developing Community Chest organizations came from business leaders. For example, in Cleveland, the Chamber of Commerce had established a fund-raising review committee before World War I to provide information to business leaders about the qualifications of various independent fund-raising solicitations. Leaders of the Chamber of Commerce, in turn, were actively involved in the organization of the Community Chest, and they served as leaders in the annual citywide fund-raising campaigns.

Executives and board members of some of the established service agencies objected to the combined fund-raising plan, convinced that they could achieve better results for their organization on an individual appeal basis. However, many of the business leaders committed themselves and their organizations to the support of a once-a-year combined campaign, refusing to contribute to individual appeals.

In most communities, campaign goals were established initially by combining the funding requests of all the organizations that agreed to be included in the solicitation. Almost immediately, however, the leaders of the Community Chest began to establish procedures to review the budgetary requests of the individual service organizations, asking for information about past and proposed future operating budgets, as well as information about the services provided. This information was then used by a volunteer committee of civic leaders to make decisions about allocating the contributions that were received.

Faced with pressures from the business community to join the once-a-year campaign and with requests for financial information about past and future plans, service agencies banded together in councils of social agencies. During the 1920s, Community Chest organizations began to turn to these councils to carry out a variety of social planning activities, including community needs-assessment surveys to determine the need for new services, as well as an occasional in-depth study of an existing service agency that was having financial or management problems (Steiner 1925).

Initially, Community Chest campaigns raised funds from a small group of wealthy individuals, from individual households throughout the community, and from business organizations. In the 1950s, with the development of large industrial firms in which workers were members of industrial unions, systematic efforts were made to raise funds from all corporate employees, using a payroll deduction procedure (Brilliant 1990). In cities such as Detroit, the annual campaign was supported by both corporate executives and labor union officers. Both wage and salary employees were encouraged to sign an agreement for regular payroll deductions representing contributions to the Community Chest (later the United Fund and then the United Way). Pressure was often applied to employees so that a particular production unit or business firm could claim that 100 percent of their employees had contributed, even if only at the level of one hour's wages per month.

During the 1950s, there was also an effort by the Community Chest movement to combine fund-raising for local service agencies with fund-raising for nationwide causes such as the American Red Cross, and national health research organizations such as the American Heart Association. The national health organizations, in particular, were criticized for having high fund-raising expenses, for taking funds out of the local community, and for competing with the Community Chest in recruiting local volunteers. In several communities, the Community Chest organization established a local health research foundation to compete with the fund-raising appeal of the March of Dimes, the American Heart Association, and others. As the competition became more intense in some of the larger cities, the American Red Cross agreed to become a partner in the local fund-raising effort, which was renamed the United Fund, as did some of the smaller health campaigns. The American Heart Association, the March of Dimes, and the American Cancer Society remained independent with their own nationwide campaigns.

During the period after World War II, the Community Chests and Councils of America, a national federation of local community chests and councils of social agencies, which ultimately became the United Way of America, took on increased importance in establishing national visibility for the annual fund-raising campaign. The United Way of America provided various forms of support and training for both staff and volunteers in local campaign organizations (Brilliant 1990). It also began to negotiate with the leaders of nationwide corporations having businesses in many different communities in an effort to gain their support for participation in the local fund-raising campaign by each of their local units.

Local United Way organizations reduced their investment in community-wide social planning activities when federal funds for social programs began to be important in local communities during the 1960s and 1970s. These included the War on Poverty community action programs, community mental health programs, model cities projects, and federal–state funding for social services for households receiving Aid for Families with Dependent Children (AFDC) payments. In many instances, the existing council of social agencies was merged with the United Way organization, or funding support for the council was withdrawn (Brilliant 1990). Emphasis was placed on quality control studies of individual voluntary nonprofit agency operations rather than on comprehensive community-needs assessments and social problem studies.

Other forms of combined fund-raising also emerged. In a number of large cities in which African American citizens felt that the traditional United Way–supported agencies were not serving their communities, alternative Black United Way campaigns were initiated (Davis 1975). In response to the numerous fund-raising campaigns that wanted to solicit funds from large groups of federal employees, including federally funded defense industry businesses, a once-a-year internal solicitation process was established through which individual employees, using the payroll deduction process, could make contributions not only to the United Way but also to a wide variety of individual nonprofit organizations. Recently, the policy of individual organization designation has been extended from federal employee groups to other large employee groups such as state employees. The use of contribution designation increases the importance of the positive public visibility of the individual service organization. In Texas in 2000, state employees could choose among 400 different organizations in designating their contribution in the once-a-year campaign for nonprofit service organizations.

To offset the loss of a sense of direct connection between contributors and particular service programs, United Way organizations also established procedures through which individuals could designate specific agencies to be the recipients of their contributions. However, the opportunity for contributors to designate contributions has reduced the overall budget review and allocation authority of the United Way. The role of large corporations in federated fund-raising, including corporate contributions, individual contributions from corporate leaders, and comprehensive employee participation through payroll deductions, make them a significant factor in funding allocations. This corporate influence may support the expansion of funding support for organizations serving outlying suburban areas where employees live, while funding support to organizations serving economically depressed central city areas is held constant or reduced (Marx 1997).

Beginning in the 1950s, many of the existing service agencies that received funds through federated fund-raising, such as the local family service agency, began to expand into outlying city neighborhoods and suburban communities, where they were able to collect fee payments from service users (Cloward and Epstein 1965). As income from fees increased, there was a decrease in the proportion of United Way support in their total operations budget and, in turn, in the influence of the United Way on agency policies and program structure.

Originally, Community Chest funds were provided as general budgetary support. However, with a lower percentage of total budgets being provided through the United Way, United Way funding now is often designated as a contract, with the United Way allocation process identifying those program components in the total agency budget that are considered most important for community-wide support through the United Way. Like other contract funding relationships, support through federated fund-raising structures makes substantial demands on the organization, in addition to the expectation that organizational personnel will provide active support for the annual United Way campaign. These include demands for detailed financial reports that identify the purposes for which the United Way funds have been used. Moreover, United Way service organizations may be expected to undergo regular visits by a volunteer committee of community leaders and, periodically, an in-depth program audit.

The federated fund-raising constituency represents a general community consensus about the types of services that deserve broad community support on a voluntary basis. Service programs that are particularly controversial, or that do not have a broad base of community support, may not be included as financially participating members in the United Way on the grounds that their inclusion could result in a drop in contributions across the community. These excluded programs have included Planned Parenthood programs that provide referrals to abortion services, counseling services for gay and lesbian adolescents, and, initially, service programs for individuals with human immunodeficiency virus

(HIV) infection or acquired immunodeficiency syndrome (AIDS). Many times, such services have found it possible to establish their own financial support base that has more than replaced what might have been a very minimal level of support had they been included in a federated fund-raising campaign.

Taxes and Legislative Appropriations

Funding action by legislative bodies involves two related actions. The first action is the decision to levy a tax of some form on individuals/households, property, or corporations or other forms of business activity. The second action is the definition of the structure for producing a governmental service. The initial action is a *determination that a tax is required* to support some set of activities that are required for the "common good" (Olson 1971). The crucial issue is that the levying of any tax includes invoking the police powers of the relevant polity to enforce the collection of the tax, regardless of whether a particular taxpaying source approves or disapproves of the activities to be supported by the tax payments. It is not possible for an individual or a corporate taxpayer to select the particular governmental activities that will be supported by their particular tax payments, which is unlike the current United Way procedures for designating contributions.

Support from a tax source for any type of service involves a significant degree of economic "coercion" on the sources from which the tax payments are made. Although there are many protections in the constitutional structure of the United States for the individual rights of political minorities, there are few limits on the power of the political majority to levy taxes. The ultimate constituency for governmentally funded programs is the total group of taxpaying/voting members of the relevant governmental unit, including those who support, and those who object to, a particular service program.

One essential distinction between a public/governmental service organization and a voluntary nonprofit service organization is that, in principle, the governmental service has the support of a constituency sufficiently large to gain approval for imposing the costs of such service on the total population, including those persons who are opposed to supporting such a service (Boulding 1973). However, the political requirements for adding funding for a particular service or program to the existing tax burden will vary widely among political entities. Some programs may not be directly supported until there is some evidence that a high proportion of the total electorate support such action. However, other programs receive direct support from tax sources because the initiators include a small group of highly visible and politically influential individuals.

The *determination of an organizational structure* for providing tax-supported organizational services involves a choice between direct operation by a governmental organization or the provision of services through a grant of funds to, or a contract with, a quasi-governmental nonprofit, a voluntary nonprofit, or a for-profit service organization. Governmental funding support may also be provided indirectly through vouchers (for example, food stamps) or by providing for an income tax deduction for personal expenditures related to specific service expenditures (for example, child care).

DIRECT GOVERNMENTAL OPERATION Some governmental human service organizations have specific authority to levy a tax to support their activities. Depending on state law, local school districts may directly levy such a tax. Other special-purpose districts such as a hospital district or a community college district may have similar taxing authority. In these instances, the governing board serves as a de facto legislative body for the purpose of establishing a tax rate and collecting the assessed taxes. That board also serves as the operating board of directors that establishes policy for the use of the tax funds.

Other legislative bodies that are involved in providing direct funding for human service programs include Congress, state legislatures, county governance bodies, and municipal councils. The provision of direct financial support for a governmental service program through the actions of legislative bodies, including federal, state, and local bodies, involves particular forms of contingencies or constraints. Legislative appropriations are normally for fixed periods of time, generally one year, but two years in states that adopt a biennial budget. Much of the management work cycle is, in turn, organized on a one-year basis, including budget development and submission, statistical reports on service activities, legislative hearings, legislative debate, legislative action, and then release of funds.

Legislative oversight may involve regular hearings associated with the appropriation process, or special hearings when some unusual issue or problem is involved. Legislative appropriations may include budget notes or riders that involve specific directives to the service organization, some of them added at the initiative of a single member of the legislature.

In most states, budgetary requests from state agencies are coordinated through the governor's administrative staff. That staff may issue advance directives restricting the budgetary requests from individual organizations. A county executive, mayor, or city manager may take similar action. At the federal level, the Office of Management and Budget (OMB) performs a similar function on behalf of the president. After legislative action has been completed, a process of releasing funds for current operations is carried out with individual service agencies on the basis of the detailed instructions that accompany the budget document.

The processes of budgetary planning and budgetary administration become additionally complex when a governmental service agency is dependent on both federal and state appropriations—for example, in the Medicaid program, in which a federal–state financial match is involved, or in the mixture of federal block grant funds and state-appropriated funds in the TANF program. Funding cycles may not coincide, and, particularly at the federal level, budgetary allocations may not be final until well after the beginning of the next federal fiscal year.

The decentralized governance structure in the United States introduces special complexities when tax funds are appropriated at one level but administered at another—for example, when federal funds are administered by a state agency, or state funds are administered by a municipal department. The separation of governance authority between the several levels of government means that an administrator at one level cannot issue direct instructions to a specific administrator at another level.

The president of the United States (or his agent) cannot direct a governor or the administrator of a state-level agency to organize a state-level program that includes federal funds in a particular way. Governors or their staff members cannot tell mayors in charter, or home-rule, cities exactly how they should administer the juvenile delinquency prevention program that includes state funds. Governors do not issue administrative orders directly to county administrators, even though counties are created by, and ultimately controlled by, state legislatures.

Linkage and coordination processes across these various levels of government are achieved by conditions formally attached to funding rather than through administrative control. This allows the possibility of a significant degree of variation, or flexibility, in program design and operation, but it also creates a very complex system of control and accountability. In many instances, the controls take the form of general guidelines that are part of the legislative appropriation. In most instances, the legislation also requires the preparation of detailed regulations reflecting the intent of the legislative body and the intent of administrative officials at the governmental funding level. The adoption of these regulations often requires public announcements and public hearings before they are official, which delays the implementation of the funding legislation. The legislation may also require the preparation of a detailed operational plan by the service-producing organization, this plan being subject to review and approval at the funding level before program operations can begin. Congress, in an effort to strengthen accountability for the use of federal funds, passed the 1995 Government Performance and Results Act, requiring federal agencies to account for the results of federal program funding (see chapter 11). In turn, the federal agencies look to state and local governmental authorities to provide information that they must obtain from contractee organizations providing the funded services.

Once a program becomes operational, reports are required to document that the funds are being spent in a manner consistent with the legislation and with the regulations that have been established. Representatives of the level from which funding is coming may visit the program to ensure that regulations are being followed. The funding organization may raise objections or limit further funding if there is a discrepancy. In turn, the operational organization may file an appeal of such action, or call on the legislative representatives from their area to put pressure on the funding agency to change its decision. Finally, at some point after the funds have actually been used, auditors from the funding level may review the financial and program records of the operating organization and impose penalties if it appears that the funds were used inappropriately. These too may be appealed.

This process is complex and time consuming even when there is general agreement between the funding organization and the operational organization about the purposes of the program. When there is political disagreement, either between legislative bodies at different levels or between elected public officials at different levels (for example, between a governor and the mayor of a large city), then there may be additional complications. For example, Congress may mandate that every state establish a particular type of specialized service, such as subsidized lunch programs for children from low-income families through the public school system, without appropriating sufficient federal funds to meet the full costs of such services. Governors or state legislators in a particular state may refuse to implement such programs because they object to the program in principle, or because of the amount of state-level funds that may be required. It may ultimately require a lawsuit by interested advocacy groups in the federal court system to compel the state government to act. Even more dramatic actions were required in the 1950s and 1960s to compel some states to comply with federal court decisions striking down systems of racially segregated, publicly supported education.

Indirect program control can also be exercised by attaching conditions to a funding stream to persuade another level of government to undertake programs or adopt policies that would otherwise be unlikely to be approved. In 1967, Congress adopted changes to the AFDC program that provided that the federal government would pay 90 percent of the costs of family planning services for mothers in households receiving AFDC benefits. The Congressional objective was to reduce the number of children born to such mothers, using the high rate of matching funds to overcome objections that legislators at the state level might have to administering a program that promoted birth control. More recently, states were persuaded to expand the coverage of the Medicaid program to include all pregnant women and young children in income-eligible households as a condition for continuing to receive federal matching funds for the entire Medicaid program, even though such expansion could also require additional matching funds from the state.

Tax funds that are specifically designated to flow directly to nonprofit service organizations, or to separate governmental entities such as school districts or public universities, to support special projects involve similar complexities. The administrator of the operational organization is not directly or personally accountable to an administrative official at the funding level. Control is exercised through a structure of regulations, detailed specifications of the purposes for which the funds are provided, detailed reports on the use of the funds, and postoperational audits.

This complex system of governmental funding of human service programs, including health-care services, educational services, social services, and criminal justice services, contributes to ambiguous attitudes toward such services, not only by users and the general public but also by many of the persons directly involved in the administration of such programs. In nearly all program areas, the complexity of conditioning regulations increases over time as administrators and legislators at the funding level attempt to correct problems in individual programs through the adoption of more and more detailed regulations that are then applied to all program operations. The ultimate result of this "regulation creep" may be legislative action to terminate a funding stream, or to convert it into a "block grant" that becomes a direct transfer of funds to the operational level with only minimal accountability and reporting conditions attached.

TAX-SUPPORTED FUNDING FOR NONPROFIT AND FOR-PROFIT SERV-ICE ORGANIZATIONS There has been an expansion of procedures through which tax-supported governmental bodies provide grants or contracts to quasi-governmental nonprofit or voluntary nonprofit service organizations, or in some programs to for-profit service organizations. The expanded role of governmental funding for nonprofit organizations is illustrated by the report that in 1994, 58 percent of the revenues of United Way agencies within the city of Chicago came from governmental sources (Grønbjerg et al. 1995). The decision as to which specific organizations, and which type of service, receive funding is usually an administrative decision rather than a legislative decision. This blurs traditional distinctions between service programs that receive governmental funding support because they have broad public support, and service programs, designated through administrative decision making, that do not necessarily have such popular support.

There are essentially two elements involved when a system is established through which a governmental, tax-levying body provides funding support for a specific type of service through grants or contracts. The first element is the designation of the *authority*—that is, the governmental or semi-governmental organization that has the power to authorize the provision of such services, to determine the specific characteristics of the service to be provided, to determine who can receive such services, to make arrangements for the production of such services, and to oversee and monitor the provision of such services.

A county health department may serve as a health-care authority for the purpose of providing hospital care to indigent persons, and, in turn, establish contracts to purchase hospital services for particular groups of individuals, as needed, from a nonprofit or a for-profit hospital. Under the Medicare program, the federal Health Care Financing Administration (HCFA) is the authority with responsibility for establishing a program to provide health care for persons sixty-five years and over who are covered by the Social Security system. However, HCFA does not actually provide any of those services. Instead, HCFA purchases such care from individual health-care providers, from individual health-care service organizations such as hospitals and home health organizations, or through managed health-care firms, and it also contracts with state level organizations for managing the payment system for such services.

The second essential element in implementing a governmental service program through grants or contracts is the *provider*—that is, the producer of the service. One alternative, previously noted, is that the authority also serves as the provider—for example, the county health department is the authority for the provision of hospital care for particular individuals, and it is the provider as it directly operates a public hospital that delivers the services. Many governmental operations have traditionally combined authority and provider functions—sheriff departments, court systems, the state mental health authority that directly operates psychiatric hospitals for the care of persons with limited income who have severe and chronic mental disabilities, and the state child welfare agency that directly operates a child protective services program. In a similar way, school districts combine both educational authority and provision of education.

However, the role of governmental authority and that of provider can be separated. Some parts of government have nearly always been limited to the role of authority—for example, in the instance of the construction of major governmental buildings or highways that are funded through a governmental authority but normally built by independent contractors. However, the most recent development in the separation of authority and provider roles is the rapidly expanding use of grants and contracts, or out-sourcing, rather than direct operation, for the provision of tax-supported human service programs.

Some forms of out-sourcing or privatization in the provision of tax-supported human services have existed for a very long time—in particular, the tradition of state and local governments as public authorities contracting with voluntary nonprofit residential child-care institutions for the care of children who are wards of state or local governments (Rosenthal 2000). In the past two decades, however, there have been important shifts in the authority–provider relationships in many areas of governmental human service provision.

An important step in the move toward expanded privatization came with the expanded use of quasi-governmental nonprofit organizations, particularly in the 1960s. The federal government, through the War on Poverty, made grants to nonprofit and quasi-governmental community action agencies. And the federal government made grants to quasi-governmental community mental health centers as a method of expanding and diversifying the organizational resources for providing mental health services. The regulations established by the federal government also ensured that these organizations were separated from direct political or administrative control by city and county governments. There was also an expanded use of contracts with voluntary nonprofit child welfare services by state child welfare organizations following the 1962 social service amendments to the Social Security Act that provided additional federal funding for child welfare services (Rosenthal 2000).

These human service quasi-governmental organizations did not have the independent taxing authority that hospital districts, school districts, or conservation districts had, and thus they were controlled by the requirements of the external funding authorities. They had governing boards that were appointed by external sources rather than being self-perpetuating, but otherwise these boards functioned much like the boards of directors of voluntary nonprofit service organizations.

Although there was considerable discussion in the 1980s about privatizing municipal services such as trash collection, the major development in human services came in health care. In a number of cities, indigent health care was traditionally operated under the *authority* of the municipal or county government that also provided the service through a municipal or county hospital, with very limited collection of any fee-for-service payments.

Public hospitals became actively involved in collecting fee payments with the advent of Medicaid and Medicare in 1965. In turn, they required more financial independence from municipal or county governments to be able to establish the cost basis of their services for rate setting purposes, and to function as self-sustaining economic units. By the end of the 1990s, many of these public hospitals had either been closed, with arrangements to pay existing nonprofit or for-profit hospitals for the costs of providing care for eligible persons, or the hospitals had been leased or sold to a nonprofit, or for-profit, health-care corporation. The municipal or county government continues to be responsible for only a limited authority function, using whatever health-care funds continue to be under its immediate control to purchase hospital services and other health-care services directly from a variety of health-care providers, or indirectly through managed-care contractual arrangements.

This separation of *authority* from *provider* functions, with the use of nonprofit, quasi-governmental organizations, and for-profit firms as service providers, is proceeding relentlessly through all areas of governmental activity. Included are the contractual purchase of naval vessels rather than construction in navy shipyards, contractual waste collection services, independent charter schools receiving public educational funds, managed-care contracts for the provision of health-care services rather than the operation of municipal public health clinic services, managed-care contracts for the provision of mental health services rather than direct provision of such services by the staff of a community mental health center, contractual arrangements for the care of dependent and delinquent adolescents who are under the legal guardianship of a state child welfare agency, contractual operation of adult prisons, contractual operation of a variety of substance abuse treatment programs, and contractual arrangements for the provision of job training and job placement for adult caretakers receiving support payments under the TANF program.

The rapid expansion of privatization reflects a variety of forces (Starr 1985). The original concept of the governmental service organization, or governmental bureau, included an expectation of long-term, stable operations, and, in turn, long-term stable employment. Civil service procedures were established at all levels of government in an effort to prevent the use of employment in governmental service organizations for political patronage purposes. These procedures protected existing employees from being discharged, or arbitrarily reassigned, for political reasons. One indirect result was that existing organizational and program structures were also largely protected from pressures to change.

Employment in a single governmental organization could be a lifetime career—for example, for many persons in prison administration or in public schools. By the end of the 1940s, a similar pattern of protected employment had developed in many state and county public assistance programs and child welfare programs, as well as in public hospitals, state schools for the mentally retarded, and state psychiatric hospitals. In many instances, support staff had more continuity of employment than the professional staff members (who were more likely to change jobs) and therefore more seniority in the employment system. These long-term support staff members often had de facto control of defining the institutional memory—"How things are done here." In a number of states, these long-term employees became members of statewide public service employee unions and had better connections with political leaders in their communities, and with the legislative appropriation process, than the professional staff or even senior managers.

However, such stable, long-term governmental service operations had several liabilities. Such organizations were often slow to adopt new technologies, or, in the case of computer systems, they had sometimes invested in a mix of incompatible systems that could not communicate with each other, in part because of rigid competitive bidding requirements. These organizations were often slow to respond to changes in the organizational environment, including demographic changes, particularly if seniority was the sole criterion for promotion. Some of the governmental service organizations also tended to expand at middle management levels as promotions were used to recognize exceptional performance because individual in-grade pay increases, beyond the defined pay scale, were largely unavailable.

In part, these operational problems were a function of legislative limitations, but in part they were also the consequence of internal organizational forces. Public employee unions made demands for improved fringe benefits and across-the-board pay increases, together with protection of existing employment structures. Stability and predictability, rather than the possibility of high entrepreneurial income, was a major attraction of public employment. Persons in the general community, including service users and their families, sometimes viewed public employees as the primary beneficiaries of the service organization, particularly if the availability of services to the general public was restricted because of budgetary constraints without a reduction in staff.

In small town and rural areas, public service employment, particularly in the public school system or in large residential institutions, including prisons, state schools, and psychiatric hospitals, was often one of the most consistent and dependable forces in the local economy, independent of the quality of services being provided. This was reflected in the politics of governmental budgets, particularly when members of legislative bodies from stable rural and small town areas had more seniority than members from rapidly changing, politically volatile urban areas. Moreover, officials in public policy positions often had a very limited choice, either to fund an existing, often inadequate, program, or to have no service resource at all.

The pressures for privatization and, in turn, a reduction in the number of permanent governmental employees came both from within government and from outside interests. Political opposition to imposing increased taxes resulted in freezing, or cutting, governmental budgets—federal, state, and local. The growing number of entrepreneurial for-profit human service industries, in health care, mental health care, and criminal justice, viewed existing pools of governmental funding as potential growth opportunities. Many of these industries could point to lower unit costs for similar services—slimmer management staffs, less generous fringe benefits, less strict personnel policies and procedures, and the use of contemporary technologies.

The result of all these developments has been a rapid growth across all governmental levels in the separation of authority functions from provider functions and the use of POSCs to provide specific tax-supported services (Green 1998). In turn, a new political constituency supporting increased expenditures for human service programs has been created, consisting of contractee organizations, trade associations of such organizations, as well as members of boards of directors with political connections and associations of employees in contractee organizations. The participants in this constituency are able to be much more aggressive in legislative lobbying than the executive and staff members of the public authority through which the funding is to be channeled.

PURCHASE-OF-SERVICE CONTRACTS The introduction of governmental contracting for human service programs has brought new complexities for both the funding source and the organization receiving a contract (Salamon 1989; Grønbjerg 1993). POSCs can be based primarily on specifications for the service process (process contract) or they can be based on the expected results—outputs or outcomes (performance contract) (Green 1998). The contracting processes involve not only formal interfaces between different types of organizations but also interfaces between different types of policy-making constituencies—on one hand, legislative bodies and elected public officials, and on the other volunteer boards of directors, and in some instances corporate boards of directors. New structures for coordination and for accountability are required (Kettner and Martin 1985). Procedures involved for policy decision making by the authority organization and for sharing information with providers require explicit contract provisions covering joint decision making and communication. Contract provisions defining the legal authority of the funding organization to change program policies, with or without advance notice to the organization providing the services, are required. Issues of the assignment of organizational responsibility in the instance of injuries to service users have to be dealt with.

Although POSCs may provide important program funding for a service organization, all such contracting procedures involve substantial constraints on the contractee organization (Smith and Lipsky 1993; Green 1998). When the organization receiving the contract is a private, nonprofit organization, these constraints include limits on the authority of the board of directors to control operational policies in the organization for which they are legally responsible. These constraints may be specified in legislation, in regulations adopted to implement legislation, or in procedures established administratively by the funding authority. These may be specified at another level of government and may not be open to negotiation, or modification, by the funding organization.

Because of time limitations and deadlines, boards of directors of service organizations may not have an opportunity to be fully informed about these constraints before being asked to approve a POSC. These constraints may take the form of explicit mandates (you *will* serve the following groups of individuals: individuals with particular mental illness conditions who are defined as being a member of a "priority population") or explicit constraints (you will *not* provide services to the following groups of persons: immigrants without official documentation).

A number of different factors may affect the quality of contract performance by contractee organizations, including clarity between the contracting authority and the contractee as to what is being sought through the contract, and the frequency of contact between the contract manager and the contractee management (Peat and Cosley 2000). An effective system of contract accountability requires reporting procedures, and procedures for review, or audit, of those reports (McDonald 1997). These procedures must deal with the authority of the funding body to obtain information, and the extent to which information dealing with individual service situations is confidential or privileged and, therefore, not available to the funding organization, even if payment under the contract is tied to evidence of the services provided. Contracts with for-profit organizations have to deal with the issue of access to proprietary information that may be defined as affecting the competitive position of the service organization.

One of the implicit consequences of the separation of authority and provider functions with the use of contracting procedures is that the governmental funding authority may be expected to produce "public goods"—that is, benefits to the general community. However, the direct service organization receiving the funds, particularly the for-profit firm, is accountable under the contract only for producing "private goods" benefits for individual service users (Salamon 1993). This is only one of a number of potential sources of strain and conflict within the contractual relationship.

Much of the contracting in human service programs that has existed in the past—public child welfare organizations contracting with residential treatment centers—has been sole-source, or "closed," contracting (Grønbjerg 1993). The funding authority negotiates the terms of a contract with a single provider organization, or perhaps with several "recognized" organizations individually, formalizing funding arrangements for a given time period in what is an ongoing working relationship that has extended over a number of years.

In sole-source contracting by public authorities with nonprofit service organizations, there is often an assumption that the organization should be expected to subsidize, in part, the costs associated with the contracted services from its own "charitable" resources. Therefore, the funding provisions are often set at a level that is acknowledged to be below the actual costs of providing the services (Kettner and Martin 1996).

There is an additional level of complexity when competitive, or "open," bidding for POSC is introduced. The complexities include the establishment of legal procedures for preparing and submitting bids; the avoidance of any appearance of preferential treatment for any individual bidder, including contacts between staff members of the funding authority and the organizations submitting bids, except as all bidders, or potential bidders, are part of the same process; formal procedures for the evaluation of proposals; and confidentiality of financial information included in a bid.

If both nonprofit and for-profit organizations are able to submit proposals on an equal basis, the bidding specifications must include provisions for inclusion of the costs of organizational overhead and corporate profit for the for-profit organization, as well as for the potential tax liabilities for which only for-profit firms may be responsible. These financial allowances for for-profit firms, however, may be excluded in making the cost comparisons used in determining the successful bidder.

Several organizations must invest personnel and financial resources in the preparation of detailed bid proposals under competitive bidding procedures. Provisions must be made in the bidding procedures for review of the bidding decisions and even for legal appeals of the outcome of the bidding process. If competitive bidding procedures are intended to increase the possibilities for program flexibility and adaptation, then provisions must exist not only for competitive bidding but also for contract termination, and for contracts to be switched from one service-providing organization to another from one bidding cycle to the next.

Financial provisions may be included in the contract for reimbursement to the service provider if a contract is cut back, or terminated, before the contract period is completed, even if the cause is a legislative reduction in the governmental funds available for such services or an unexpected reduction in the number of persons expected to use the service. Some POSCs, however, are intended to make the contracting service provider assume most, or all, of the financial risks that may be involved, including unexpected increases in costs (health insurance costs for staff members), or lower than expected levels of service utilization resulting in lower payments from the contracting organization.

The establishment of competitive bidding processes does not ensure that there will, in fact, be competition. The competitive bidding process assumes that there is more than one organization that has, in advance, the financial and personnel resources to prepare bid submissions and to operate the service program if there is a contract, and to survive if a contract is not received. Larger and more diversified organizations have an advantage. Organizations that have an existing contract have inherent advantages over competing organizations. For-profit organizations may have access to operating lines of credit that nonprofit organizations do not have, and these can be used to cover gaps in funding cycles.

The establishment of the initial contracting procedures involves complex boundary-spanning processes between the funding authority and the potential bidders. Similar boundary-spanning procedures are required for the establishment of the procedures that will be used to govern quality control and evaluation, including access to service data and case information if a contract is offered. These boundary-spanning negotiations normally involve the executive and other agency staff persons in the provider organization. After the negotiations, the nonprofit board of directors may be presented with a completed contract document accompanied by a request to act promptly in order to meet a deadline established by the funding organization.

The 1990s brought a rapidly changing and complex set of relationships between governmental funding sources and nonprofit, as well as for-profit, provider service organizations. As funding and contracting organizations, governmental authorities must deal with a wide range of policy and administrative issues for which there are limited precedents. Central to these issues are those of equal treatment in the contracting process, and of the balance between program flexibility and accountability for the use of public funds. But most important is the issue of the accountability of provider organizations, and ultimately the governmental funding organization, for the quality of services provided. Among the consequences for the nonprofit contractees are an increase in the authority and responsibility of the executive, in comparison with the board of directors (Saidel and Harlan 1998), and an increasingly complex pattern of financial management. This can result in pressures for organizational consolidation in order to create the larger pool of financial resources required to operate in a competitive marketplace-like environment.

Foundation Grants

Foundations are a widely recognized source of special-purpose grants, although grants may also come from other sources, including governmental bodies. Grants may be similar in some characteristics to contracts, but they generally are not legally constrained and involve less detailed specifications of the ways in which the funds may be used. Foundation grants have been an increasingly important source of funding support for nonprofit, and sometimes governmental, service programs, as foundation endowments have increased and as funding from governmental sources has been reduced or has involved severe constraints (Clotfelter and Ehrlich 1999).

The creation of charitable foundations as a way for persons with wealth to establish an ongoing source of financial support for activities in which they are interested has a long history. In the late 1800s, the creation of charitable foundations by wealthy individuals became one response to public criticism of the existence of extreme wealth in the midst of the exploitation of industrial workers and widespread poverty. Many of the largest of the current national foundations reflect wealth created through successful business activities in the past—Russell Sage Foundation, Ford Foundation, W. K. Kellogg Foundation, Pew Charitable Trusts, Carnegie Foundation of New York, Rockefeller Foundation.

The original bequests that established these and other foundations were generally invested in stocks and bonds. The result is that the current values of foundation endowments is many times larger than the original bequest. Current foundations also include those established by business firms as a method for using tax-exempt corporate contributions to provide support for community services in communities where business activities are centered, and for other projects that have the support of corporate leaders.

A more recent version of the charitable foundation is the community foundation that is established to administer a number of small or medium-sized charitable bequests focused in a single community, such as the Cleveland Foundation, one of the earliest of such community foundations. Still more recent are the foundations being created when private, nonprofit hospitals are purchased by a for-profit health-care firm, such as Columbia-HCA (Health Corporation of America). The purchase price and any endowment funds that are associated with the institution are converted into a charitable foundation, often administered by members of the original board of the voluntary nonprofit hospital (Maynard and Poole 1998).

Foundation boards of directors have wide discretion in the use of the foundation resources. Some foundations have explicit political or philosophical objectives, with foundation support for nationally recognized researchers and for writers supporting specific policy positions. However, the federal government has substantial authority in relation to the financial administration of foundations, since they are exempt from federal income tax payments on the income earned from invested funds. Because of a concern that some foundations were being used to shelter large amounts of personal and business income from tax obligations with a very limited record of grant making, Congress included in the Tax Reform Act of 1969 a requirement that philanthropic foundations pay out each year the income from endowment investments and, in addition, 5 percent of the core endowments themselves. However, in recent years, even with these requirements, the value of the invested endowment in many foundations has continued to increase as a result of careful attention to investments, even while expenditures in the form of grants have also continued to increase.

Members of a family that has created a charitable foundation, or unpaid members of a board of directors, often serve as the grant decision makers in many of the small to medium-sized foundations, reviewing each of the many requests received. Larger foundations employ professional foundation management staff. The foundation staff members, in addition to overseeing the investments of the foundation, screen requests for grants against criteria set by the foundation board, investigate the background of those persons and organizations making requests, oversee the payment of approved grants, monitor the performance of organizations receiving a grant, and review periodic reports from grantees.

Members of foundation boards of directors and the grants management staff constitute an important funder constituency, at both local and national levels. Moreover, the development of an active pattern of networking and conferencing involving foundation board members and foundation staff members means that this is, in many ways, a semi-organized constituency. At a national level, this constituency, operating through such organizations as the Council of Foundations and Grantmakers in Health, can have an important influence on policy and funding decisions in the federal government. This is accomplished through research reports and other publications, through the active involvement of foundation board members and staff members in federal advisory bodies, through the sponsorship of conferences dealing with national policy issues, and through the choice of projects receiving financial support through foundations.

Foundations are limited to making grants to tax-exempt organizations, including voluntary nonprofit organizations, semi-governmental nonprofit organizations, and governmental bodies, or to individuals as part of a larger program of grants—for example, scholarships to university students. Traditionally, charitable foundations have acted on requests initiated by outside sources. More recently, however, many foundations have established their own program priorities and have begun to solicit applications that fit those priorities.

Foundations can influence program development at state and local levels by deliberately providing program grants to support specific types of organizations or programs that may have difficulty in obtaining financial support from traditional sources. In the late 1950s, the Ford Foundation initiated "grey areas" projects in five cities and one state (North Carolina) as part of a larger effort to address problems in central city areas. This initiative contributed directly to the establishment of the President's Committee on Juvenile Delinquency and Youth Crime in 1961. The demonstration projects funded by the President's Committee, in turn, led to the inclusion of community action programs in the War on Poverty legislation under President Johnson. Many foundations that do not have specific developmental objectives do have an established set of funding priorities, as well as explicit criteria as to the type of grant proposal that they will consider. Many foundations have now established web pages that provide information about program priorities and grant application procedures.

Foundations generally provide time-limited grants focused on new program development, support of a time-limited research project, funding support for a particular event, and so forth. Most foundations do not provide funds for the continuation of ongoing service programs unless it is a program that has been deliberately initiated by the foundation. Many foundations also do not provide funds for "bricks and mortar"— that is, for physical facilities; however, some foundations restrict their grants to such building projects.

Foundations have a strong power position vis-à-vis organizations making requests, because they receive more requests than they have resources for. That makes it possible for the foundations to require the preparation of detailed plans for a proposed program or activity. There are often other requirements, such as the raising of matching funds, periodic reports on progress once a grant is made, and provisions for evaluation of the outcomes achieved with the grant funds. A foundation may require commitments that alternative sources of future funding will be developed for a service program initiated with foundation funds. Representatives from requesting organizations may be asked to meet with foundation program officers, or program officers may make a site visit. Foundations may also have a grant review cycle that involves a lag time of several months before there is a final decision.

Although the funds provided through a foundation grant can make an important addition to organizational resources, they may also require a substantial investment of personnel and time resources (Grønbjerg 1993). A three-year grant for a new, or experimental, program often involves a developmental period for the first year, a second year of full-scale operation, a third year of evaluation, and a potential phase-out. Additional fund-raising activities must be initiated or existing financial resources must be diverted to the continuation of the grant-initiated program if the foundation-supported activity is to be maintained rather than being phased out. The new program may become a high priority for the service organization at the expense of existing program components, either because of the effectiveness of the program or because of the status and visibility of the foundation constituency that makes it important for the service organization to maintain the program.

Investment Income

Long-established nonprofit service organizations may have a funding stream from endowments created from past contributions that were not used for ongoing program operations. In many instances, these endowments were created through large contributions from individuals who had a particular interest in a given organization, or from their estates. Many voluntary nonprofit service organizations actively seek such endowment contributions to increase the size of the endowment and the level of consistent annual income from the endowment investments. Income tax and inheritance tax regulations complicate the making of such contributions, but they may also provide positive financial incentives for the donor.

Where organizational endowments do exist, the management of such funds may be one of the important responsibilities of the nonprofit board of directors. The endowment, like the board of directors, becomes part of the legal continuity of the organization. The board of directors is particularly accountable for the prudent investment of such funds and the prudent use of the income from such funds. A board officer, such as the board treasurer, may be assigned direct responsibility for overseeing the investment of the endowment funds.

In organizations with large endowments, organizational staff specialists may handle the investments. However, the foundation may also contract with an outside organization to handle investments. The board of directors establishes the guidelines for investments, balancing growth against the need for current income, and deciding whether to exclude some types of investments when such an action would be consistent with the mission of the service organization. Thus the American Cancer Society avoids investments in tobacco companies.

The income from endowment funds, even if only a small part of the total budget, can be particularly crucial because it is one of the limited sources of funding that the board and staff may be able to use flexibly for expenses not provided for in more constrained forms of the funding. However, the temptation to seek high returns on investments has, on occasion, left service organizations with a serious shortfall when such investments have collapsed.

In some instances, nonprofit service organizations may receive funding prior to incurring the costs for which the funding is to be used. This can occur in organizations that conduct a major membership funding campaign once a year, or that have a substantial profit from a special fund-raising event. This may provide an opportunity for short-term investments in certificates of deposit, which are covered by governmental insurance against any loss in value, or other interest earning investments, rather than being deposited in the corporate checking account.

Nonprofit service organizations may also have access to other forms of investment income. In some instances, an organization that has an operating surplus at the end of a given year may place those funds in a special operating-reserve investment account against the possibility of unanticipated funding requirements at a later date. Such funds may also be placed in a special reserve for capital expenditures that do not lend themselves to a special fund-raising effort. These may include periodic building maintenance costs or equipment replacement. Governmental service programs, on the other hand, are usually not able to retain any operating surplus or to establish reserve funds under the control of the service organization.

Funding sources may attempt to limit such opportunities for investment income by advancing funds throughout the year rather than all at one time, or by requiring that such investment earnings be credited against the funding commitment. On the other hand, some funding sources provide reimbursement only after expenditures have occurred and the provision of services has been documented, thus retaining any potential income from short-term investments for themselves.

For-profit organizations have much greater flexibility in managing funds to produce investment income. In managed health-care organizations, as well as in traditional indemnity health insurance companies, premium payments are received before health-care expenditures are required. Surplus funds may be placed in short-term high-interest investments in the interim, particularly if payments to individual service providers are deliberately delayed. For-profit organizations are able to smooth out variations in income flow through bank loans against anticipated income. Such organizations are also able to expand their programs in response to new opportunities through commercial loans based on the financial record of the business, with physical facilities used as loan collateral, or through the sale of additional shares of stock. These financing strategies are generally not available to either nonprofit service organizations or governmental agencies. As a response to the financing options that are available to for-profit organizations, some nonprofit organizations, particularly in the health-care field, have converted to for-profit status (Goddeeris and Weisbrod 1997).

SUMMARY

Legitimators and funders are critical organizational constituencies that have ultimate control over the continuing existence of voluntary nonprofit and governmental service agencies. They are also characteristic of for-profit human service firms if the terms include shareholders, banks, and other sources of commercial credit, and government regulatory authorities. The constraints imposed by legitimators and funders are major factors in the ability of the service organization to fulfill its mission and meet its operating objectives.

Many changes are taking place in the pattern of human service funding within the United States. Privatization highlights the role of governmental bodies as primarily funding authorities and expands the role of nonprofit and for-profit service organizations as providers (Salamon 1995). Contracts for service provision have become the most important source of funding for many nonprofit organizations. Contracting shifts the funding relationship between governmental bodies and service organizations (both nonprofit and for-profit) to a more business-like relationship. Consolidations and expansions are taking place among nonprofit service agencies so that they can be more effective in this complex funding environment. Executive responsibilities for financial management are becoming more complex, and computer-based accounting systems are becoming essential. Voluntary nonprofit boards of directors are often being expected to carry an expanded responsibility for contributions, although their role in managing purchase-of-service contract relationships is constrained.

Nonprofit organizations, including quasi-governmental nonprofits, often draw funding support from a variety of funding sources. Relationships between the organization and the several funding constituencies must be a central concern of organizational leadership, including members of boards of directors. Leaders of nonprofit organizations have a broad spectrum of choices for future funding strategies ranging from maximizing internal fund-raising to becoming an organization wholly funded through governmental contracts. Each of these funding sources has a different constituency structure, provides a different set of opportunities, and involves a different set of constraints and expectations. Strategic planning includes an examination of funding support options and a careful analysis of the organizational implications of the several alternatives. Such an analysis should include an examination of the implications of different funding sources for the roles of the executive, the executive staff, and the board of directors.

NINE

THE HUMAN SERVICE EXECUTIVE

My only thesis is that in the more progressively managed businesses there is a tendency for the control of a particular situation to go to the man with the largest knowledge of that situation, to him who can grasp and organize its essential elements, who understands its total significance, who can see it through—who can see length as well as breadth—rather than to one with merely a dominating personality or in virtue of his official position.
—Mary Parker Follett (in Graham 1995:175)

All managers have two jobs—handling today's issues and getting ready for the future.   —Rosabeth Moss Kanter (1997:3)

THERE ARE two highly visible and distinctive models of the organizational executive. The most widely recognized model is that of the chief executive officer (CEO) of the for-profit corporate firm. The corporate executive role combines policy making—as a member of the corporate board of directors—and implementation—as the senior manager. Conceptually, this version of the CEO role is applicable in the small, entrepreneurial firm and in the multinational corporate giant. And ultimately, a single yardstick measures the effectiveness of executive performance in the for-profit corporation—financial returns to the owner shareholders.

The second widely recognized executive model is that of the career generalist public administrator—the federal department executive, the state agency administrator, the city manager (Gortner, Mahler, and Nicholson 1987). According to traditional principles of public administration (Wilson 1887), the public administrator is responsible for policy implementation but is not a policy maker. Members of elected legislative bodies and those elected officials who may also be organizational managers, such as the president of the United States, make policy. This public administration role is, conceptually, a more complex version of the executive role than the for-profit executive (Gortner, Mahler, and Nichol-son 1987), because a number of different yardsticks are used to measure the effectiveness of the performance of the public administrator.

These yardsticks include consistency of implementation with legislative intent, continuity of the governmental organization, break-even financial management (that is, operating within the limits of available financial resources), maintenance of a consistent pattern of operation in which all members of the general public are dealt with evenhandedly on the basis of specific rules and regulations, and contribution to maintaining trust in the implicit political "contract" between the general body of citizens and the administrative structure of government. However, in the instance of the generalist public administrator, as for the corporate CEO, the quality of the products/services produced by the organization, while important, is not, in reality, the ultimate yardstick for judging executive performance.

Analyses of the executive role in voluntary nonprofit, quasi-governmental nonprofit, and governmental human service organizations draw, in varying degrees, on both the model of the corporate CEO and the generalist public administrator. The position of human service executive is shaped, in part, by the organizational characteristics that nonprofit and governmental human service organizations share with other types of formal organizations. These include, in particular, service-producing organizations (Fitzsimmons and Fitzsimmons 1994) that are also professional bureaucracies (Mintzberg 1979). But the human service executive role is also shaped by the distinctive characteristics of human service organizations (see chapter 2).

Human service executives in both nonprofit and governmental organizations, like corporate executives, are usually active participants in the process of organizational policy formation as well as in policy implementation, even though the executive position is not formally defined as a policy-determining position. Most policy action issues in human service organizations come to a policy board or a legislative body as a recommendation from the executive, and with the executive as participant in the policy discussion. In the nonprofit service organization, in particular, the interaction between the executive and the volunteer board of directors in establishing organizational policies, without the executive being a voting member of the board, is a distinctive element of the executive role (Menefee 1997).

Like the generalist public administrator, human service executives are responsible for the congruence of implementation to enacted policy, whether or not it is the policy that they have recommended. They are also responsible for organizational continuity, and for break-even financial performance. And, like the generalist public administrator, the human service executive has no direct personal economic stake in the financial performance of the organization. That is, executive salaries, in nonprofit as well as in governmental human service organizations, do not increase in proportion to the size of the organizational budget, nor do they include special bonuses based on financial performance (Gibelman 2000a).

However, the role of the executive in human service organizations is, in many ways, a more distinctive role and even more complicated than either of the two more widely recognized roles (Austin 1989). One of the critical differences is that the most important yardstick for judging executive performance in a human service organization is the quality of services produced by the organization as well as the quantity of those services (Patti 1988). Another distinctive characteristic of the role of the human service executive is that the executive must often deal with the interface between two distinctive social structures—the service production organization and the organized human service profession (see chapter 7).

THE EXECUTIVE POSITION

The referent in this discussion is *the executive*. In new, start-up organizations, and in many small, simple-structure organizations, a single executive often handles all the executive functions, together with some direct service functions, or executive functions are divided between an employed executive and members of a board of directors. However, it is important to note that in many, if not most, medium-sized or large human service organizations, the executive component involves at least two persons, and sometimes more. That is, the complexity of the executive functions, as described later, in the contemporary social, political, and economic environment, frequently requires more than one individual to carry out the executive functions—often individuals with different sets of skills and different priorities.

Characteristics of the executive position have been analyzed in a variety of ways. The approach used in this analysis is based on the concept that the executive position, and the preferred style of executive performance, involves an interactive, adaptive, "contingency" process involving the executive, the operational characteristics of the particular organization, and the situation of that organization in its environment.

There is no single, universal definition of the characteristics of the human service executive position. Human service organizations producing similar products but in different environments may require different mixes of elements in the executive position. Human service organizations include those that are essentially professional group practice arrangements, in which the manager has a subordinate power position (Mintzberg 1983), as, for example, a general hospital in which the medical staff selects the hospital administrator. However, in most governmental and nonprofit human service organizations, the executive has major responsibility and authority for the organization as a whole, although the ultimate policy authority—the governmental legislative body or the nonprofit board of directors—is separated from the role of the executive. Different individuals may shape the specific elements in the executive position in different ways. The following discussion examines an inclusive model that may be useful, however, in analyzing the mix of elements in the executive position in a given organization at a particular time.

THE "COMPETING-VALUES" MODEL
OF MANAGEMENT FUNCTIONS

One inclusive framework for the analysis of the management functions in human service organizations and the position of the executive is the competing-values model presented by Quinn and Rohrbaugh in "A Spatial Model of Effectiveness Criteria: Towards a Competing Values Approach to Organizational Analysis" (1983) and by Quinn in *Beyond Rational Management: Mastering the Paradoxes and Competing Demands of High Performance* (1988:48) (figure 9.1). This analytic framework is built around two dimensions that represent competing orientations, or values, in the organizational context: (1) control–flexibility and

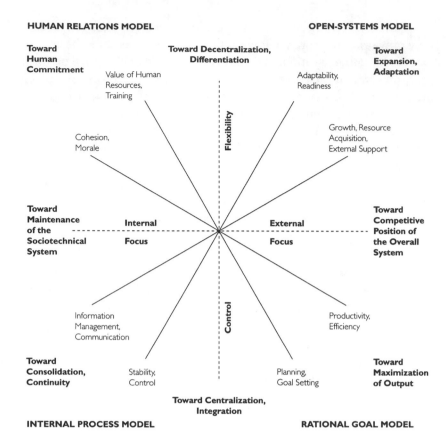

HUMAN RELATIONS MODEL

OPEN-SYSTEMS MODEL

Toward Human Commitment

Value of Human Resources, Training

Toward Decentralization, Differentiation

Adaptability, Readiness

Toward Expansion, Adaptation

Cohesion, Morale

Flexibility

Growth, Resource Acquisition, External Support

Toward Maintenance of the Sociotechnical System

Internal Focus

External Focus

Toward Competitive Position of the Overall System

Information Management, Communication

Control

Productivity, Efficiency

Toward Consolidation, Continuity

Stability, Control

Planning, Goal Setting

Toward Maximization of Output

Toward Centralization, Integration

INTERNAL PROCESS MODEL

RATIONAL GOAL MODEL

FIGURE 9.1. The competing-values framework: Effectiveness.

With permission from Quinn, Robert E. 1988. *Beyond Rational Management: Mastering the Paradoxes and Competing Demands of High Performance.* San Francisco: Jossey-Bass.

(2) internal–external. The combination of these two dimensions distinguishes four sectors of executive activity with different, and often competing, requirements for organizational effectiveness: (1) human resources mobilization and motivation, (2) organization and control of production processes, (3) resource acquisition and adaptation to the task environment, and (4) goal-oriented management.

These four sectors are used by Quinn and Rohrbaugh as a framework for assessing organizational effectiveness. Rojas (2000), in an analysis of four different frameworks, identifies this one as the most useful for assessing organizational effectiveness. This competing-values analysis has been applied to the assessment of the performance effectiveness of the human service organization (Edwards, Faerman, and McGrath 1985; Edwards, Austin, and Altpeter 1998). In combination, these four sectors deal with the two major criteria for assessing organizational results—quality of services produced and continuity of the organization (Austin 1989).

This analytic framework can also be used for examining the component skill requirements of the executive position in human service organizations (figure 9.2) (Quinn 1988:86). No single executive position involves equal emphasis on all four of these sectors. In any given organization, the executive may be primarily involved in some sectors while other persons who are part of the executive component may carry major responsibility for other sectors. Yet it is the executive who is ultimately responsible for the effectiveness of organizational performance in all four sectors. The following material, based on work by Quinn (1988), summarizes some of the key requirements of executive performance associated with each sector.

Human Relations—Mobilization and Motivation of Human Resources

One of the major sectors of executive responsibility involves the mobilization and motivation of the personnel who constitute the human resources of the organization (Weiner 1991). "Managers have the fundamental, enduring job of mobilizing and motivating individual human talent in pursuit of collective ends" (Kanter 1997:6). This "talent" includes employees, but it also includes, in many human service organizations, volunteers. Given the role of co-production in human service organizations, service users are, in reality, also part of the human resources of the organization (Fitzsimmons and Fitzsimmons 1994). This sector is particularly critical in labor-intensive human service organizations, in which most of the services are produced and delivered through person-to-person interactions. In the competing-values model, the performance values in this sector are defined by the dimensions of *internal* and *flexible*.

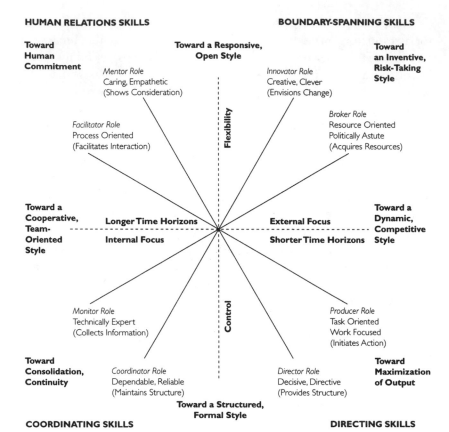

HUMAN RELATIONS SKILLS

BOUNDARY-SPANNING SKILLS

Toward Human Commitment

Toward a Responsive, Open Style

Toward an Inventive, Risk-Taking Style

Mentor Role
Caring, Empathetic
(Shows Consideration)

Innovator Role
Creative, Clever
(Envisions Change)

Facilitator Role
Process Oriented
(Facilitates Interaction)

Broker Role
Resource Oriented
Politically Astute
(Acquires Resources)

Flexibility

Toward a Cooperative, Team-Oriented Style

Longer Time Horizons

External Focus

Toward a Dynamic, Competitive Style

Internal Focus

Shorter Time Horizons

Control

Monitor Role
Technically Expert
(Collects Information)

Producer Role
Task Oriented
Work Focused
(Initiates Action)

Toward Consolidation, Continuity

Coordinator Role
Dependable, Reliable
(Maintains Structure)

Director Role
Decisive, Directive
(Provides Structure)

Toward Maximization of Output

Toward a Structured, Formal Style

COORDINATING SKILLS

DIRECTING SKILLS

FIGURE 9.2. The competing-values framework of leadership roles.

With permission from Quinn, Robert E. 1988. *Beyond Rational Management: Mastering the Paradoxes and Competing Demands of High Performance.* San Francisco: Jossey-Bass.

The focus in this sector is on the role of the executive in dealing with those individuals who are internal to the organization, including service users, whose competencies directly shape the service production process. Symbols and traditions, the use of special events, and definitions of the organizational mission and of organizational values are all elements of the organizational culture that may be significant in motivating these individuals.

Quinn (1988) identifies two manager roles in this sector: mentor and group facilitator.

> *Mentor:* The manager is also expected . . . to engage in the development of people through a caring, empathetic orientation. . . . He or she listens, supports legitimate requests, conveys appreciation, and gives compliments and credit. . . . The leader helps with skill building, provides training opportunities, and helps people develop plans for their own individual development.

> *Facilitator:* The facilitator is expected to foster collective effort, to build cohesion and teamwork, and to manage interpersonal conflict. . . . Expected behaviors include intervening in interpersonal disputes, using conflict reduction techniques, developing cohesion and morale, obtaining input and participation, and facilitating group problem solving.
>
> Quinn (1988:41–42)

In many human service organizations, the employed staff includes members of one or more professional disciplines, an important factor in the decentralized pattern of interpersonal relationships to be dealt with (see chapter 7). One of the important internal dynamics may be competition among professional groups for control over power positions within the organization and, therefore, for access to resources (Mintzberg 1983:401). Perceived distinctions between organizational employees and members of organized professions, or between service providers and support staff, may also be important factors that must be dealt with in the effective mobilization of personnel resources for service production. Even more critical may be perceived distinctions between employees and service users, including gender, ethnic, income status, or wellness distinctions that may constitute barriers to effective service co-production.

The processes of human resources mobilization and motivation are often identified, as they are in the Quinn framework, with the terms *human relations skills* and *commitment,* or with an emphasis on *cohesion/morale,* as in the Blake and Mouton managerial grid (1964). The human relations model for human resource mobilization and motivation, emphasizing group processes, team-building, and participatory decision making (McGregor 1960; Argyris 1964; Ouchi 1981), has been advocated as being particularly congruent with, and supportive of, the humanistic and service orientations of human service practitioners (Fallon 1978). A strong emphasis on the importance of organizational mission and commitment as the primary sources of employee motivation may also be associated, in part, with the fact that few human service organizations, for either ideological reasons, structural reasons, or financial reasons, use tangible motivations, including financial rewards or rapid career advancement, as major methods of individual motivation.

Under the participatory human relations model, a primary role of the executive may be viewed as being the "team leader." Although there may be important functions for time-limited, special-purpose teams (Bailey 1998), it is not clear that the human relations model of management, focused around the approaches used to improve *work group* performance in industrial production, including T-groups, management by objectives, parallel organizations, and quality circles, is the relevant model for the mobilization and motivation of personnel throughout human service organizations.

> The participative style is more conducive to creative or innovative solutions and leaves participants more satisfied with the decision that is ultimately reached. However, it does so at the expense of efficiency and, occasionally, the internal harmony of the group. This is because participation is prone to generate more diverse opinions, hence more conflict and confusion in the decision-making process—all of which takes more time—than does centralization.
>
> Howell (1976:85)

In the human service organization, the quality of service often depends on the competence and commitment of individual service providers interacting with individual service users in a co-production process, rather than on the work group or work team. Indeed, decentralized individual responsibility, or professional autonomy, may be more important in motivation than elaborate group participation processes in an organization in which ultimate authority is, in reality, highly centralized. To the extent that a model of participatory decision making refers only to service specialists, the interests of other stakeholders, such as support staff personnel and service users, may be undervalued. Moreover, critical as it is, the mobilization and motivation of organizational human resources is only one of four critical sectors of executive performance.

Internal Process—Organization of Production Processes

Given the labor-intensive, individualized nature of most human service production activities, the systematic organization of service activities and the monitoring of service production are also major functional elements in the executive position. In the competing-values model, this sector is defined by the dimensions of *internal* and *control*. This sector involves the technical areas commonly dealt with in discussions of management tasks (the organizing, staffing, directing, coordinating, reporting, and budgeting functions of the classical model of public administration)— that is, budgeting and fiscal controls, time control and scheduling procedures, information and communication systems, personnel administration systems, the structure of formal authority and reporting systems, technical training programs, evaluation and quality control, technical equipment, and management of facilities. These tasks, which are primarily associated with bureaucratic structure in the professional bureaucracy (Mintzberg 1979), are normally described as being defined and enforced centrally in order to establish consistency of procedures throughout the organization and consistency in communications with external constituencies. The tasks are often governed by written directives and operational manuals.

Quinn (1988) identifies two manager roles in this sector: monitor and coordinator.

> *Monitor:* A manager is expected to know what is going on in the unit, to determine if people are complying with the rules, and to see if the unit is meeting its quota. The monitor . . . is good at quantitative analysis. Behaviors in this role include handling paper work, reviewing and responding to routine information, and carrying out inspections, tours, and reviews of printouts and reports.

> *Coordinator:* A manager is expected to maintain the structure and flow of the system. . . . Behaviors include various forms of work facilitation such

as scheduling, organizing and coordinating staff efforts, handling crises, and attending to technological, logistical and housekeeping issues.

Quinn (1988:39)

The executive has responsibility for making certain that there are *established procedures* for determining if the service production activities within the organization are consistent with the mission and goals of the organization, with applicable professional and regulatory standards, and with the requirements and expectations of funding and policy-making sources—both internal and external. Procedures for establishing financial accountability are particularly critical as human service organizations become increasingly dependent on multiple external funding sources, each with distinctive accountability requirements. Failure to deal with financial accountability effectively can lead to the dismissal of the executive and the collapse of the service organization. Recently, the issue of legal liabilities, which leads to the problem of the procurement of liability insurance to protect the financial resources of the service organization, has become of one of the important, internal, centrally controlled management responsibilities (Reamer 1993).

The importance of these financial (*internal* and *control*) functions may lead in some situations to a preference for selecting someone with business management experience or a master's degree in business for an executive position rather than someone with professional experience in, for example, social work. An additional factor currently affecting executive selection is that the development of the private practice option in social work has provided experienced clinical practitioners with an alternative to the concept of internal organizational promotion as a personal career objective.

In a small organization, such as a nonprofit start-up, the executive may carry out many of the tasks involved in this sector directly, in particular the handling of crises. However, these are also the executive tasks that are, in larger organizations, most likely to involve technical staff specialists, and sometimes very sizable staff components—for example, in financial management or personnel administration. This is also an area in which rational and systematic procedures often have their widest application. Indeed, rational models of management focus almost entirely on technologies applicable to this sector.

In the past two decades, computerization has become a major feature in all technical areas, reflecting the fact that these areas often involve structured decision-making choices among known alternatives—the available combinations of direct salary and fringe benefits for staff compensation; the possible variations in employee work schedules and user demand schedules that can be fitted together, using queuing theory, to design the most efficient workload schedule for direct service personnel; the choice of a communication system or of computer software programs for service user records and financial accounting; the design of organizational facilities; and procedures for handling organizational funds.

These are also areas in which consistent decisions, centrally controlled, appear to have a direct connection with efficiency. It is in these areas that command-and-control techniques developed in goods production industries have most frequently been applied. Many of the recent developments in the managing of health-care services under health maintenance organizations are efforts to apply such centralized decision-making procedures to a complex, multiorganization health-care system. One result has been increased attention to the development of diagnostic coding systems, such as the *Diagnostic and Statistical Manual of Mental Disorders* (DSM-IV) for diagnosing mental illness conditions, and best practice protocols, or practice guidelines, for dealing with particular medical conditions.

An initial example of diagnostic codes and related protocols was the establishment, as part of the Medicare program, of diagnostic-related groups (DRGs) to define the expected length of hospitalization for specific medical conditions. However, the effectiveness of such approaches must also be judged by their impact on the equally important processes of motivation and commitment among the people involved in the organization. The development of the concept of sociotechnical design represents one effort to combine the objectives of efficiency and personnel motivation (Barko and Pasmore 1986).

In human service organizations, in particular, this sector also involves complex decisions about program organization, or the structure of production roles involving professional specialists, and professional technology (see chapter 4). These program structure and technology issues include decisions about the most effective and efficient procedures through which specialized professional personnel participate in the implementation of "intensive" technology (Thompson 1967), as well as decisions about the roles of service users, service generalists, paraprofessionals, and support staff, as well as volunteers.

The application of new technologies, either in internal control procedures or in service provision technology, may require substantial restructuring of the staff organization, including the termination of existing personnel and the employment of new personnel with different skills. However, efforts to avoid such changes may make the organization less effective in responding to the needs of service users. The management of such structural change processes makes additional demands on the organizational executive and often also on the policy-making body (see chapter 12).

Given the complexities and uncertainties of professional production activities in human service organizations, executive performance in this sector is often viewed as being based primarily on the background of professional experience of the executive rather than on knowledge about more general management technologies, including financial management. Executives in human service organizations, including social service executives and educational executives, are often selected on the basis of professional education and previous professional experience. That is, the executive is viewed as the ultimate professional supervisor. However, although such a background may be a necessary qualification for a human services executive, it is often not a sufficient qualification. Also important is an understanding of the technical requirements involved in the systematic organization of service production and organizational accountability, as well as the competencies involved in the other three sectors of executive performance. However, in many instances, the appointment of a senior professional practitioner to an executive position is not accompanied by any systematic orientation to the particular requirements of the position.

Open Systems—Resource Mobilization and Organizational Adaptation

Given the extent to which human service organizations, nonprofit and governmental, are environmentally dependent (see chapter 2), the executive is constantly involved in activities that cross the boundaries of the organization. These include, among others, financial resource procurement, personnel recruitment, the establishment and maintenance of organizational legitimation, making adaptations in organizational programs in response to environmental changes, managing external requirements for reporting and accountability, negotiation of informal and formal interorganizational agreements on user referral with other service network organizations, cost-sharing in joint projects, and participation in advocacy coalitions.

In the competing-values model, this sector is defined by the dimensions of *flexible* and *external*. It involves dealing with individuals and organizations that are external to the formal boundaries of the organization and not under the control of the organization. Moreover, in dealing with such individuals and organizations, the manager needs to be flexible in defining role boundaries, adaptive, and willing to take risks.

Quinn (1988) identifies two manager roles relevant to this sector: innovator and broker.

> *Innovator:* As an innovator, a manager is expected to facilitate adaptation and change. The innovator absorbs uncertainty by monitoring the outside environment, identifying important trends, and conceptualizing and projecting needed changes. . . . The innovator role requires the manager to rely on induction, ideas and intuitive insights. . . . The manager is expected to be a creative, clever dreamer who sees the future, envisions innovations, packages them in inviting ways, and convinces others that they are necessary and desirable.

> *Broker:* The broker is particularly concerned with maintaining external legitimacy and obtaining external resources. Here the manager is expected to be politically astute, persuasive, influential and powerful. . . . The manager is expected . . . to represent the company and market its products or services, to act as a liaison and spokesperson, and to acquire resources.
>
> Quinn (1988:41)

This sector involves, in particular, the *external, political*, or *open systems* dimension of executive performance, least subject to technical rationalization, or computerization. In periods of system turbulence (Emery and Trist 1965), surveillance of the task environment and the gathering of intelligence about societal changes becomes essential for effective organizational performance, and, indeed, for organizational survival. This sector also includes, as part of the broker role the processes of collaboration, participating with representatives of other organizations in joint initiatives. Goldman and Kahnweiler (2000) report that nonprofit executives who report success in interorganizational collaborations are flexible—that is, they can tolerate ambiguity about the specific boundaries of their role.

The quality of executive performance may be viewed as involving political or negotiating skills and an understanding of the nature of power relationships in the task environment. It is also the sector in which short-term, contingency decision making by the executive may frequently be required, in contrast to the systematic, and longer-term, internal participatory decision-making processes that may be important in human resource mobilization and motivation, or in the establishment of highly structured accountability procedures, including computerization.

This is, perhaps, the sector of activity least likely to be fully delegated to another member of an executive component. However, it may also be the sector that policy makers, both volunteer and legislative, also define as their particular area of activity, with explicit limits being placed on the scope of activities of the executive. For example, the executives of governmental human service organizations are often restricted in their authority to initiate direct lobbying contact with individual members of legislative bodies that control the definition of their legal authority and their operating budget.

The effectiveness of the process of contingency decision making, or strategic adaptation, whether carried out by policy makers or the executive, or both, may be severely constrained by considerations involving the other executive performance sectors. Executive participation in cultivation of potential funding sources or in extensive external advocacy activities, even if successful, may be perceived as limiting the availability of the executive for internal mentoring and group facilitating tasks. Or such activities may involve neglect of critical internal monitoring and reporting responsibilities. Moreover, successful opportunity-seizing initiatives by the executive, involving responses to short-term funding opportunities, may be inconsistent with overall organizational goals, may require substantial expenditures for the development of new technical production procedures, and may disrupt the cohesiveness and morale of organizational participants.

Rational Goal-Directive Management for Goal Accomplishment

A fourth sector of executive performance is the goal-oriented process of improving both effectiveness and efficiency in producing services that are responsive to the market of needs in the larger society as well as enhancing the relative position of the organization in its environment. In the competing-values framework, this sector is defined by the dimensions of *external* and *control*. This sector encompasses organization-centered activities identified as goal setting and productivity improvement, in which the executive has a central leadership role. Although a variety of individuals and groups may participate in the process of goal setting, the executive is ultimately, and centrally, accountable for the quality of services produced (Hawkins and Gunther 1998) and the consistency of service design (see chapter 4) with organizational mission and goals.

Again, Quinn (1988) identifies two manager roles in this sector: producer and director.

> *Producer:* A producer is expected to be task oriented and work focused and to have high interest, motivation, energy, and personal drive. Here a manager is supposed to accept responsibility, complete assignments, and maintain high personal productivity.

> *Director:* As a director, a manager is expected to clarify expectations through processes such as planning and goal setting and to be a decisive initiator who defines problems, selects alternatives, establishes objectives, defines roles and tasks, generates rules and policies, evaluates performance, and gives instructions.
>
> Quinn (1988:40)

The definition of goals and objectives is particularly important because human service organizations are created to accomplish particular societal objectives; they are created as goal-achievement organizations. For externally dependent human service organizations, this includes, as part of strategic planning, efforts to estimate future developments in the environment, including the user environment, as well as future developments potentially affecting the availability of financial and personnel resources, technological developments, and political and legislative initiatives (Bryson 1994).

The central role of *service quality* as a goal that is consistent with the value traditions of human service organizations has been highlighted by the development of the concept of total quality management (TQM) in the for-profit sector (Gummer and McCallion 1995; Gunther and Hawkins 1996; Boettcher 1998; Hawkins and Gunther 1998) (see chapter 11). TQM involves "the application of quantitative methods and human resources to improve the materials and services applied to an organization, all the processes within an organization, and the degree to which the needs of the customer are met, now and in the future" (Martin 1993:10). As part of the TQM concepts, *customers* are defined as including other organizations and individuals with which the service organization carries out exchange transactions, as well as the ultimate service user (Chism 1997).

The goals of the human service organization also include *organizational continuity*. This requires developmental, and defensive, strategic planning. Organizational continuity takes on a high value in nonprofit and governmental human service organizations. Unlike the successful for-profit service organization, the "sunk" costs involved in the original effort to create a service organization and the good will represented in the community legitimation of the organization cannot not be "sold" to another set of owners, or be converted to a set of financial resources to be used for another purpose. [One exception to this involves the payments that have been made by for-profit health-care organizations when a nonprofit hospital is acquired. In this instance, the assets of the nonprofit corporation have often been converted into a community-level "foundation" that may have a general community health improvement mission (Maynard and Poole 1998).]

The range of task responsibilities of the executive within the four functional sectors previously described includes the interpersonal processes of personnel motivation, the technical competencies involved in organizing and monitoring production, the political processes involved in dealing with the task environment, and the analytic and leadership processes involved in productivity improvement and goal accomplishment. As Quinn emphasizes, these four task sectors involve competing values and paradoxes (1988:xv), since the conceptual orientation and skills most needed in one sector may be quite different from those required in another sector.

Particularly important for the executive is an understanding of the tensions that can exist—for example, between maximizing participatory processes to reinforce motivation and commitment among staff personnel, and being directly and personally involved in the systematic analysis of financial, social, and political forces that may shape the goals of the organization in ways that are not consistent with staff preferences. Similar tensions exist between the carefully controlled application of technical knowledge about the most effective and most efficient production methodologies, and the highly interactive, and unpredictable, political support–building processes that go on with critical external constituencies.

As Follett noted, it is a critical function of executive leadership to pay attention to the *whole* of the organization as well as to the balance among the *parts*. This includes attention to the future as well as to the present and to organizational continuity as well as to organizational effectiveness. Although the production of effective and useful services for individuals in need of those services is the primary objective of organizational activity, the human service organization itself is an essential tool for that production. It embodies past investments not only in facilities and equipment but also in the efforts involved in creating and maintaining the organization over time. It is a critical resource for service production in the future in response to the needs of future service users. Executive attention to continuity and development of the organization as a community resource is, therefore, as important as the attention that is given to current production activities.

The ultimate responsibility of the executive is to understand these tensions and paradoxes and to deal with the competing pressures that each of four sectors represents. The distribution of time and energy among these four task sectors varies from time to time within any one organization, depending on the "life cycle" position of the organization (Hasenfeld and Schmid 1989). The distribution of time and energy also varies among different organizations in different environments. Responsibilities may be divided up differently among the individuals who are part of what is often a multiperson executive component. Individuals who are part of a multiperson executive component bring different mixtures of skills. In many organizations, senior support staff persons, such as an executive assistant, are realistically part of the executive component. Moreover, in multiple-program-component organizations and sizable technical support units, the component managers also carry some part of these executive functions. Fundamentally, however, it is the responsibility of the executive in the human service organization to have an overview of the pattern of activities in all four sectors and to determine the extent to which the requirements of effective performance are being met in all four sectors.

EXECUTIVE STYLE

Discussions of executive style have often been based on one of two traditional models developed within the business community. Taylor's *scientific management* model (Taylor 1947), often described as a normative, rationalist approach to management (Peters and Waterman 1982), views the executive as a systematic analyst, focusing primarily on production technology, economic analysis, and a centralized command-and-control organizational structure with organizational motivation based on tangible rewards. The model of *human relations management*, as set forth initially by Elton Mayo and colleagues (1933), views the executive primarily as the designer and initiator of an interactive motivational process of participatory decision-making groups involving teams of production workers, with motivation involving psychological factors as well as tangible rewards (Ouchi 1981). In both models, the objective is to increase production efficiency while being consistent with the goals of the business firm.

Both of these models are rooted, fundamentally, in a structure of industrial goods production in the United States in which there is an assumption of a clear-cut separation between managers and workers. Not only does this separation involve differences in roles and responsibilities but, in actual practice, it has involved differences in socioeconomic backgrounds, and often differences in ethnic/cultural backgrounds, between these two groups of organizational participants. This pattern of separation has been reinforced in the United States by an absence of upward mobility opportunities involving a cross-over from industrial production roles to management roles, with industrial managers being recruited largely from among college and university graduates without production experience (Reich 1983).

This pattern of separation includes an assumption that managers have all of the strategic and tactical knowledge required for effective production, whereas workers have only operational knowledge. Consistent with this model is an assumption of a fundamental conflict of interests between bosses and workers that must be systematically managed by executives, who control strategic and tactical knowledge, in order to achieve efficiency and effectiveness in production. Scientific management and human relations management are essentially alternative approaches, designed by management, to deal with the conflicts and alienation that develops out of this separation of interests.

As Child (1995) comments, the management philosophy of Mary Parker Follett rejected the assumptions of the human relations model, as well as those of scientific management:

> Mayo's approach appealed directly to managers, conveying as it did a welcome and straightforward message. It ascribed a privileged rationality to managers that legitimated their authority. . . . There was a significant divergence between Follett's concept of constructive conflict . . . and Mayo's deep abhorrence of conflict in any form. Follett believed that people at all levels in an enterprise could come rationally to accept the "law of the situation" and that, therefore, through discussion, a mutually acceptable and innovative integrative solution could be found to many conflicts. She anticipated that integration could be achieved through participation in decision making, on the basis of the functional knowledge that each party to an issue could offer. Mayo and his colleagues. . . assumed that ordinary employees were largely governed by a "logic of sentiment," which was of a different order from managers' rational appraisal of the situation in terms of costs and efficiency. Conflict with management was thus an aberration that threatened the effectiveness of organizations.
>
> Child (1995:88–89)

Contemporary versions of both these models have been promoted as a solution to issues of effective executive performance in human service organizations. A great deal of attention was devoted in the 1970s and 1980s to the executive application of the principles of "rational management" in human service organizations, including the introduction of cost–benefit analysis and large-scale, computerized record keeping systems, frequently with a substantial sacrifice of motivation and commitment among direct service workers. More recently, many of the concepts of rational management have been applied in the field of managed health care.

Alternatively, application of "human relations" methods has often been advocated as the humane solution to problems of motivation (Argyris 1964; Fallon 1978). However, although participatory processes among organizational members may be valuable for a number of reasons, any consistent connection between the intensity of such processes as a regular, ongoing part of organizational life and increased service productivity or improved service effectiveness is difficult to establish. Indeed, as Mintzberg (1979) has pointed out, professional bureaucracies are generally marked by an individualistic pattern of work activities rather than by work teams.

Both of these traditional models of administrative style have limited applicability to human service organizations, because several of the underlying assumptions do not apply. The basic assumption of a fundamental, structural conflict of interests between managers and direct service personnel is not relevant in human service organizations (although the actual situation in some individual organizations may appear to support such an assumption). In most human service organizations, managers and direct service personnel share some form of common professional identity and experience as well as a shared commitment to the public service mission of the organization. Most executives and other administrative personnel are recruited from among persons with at least some form of direct service—front-line experience. Systematic socioeconomic and ethnic/cultural distinctions between managers and direct service workers are less likely to be a major factor, although there are often significant differences within human service organizations between the percentage of front-line workers who are women and the percentage of managers who are men (Chernesky 1998).

The "intensive" (Thompson 1967) or individualized and interactive nature of human service production technology, whether it involves handling an individual child abuse family situation, teaching a classroom of elementary students, or providing nursing care for a terminally ill patient with acquired immunodeficiency disease, works against the model of increasing efficiency solely through the application of standardized production technology. Moreover, the level of personal commitment among both direct service employees and volunteers to the organizational mission and goals, and personal concerns about the needs of service users are more likely to be major factors in the effectiveness (and efficiency) of human service production than group motivational exercises.

Given the differences between large-scale industrial goods production firms and human service organizations, models of executive style other than scientific management or human relations are essential for understanding the requirements of effective management in human service organizations. The *managerial grid* by Blake and Mouton (1964) is one of the more widely recognized behavioral models of executive style that attempt to overcome the dichotomy between task-oriented scientific management and motivation-oriented human relations. The grid combines two dimensions, one dealing with productivity/efficiency and the second dealing with morale/cohesion, in effect combining the scientific management emphasis on technology and the human relations emphasis on interpersonal processes and motivation. The preferred "9,9" executive seeks to maximize effective production by mobilizing organizational human resources.

These two dimensions, however, refer only to the competencies required in the internal quadrants of the Quinn model, human relations and internal processes. They focus primarily on executive competencies and behavioral styles involved in *intra*organizational processes. The grid does not deal directly with the political and cognitive executive styles that are essential in the external processes involved in maintaining the resource flow from the task environment, and in goal-oriented planning and development for the organization. Indeed, as Menefee and Thompson point out, "It becomes apparent that the [social work manager's] role has shifted from one focused primarily on internal operations to one that is strategically oriented" (1994:14).

Interactive Leadership as an Executive Style

One relevant behavioral model for the human service executive is that of *interactive leadership*. Leadership is a widely used but seldom defined concept. A full discussion of interactive leadership as an executive style is beyond the scope of this chapter, but two key elements can be emphasized.

One element is the inclusive focus of attention by the executive on the total organization and its context—that is, a total situation approach, as described by Mary Parker Follett at the beginning of this chapter, including the full range of organizational functions as described earlier in the competing-values framework. This involves the management of a complex process of interpersonal communication that emphasizes the unity of the organization in the face of the organizational forces that tend to fragment and divide. Sayles describes it as the "recombination of elements separated by the division of labor" (1979:26). It includes an emphasis on the purposes of the organization as a whole, including attention to the symbols and traditions that embody the social values and social goals that underlie the existence of the organization, particularly in nonprofit and governmental service organizations.

A second element in the model of an interactive style of executive leadership has been described in the writings of Sayles (1979) and Peters and Waterman (1982), and it is consistent with the earlier teachings of Mary Parker Follett. This involves an emphasis on intense personal interaction between the executive and other people throughout the organization including service users. It includes interaction with individuals as well as being part of a variety of group processes. "It would appear that both to learn about social systems and to cope with them the appropriate working level is the process level. This means that managers and researchers alike need to concentrate on the behavioral interaction that underpins organizational life" (Sayles 1979:8).

Sayles suggests that the central concept of executive behavior is "action in time"—that is, a never-ending series of contacts with other people that have as their focus two elements of system management: *contingency responses* and *reduction of uncertainty* (1979). Peters and Waterman (1982:89) describe the core focus of executive activity as "managing ambiguity and paradox," whereas Quinn (1988) focuses on "mastering the paradoxes and competing demands of high performance." All of these authors are critical of the scientific management/rational model for executive behavior, focusing instead on an evolving, interactive, problem-solving approach that includes the use of participatory groups but also includes a high level of individual, one-to-one initiating activity on the part of the executive.

A particularly critical element in the interactive pattern of leadership in human service organizations involves the relationship of the executive to professional specialists. "The growth of a service economy of knowledge workers makes professionalism a more salient part of business suc-

cess in more companies—particularly the kind of professionalism familiar in human service occupations" (Kanter 1997:14).

The relationship between the executive role and the professional role
can become particularly complex when the executive comes from a professional background. In some settings, the executive as professional may
function as the senior manager, the senior practitioner, the ultimate professional supervisor, and the professional consultant (and even as the
part-time practitioner). However, monopolizing the role of senior professional specialist as well as that of senior manager may seriously limit
the ability of other professional practitioners in the organization to function independently. Moreover, a preoccupation by executives with maintaining or enhancing their own personal professional identity may mean
that inadequate attention is given to organizational members who are
not part of the same profession. Alternatively, other executives who
come from a professional background may suppress their professional
identity, and avoid personal relationships with individual professional
practitioners in the organization, in favor of a technically oriented identity as a manager, using a command-and-control approach to the organization of service production activities.

Neither of these two models, the executive as senior professional
practitioner nor the executive as the pure manager, is really consistent
with the model of interactive executive leadership. The interactive
human services executive who is also a professional specialist can maintain a professional identity while allowing other members of the professional staff to carry major responsibility for professional leadership.
However, interactions with staff members from a common professional
background should be balanced by similar interactions with all other organizational members.

MANAGERIAL ETHICS

The executive who is also a member of an organized profession faces the
personal issue of the relationship of management decision making to the
code of ethics of that profession (Levy 1982; Reamer 1995). There are
general definitions of ethical behavior written into law in connection
with many of the decision issues that any human service executive, or

other manager, must deal with. These include prohibitions against the diversion of organizational funds for personal benefit, against sexual harassment or discriminatory treatment of organizational personnel, against the mistreatment of individuals receiving services, against discriminatory treatment of particular categories of service users, and against fraudulent misrepresentation of organizational activities in reports to funding bodies.

Such legal provisions exist, in part, because there is no universal code of ethics for organizational executives, including executives of human service organizations. Nor is there any inclusive mechanism for enforcing ethical mandates that might apply to human service managers, other than the courts. Indeed, the courts become an increasingly critical factor in the enforcement of fundamental ethical mandates for managers as the size and scope of human service organizations increases, and as the role of for-profit human service organizations expands.

The specific provisions of a professional code of ethics, such as the National Association of Social Workers (NASW) *Code of Ethics* for social workers (National Association of Social Workers 1996) or the codes of ethics associated with state licensing laws, often go beyond what is covered by legal prescriptions. Such provisions may provide support for the executive, who is a member of a profession, in conflicts with external constituencies—for example, over the confidentiality of professional records dealing with individual services users. Moreover, many of the provisions in the NASW *Code of Ethics* that deal with interpersonal relationships are broadly applicable to all relationships within the organization (Levy 1982). The NASW *Code of Ethics* does include a section that specifically covers administration dealing with advocating for adequate program resources, evenhanded administration of resources, and maintaining a work environment that is consistent with the *Code of Ethics*. However, there is debate about the extent to which professional codes of ethics, designed primarily for direct service practitioners, are really applicable to the critical choices that executives face (Congress 1997; Gummer 1997).

As Reamer (1995) and Gummer (1996) point out, the social work code of ethics, for example, does not provide ethical guidance for the manager in dealing with such "conflicting value-tensions" (Weiner 1990) as the allocation of limited resources between organizational maintenance requirements and service needs—that is, between the needs of current service users and the potential needs of future users, or between even-handed application of rules and regulations and the recognition of the individual circumstances of particular service users. Additional dilemmas that are not covered by the code include the choice between governmental and private sector organizations for providing contracted services, administrative compliance with democratically established laws and regulations that create disadvantages for some individual service users, and conflicts between the economic self-interests of organizational employees, including professionals, and the needs of service users.

In practice, no procedures are provided by a professional association or by a licensing board for bringing charges of unethical behavior against an executive who is also an active member of a profession for decisions made as an executive. Professional codes of ethics also do not deal with the special responsibilities that executives carry for monitoring the ethical performance of all service personnel within the organization, including those who may not be personally accountable to a specific professional code of ethics.

Executives in nonprofit service agencies may have to deal with decisions about participating in a publicly funded service contract that provides expanded service benefits for eligible individuals while explicitly excluding other persons with similar needs who do not meet legally defined eligibility criteria. Similar issues are involved in contracts with managed care for-profit organizations (Reamer 2001). In deciding which provisions of the professional code of ethics might be viewed as being applicable (for example, the section of the NASW *Code of Ethics* that states that the primary responsibility of the professional practitioner is to clients), the executive must also deal with the interests of other organizational constituencies, including funders and members of relevant policy-making bodies, constituencies that may have different views about the ethical issues involved (Gummer 1996, 1997). Moreover, the executive must balance a professional commitment to a professional code of ethics and the obligation of a nonprofit or governmental executive to respect the policy authority of an official board of directors.

There are, however, two ethical guidelines that are particularly relevant for organizational executives and other managers. The first is *honesty*—in particular, the communication of the most consistent and dependable information available about the organization and its services with both internal and external constituencies. The second involves the fundamental obligation of the service organization to the service users: to make certain that the services of the organization *do not harm the service user* and that the service user be provided the best available information about *the effectiveness of the services being provided* (Gambrill 2001).

WOMEN, PERSONS FROM AFRICAN AMERICAN, AMERICAN INDIAN, LATINO, AND ASIAN AMERICAN BACKGROUNDS, AND GAYS AND LESBIANS IN EXECUTIVE POSITIONS

Any analysis of the position of human service executive needs to give specific attention to the dynamics affecting women, persons from African American, American Indian, Latino, and Asian American backgrounds, and gays and lesbians in executive positions. Many of these dynamics may also affect executives who have a disability condition. In most human service sectors, women are the largest group of organizational employees. They are often the largest group of service users as well, either directly or representing the interests of a child. Similarly, there are more persons from African American, American Indian, Latino, and Asian American backgrounds among employees and service users in both nonprofit and governmental human service organizations than in most other organizational sectors of society. Increasingly, individual organizational participants are also identifying themselves as gay or lesbian in sexual orientation.

The number of women who have organizational experience and are seeking executive positions is steadily increasing (Chernesky 1998), as is the number of men and women from African American, American Indian, Latino, and Asian American backgrounds, and persons who identify themselves as gay or lesbian. In many organizations, there continue to be barriers to executive positions, and these barriers involve stereotypes as well as institutionalized sexism, racism, and homophobia (Weiner 1990; Gibelman 2000a). Similar barriers may affect access to executive positions by qualified individuals with a disability. Patterns of persistent economic inequality can also be seen in the level of executive salaries between men and women (Huber 1995). However, a steady process of change will occur in the ethnic and gender patterns of executives across all types of human service organizations in social services, education, health care, and criminal justice (Alexander and Kerson 1980), regardless of the status of official affirmative action policies and programs. Also, opportunities will increase for individuals with a disability, and a greater diversity of personal lifestyles among executives will be seen in the future.

However, executive positions in human service organizations, as well as in much of the rest of society, are still perceived as being embedded in a White, male, heterosexual culture (Chernesky 1983, 1998; Dressel 1992). Executives from African American, American Indian, Latino, and Asian American backgrounds are often under pressure to adapt, in varying ways and to varying degrees, to the characteristics of this culture (Arguello 1984), as are women and gays and lesbians. One of the factors in the resistance of many White heterosexual men, who are otherwise reasonable individuals, to the demographic changes that are now taking place within many organizations is anxiety over the possibility of having to adapt to different expectations in organizational settings in which *it is not taken for granted* that the White, male, heterosexual culture is dominant at the executive level. Anxiety may be particularly acute in male-dominated organizations that have traditionally been organized as a hierarchical, command-and-control structure in which a gender change in leadership positions is accompanied by a change to a low-profile, interactive management style. Such culture changes have already occurred in some human service organizations in which women predominate in executive and in policy-making roles as well as in direct service roles (Hyde 1992).

The body of publications that deal with the pressures facing women, both in gaining access to executive positions in human services and in functioning effectively in those positions, is increasing (Austin, Kravetz, and Pollock 1985; Martin and Chernesky 1989; Haynes 1989; Weiner 1990; Chernesky 1998). Padgett (1993) distinguished between research studies that focused on the role of individual factors and those that focused on the role of situational factors affecting the access of women to managerial positions, and between those that used a liberal feminism ideological framework and those that used a radical feminism ideological framework in interpreting the relationship of women to organizational management. The body of published material is more limited that deals specifically with the experiences of persons from African American, American Indian, Latino, and Asian American backgrounds in gaining access to managerial positions (Arguello 1984; Rincon and Keys 1985).

Among all the issues potentially involved in the situations of women, persons from African American, American Indian, Latino, and Asian American backgrounds, and gays and lesbians who are in executive positions, two are touched on briefly here. One issue is that of the relationship of such individuals to the White, male, heterosexual executive culture, and the personal problem of "marginality," or identity ambiguity. The other issue involves the role of executives who belong to any of these groups in bringing about changes in their organizations—in particular, in implementing nondiscriminatory employment objectives.

Marginality

There are many pressures to conform to the informal expectations of the White, male, heterosexual executive culture and to suppress patterns of personal behavior that are not viewed as consistent with that culture. One alternative is to attempt to become wholly accepted within that dominant culture and to adopt the symbols, language, and values of that culture, while curtailing personal involvement in, or identification with, a different cultural background. This may be viewed as the best option for career success, but it may also have very high personal costs. Moreover, regardless of the quality of individual performance in an executive position, it is very difficult for individuals who are not inherently part of a particular culture to completely "pass"—that is, to become a total participant in the informal elements of that culture.

Therefore, the individual risks cultural marginality—that is, risks becoming an individual without a stable self-definition of cultural identity, a person who is caught between efforts to adapt to the dominant culture with only partial success and isolation from the culture of origin. This has often been a problem for first-generation children in immigrant households. The stresses of marginality may be intensified by the pressures on an individual who is functioning constantly in a setting in which a different cultural group is dominant, even if there are no overt expressions of discrimination or antagonism. Moreover, in conflict situations within an organization, "marginal" individuals, even at the executive level, may find themselves unexpectedly isolated, without systematic sources of support, either personal or political.

One way of dealing with the potential stresses of marginality can be to de-emphasize adaptation to the dominant culture and to emphasize one's own distinctive cultural background while maintaining a strong, culturally congruent support system in which one is not a "marginal" person. But it is important that such a support system does not make unusual demands on the time or resources of the individual, or embody values that are significantly in conflict with the dominant organizational culture, both of which may substantially increase the stress level for the individual. Also, asserting a distinctive and separate cultural identity increases the risk of being isolated or ignored, particularly in informal and unofficial decision-making processes that are dominated by White, male, heterosexual staff members.

Another personal alternative is to make an explicit decision to maintain dual cultural identities. This entails establishing a place for oneself in the dominant executive culture by giving serious attention to the informal expectations within that culture, as well as to the formal requirements of role performance, while also investing substantial time and effort in maintaining an identity that is rooted in the culture of origin. Such a decision involves extra costs in time and money. Moreover, although this may provide an alternative framework for personal identification, special psychological costs are involved when there are situations in which the cultural expectations or values of different cultural groups are in direct conflict.

These stresses of dual cultural identity and dual cultural connections can be particularly acute when policy or administrative decisions represent conflicts between important values—for example, between individualized responses to individual service situations and consistency with established rules and procedures (Weiner 1990). Support by executives who are not part of the dominant culture for case decisions that benefit individual service users, but that conflict with existing rules and regulations and the principle of absolute distinctions between right and wrong, may be criticized as biased, or special-interest pleading. This is particularly likely to happen when women or individuals from diverse ethnic or sexual-orientation backgrounds are involved as service users. However, support of across-the-board enforcement of rules, rules that may, in reality, reflect institutional racism, sexism, and homophobia, may be viewed as a refusal to recognize the real problems of real people and as denial of one's own cultural background.

Action Against "Institutional Isms"

A second potential source of stress involves the relationship of individual executives from American Indian, Latino, African American, or Asian American backgrounds, as well as women executives in general, and gays and lesbians, to changes going on within human service organizations, such as the use of recruitment initiatives to increase ethnic and gender diversity in administrative positions, or conflicts over implicit discrimination against gays and lesbians. Norms of administrative impartiality may argue against explicit personal support for efforts to bring about such changes within the organization, even though personal commitments to principles of social justice, together with the expectations of organizational affirmative action objectives, may argue for active executive support of such changes.

In some instances, efforts to change existing institutional patterns that have negative consequences for members of one population group may be viewed as being hostile to a different group. Deliberate efforts to recruit women, and men, from Latino backgrounds for administrative positions, in an organization with no persons from such backgrounds, may be viewed as being potentially discriminatory against White women who are current staff members seeking career advancement.

Proactive initiatives by any executive, including White, male, heterosexual executives, to support changes in the characteristics of the administrative staff often involve significant personal cost. Such efforts may involve career risks when, for example, recruitment efforts conflict with the preferences, even if unexpressed, of other persons in executive and policy-making positions, including members of a policy board. Again, such efforts may be attacked as special-interest advocacy. However, the failure of persons with executive power and authority in human service organizations to play an active role in bringing about increased diversity among administrative staff members may well be viewed by others, both within the organization and in the community, as clear evidence of institutional racism and sexism.

In general, leadership expectations, and stresses, for persons from American Indian, Latino, African American, and Asian American backgrounds in executive positions, as well as for women, and gays and lesbians, are likely to be more complicated and more intense than those for persons who are part of the dominant White, male, heterosexual executive culture during the demographic, social, and political changes that will take place during the next twenty-five years in the United States. This requires simultaneous attention to the sources of extra stress, as well as to the development of personal supports, including mentoring relationships and peer support networks, that may help in coping with such stresses (Weiner 1990).

SUMMARY

The position of human service executive is a complex, multifaceted role that is shaped in part by the traditions of for-profit business management and public administration. However, it also involves very distinctive task expectations that require both flexibility and control, exercised both internally and externally. Interactive process skills are critical, but the most important skill is the conceptual ability to comprehend the "total situation" of the organization in its environment.

The human service executive must deal with many important challenges in this era of commercialized health care, increasing electronic and biological innovation, demographic transformation, and governmental devolution and privatization. Two particularly important challenges involve (1) the interface between organizational pressures and professional ethics and (2) the imperative to increase the cultural and lifestyle diversity of the executive and management cadre and to provide full opportunity and support for personal and career development across such diversity.

TEN

BOARDS OF DIRECTORS AND
ADVISORY COMMITTEES

The first lesson to be learned is that nonprofits need a clear and functioning governance structure. They have to take their governance seriously and they have to work hard on it. . . . Making the organs of governance effective in the nonprofit institution and creating the proper relationship between them should therefore be considered a priority task of executive officers.

—Drucker (1990a:8, 13)

The nonprofit board has always been important, but greater national attention is being focused on its role than ever before. This scrutiny has been precipitated by escalating demands for the services that nonprofits provide, intense competition for funds from private and public sources to finance those services, and growing recognition that the success of nonprofit organizations in delivering services will be influenced by the effectiveness of their leaders. . . . It is the board which is ultimately responsible for ensuring that the organization fulfills its mission. —Axelrod (1994:119–120)

I N EVERY formal organization, there is a component that has the fundamental responsibility for defining the institutional relationship of the organization to its environment—that is, for establishing the "policy framework." In nearly all formal organizations, the official policy-making component is a group of individuals. In nonprofit human service organizations, including both voluntary nonprofit and quasi-governmental nonprofit, this policy-making group is identified as a board of directors (reflecting a tradition taken over from the business world), or a board of trustees (taken from the concept of a trust or charitable foundation) (Siciliano and Spiro 1992). The board of directors is the formal, legal embodiment of the service organization and its mission. Collectively, the board members are in positions of trust with fiduciary responsibility for the organization (Siciliano and Spiro 1992). And it is the board of directors that provides legal continuity of the organization over time, regardless of changes in the membership of the board.

The ultimate policy-making body for governmental service organizations is generally an elected body—city council, county commissioners, state legislature, or a board of directors or board of commissioners established by such an elected body to oversee a public commission or a quasi-governmental nonprofit service organization. In the instance of school boards or hospital districts, the members of the board may be elected directly by the voters in a local community. (In a limited number of instances, a single elected public official is both the primary policy maker and the executive for a specific governmental organization.)

Many elements of the functions of nonprofit boards of directors also apply to quasi-governmental nonprofit boards, but there may also be important differences. New members of such boards may be appointed by one or more external sources rather than by the board members themselves (Robins and Blackburn 1985). Such quasi-governmental boards may also be specifically constrained by policies and directives established by the appointing source, or by particular funding sources. Such quasi-governmental boards may or may not be directly responsible for selecting the organizational executive. However, in spite of these differences, both voluntary nonprofit and quasi-governmental nonprofit boards of directors will be referred to as *nonprofit boards* in the following discussion. The structure of the nonprofit board of directors provides a mechanism for focusing ultimate responsibility for the service organization and its performance on a particular group of individuals. In general, the individual members of that group are shielded from direct legal and financial liability for the actions of the organization, although such protection has been eroded in recent court decisions (Zelman 1977; Siciliano and Spiro 1992; Tremper 1994). The following discussion also includes some consideration of differences between nonprofit boards of directors and those in for-profit businesses, since the differences in governance structure are central to differences between these two types of human service organizations.

THREE TRADITIONS

The development of the current pattern of boards of directors in nonprofit human service organizations draws on three traditions from the past. One tradition is the voluntary membership association that took many different forms in early American life but was perhaps most widely reflected in the self-governance structures of congregation-based Protestant churches. Voluntary associations are initiated by a small group of interested persons with a division of organizational tasks among the members, a process of structured group decision making, and a tradition of rotating leadership responsibilities. Today, such voluntary associations are found in every aspect of community life, including a large number of religious associations or congregations (Knoke 1990).

Community-level associations are largely self-financed, and many of them do not involve an employed staff. However, local membership associations such as church congregations usually do have employed staff members, and associations such as the American Association of Retired Persons or Rotary International may be national or international in scope and involve large support staffs. Membership associations are often described as being a particularly important type of "mediating structure" between individual citizens and the formal structures of societal governance. Many board members in human service organizations have had previous organizational experience as officers of voluntary associations, including church congregations (Ammerman 1997).

A second tradition, previously noted in chapter 1, is the philanthropic board, modeled on the board of directors of the for-profit firm. The early philanthropic board was headed by an important civic leader who served for an indefinite number of years and who often functioned as both president of the board and as de facto executive. This was generally an individual who also provided major financial support and who, as board president, controlled the agenda and the decision-making procedures of the board. The philanthropic board was the prototype for the contemporary board of directors of the nonprofit organization.

A third tradition is the governmental commission, a small body of citizens appointed by an elected body (or directly elected, in some instances) to carry responsibility for a particular public task with delegated authority independent of the appointing body. Examples include public utility commissions, public housing commissions, and park commissions. Joint-powers commissions provide a structure through which more than one governmental body can participate in the sponsorship of a shared governmental activity such as a metropolitan system of parks. In some instances, such as the commission form of municipal government, elected officials with independent administrative authority also function collectively as the legislative, or policy-making, commission for the municipality or county. Although some of these commission-member positions include a salary, the majority involve unpaid civic service.

All three traditions have contributed to the development of a complex network of organized civic activities in the society of the United States. These intermediary, or mediating, organizations, which function between the individual or household and government, contribute to the diversity and richness of the civil society. They also function to bring individuals together in varying degrees, cutting across the lines of ethnic and cultural identities, religious identities, occupational identities, sexual identity, ideological identity, and economic position. These cross-cutting linkages constitute a form of societal insurance against the polarizing forces of such identity differences, differences that underlay the Civil War in the 1860s and the violence of the 1960s and that have often had violent consequences in other nations.

The participation of individuals as members of boards of directors of human service organizations has an important integrative civic function quite apart from the governance function that they serve for a single organization. Some boards of directors exercise great power in American society. These include the boards of directors, or regents, that are the governing bodies for academic systems or for major research universities, both public and private. They also include the boards of large national foundations that have almost complete discretion in the use of the foundation funds, and the boards of large national/international organizations such as the Red Cross. But most boards of directors have responsibility for a single organization serving a single community, and this is the context in this chapter.

The three historical traditions noted here contribute to a diversity of governance structures and governance authority in human service organizations (see chapter 4). However, there are also common elements across these varied boards of directors or commissions. Members of the governing boards of nonprofit human service organizations do not receive financial or other *direct* personal benefits in return for their services, although there may be a variety of indirect benefits, including increased personal prestige within the community (Silk 1994). Such service requires that these individuals behave in ways that are contrary to the general assumption that economic self-interest is the primary motivation for individual action in a marketplace economy, even if public recognition may have some ultimate economic benefit for some board members.

Collective social values, rather than individual self-interest, are expected to provide the normative framework for the decisions made by these boards of directors. Some individual board members, including those who serve on several boards, may, in fact, view themselves more as volunteers participating in the cross-cutting network of civic activities noted earlier than as members of a decision-making governance board with fiscal and legal responsibilities for a single organization. The large-scale existence of noneconomic volunteer service across the society reflects the availability of very substantial "slack" (or not fully committed) resources of personal time and money within a highly productive economic system.

In contrast to members on nonprofit boards, members of for-profit boards of directors usually receive economic benefits from their services as a board member, benefits that result in part from their being shareholders in the firm. This general distinction between the financial position of members of the nonprofit boards of directors and the financial position of members of boards of directors of for-profit firms is an example of the ways in which general institutional patterns in the society shape processes within a large number of individual organizations.

In nonprofit human service organizations, the executive, who receives financial benefits from the organization as a result of board action, is not a voting member of the board of directors. Similarly, in governmental commissions or authorities, senior administrative officers are normally not voting members of the board or public commission to which they are accountable. However, in for-profit firms, the CEO and other senior administrative officers are normally voting members of the board of directors of the firm, and the CEO may serve as the chair of the governing board of directors.

FUNCTIONS OF THE BOARD OF DIRECTORS

The formal and fundamental role of the nonprofit board of directors is "governance"—that is, the establishment of the policy framework for the organization (Axelrod 1994). However, the activities of the board of directors are not limited to taking action on formal policy decisions. "The worst illusion ever perpetuated in the nonprofit field is that the board of directors makes policy and staff carries it out. This is just not so. The board, with the help of the staff, makes policy, and the board, with the help of the staff, carries it out" (O'Connell 1985:44).

The pattern of board decision-making activities can be very diverse, with board members being involved in a wide variety of decisions, some of which may be largely technical. Thus boards may act on the arrangements for the rental of office space or the awarding of a contract for insurance, confirm the arrangements for the investment of endowment funds, establish the operational plans for a board-sponsored fund-raising event, or make changes in the definition of the organizational mission. Other decisions deal directly with the achievement of the fundamental purposes for which the organization has been created. The total pattern of board activities includes three distinct functions, functions that may often be contradictory.

The first of these board functions, an inward-facing function, is that of control and *oversight*—the process through which the executive and other members of the organizational staff are held accountable for their performance and the performance of the organization (Zald 1969). In this function, the board represents stakeholder constituencies by overseeing organizational operations and reporting on the performance of the organization through a variety of media outlets. These constituencies may include governmental bodies that contract with the organization for the provision of particular services, contributors from the general public, funding bodies such as the United Way, regulatory and licensing bodies, and the public. The board is also expected to represent the interests of current and potential service users as a group. To carry out this function, the board requires a variety of reports, both written and verbal, from the executive and the operational staff.

Participation in the development of plans for the evaluation of service effectiveness is becoming an increasingly important element of board oversight in both nonprofit and quasi-governmental nonprofit organizations that are administering tax-supported services, either directly or through contracts. In part, this responsibility is similar to that of the board of directors for the selection of an auditor, which is part of the oversight responsibility of the board. However, the design of effectiveness evaluation involves board members in decisions about the selection of effectiveness criteria and about the method of carrying out an effectiveness evaluation (see chapter 11). The oversight function also includes giving attention to the implications of developments in the organization-al environment for the future of the organization and participating in forward-looking strategic planning (Bryson 1994).

A second board function, an outward-looking function, is organiza-tional *advocacy*—that is, acting as a supporter and promoter for the or-ganization and for the services that it produces (Zald 1969). In carrying out this function, members of a board of directors may work closely with organizational staff members in developing promotional information, representing the organization to sources of legitimation and resources, and defending the organization against external criticism and attack. An important support and advocacy role of the board of the nonprofit or-ganization in the current organizational environment has often been fund-raising, including representation of the organization to funding bodies such as governmental contracting authorities (Harlan and Saidel 1994). However, the board, as a body of civic volunteers, may also have an important external public policy role by serving as an advocacy body in connection with governmental policy making on issues that are relat-ed to the mission and goals of the organization. This policy advocacy role may be carried out by individual members of the board, or it may take the form of organized action in the name of the board, with techni-cal support from organizational staff members.

In newly established organizations, the board members, who may in-clude some of the persons responsible for the original establishment of the organization, may view the advocate/support role as clearly the most important. The shift from being primarily an advocate board to begin-ning to incorporate oversight functions is an important milestone in new organizations (Koroloff and Briggs 1996). This shift may be accompa-nied by changes in board membership.

There is also a third function of board members, that of *consultation*. In this function, the board members serve as advisors to the executive and to other organizational staff members on a wide variety of program and organizational issues. The provision of such advice may be based on the personal background and experience of the board members, on the distinctive technical and professional knowledge of individual members of the board, or on the connections of individual board members with sources of information and influence in the community. One of the com-plexities of the board–staff relationship is that advice from individual members of the board may be contradictory. Also, the advisory function may be confused with the oversight function, with the result that staff members might interpret as suggestions what board members intended as explicit instructions or directives.

These three ongoing board functions overlap, and may, at times, be in conflict. Information that becomes available to individual members of the board through participation in fund-raising and other organizational promotion activities may raise questions that are relevant to the oversight function of the board. Vigorous pursuit of information relevant to the oversight function may raise questions among members of the organizational staff about the enthusiasm of board members in supporting the organization. Friendly advice may be viewed by staff members as criticism coming from board members in their oversight function. Individual board members may participate as service volunteers in the service production activities of an organization, with the expectation that they will be responsive to the general supervision of organizational staff members. Failure to recognize that there are multiple, and sometimes conflicting, definitions of board functions can be an important source of confusion and friction among members of a board, between the board of directors and an executive, or between the board and the general staff of the organization.

In carrying out these three functions, the board of directors has a number of critical responsibilities. The board of directors in any organization has important *external* or boundary-spanning responsibilities. The board is a critical element in the connections between the organization and its *task environment*. Through the board members, the external environment is represented to organizational staff members; through the board members, the organization is represented to the external environment.

One of the external responsibilities of the board of directors is serving as the legal representation of the organization. This is a responsibility of the boards of for-profit corporations as well as of nonprofit boards. It is the board of directors collectively that provides legal continuity for the organization regardless of changes in the membership of the board or in the organizational staff. In nearly all nonprofit human service organizations, the sources of legitimation and the major sources of funding are external to the organization. It is under the authority of the nonprofit board of directors that staff members of the organization negotiate the arrangements through which legitimation and resources become available on an ongoing basis for the work of the organization. It is also through the board of directors that the organization is officially accountable to external stakeholder constituencies, including the sources of legitimation and funding, primarily through the enactment of a basic policy/program framework. Because of the responsibility of the board of directors for the legal continuity of the organization, the board has particular responsibility for looking to the future. This includes strategic planning that takes into account potential changes in the external environment (Bryson 1994).

The board of directors also has critical *internal responsibilities*. Three general arenas of decision making represent the core of the internal policy-making responsibilities of a board of directors. These are the following:

- Decisions about allocating financial resources
- Decisions about the fundamental program structure of the organization—that is, decisions about how the organization produces services for use by members of the larger society
- Selection of executive personnel—that is, selection of the person or persons who are directly accountable to the board for the operation of the organization

Green and Griesinger (1996) reported that the level of board involvement in these external and internal responsibilities was associated with the level of effectiveness of the organization, as rated by knowledgeable individuals in the community. "Boards of effective organizations tended to be more fully involved in policy formation, strategic planning, program review, board development planning and control, and dispute resolution" (1996:398).

Another critical, but infrequent, responsibility of boards of directors is the management of transitions. Usually, this means a change in the position of the executive, either mutually agreed upon or involuntary. The board becomes directly involved both in the interim management arrangements and in the search for a new executive. However, transitions can also include major changes in organizational structure or program design, including redefinition of the organizational mission and goals, mergers, physical relocations, the ending of particular program operations, and the initiation of new operations. It is the formal decisions by the board of directors that legitimate these transitions, although the details of the changes may be the responsibility of management staff.

Wernet (1988), in a study of twelve nonprofit organizations—children's residential treatment centers, child guidance clinics, and family service agencies—identified a mixture of board leadership, executive leadership, and partnership patterns in dealing with eighteen decision processes involving transition.

BOARD ACCOUNTABILITY

As indicated previously, it is the board of directors that carries legal responsibility for the activities of the organization (Zelman 1977). It is the board of directors that constitutes the legal channel of accountability between the organization and those constituencies that have legitimated the organization or provided the resources that are required to provide a particular set of services and to maintain the organization (Chisolm 1995; Hammack 1995).

A central issue in all nonprofit human service organizations is the way in which the organization is responsible to, or is held accountable to, these constituencies for the quality of organizational performance (Lawry 1995). The formal pattern of accountability is quite clear when the manager of a governmental organization is directly accountable to a governing body that is elected by members of the community—for example, the accountability of the executive of a county child welfare department to an elected board of county commissioners, or the accountability of a superintendent of schools to an elected school board. Moreover, the actions of such an elected policy board are generally controlled by specific rules and regulations and are open to inspection by the public and the media. In a similar way, the official line of accountability of the board to the membership is quite clear when the members of a membership association, such as a religious denomination or a national professional association, create a board of directors to oversee the activities of an employed staff.

However, such examples among human service organizations are the exception. The line of accountability for a nonprofit board of directors is often obscure, whether it is a nonprofit child guidance clinic, a nonprofit youth membership organization, a nonprofit health services organization, or a philanthropic foundation with a self-perpetuating board. To a very large degree, accountability of the board of directors in such organizations is highly dependent on relationships of trust, rather than on relationships of contract or external control (Kearns 1996). This means that the behavior of the board of directors is governed by personal ethical standards rather than by externally established rules and regulations or enforceable agreements (Lawry 1995), even though, in theory, states have oversight authority in the case of state-chartered organizations, and the Internal Revenue Service has oversight responsibility in the case of tax-exempt organizations. Moreover, the boards of voluntary nonprofit organizations are similar to the boards of for-profit organizations in having rights of organizational privacy and in being exempt from those requirements for open meetings and public disclosure that generally apply to governmental and quasi-governmental organizations.

The ethical standards for members of nonprofit boards include those that represent a societal, or communal, consensus, and those that are specifically embodied in the purpose for which the organization was established. Unlike for-profit organizations, which have in common economic gain as their principle purpose, voluntary nonprofit and governmental human service organizations are established around a noneconomic purpose, or a mission. "An organization's mission, in tandem with its mandates, provides its raison d'étre—the social justification for its existence. For a nonprofit organization, this means that there must be identifiable social or political needs that the organization seeks to fill. In particular, nonprofit organizations must basically serve some important public purpose that would not otherwise be served" (Bryson 1994:159–160). This mission represents the set of understandings that justify the provision of external funding support for the organization, as well as justifying the nonreimbursed service of the members of the board and service volunteers. The mission also serves to justify the "less-than-marketplace" terms of compensation under which members of the operational staff agree to join the organization.

It is the board that carries the ultimate ethical responsibility for ensuring that the operations of the organization are, indeed, consistent with the mission of the organization. However, this ethical responsibility for consistency between the organizational mission and organizational operation is shared with staff members who are expected to bring to the organization a set of professionally based ethical standards, or a personal set of ethical standards.

A high level of motivation may unite the members of the board and the staff when there is a high degree of consensus about the organizational mission and the implications of that mission for organizational activities. However, there may also be serious internal dissensus and conflict when there is not a consensus about the implications of the organizational mission, or when the realities of organizational operation, and survival, appear to conflict with the implications of the mission. Boards of directors are often more cautious than staff members, in part because of the fiduciary responsibility of the board for the conservative use of community resources and for the continuity of the organization, and in part because of the conservative ideological social-policy perspective of most nonprofit board members (Kramer 1975).

Whether the human service organization is a voluntary nonprofit human service organization or a quasi-governmental nonprofit organization, such structures are created with the objective of providing a significant level of organizational independence and flexibility. In many instances of quasi-governmental nonprofit human service organizations, there is a specific intent to exempt a particular type of service organization from the detailed rules and procedures that govern the core operations of standard governmental bureaus. In the world of voluntary nonprofit organizations, the objective is to encourage diversity and initiative by exempting such organizations from direct oversight or control by other organizations. However, autonomy and flexibility also make accountability more complex and make it possible for serious abuses or accountability failures to occur involving the governing board (Gibelman, Gelman, and Pollack 1997).

One form of board wrongdoing includes self-serving actions by individual members of a board of directors or by the board collectively. Examples include the direct involvement of members of the board in financial decisions that benefit individuals they are closely associated with, such as decisions about the purchase of organizational insurance, or the selection of senior managers on the basis of personal relationships with members of the board. Self-serving actions can also include the provision of expensive benefits to board members, often in connection with meetings of the board.

Board wrongdoing can also include failure to exercise oversight over the financial affairs of the organization, with the result that resources of the organization are depleted and the organization is unable to continue to provide the services for which it was established. Another critical form of board wrongdoing is the failure of the board of directors to carry out systematic oversight of organizational performance. This can include failure to exercise supervision over the actions of the organizational executive.

A recent high-profile example involved the United Way of America (Brilliant 1990; Glaser 1994).

> *In 1995, the Federal District Court of Virginia convicted William Aramony, previously the CEO of the United Way of America, on twenty-five counts of conspiracy, mail and wire fraud, filing of false income tax returns, and transactions involving criminally derived property. The criminal indictment also accused Mr. Aramony of using his position to seek sexual favors from other United Way employees. Mr. Aramony served as the CEO of the United Way of America under a board of directors that included executives from Fortune 500 corporations. During this period, there was a steady growth in the support of the United Way movement among national corporations. Among the reported examples of executive malpractice were the maintenance of an expensive apartment in New York City where the board meetings were usually held, lavish expenditures on travel, and the establishment of spin-off subsidiaries, headed by friends or family members. The justification offered by Mr. Aramony, and accepted by at least some members of the board, was that his personal style of administration was consistent with the operational style of the corporate executives with whom he was dealing.*

In addition to the routine reporting procedures that are being required by external legitimation and funding sources, the scope of external monitoring of nonprofit organizations has increased as the service activities of such organizations have expanded, and also as a response to highly visible failures in board performance. Such monitoring may include lawsuits by persons who have been directly affected by an action of the service organization, legal action initiated by a state attorney general under the statutes governing nonprofit organizations, action by an accrediting body, investigative action by a funding source, or investigative reporting by news media. Furthermore, more intensive governmental regulation of nonprofit organizations has been proposed as a result of events such as the United Way of America scandal (Chisolm 1995).

CHARACTERISTICS OF BOARDS OF DIRECTORS

The characteristics of boards of directors vary in many dimensions. Important variables include size, the governance structure of the board, the personal characteristics of board members within the board membership, and the degree of diversity among them.

Size

Boards of directors in human service organizations come in three sizes: executive boards, governing boards, and support boards. *Executive boards* generally have a membership of ten or fewer persons. One example of an executive board is the elected school board, which in most communities has ten or fewer members. Some voluntary nonprofit service organizations, philanthropic foundations, and public commissions may also have boards of this size. The executive board generally functions as a unit, with the full membership making the significant decisions although there may be small subcommittees with specialized assignments. The board may meet at least once a month, and frequently more often, depending on the scope of authority that is delegated to the board chair. Normative expectations are that all board members will be present for each meeting of the board. With a board of this size, there is an opportunity for each board member to participate actively in all board discussions.

The *governing board* has ten to twenty-five members. This is the typical nonprofit service organization board, and many quasi-governmental nonprofits and public commissions have a similar structure. This board size provides an opportunity for representation of a variety of constituency interests while maintaining a pattern of active participation on the part of most members. Governing boards often have an executive committee consisting of officers and additional members from the board as a whole. The board may meet once each month, or even less frequently, with the executive committee authorized to act for the board between meetings. The governing board is likely to have greater diversity in participation patterns than the executive board. Some members attend every meeting and actively participate in most discussions, whereas others attend regularly but do not participate actively, and there are a few members whose attendance and participation may be less frequent but who represent important constituencies or who assist the organization in other ways. The governing board often has a regular set of subcommittees, including both *functional* committees—for example, finance, nominating—and *program component oversight* committees.

The *support board* has more than twenty-five members, sometimes as many as a hundred. The support board operates largely through an executive committee and subcommittees, with the full membership of the board meeting infrequently and having limited formal authority. The support board, in particular, is likely to include members who attend infrequently, if at all, but who represent important constituencies including funders and civic leaders, who primarily assist in the public legitimation of the organization through the inclusion of their names on the organizational letterhead.

Board Structure

The basic organizational structure of most boards is similar to traditional patterns within voluntary associations. Board officers generally include a chair, vice-chair, secretary, and treasurer or finance chair. The degree of internal elaboration of board structure is dependent in part on the board size, and in particular on assumptions about the time investment that board members are prepared to make. Most organizations have some form of a finance committee with particular responsibility for monitoring the flow of financial resources, or such responsibility is assigned to the board treasurer. Self-perpetuating boards normally have a nominating committee with responsibility for recruiting and recommending new board members.

Board structure is often determined by assumptions about the nature of the relationship between the board and the program operations of the service organization. Boards that are organized for the maximum time efficiency of board members assume that all aspects of the organizational operation are reported to the board through the executive and that the executive is the only member of the management staff that board members deal with consistently in an official capacity. Other administrative officers are involved in meetings of the board through the executive.

Boards that are organized for maximum involvement of the members of the board, and that assume more extensive participation by board members, may have a structure of board committees that parallels the program structure. Thus each program department has a board subcommittee that meets regularly with department administrators. The subcommittee may then become the channel for input to the full board in regard to the particular program department.

An executive-centered framework of communication with the board may require that differences in perspectives on program and policy issues among organizational staff members be resolved, or suppressed, before an issue is taken to the board. Alternatively, the executive controls the manner in which alternative proposals are presented to the board. A program subcommittee structure allows program unit directors direct access to members of the board. One consequence is that differences in perspectives among members of the administrative staff may become differences among subgroups within the board as program subcommittees become advocate voices in support of the program department with which they are associated. This can result in persistent internal conflicts within the board—for example, over budget allocations among various program departments, or over the allocation of office and program space— rather than a consideration by the full board of the strategies involved in the total operation of the organization.

Board Member Characteristics

Although the characteristics of the board members of human service organizations can vary widely, the most prevalent pattern across all such organizations is that the majority of board members are White men, college educated, from business and professional backgrounds, and between forty and seventy years old. The second largest group consists of women with similar age, ethnic, and educational background characteristics. A limited number of human service boards have only women as members, and some boards have only persons from African American, Latino, Asian American, or American Indian backgrounds. The board members of many human service organizations have personal characteristics that are quite similar to those of middle- and upper-level management in corporate firms and in governmental bureaus.

As Kramer (1975) notes, the characteristics of typical board members suggest that there are significant power and status differentials between the board members and the executive of a nonprofit or quasi-governmental nonprofit service organization. This suggests that a high level of controversy could exist when there are social policy and ideological differences between the executive and some or all of the board members, as Kramer notes in a summary of three existing studies of board and executive social policy beliefs. However, such controversies are relatively rare. Kramer notes that the self-perpetuating system of selection for board members helps to perpetuate a board culture that includes the avoidance of ideological conflict. Moreover, board membership in a single organization is not a highly salient role for most board members. It is more generally viewed as one part of a general commitment to public service. However, when a board member has a high attachment to a particular organization—for instance, as an active volunteer or a major financial supporter—there may be more readiness to engage in controversy.

Often, an overlap exists between the characteristics of board members and the characteristics of persons who have access to major sources of organizational funding, including wealthy individuals, corporate executives, and public officials, or their spouses. There is also likely to be little similarity between the characteristics of board members and the characteristics of persons using the services produced by these human service organizations. This is true of gender characteristics where women predominate among users, either as direct service users or as the family surrogate acting in behalf of children and dependent older family members. It is also true for age characteristics where service users tend to be either younger or older than the predominant group of board members. Similar differences often exist in terms of income/asset characteristics and ethnic background characteristics between service users and board members. Exceptions occur when an organization draws board members from within an explicit and narrowly defined service population.

This pattern of board membership reflects the fact that among all the stakeholder constituencies, the most significant constituencies operationally are those that control the flow of essential resources—legitimation and funding. The central public or external responsibility of the board is the establishment of policies governing program operation that can be accepted by external sources of funding as the basis for providing such funding—whether large grants or individual contributions. Increasingly, this includes responsibility for anticipating changes in funding sources and making strategic decisions about the future direction of organizational development (Stone, Bigelow, and Crittenden 1999).

The member characteristics of a traditional board of directors reflect, implicitly, an assumption that the board is actually a body of trustees—that is, a group of trusted individuals acting in behalf of the interests of the community. During the 1960s, there was an increased emphasis on the inclusion of service users and residents of lower-income neighborhoods on human service policy boards, with the assumption that they could be trusted specifically to represent the interests of actual or potential service users. This was in part a response to the civil rights movement, and in part it was a response to the experience of several large-scale social change initiatives in central city communities that had been unsuccessful, partly because of neighborhood rejection. The provisions for "maximum feasible participation" in community action agencies and similar provisions in the model-cities program brought attention to this issue in many types of nonprofit human service organizations (Matusow 1984).

Since then, many human service organizations have given substantial attention to creating a diverse representation of stakeholder constituencies in the governing board (Fletcher 1997). Alternatively, this objective has been addressed by creating advisory councils or advisory committees with limited formal authority (see later). The objective may be either to include a wider range of perspectives in board discussions or to have explicit representation of specific constituency interests, including representation of service users or community surrogates of potential users. The objective may also be to include a more diverse age range among board members or to include among the board members individuals from a more diverse range of ethnic and cultural backgrounds. In some instances, the legislative creation of a board of directors for a quasi-governmental nonprofit organization may include explicit mandates for the inclusion of service users, or of representatives of other constituencies such as specific professional groups, or of businesses potentially affected by the actions of the service organization.

Most voluntary nonprofit boards are self-perpetuating with an internal nominating committee that makes recommendations to the full board for the election of new board members. The nominating committee may also have responsibility for recommending a single slate of nominees for board officer positions. The pattern of self-perpetuation in voluntary nonprofits is in contrast to many quasi-governmental nonprofits or public commissions in which the members are appointed by external sources. Efforts to diversify voluntary nonprofit board membership may be handled directly by the internal board-nominating committee through the active recruitment of potential members to be considered by such a nominating committee, through the selection of individuals from a slate of nominations by outside groups, or by recommending a process of direct election from an external constituency.

The effectiveness of efforts to include new board members whose personal characteristics differ from the dominant characteristics of existing board members, or to ensure the continuing participation of such persons, depends on a number of factors:

- *The process for selecting new members.* In most self-perpetuating boards, new nominees are selected by the nominating committee from among persons who are known to the existing members of the board—that is, persons who travel in the same occupational or social circles as current board members. Given the degree of social, occupational, and economic stratification that exists in the United States, as well as de facto residential segregation, current board members are likely to suggest new members who are similar to themselves. This pattern is reinforced by the emphasis on consensus decision making within most boards.
- *The social culture of the board.* The extent to which the board members participate in informal and socializing activities apart from the formal meetings of the board can often determine the extent to which board members from different social and cultural backgrounds feel accepted and comfortable in their role as a board member. This may involve the issues of where board meetings are held and the extent to which there are related social events that are held in the homes of board members, events that may serve to highlight social and economic distinctions among board members.
- *Financial expectations.* As the role of nonprofit boards in fund-raising increases, expectations often increase for members of the board to participate financially, either directly, or through the provision of resources, including personal time, that are needed to organize large fund-raising activities, or by providing access to persons who do have such resources. To the extent that nontraditional board members do not have such personal resources or connections, their comfort level is diminished and their influence within the board may be affected.
- *The "rule of two."* The introduction of a person whose personal characteristics differ markedly from those of the general membership of

the board should normally be accompanied by the introduction of at least one more person who shares similar characteristics (Martin 1985b). The appointment of a single token board member, whether the tokenism is in terms of gender, age, economic status, or ethnic background, may be expected to have little substantive impact on board discussions and decisions (Pearl and Bryant 2000). Two persons who share some common element of identity may establish a mutually reinforcing subgroup in board discussions, increasing the visibility of shared concerns, even if these individuals do not take sharply different positions on most of the issues before the board. Moreover, two members can provide the appearance of continuity of constituency board participation even if one or the other is unable to be present at all meetings, and even if they do not agree on the issues before the board. Such a subgroup can also provide an opportunity for discussion of mutual concerns outside the board meeting and the development of political strategies for influencing board action with shared responsibility for the recruitment of support from other members of the board.

Constituency Representation

Another critical element in the appointment of a nontraditional member to a board of directors is the nature of the representation role, which is involved implicitly or explicitly. In many instances, efforts to diversify board membership characteristics include assumptions not only that the new board members will bring their own personal perspectives into the board deliberations but also that they will represent a stakeholder constituency that is not represented within the current board membership (Fletcher 1997). There may, however, be simplistic and inaccurate assumptions about representativeness on the part of other members of the board (Alexander 1976; Pearl and Bryant 2000). A number of different forms of representation may be involved in board membership. Each form of representation has different implications for the role of an individual in the board deliberations.

The most common form of assumed representativeness is that of statistical, or categorical, representation (Alexander and McCann 1956). That is, the individual involved is assumed to represent some significant population category because of individual personal characteristics. Thus a girl who is a senior high school student, and also a class leader, is selected to serve on an organization board on the basis that she will represent adolescent girls in the community. A seventy-five-year-old retired banker, with a vacation home in another state, is appointed to the board to represent senior citizens. A physician from an African American background is assumed to represent African Americans in the community. In these instances, there is no organized stakeholder constituency, no provision for systematic interaction with other persons in the same category, and no assurance that the categorical trait for which the person was selected is actually the most salient for that individual in board discussions. For example, the African American physician may, in fact, reflect the interests of the community medical establishment rather than the interests of local residents who come from African American backgrounds.

A second form of representation involves the individual who is interested in the work of the service organization and who is also known to be a member of a community association, a manager in a local business firm, or a member of a religious congregation. In selecting such a person, a board nominating committee may assume that that individual will serve as a channel of communication, bringing the perspectives of the members of a particular organization and taking back information to those persons. However, there may be little consistency in such communication, and, indeed, the individual may not reflect at all the perspectives of other persons in that organization.

A third form of representation involves the individual who is designated by the members of an existing constituency group but with no formal provision for accountability to that group. Thus a neighborhood association may designate one or more individuals to serve on the advisory board of a public library branch or a family counseling agency neighborhood outreach program. Or a city council may designate specific individuals to serve on the board of the community mental health center. However, there is no consistent expectation that these individuals will report back to the neighborhood association, or the city council, or in any way be held accountable for their position on the decisions made by the board of directors.

A fourth form of representation involves an individual who is selected by the members of an organized constituency with an expectation of regular communication. Thus the Gray Panthers may appoint an organizational officer to serve on the board of a senior citizens center with the expectation that there will be regular reports to the Gray Panther membership and that the opinions of the Gray Panther members will be shared with the other board members.

A fifth form of representation involves the constituency delegate. In this instance, the individual is selected by a constituency association and is expected to consult with, *and to be bound by*, the position of that association in voting on any substantive policy issue. For example, an association of parents whose children have chronic, long-term disability conditions may appoint an "instructed delegate" to the board of an organization providing services to their children, with the understanding that that person will not participate in any policy decision until there has been consultation with other members of the association and until the recommendation of the association has been determined on the issue. Labor unions have often insisted that a board member who is publicly identified as being a union member should be an official delegate selected by and accountable to the union.

A sixth form of representation involves the individual who is elected by the members of a local constituency. Although the use of such representation is infrequent, it was used in community action agency boards in the 1960s. Moreover, it is frequently used in public commissions that have a geographic base, such as water district commissions or hospital district commissions. Although the degree of formal reporting accountability of such elected representatives may vary widely, their actions are subject to public scrutiny.

Differences in assumptions about the nature of representation can cause serious misunderstandings within a board. For example, support by an individual perceived to be a categorical constituency representative for a particular board decision, such as a decision to establish a new service location in an underserved part of the community, may be assumed to be an endorsement of that policy by other community members with similar characteristics (Alexander 1976). Or the reluctance of a delegate board member to support a particular program initiative until after there has been an opportunity for consultation with a constituency organization may be interpreted by other board members as a personal objection to the proposal or a personal effort to block the proposed action.

Failure to take these issues into consideration may mean that efforts to create a greater diversity of perspectives within the board do not succeed.

The new board member either may become inactive or may simply join the general board consensus without contributing a distinctive perspective. A personal sense of social acceptance by the board can become an important issue when the new board member is, in reality, a single individual, representing only her- or himself. However, when the new member is a formal representative of an external constituency and is accountable to that constituency, active participation in board decision making may persist, regardless of the level of social acceptance that the individual experiences.

The issue of representing service users is particularly difficult to resolve. For most service organizations, the user constituency is not cohesive or organized and is, therefore, unable to select a true representative, or to hold such a representative accountable. Moreover, a single, token representative will, most often, have limited impact on significant board decisions that affect service users. Other methods of obtaining service user input may be more effective, including surveys, focus groups, panel presentations to the board, and board member participation in a user public hearing (see chapter 6).

BOARD PROCESS

Life Cycle of the Board of Directors

Boards of directors of voluntary nonprofit service organizations, in most cases, have "life cycle stages," although the experience of any one organization may vary (Dart et al. 1996). The most critical periods for the board of directors are the periods of transition from one stage to another. To the extent that a quasi-governmental nonprofit organization or a public commission has a relatively stable board of directors over an extended period of time, the pattern of transitions may be similar to that in stable nonprofit organizations. However, if the external appointment of board members results in frequent changes in board memberships and internal controversies, the pattern of organizational transitions may be quite different.

In the initial stages of organization, the initiators of a new service organization often have a dominant role. This is particularly likely to occur when a formal, nonprofit, start-up service organization emerges from what has been a voluntary membership association or a social movement collective (Hyde 1992). Such a transition may be the specific objective of the members of the association, or it may occur when a voluntary association receives funding to create a service activity. The initiating leaders in such a transition may be incorporated as the board officers in a newly incorporated nonprofit organization, or they may become the executive staff in the new organization with a group of friends and supporters as the initial members of the board.

Throughout this initial period, personal relationships among the program initiators are central to the development of the organization. The board may become the dominant force in the organization, with board members actively involved in many aspects of organizational development, including being active as service volunteers (Zald 1969). Alternatively, when the program initiators become the program managers, the board function may be primarily that of an advocacy, support, fund-raising body, leaving most, or all, of the details of program development to the original initiators as the administrative staff.

The first organizational transition generally occurs when the initiating leadership is replaced. This may result from a change in board leadership as the board membership is expanded to establish a stronger community support base. New board members may bring new perspectives about the program structure or may represent other constituencies that expect the board to take on a greater oversight function. A change in board leadership may come easily and naturally, or it may be forced by new members of the board, some of whom may represent, directly or indirectly, external funding sources.

Alternatively, the transition may come when the original executive is replaced, either voluntarily or involuntarily. An assumption by the original initiators that the program is, in reality, a personal creation can lead to the exclusion of board members from meaningful decision making until a program (or funding) crisis pushes the board members into taking action. There are, of course, exceptional situations in which the original creators of a service program serve as the ongoing, and successful, leaders of a service organization over many years.

Many organizations are able to manage this initial process of leadership transition by creating ceremonial events that recognize and celebrate the contributions of the organizational founders. However, under a worst-case scenario of transition, there is a major rupture, and the program initiators leave with the objective of re-creating the organization in their original image. Similar processes can occur within a governmental commission, particularly when the original advocates for the establishment of such a commission constitute the original members of the governing body or are appointed as senior managers. Similar difficult transition processes can also occur within start-up for-profit service organizations, particularly when venture capitalists finance the expansion of the organization and then take over control of the organization to ensure that their financial objectives will be met.

Following the initial organizational transition, new organizations may have an extended period of growth and development within the "environmental niche" in which they first emerged. Board members and management leadership may be active partners in developing funding resources and implementing program development plans. During this period, board members are likely to become more involved in oversight functions as the requirements of accountability to external legitimation and funding sources take on more importance. There may be less personal involvement with program activities as the decision responsibilities of board members take more time. The intensity of personal relationships involving board members and senior staff members that marked the beginning stage of development is lessened when there are changes in board membership as well as among the management and professional staff members.

In some instances, the period of initial organizational stability may be transformed into a long-term pattern of stable operation marked by substantial continuity in both board and management leadership. This continuity is often supported by a relatively stable and predictable external environment. Board members may become accustomed to a smoothly operating organization with few critical or decisive decisions to be made. This is particularly likely to occur when there is access to dependable sources of funding with some opportunity for regular increases.

However, such long-term stable conditions are more likely to be an exception than the rule. More often, the organization is faced periodically with significant transitions or transformations. These may include program and goal changes, major changes in funding patterns, and mergers. Such transitions are periods in which the responsibility of the board is sharply increased (Zald 1969). One critical form of transition involves the death, retirement, or departure of a long-time executive, particularly one who has had a dominant leadership role in relationships with the board. Suddenly, the board is faced with the responsibility of taking an active role in the processes of transition and of making a series of interim decisions, many of which were previously dealt with by the executive.

In such situations, a new executive selected by the board may find that it is difficult to satisfy the expectations of board members, in addition to any problems that may emerge in staff relationships (Hernandez and Leslie 2001). Perspectives may emerge among board members and administrative staff members that had previously been suppressed. The selection of a new executive by the board may have been based on a need for fresh ideas and pushing ahead with what was perceived as an overdue need for changes in organizational operation, either in terms of service programs or administrative practices. Some of these changes may be urged by external funding sources. However, the initiation of such changes may also appear to imply criticism of the preceding executive, whose virtues become magnified and whose limitations are diminished in the memory of both board members and staff. And long-term senior program staff members, who may have more job security than the new executive, may have personal connections with key board members that bypass official channels of communication. The term of service of the initial successor to a really long-time and popular executive is often quite limited, with diminishing confidence in the executive and with increasing controversy within the board that, in part, may reflect conflict among staff members.

Other critical organizational transitions may occur when there are changes in the external environment that affect legitimation—intensified requirements for organizational licensing or accreditation—or that affect funding. Changes in the ecological niche may result in sharply diminished funding resources, or in the emergence of new organizations that create a competitive environment (Wernet and Austin 1991). The board may be faced with making substantial program and personnel cutbacks to adjust to a lower level of funding, or, even more difficult, it may be faced with a major operational deficit because an adjustment to reduced funding was not dealt with in a timely fashion. In other instances, changes in funding or in organizational leadership may lead to consideration of an organizational merger, or, in the current environment of commercial development of human services, including health care, they may lead to consideration of a potential buyout of a nonprofit organization by a for-profit firm.

Other critical transitions may involve major program transformations—from a residential treatment center for children to a community-based, day-treatment, foster-care and adoption service—that may involve serious disagreements within the existing staff as well as uncertain estimates about the potential demand for such services and future funding possibilities. All of these transitions involve high levels of uncertainty for board members and serious threats to the normal consensus decision processes of the board. It is in these transition periods that the full force of responsibility involved in board membership becomes most apparent (Wernet 1988).

A final stage in the life cycle of a board of directors comes when a particular organization can no longer continue to operate effectively, as a result of either internal mistakes or, more likely, upcoming changes in the external environment identified through a strategic planning process. The board of directors then becomes involved in the decisions that must be made when terminating staff operations, preserving, or disposing of, the remaining assets of the organization, and complying with the legal requirements of final accountability. This includes dealing with the sense of loss among persons closely identified with the organization, including recriminations from those persons, including financial supporters and service users, who feel that such an ending was not required and that they are being unjustly abandoned.

The Board Chair

The chair of the board of directors is structurally the most important board position (Dorsey 1992). It is also a very unusual position, quite different from the chairman of the board in a for-profit firm. The ultimate source of leadership authority within the nonprofit or quasi-governmental human service organization rests with the board chair, but it is the executive who often provides continuity of leadership over time, and who, in fact, may be actively involved in the process of selecting a new board chair. The division of responsibilities between these two positions is shaped by the structural separation between the board chair, an unpaid but influential leadership position in the organization, and the executive, a paid leadership position but one without a vote in the board decision processes.

How a board chair prioritizes the use of personal time among several potential areas of responsibility has important consequences for the board operation, for the executive, and for the service organization. The potential areas of responsibility for the board chair include the following:

- Management of the board decision processes within meetings
- Management of personal relationships within the board
- Representation to other organizations, in particular to funding sources
- Representation of the organization to the general public
- Representation of the board to the executive and staff
- Consultation to the executive
- Leadership in board member training and board development
- Fund-raising leadership within the board
- Advocating for, and developing support for, particular decision outcomes in board discussions

The board chair may choose to function solely as a presiding officer for meetings of the board, focusing on the formal meeting procedures, and dealing with the executive only to submit formal reports to the board. Other areas of responsibility may be assigned, or left by default, to other members of the board or to management staff. Alternatively, the board chair may take an active role in all internal aspects of the board process, including a program of board development (Axelrod 1994), and in the working relationship with the executive, but without taking any responsibility for the relationship of the organization to its environment.

However, a board chair may also take on responsibilities in all the areas just identified, being an active leader within the board processes, having an intensive working relationship with the executive, and serving as the principle spokesperson for the organization in the community. Since there are few formal guidelines for a board chair, the pattern that emerges with any single board chair is likely to be a combination of the experience of that person in other organizations, observation of the preceding board chair in this organization, the personal abilities and interests and the time and money resources of the chair, and occasional discussions with the executive about the division of responsibilities.

Board Decision Processes

The board of directors is primarily a decision-making body. Even on technical issues, such as the purchase or leasing of operating space, it is the decision of the board that makes such actions legal and binding. In other areas, such as employment agreements with new staff members, it is a formal delegation of such authority to an executive officer that makes such actions official. Central to the operation of the board are the decision processes used by the board.

Board decision making follows essentially two patterns, which are related to the base of authority for individual members of the board. The predominant pattern of decision making occurs through *negotiated consensus* when new members of a board are elected by the current board members, or when they are elected by a general membership body associated with the organization based on nominations from the board. A study of nonprofit board effectiveness by Herman and Heimovics (1994b) reported that 91 percent of the sixty-four boards surveyed reported using consensus decision making. The second pattern, *contested majority vote* decision making, which involves approval by a majority vote but with a dissenting minority, can occur when board members are appointed or elected from outside sources, often for fixed terms of service.

The members of the board of directors of a self-perpetuating nonprofit organization, in which board members are appointed as individuals without accountability to any specific external constituency, face strong internal pressures to act through negotiated consensus. There is also a preference for low-risk action proposals that are unlikely to generate strong objections from individual board members. Since a major function of the board is to represent the organization to the community, including the provision of leadership in fund-raising, it is of critical importance that the board present itself to the community as a unified body. Persistent and visible dissension within such a board may limit its ability to function effectively as an organizational support and advocacy body. It may also create doubts on the part of external funding sources about the stability of the organization.

A major function of the chair of the self-perpetuating nonprofit board is, therefore, to facilitate the negotiation of a consensus on critical policy issues. Group pressures within the board are exerted on individual members to support a consensus decision, or, at a minimum, to remain silent. Individuals who find themselves frequently in disagreement with the majority of the board members are likely to have limited influence on board decisions. Since service on such a board is voluntary, such individuals are likely to become less active, or in fact to leave the board, rather than be consistently identified with decision outcomes that they do not support.

The pattern of negotiated consensus decision making also influences the process through which a nominating committee selects new board members. A significant criterion for selection is whether the backgrounds that new board members bring are likely to be compatible with the existing board consensus—that is, whether the new board members will "fit in." This creates a strong bias in favor of choosing new board members who are similar in personal characteristics to the current board members, with the assumption that they are likely to have similar views on future issues to come before the board.

The executive in the nonprofit service organization also has a strong investment in helping the board develop a negotiated consensus decision-making style, particularly in those organizations in which the executive serves at the pleasure of the board without a formal contract. A majority positive, but sharply divided, vote on a major program or policy proposal advocated by the executive may well be viewed as departing from the negotiated consensus tradition and therefore as a major threat to the ability of the board and the executive to work together in a consensus-based collaborative consultative relationship. The negotiated consensus decision process often requires an extensive proposal development process in which objections from a single board member may require modifications in an initial proposal.

However, when individual board members are appointed by an external source, or when they are explicitly accountable to an external constituency, as, for example, in an elected school board or an externally appointed community mental health board, then there can be a series of majority vote decisions, with persistent dissenters, as long as there is a general pattern of agreement between the majority of the board members and the executive. However, in some instances, the persistent dissenters may be able to mobilize public support for their position from constituencies they represent, enlarging the arena of action on a particular proposal and limiting the ability of the majority to act.

Relationships Between Board Chair and Executive

One of the most critical human relationships in most nonprofit and quasi-governmental nonprofit human service organizations is that between the board chair and the executive. Although in some instances of an elected or externally designated board, an executive can function without the support of the chair—if the executive has the support of a majority of the board members—such a situation is most unlikely. In most boards of directors, an antagonistic relationship between the executive and the chair is intolerable and can be resolved only by the removal of one person or the other. This can mean that for the executive, the most important internal board decision is the selection of the board chair.

The operational relationship between the board chair and the executive is an interactive relationship that in actual practice may take three different forms depending on the organizational traditions and the characteristics of the two individuals involved. These are a chair-dominant relationship; an executive-dominant relationship; and a chair–executive partnership. All three models are viable organizational forms, even though the board chair generally has greater status and power in the community than the executive. There is no single, pure pattern; each pattern can result in an effective organization given a match with the expectations of the key persons involved. Kramer (1975) indicates that the executive is more likely to have a higher power position in the relationship when the organization is large and complex, when the services are highly professional, when the issue is programmatic or professional, and when the executive has long tenure and high professional status.

How responsibilities are divided between the board chair and the executive of a given board can provide a clue as to its style—for example, whether the board chair or the executive is the primary spokesperson for the organization in funding relationships, or whether the chair or the executive has the most influence in establishing the working agenda for meetings of the board. A potential area for creating a working partnership is the development of a strategic model for board meeting agendas that focuses the leadership of the board chair and the work of the board on issues that are central to the real responsibilities of the board rather than on the details of the organizational operation (Inglis and Weaver 2000). A key concern in establishing an agenda for board action is the determination of which policy issues are substantive and require board action, and which are important administrative issues that are to be decided by the executive (but also to be reported to the board).

One of the most important fiduciary responsibilities of the chair, under any conditions, is providing for the periodic review and evaluation, by the board, of the performance of the executive. "One principle is that the board should be in a position to evaluate the executive; that means that the board, or at least its officers, should have the information that will enable it to judge executive performance. Another principle is that this evaluation should be formal, and regularized, and so carried out that the position of the executive is not made untenable" (Stein 1985:195–196).

The most serious source of difficulty in the board chair–executive relationships is likely to result from changes in the occupants of either role. A new board chair may bring different expectations about the responsibilities of that position and of the executive, often based on experiences in other organizations. A new executive may bring different expectations about the role of the chair based on work experience in another setting. Since there is no clearly prescribed protocol for the chair–executive relationships, differences in expectations may not be identified or explored until serious differences in underlying assumptions have surfaced.

Relationships Among Board, Executive, and Staff

The relationships among the members of a board of directors, the executive, and other organizational staff members are often perplexingly human and sometimes consistently troublesome (Stein 1985; Green et al. 2001). The fact that board–executive–staff collaboration actually works effectively in most voluntary nonprofit and quasi-governmental human service organizations is testimony to the ability of individual people to overcome the contradictions that are built into the organizational structure and the power imbalances that exist in the relationships among key individuals.

Executives and other managers establish implementation procedures called for under the policies enacted by the board of directors. In nonprofit human service organizations, a structural separation exists between the group of individuals who have ultimate policy accountability and the group of individuals who have the responsibility for the implementation of those policies and for management of the day-to-day activities within the organization. In contrast, in the for-profit firm, these two functions overlap, with senior management executives normally being both voting members of the policy-making board and implementers of policies.

Traditional statements about the division between the policy-making responsibilities of a board of directors and the implementation responsibilities of the organizational executive and staff members ignore important realities (Drucker 1990a; Axelrod 1994). In actual practice, this structural separation of responsibilities in nonprofit human service organizations does not result in a rigid separation of operational roles and activities. The policy issues that come before a board are generally in the form of recommendations by the executive or other organizational staff members or are developed collaboratively between the executive and board members. Managerial staff provide most of the information that board members consider in making a policy decision, and management staff members usually participate in policy discussions.

The program and financial accountability for which the board is ultimately responsible requires knowledge by individual board members about the specific cost elements of program operation. This may result in detailed board recommendations dealing with specific budgetary/program implementation items. Moreover, board members and staff members often work together as partners in the planning and implementation of major fund-raising events, particularly in voluntary nonprofit organizations.

At the heart of the complexities of the board–executive–staff relationships are three principles that are part of the traditions involved in the provision of human services through nonprofit and governmental organizations. The *first principle* is that the ultimate accountability of human service organizations, both nonprofit and governmental (but not for-profit), should be to the community through the board of directors or a governmental policy body. The *second principle* is that a single manager, or executive, should be ultimately responsible for organizing the work of other persons to produce effective results from the efficient use of funding, personnel, and other relevant resources.

The *third principle* is that the expertise of professional specialists should be deferred to in areas of professional competency. Thus the expertise of architects and engineers is drawn upon for the detailed design and construction of a hospital rather than being determined by the policy authority of a board of directors or the management authority of the executive. The medical expertise of physicians is drawn upon to define the procedures to be followed in the intensive care unit of the hospital rather than the judgments of board members or of a nonmedical hospital administrator.

Although these three guiding principles are clear and explicit, areas of overlap in their application create operational ambiguity. The overlap between the first and second principles involves the issue of micromanagement, or the extent to which a policy body should become directly involved in the details of policy implementation—that is, whether a board of directors that has approved a general program proposal should also have the authority to review and modify specific details of the operational plan prepared by the management staff.

The overlap between policy authority and professional authority involves the issue of how much a policy board should be constrained in the choices it makes by the technical knowledge of professional specialists. That is, should the board of a private adoption agency be constrained to follow the formal recommendations of a social work adoption specialist in regard to transracial adoptions or the criteria for selecting adoptive parents. Or should a community mental health board should be constrained to follow the recommendations of a psychiatrist in defining agency policy for the administration of psychotropic medications, rather than the recommendations of the nonmedical executive.

The overlap between professional authority and managerial authority involves the authority of an executive to define the work procedures of professional specialists. For example, should the executive, or, alternatively, staff professionals, have the authority to define the treatment methods to be used with aggressive adolescents in a residential treatment center. This also involves the issue of direct access of professional staff members to the board of directors. Stein (1985) suggests that although the executive should have control over the pattern of access of staff members to the board of directors, there should also be defined channels through which staff concerns can be brought to the attention of the board. One such channel would be the periodic review and evaluation of the performance of the executive by the board of directors.

The board has the ultimate responsibility to define the application of these three principles when problems arise from areas of ambiguity, recognizing that the other parties involved may choose to appeal a board decision to potential sources of legitimation and support outside the organization. However, in the current environment of litigation, a board's decision to substitute its own judgment for that of the executive or professional specialists could provide the basis for legal challenges if that judgment results in ineffective or even harmful service outcomes.

The formal separation of the board, executive, and staff roles in non-profit organizations creates power and authority issues that are different from those in for-profit firms (Leduc and Block 1995). Some writers support the concept of strong board leadership on the basis of the formal responsibility of the board for establishing basic organizational policy (Carver 1990; Axelrod 1994; Houle 1997; Holland 1998). Others view the relationship between the board and the executive as interactive, with the primary leadership responsibility resting with the executive (Drucker 1990a; Herman and Heimovics 1994a).

This uncertainty about the appropriate relationship is influenced, in part, by the fact that in most nonprofit human service organizations, an individual board chair serves for a limited number of years, whereas the executive may serve indefinitely, given satisfactory service. New board members in nonprofit human service organizations and governmental commissions may have considerable public service experience, but they often have limited knowledge about the operations of the specific organization for which they will be making policy decisions and thus may have to rely heavily on the executive for information.

Zald (1969) points out that relationships between the board of directors and the executive involve power differences, differences that are often connected to the pattern of organizational funding. The role of the executive and other staff members is strengthened in interactions with the board if sources of funding are dispersed and organizational fund-raising is tied to a strong vision of a community service need rather than to the personal connections of board members. However, if individual board members are connected with major funding sources for the organization, their position vis-à-vis the executive and other staff members is strengthened. If board members are connected with powerful external constituencies, the power of the board is strengthened in contrast to a board in which individual members have few connections with external constituencies. However, in a large board, connections with different external funding constituencies may result in the creation of "cliques" among board members identified with these different funding sources (Zald 1969).

The role of the executive, and of the staff generally, is strengthened in an organization with a complex organizational structure and a highly technical service production process, as well as in the case of residential, or "total," institutions (Senor 1963). The power of the executive is strengthened and the power of the board is weakened in organizations in which board members have few contacts with the work of the organization and receive information only through the executive (Senor 1963).

Under conditions associated with the mixed economy of human services, the board–executive–staff relationships have become even more complex. Many forms of external relationships involving funding support through contracts and third-party payment agreements are negotiated directly with the executive with little or no board participation, although there may be official board sanction of a final agreement (Levin 1985; Harlan and Saidel 1994). The external funding sources then deal directly with the executive and the management staff in the implementation of the terms of the agreement, without the board having any independent authority to modify the agreement.

Tensions involving board–executive–staff relationships can develop from the overlap between the oversight functions of the board and the support/advocacy functions. Staff members, in general, regard the role of the board as being one of advocacy and support, built around interests shared by staff members and board members in the organizational mission. Staff members often perceive the primary responsibility of the board to be representation of the organization to funding sources and other external constituencies in order to garner the funding support and public endorsement that can make it possible for the staff to accomplish the goals of the organization. Moreover, the board members are expected to serve as allies if there are criticisms of the work of the organization.

Board members are, in varying degrees, aware of their oversight responsibility for the accountability of the organization to other stakeholder constituencies, even though they are also committed to the support of organizational staff members in the achievement of organizational goals (Lawry 1995). This oversight responsibility requires that board members seek information, ask questions about the information they receive, press for information on the effectiveness of the services being provided, and examine financial operations carefully. In particular, the board is ultimately accountable for the effective and efficient use of funds from sources outside the organization. This may require serious questioning of particular elements of service provision. One oversight tool available to a board is a performance audit, which is a specific look at one area of organizational activity, assessing the speed, quality, integrity, and intelligence with which a board decision has been implemented.

Board members are perceived as having the ultimate power to make the decisions that determine the general division of funds between program operations and personnel support, as well as for decisions that may affect the economic position of individual staff members. Nonprofit and governmental human service organizations generally do not have provisions for profit sharing or year-end bonuses, and as a result it is not expected that there will be any substantial connection between individual productivity effort and financial incentives. The economic framework for staff personnel is determined by the board's action on an operating budget. The dynamics of the board–executive–staff relationships are affected by the trade-off between minimizing personnel costs to extend service availability, and responsiveness to financial expectations of members of the staff.

Although some human service organizations do include a formal staff union that may play a role in determining the trade-off between the level of personnel expenditures and expanded program expenditures (Peters and Masaoka 2000), in the majority of nonprofit human service organizations and in many quasi-governmental and governmental organizations there is not a collective bargaining relationship between the staff and the board. The board members may be perceived as the ultimate authority in salary and pay decisions even though the members are acting on recommendations from the executive. The role of the board in such personnel matters means that although board members are partners with the executive and other staff members in the agency mission, they are also the ultimate bosses in personnel policies.

Board–executive–staff relationships may be particularly complex in human service organizations in which the executive is also a professional specialist. When a disagreement occurs between the executive and the board, it is often not clear whether the executive is asserting professional authority, which, in principle, is not subject to policy dictation, or management authority, which, in principle, can be defined by the policy body. If the policy action is viewed by an executive who is a professional specialist as being contrary to professional principles and ethics, then that person may feel compelled to resign. However, if it is viewed as an issue of organizational procedures, the executive may disagree but feel that it is appropriate to recognize the formal authority of the policy body. The staff may perceive the executive as having a primary responsibility for representing a professional perspective on program and policy decisions, and, indeed, for representing the interests of the professional staff members. Board members may perceive the executive as having primary responsibility for managerial recommendations and managerial decisions that affect the well-being of the organization and its status in the community, including the efficient use of financial resources, consistent with, but not determined by, professional identity and affiliation.

Writings about board process often indicate that one major responsibility of the executive is the initiation of a board development program. Such a program educates new board members about the mission and program of the service organization, assists the board in developing an efficient and effective decision-making process, and contributes to developing an understanding by the board members of the larger context for specific policy decisions (Axelrod 1994; Chait, Holland, and Taylor 1996; Holland 1998). This board development program may also be intended to contribute to the process of negotiated consensus decision making by providing in-depth exploration of critical decision issues prior to formal action by the board. Another important part of the board development process is the establishment of a process through which the board evaluates its own decision-making process and the fulfillment of its functional responsibilities.

ADVISORY COMMITTEES, COUNCILS, AND PANELS

Human service organizations often establish advisory committees or advisory councils. In some instances, these are required as a condition of receiving external funding support. For the funding source, such a condition may be intended to ensure the inclusion of opinions not represented on a board of directors or to provide for accountability to particular constituencies that are not represented on the board. Advisory committees may be appointed by a board, by an organizational executive, or by the director of a program component (Rosenthal and Young 1980). Advisory committees in nonprofit organizations normally have no legal status in comparison to the board of directors—that is, they do not carry a fiduciary responsibility (Saidel and D'Aquanni 1999).

As boards of directors of nonprofit organizations become more heavily involved in financial planning, advisory bodies may provide advisory support in functional areas that the board is not able to accommodate and may assist in maintaining connections with the service community. Saidel and D'Aquanni (1999) point out such advisory bodies may be helpful in three areas:

- In linking the organization with its community, including service users
- In complementing and strengthening governance
- In providing organizational assistance

In a variety of ways, advisory committees may extend the network of persons who are familiar with the service organization and are able to interpret the organization to members of the community. In particular, an advisory body may serve to involve individuals who may be interested in the work of the organization but are not able to undertake the intensity of involvement required by the board of directors. However, any advisory body requires substantial attention from the executive or other administrators. Indeed, in some instances, an advisory body may create serious difficulties for the organization.

An advisory body may have no formal internal structure and meet only at the initiative of the appointing person, and that person determines the agenda and serves as chair or presiding officer of the meeting. On the other hand, such a body may have a distinctive structure, with a chairperson who has a significant degree of responsibility for the timing and agenda of meetings. Although some advisory bodies may have an official and fixed membership, the membership of many advisory bodies is often quite general, with new members appointed from time to time and alternates attending meetings in the place of officially designated members. One important consideration in establishing an advisory committee is whether it is expected to represent a particular stakeholder constituency, such as residents of a particular neighborhood, or to include a cross-section of persons from various constituencies. The character of the representativeness of the members of an advisory body involves the same complexities as the representativeness of board members discussed earlier. As Onken (2000) reports, a service user advisory body may selectively include persons for whom treatment has been successful and who have social skills comparable to those of members of a board of directors. Such persons may fail to represent the concerns of those with less successful outcomes who have immediate and urgent personal survival problems.

An advisory body, on occasion, may become a complex element in the governance structure of a human service organization. There are two general perceptions of the function of an advisory committee. The first perception is that it is *outward looking*, created by the organization so that the members can receive information from the service organization, ask questions for clarification, and disseminate the information to particular constituencies or audiences. These constituencies could include a group of service users, other service organizations, community influentials, members of a profession, or corporate executives.

With such a perception of the advisory function, the meetings may be primarily occupied with presentations about the organization and its services. Such presentations may include staff presentations, visual and printed reports, and testimonials by service participants. Participation by individual members of the advisory body often diminishes, or disappears, over time, to the extent that such unidirectional show-and-tell presentations provide little opportunity for actual advice-giving responses by the members of the advisory committee. Alternatively, other individuals with limited responsibilities and authority may replace attendance by senior executives or leadership persons from other organizations. Moreover, passive participation can result in negative evaluations of the information that is presented and the dissemination of such evaluations to various organizational constituencies.

A second perception of the advisory group is that it is *inward looking*, that the members have, in fact, been invited to provide collective advice to the organization. However, the process of advice giving can turn out to be relatively complex. An advisory body that includes representatives from a number of different constituencies may present particular difficulties in providing collective advice. Moreover, to the extent that an advisory group is provided with only general information about the organization's activities, any advice that is offered may not be consistent with the constraints that are part of the financial support arrangements for a particular program activity.

The advice from various members of the advisory committee may also not be compatible with, or may conflict directly with, decisions that have already been made by the executive or by the board of directors. Efforts by an organizational executive to explain why such advice cannot be followed may be viewed as excuses or defensive rationalizations. Moreover, consistent failure to follow advice when it is offered may also be met by dwindling participation in advisory group meetings. Alternatively, the result could be a significant degree of alienation and anger among the members of the advisory group, which is then communicated to the several constituencies represented by the advisory group members.

It is also possible that a power contest may develop between an advisory body that has its own organizational structure with a chairperson who controls the timing and agenda of meetings, and whose advice is not followed, and the organizational executive, or between the advisory body and the board of directors. In such a situation, the chair of the advisory body may appeal directly to the full board of directors, to external constituencies, or to the news media in an effort to require the organization to respond to the advice being offered.

Although an advisory committee is often thought of as a collective body, it may also be viewed as primarily a group of individuals, or an *advisory panel*, offering individual advice and counsel rather than collective advice. Interested individuals may be invited to serve on such a panel rather than as members of a committee. Such an advisory panel can also serve as an expanded audience for detailed reports on organizational activities. The members may meet together only at the initiative of the executive or the board of directors. However, official recognition of such a panel of individuals may provide organizational access to specialized information and valuable individual advice, as an alternative to the collective advice that might be shaped by the happenstance of attendance at an advisory committee meeting. A failure to recognize the importance of the distinction between collective advice giving and individualized advice giving can result in a struggle for control over organizational policy without providing the specific forms of advice that could be particularly important for the organization.

SUMMARY

Boards of directors are central to the effectiveness of nonprofit and quasi-governmental nonprofit human service organizations as well as many governmental organizations. Boards of directors are the legal embodiment of the service organization and are ultimately accountable for the operation of the organization. An important distinction between nonprofit service organizations and for-profit service organizations is the structure and function of the unpaid volunteer board of directors. Nonprofit boards of directors are also important mediating and cross-linking elements in the civil society of the United States, providing a variety of civic leadership development opportunities. The effective governance of nonprofit human service organizations is ultimately shaped by a complex set of personal ethics and civic values rather than financial, marketplace values. These values are also central to the effective functioning of the civil society more broadly.

Human service boards of directors have very diverse characteristics in size, structure, and membership, and in the pattern of representative connections to significant constituencies. Human service boards of directors are often viewed as representing the interests of the community, or of the larger society, although most such boards are not representative of their community, and, in particular, are not directly representative of the constituency of service users. Efforts to achieve greater diversity among the members of self-perpetuating nonprofit boards of directors are often constrained by the internal dynamics of such boards.

Relationships between the board of directors and other participants in a human service organization involve both formal structures and complex personal interactions. Particularly complicated is the relationship between the board of directors and the executive, as the executive has a major role in the development and functioning of the board but not a formal role in board decision making, and is subject ultimately to control by the board. Changes in funding patterns for nonprofit organizations have increased the relative power of the executive and the organizational staff in relationships with the board of directors. Advisory committees, councils, and panels can expand the involvement of relevant constituencies in the work of the human service organization. However, such bodies may also increase the complexity of organizational governance.

ELEVEN

ACCOUNTABILITY

The end of the twentieth century marks a critical period for nonprofit organizations. It is not only that they are facing funding shortages. Not having enough money is a chronic problem. . . . Now, however, growing pressures are compounding the problem created by budget concerns:

• *The demand for services is increasing as funds decline.*
• *Funders are no longer willing to allocate funds simply on the basis of showing the need for the services an agency supplies. . . . The watchwords of the day are* accountability, impact, outcome effectiveness, quality service.
• *Funders are not the only ones using these watchwords. The recipients of services are no longer willing to accept what is provided if they are not satisfied. They, too, are organizing to demand client satisfaction.*

—Murray and Tassie (1994:303)

THE ACCOUNTABILITY of service organizations for evidence of service effectiveness is a recurrent issue in human service programs. Traditionally, a combination of the mission statement for nonprofit service organizations and the legislative mandate for governmental organizations, plus quality assurance control through staff training, professional education, and professional standards of practice (Wells and Brook 1988), have been taken as evidence of the quality, and presumed effectiveness, of the services provided for the service user. However, there are now increasing expectations for information about service outcomes, particularly as the scope of human service programs has increased dramatically together with major expansions of governmental funding for such programs. In nonprofit and quasi-governmental nonprofit organizations, decisions about the design of effectiveness assessments are a critical area of program policy that involves decisions by boards of directors as well as by executive staff members.

Much of the demand for evidence of effectiveness comes from funding sources—governmental bodies, foundations, and business firms—particularly in the health-care and education sectors. These funding sources are concerned with the effective use of limited financial resources. Without measures of service effectiveness, funding sources, in making funding decisions, are often limited to descriptive information about program objectives and qualifications of service specialists, quantitative information about past provision of services, and individual testimonies from service users.

Having only limited information encourages the pursuit of fads in the funding of services, as happens when a single example of what is widely reported as a successful program with some evidence of positive short-term results becomes extensively replicated. Such replications, however, may take place under very different operational conditions, with outcomes that often fail to confirm the original reported results. As Schorr (1997:31) points out, "Thus, the proven effectiveness of intensive individualized services is routinely diluted—and destroyed—by the pressure to reach large numbers with inadequate resources."

The increasing attention to effectiveness assessment is motivated by two concerns. First, service programs need to be improved by providing more effective services—for example, improving treatments for individuals with chronic and severe mental illness. Second, the most effective and efficient form of program intervention must be selected to achieve the best outcomes with a given level of funding—for example, to protect the future of children who have been abused in their biological families, a choice is made between the use of family preservation services and foster care placement.

However, increased attention to service effectiveness also focuses attention on the question of the actual benefits that are provided for the service user. What are the benefits for an adult from an alcoholism treatment program, or for an adolescent from residential treatment center services? What are the educational achievement benefits for a student in a public middle school or in an independent charter school? Pressure for accountability and evidence of effectiveness, even on a limited basis, can result in increased examination of the actual benefits for service users even though individual service users, in general, have a low power position in human service programs (see chapter 6). The use of total quality management, especially as a method of improving service effectiveness, focuses attention on service user satisfaction (Burton and Gummer 1995).

This chapter deals with the following:

- The historical development of efforts to assess the effectiveness of human service organizations and of service programs
- Dynamics in the design of service effectiveness evaluation
- Alternative approaches to the measurement of effectiveness
- The application of total quality management to human service organizations

THE HISTORICAL DEVELOPMENT OF EFFECTIVENESS ASSESSMENT

Early efforts to measure program effectiveness, primarily involving voluntary nonprofit service organizations, determined effectiveness largely on the basis of the quantity of *throughputs* (Murray and Tassie 1994; Kettner, Moroney, and Martin 1999), or the number of active cases (that is, the number of days of hospital care, number of service interviews or home visits, membership counts, activity participation counts) and the quantity of *outputs*, or completed services (that is, the number of closed cases, adoption placements, or hospital discharges). Such quantitative measures were often supplemented by selected personal testimonies and individual vignettes of successful case outcomes. Some youth-serving activity centers installed turnstiles to provide gross counts of the number of individuals coming through the door, who were then reported as receiving the services of the center.

Similarly, activity reports in elementary and secondary schools included attendance statistics and numbers of students completing particular courses. State psychiatric hospitals reported admissions and daily occupancy statistics, as well as the number of discharges (often reported as the number of cures). Such cure numbers were often distorted by the number of individuals who were repeatedly discharged but then readmitted. Such self-reported activity counts assumed that the provision of any service that was intended to create a positive outcome was equal to accomplishing that outcome.

This assumption of positive outcomes, based on charitable intent, was reflected in the general legal assumption that non-profit providers of well-intended services could not be sued by service users (Zelman 1977). Similarly, users of governmental services were restricted in their ability as individuals to sue state or federal governments for providing inappropriate or ineffective services.

Community fund-raising organizations such as the Community Chest, and later the United Way, used such activity counts in making decisions about allocating funds from the annual fund-raising campaign. This activity information was often supplemented by information about the credentials of service personnel, including academic degrees and records of professional practice experience. However, even with efforts to establish standard definitions of service activities, such information was generally not comparable across different service organizations. Such quantitative information was also subject to systematic distortion, if not actual manipulation. More important, these activity counts did not provide any information about the actual results, or outcomes, of the reported service activities.

During the 1940s and 1950s, a variety of efforts were initiated to determine the effectiveness of social case work services provided by nonprofit social service organizations (Zimbalist 1977). Data schedules were used to record the characteristics of families receiving social case work services. "Movement scales" were used by service providers to record observed changes in family situations during the course of receiving such services (Hunt 1948). The results of these studies of the effectiveness of social case work services were inconclusive (Zimbalist 1977). There was no standard definition of the service inputs—that is, the actual content of the service transactions. Moreover, there was no control group of "untreated" families requesting services but not provided with them. Therefore, it could not be determined if any reported changes, or absence of changes, were a direct consequence of the social case work services or possibly of other events in the family. However, these movement-scale efforts to define social case work effectiveness did contribute to the later development of the single case study methodology for use by individual service providers to chart changes in individual service cases (Blythe and Tripodi 1989; Rubin 1997) and to the development of clinical assessment tools (Hudson 1997).

Federally supported service programs that were established after the Social Security Act and other federal service program initiatives often used the throughput–output activity models of assessment. Activity reports from Aid for Families with Dependent Children (AFDC) programs included the number of eligibility determinations and the number of active cases as well as the number of closed cases. Community action programs reported the number of persons enrolled in community development activities. Community mental health programs reported service caseloads.

Program auditing was also used to judge program operations, primarily for governmental service programs. Such audits focused on consistency between legislative intent, program guidelines, and the operational characteristics of the governmental service program. The determination of eligibility error-rates through systematic sampling of state AFDC program records was used by federal officials to identify needed changes in state administrative procedures to prevent ineligible persons from receiving benefits and to prevent eligible persons from being denied benefits. This audit information was also used to levy financial penalties on states that were determined to have consistently high eligibility error rates. The concept of program auditing also included financial audits, primarily to determine if the expenditures of funds had been consistent with legislative intent and program guidelines. Although program auditing could determine the consistency of program operations with the original plan of operation, it did not include any systematic effort to assess service outcomes or comparative effectiveness.

In the 1960s, a series of federally funded demonstration programs were established to test the effectiveness of social case work services in reducing the economic dependency of households receiving AFDC payments. However, social case work services were defined only as the activities of an individual employed in a "social work" position. Across the several studies, the actual service providers included persons with a variety of educational backgrounds using personal, idiosyncratic procedures to provide services in individual service situations. These studies, in general, indicated no differences in economic self-sufficiency outcomes between households receiving the undefined and unmeasured "social case work services" and those receiving only financial assistance payments and routine administrative services (Geismar 1972). The results of these studies pointed toward the need for more careful specification of the service intervention in order to assess intervention effectiveness.

These studies, together with studies evaluating a variety of other federally supported service programs, contributed to the ongoing development of evaluation methodology (Rossi, Freeman, and Lipsey 1998). As a result of the availability of funding for evaluation studies, academic research centers and for-profit research firms developed more complex procedures for gathering information on program outcomes, including surveys of service users, as well as improved statistical procedures for analyzing the information from such surveys.

With the substantial expansion in the 1970s of federal funding for human service programs such as Head Start and community mental health centers, attention was directed to the concept of unit cost—that is, the relative cost of one service unit, or of providing services in a single case situation, under different program conditions. In addition, the relationship of costs to benefits was examined; for example, the cost of mental health rehabilitation services was compared to the presumed dollar value of the potential employment earnings of an individual after receiving those services (Buxbaum 1981; Levine 1982; Rossi, Freeman, and Lipsey 1998).

When it was not possible to place a dollar value on the potential benefits (for example, when services were provided for very young children or for older adults and other individuals not in the labor force), an alternative method of evaluation—cost-effectiveness—was used. This approach could be used to estimate, for example, the comparative costs of the use of alternative methods for achieving a particular level of preschool reading readiness (Rossi, Freeman, and Lipsey 1998).

These cost–benefit/effectiveness initiatives also included an increased emphasis on efforts to establish comparative measures of program costs in order to make financial comparisons among different forms of service provision. State budget planners and state legislators sought such information to assist them in making legislative budgetary choices (Martin 2000a). In general, however, these service unit cost measures assumed a program operation directly managed by a single organization, with the cost–benefit measures being used in decision making to determine future funding levels for that single program. The measurement of the cost-effectiveness of a network of services involving referrals and service contracts was not possible because it involved too many uncontrolled and unmeasurable variables.

These efforts to measure and evaluate program results assumed that participation in a specific service production activity was, by itself, the primary "cause" of any positive result or benefit that could be identified at the end of the service episode. Moreover, such "intermediate outcomes" were considered to be equal to "final outcomes" (Kettner, Moroney, and Martin 1999). Little effort was made to determine if other personal experiences might account for the pattern of outcomes identified among program users, or if the intermediate results at the end of a service episode persisted over time. The evaluation of Head Start programs has been one exception where there have been continuing efforts to measure long-term outcomes, particularly in connection with later academic achievement levels.

During the 1970s and 1980s, a series of class action lawsuits were brought in the federal courts in efforts to force state governments to improve the quality of services provided through governmental programs in mental health, mental retardation services, and criminal justice services. These suits focused attention on service outcome consequences in existing programs, and on the use of evaluation methods for measuring changes (including service user outcomes) resulting from court-ordered mandates for service improvements. Similar efforts were made to measure the effects of government-mandated program changes on student outcomes following educational desegregation court orders.

In 1993, the Government Performance and Results Act (GPRA) of 1993 (P.L. 103-62) was passed by Congress. It called for performance effectiveness reports for federally funded programs "to clarify what we want to achieve, document the contribution we can make to achieving our goals and document what we are getting for our investment" (U.S. Department of Health and Human Services 1995:19). This Act is an example of a *goal-attainment* effectiveness model (D'Aunno 1992; Murray and Tassie 1994; Au 1996) with the goals for effectiveness assessment being set by a funding source—in this instance, the federal government—rather than by the service organization. The congressional expectations for effectiveness assessment were intensified with the enactment of the GPRA Technical Amendments of 1998 (H.R. 2883). However, as Radin (1998) indicates in "The Government Performance and Results Act (GPRA): Hydra-headed Monster or Flexible Management Tool?" there is not agreement about whether GPRA can produce the results that are being sought by Congress. Part of the difficulty is that many of the federal agencies depend on receiving effectiveness information from state agencies that receive federal funds, and the state agencies must obtain the information from nonprofit and for-profit organizations that administer the service programs through a series of contracts.

The passage of the GPRA (in 1993) and the GPRA amendments (in 1998) reflected increasing pressure from federal funding sources for evidence of organizational effectiveness (Martin and Kettner 1997). In 2000, the federal Administration on Children and Families (ACF) adopted a rule providing state-level "child and family reviews" to be completed by every state by 2004 (National Child Welfare Resource Center for Organizational Improvement 2001). By the end of the 1990s, demands were increasing from many sources, including political leaders, for regular and frequent student testing in elementary and secondary educational programs to determine the effectiveness of public school expenditures. Health-care organizations began placing increased emphasis on the development of treatment protocols based on the measurement of treatment outcomes across large numbers of medical patients.

In response to these pressures, methodologies for assessing program effectiveness were developed more fully by the end of the twentieth century (Mullen and Magnabosco 1997; Rossi, Freeman, and Lipsey 1998). These methodologies have included the use of social science experimental models for a more rigorous test of the effectiveness of particular forms of service provision (Rubin 1997). One of the earliest uses of such experimental models was by agricultural experiment stations to determine the effectiveness of genetically improved forms of agricultural crops. In this experimental model, all relevant variables were standardized except for the modified seed. This model was then adapted to the clinical testing of pharmaceutical products. Since it is impossible to standardize, or to control for statistically, all the variables potentially affecting animal and human responses, random assignment to treatment and to placebo has been used in clinical trials of new pharmaceutical treatments. However, many forms of human service interventions cannot be tested under such controlled clinical or standardized laboratory conditions, or with a random assignment of users to treatment and placebo interventions.

In an effort to determine the relative effectiveness of a particular form of service intervention in a diverse service population, statistical procedures have been developed to control for systematic variations among service users—gender, age, ethnicity, family background, and so on, as well as for variations in the extent and intensity of the treatment intervention (Rossi, Freeman, and Lipsey 1998; Rubin 1997). However, the use of such statistical procedures requires relatively large study populations, making it difficult to carry out well-designed studies of the effectiveness of individual service programs in a single community setting.

Regardless of whether the definition of effectiveness is tied to the interests and preferences of immediate service users or to the interests of other stakeholders, including funders, a series of evaluation procedures are now available to community decision makers, organizational policy makers, and organizational executives. However, there are many practical difficulties in measuring the effectiveness of any single service program or the level of benefits for any single service user (Mullen and Magnabosco 1997; Hoefer 2000).

DYNAMICS IN THE DESIGN OF SERVICE EFFECTIVENESS EVALUATIONS

In the absence of information about outcome results of service provision, information about the quantity of services provided by a service organization has often been accepted as evidence of the effectiveness of the organization. Determining service effectiveness, rather than simply reporting service utilization, has, however, become an increasingly important issue as a result of changes occurring in the organization of human services (Austin et al. 1982; Patti 1985; Kettner, Moroney, and Martin 1999). In the field of chemical dependency treatment, the ability to make comparisons of effectiveness between alternative service providers and alternative service models has become more critical with the increasing use of competitive procurement and purchase-of-service contracts (POSCs) in developing a program of services.

Legislators seek information on the comparative effectiveness of alternative approaches to the complex challenges of child welfare services. Mental health authorities need information about the effectiveness of contracted "behavioral health" services. Foundations regularly require outcome evaluations for service programs that are initiated with foundation support. The passage of the GPRA in 1993 increased the attention to effectiveness assessment for all organizations that directly, or indirectly through contracts, receive federal funding. However, the efforts to design a plan to define and measure effectiveness in human service programs must deal with many complexities (D'Aunno 1992; Murray and Tassie 1994; Au 1996), each of which requires a series of evaluation design choices.

Level of Evaluation

One complexity is the difference between the evaluation of organizational effectiveness and the evaluation of individual program component effectiveness, both of which may, on occasion, be referred to as program evaluation. Effectiveness evaluation at an organizational level often deals with the efficient use of resources, both financial and personnel (including the ratio of overhead costs to direct service costs). It may also deal with the efficiency of internal decision processes, with cultural diversity competence, and with the relationship of the overall performance of the organization to organizational goals and objectives. It does not deal with the benefits for individual service users provided by specific service components.

Kaplan (2001) describes the "balanced scorecard" as a method of multidimensional organizational performance assessment that includes a number of perspectives: customer, financial, internal, and learning and growth. Quinn and Cameron (1983) point out that the assessment of effectiveness of the organizational operation is affected by the life cycle position of the organization. They make distinctions among four life cycle stages—the entrepreneurial (or start-up) stage, the collectivity stage, the formalization and control stage, and the elaboration–expansion–renewal stage. Each involves different organizational effectiveness criteria.

As D'Aunno (1992) points out, the loosely coupled nature of program components within individual service organizations makes it difficult to measure any type of total service outcome effectiveness at the organizational level separately from determination of the outcome effectiveness of individual program components. User participation in evaluation is primarily tied to a specific program component. In many instances, the interests of funders are connected to the function of a specific program rather than to the financial management pattern at the organizational level. Martin and Kettner (1997:26) state that the increased emphasis at the federal level on performance measurement "makes 'programs' its unit of analysis as opposed to . . . using either clients or agencies." In the following discussion, *program evaluation* refers to evaluation at the program component level.

Analytic Framework

In initiating a plan for effectiveness evaluation, choices must be made among several different analytic frameworks. This choice is one of the potentially politically contentious decisions involved in the design of an effectiveness assessment that may require the involvement of a board of directors. D'Aunno (1992) identifies the following analytic framework alternatives; they are focused primarily at the organizational level, but they may also be relevant to program component evaluation:

- A *goal attainment* framework, in which the organizational definition of program goals and objectives is used as the criterion for assessing effectiveness
- A *multiple constituency* framework (Martin 1987; Kanter and Summers 1987) [identified by Murray and Tassie (1994) as a political model of evaluation], in which the different outcome objectives of the several stakeholder constituencies—service users, funders, service personnel—are all used as criteria for assessing effectiveness, with a further determination of which of them is the most important in the functioning of a given organization
- An *institutional* framework, in which the performance of the organization is judged by accepted societal standards, as in accreditation procedures

Murray and Tassie (1994) offer two additional analytic frameworks:

- A *means achievement* framework, in which the effectiveness of specific operational activities is assessed on the basis that high-quality treatment processes are the equivalent of successful service outcomes
- A *human resources* framework, in which the proper selection of personnel, personnel training, and motivation are measured on the grounds that well-prepared personnel will provide effective services

Au (1996) recognizes these frameworks and adds one more:

- A *system* framework, in which the effectiveness of the organization is judged by the ability of the organization to survive and adapt to its environment and to obtain resources from that environment

Level of Stakeholder Conflict over Evaluation Procedures

The selection of the specific effectiveness criteria to be used and the methods for measuring them are often shaped by internal and external political economy dynamics. Murray and Tassie (1994:312–313) identify four alternative "political" conditions that may affect an evaluation process:

- The *low-profile* condition, in which there is little conflict over either the choice of criteria or the method of measurement
- The *negotiation-dependent* condition, in which there is conflict over the choice of assessment criteria but not over the methods of measurement
- The *measurement-dependent* condition, in which there is little conflict over the choice of criteria but conflict over methods of measurement
- The *maximum-complexity* condition, in which there are conflicts over the choice of assessment criteria *and* over the method of measuring such criteria

"By far the most common pattern . . . in nonprofit organizations is the 'maximum complexity pattern'" (Murray and Tassie 1994:314). This suggests that determining a plan for assessing organizational effectiveness involves, in many instances, political negotiation and bargaining among various organizational stakeholders. Moreover, as Lohmann (1999) points out, the historical record indicates that government program and policy decisions are often decided more by political factors than by the information from systematic evaluation studies. Indeed, the implementation of an effectiveness evaluation may be viewed, in some instances, as more important for maintaining organizational legitimation than as a source of detailed information for changing organizational performance.

The Influence of User Perspectives

Whether the definition of effectiveness is tied directly to the preferences of service users or to the objectives of other stakeholders is an ongoing concern. With the wider dissemination of information about human service programs, user interests have become a significant factor in promoting the measurement of service effectiveness, particularly in the health-care area, through the print media and television and more recently through the Internet. There is also a high level of parental interest in the effectiveness of alternative educational models—home schooling versus group education, alternative methods of promoting reading readiness, single gender versus coeducational classrooms. Parental initiatives have directed attention to the issue of comparative outcomes from interracial versus same-race adoptions.

The co-production participation of service users in the simultaneous production and consumption of services makes the user evaluation of service effectiveness very different from traditional measurements of the effectiveness of industrial products (Bowen and Schneider 1988). That is, in taking part in a program evaluation, users are, in effect, evaluating their own participation in the service production process. For example, student evaluations of teachers may reflect their own feelings of success, or failure, in a particular class as much as their perceptions of the effectiveness of the teaching procedures.

The Influence of Funder Perspectives

Analyses of organizational/program effectiveness and efficiency are often initiated by funding stakeholders that face the problem of responding with limited resources to expansive requests for program funding. However, such analyses are driven not only by funding efficiency concerns but also by concerns for improving the effectiveness of individual programs. The definition of the criteria for measuring effectiveness may be shaped largely by the interests of the funding source, whether this is a foundation, a legislative body, a business firm, or a community fund-raising body. These criteria may or may not be consistent with the formal definition of goals and program objectives by organizational leadership.

Both service users and service providers may have elastic, or expansive, definitions of the potential demand or need for services of all types—education, health care, social services, criminal justice, addiction treatment, community building—and of the appropriate effectiveness criteria. Of all the stakeholder constituencies, funders have the most powerful incentives for seeking a determination of the effectiveness of these services, and also of their efficiency, since all financial resources have ultimate limits. For example, governmental bodies often face a basic choice between funding existing service programs, within the limits of existing tax resources, and initiating an increase in taxes to support the expansion of particular service programs. It is, however, also possible, as Lohmann (1999) notes, that governmental bodies make decisions about funding particular service programs, such as prisons, for reasons that have no connection with either effectiveness or efficiency.

Within managed health care, the current, highly politicized power struggle among health-care funding sources, professional providers, and service users essentially involves a contest about control over the definition of effectiveness. For example, the dominant definition of hospital operation effectiveness has been the maintenance of a limit on the period of hospital care since the introduction of diagnostic related groups (DRGs) by federal Medicare authorities. DRGs involve criteria that have been adopted by other health-care funding sources and by insurance companies. In many instances, the definition of such effectiveness measures by health-care funding sources has imposed appropriate limits on the use of limited resources, both financial resources and service personnel resources. But this definition of effectiveness has been established through the use of the interactive combination of financial power and influence (or "political") power on the part of health-care funders rather than through any type of individual consensus agreement between service providers and service users.

Indeed, the effectiveness definitions of large funding sources such as the federal government (for example, under the 1993 GPRA) may override program objectives set forth in legislative language governing state and local governmental service programs such as child welfare services. To the extent that traditional nonprofit service organizations have become dependent on POSCs and other powerful external forms of funding, these organizations have largely surrendered control over the definition of service effectiveness in individual service programs to the funding sources.

The Role of Merit Goods in Effectiveness Evaluation

As noted in chapter 2, many of the services of nonprofit and governmental human service organizations (including services provided by for-profit firms administering POSCs funded by governmental sources) can be defined as involving "merit goods." The primary objective of the services is defined by a third party rather than by either the service user or the immediate service provider. The services provided through the Temporary Assistance to Needy Families (TANF) program are defined by law as having the objective of encouraging or forcing economically dependent single parents into the labor market and economic self-sufficiency. Weaver (2000) points out that at the local level, "institutional ideologies" that reflect different moral judgments about the reasons for household poverty may result in widely varying agency practices, and related definitions of effectiveness, in the TANF program in individual counties. These ideologies become the operational definition of effectiveness applied to all service situations, overriding any definition of the objectives that might be the most realistic in particular service situations.

Similar merit-goods objectives shape governmental child protection services, which under the current federal Adoption and Safe Families Act of 1997 are measured by the effectiveness of achieving, in every child protective services case, some form of "permanency" solution within twelve months, even if this requires abruptly terminating parental rights or, alternatively, returning a child to a home with a serious level of potential risk. The satisfaction of the biological parents or of the service provider as to the appropriateness of the solution are not considered, under federal regulations, to be relevant measures of organizational effectiveness, in comparison with the rate of "case closures" within twelve months.

Implementation Issues

Whatever the form of the evaluation, the final issue is whether the results of an effectiveness evaluation are actually used in modifying existing organizational procedures. One approach to evaluation is the use of an independent, outside evaluation specialist or of personnel from an organization that specializes in evaluation. These specialists carry out an evaluation plan that has been designed in advance to meet particular technical specifications. Such an evaluation normally results in a written report that is presented to the board of directors and executive staff and includes recommendations for change. The limitation on this approach to evaluation is that it often fails to produce changes consistent with the reported results of the evaluation (Hasenfeld and Patti 1992).

An alternative approach is to develop the plan for evaluation with the involvement of critical stakeholders and, in particular, the staff members of the organization who would be centrally involved in carrying out recommendations that might result from the evaluation (Fine, Thayer, and Coghlan 2000). Cherin and Meezan (1998) propose that an evaluation process should be converted into an organizational learning process by the inclusion of organizational personnel in all phases of the evaluation process. They acknowledge that such a process may have high costs in terms of the time used by key personnel but suggest that such a process is more likely to result in substantive changes in organizational procedures. A two-year study (1998–1999) evaluated the quality of 180 service outcome evaluation designs in a single city created in response to a requirement from the United Way, with independent reviewers evaluating the design quality using the program quality evaluation scale (Poole et al. 2000). A path analysis of critical factors indicated that the degree of involvement of both staff members and board members and the level of management support were the most important factors in the quality of the research design, in comparison to the openness of the agency culture to change, the approach of the funding organization, and the technical capability of the organization (Poole et al. 2001).

MEASUREMENT OF EFFECTIVENESS

Although there are ongoing concerns about the assessment of organizational or program efficiency and effectiveness—that is, the relative cost–benefit ratios of alternative ways of providing particular services—the measurement of efficiency is secondary to the measurement of effectiveness. There is no relevant measure of efficiency if particular services are, in fact, not demonstrated to be effective.

Approaches to the systematic determination of service effectiveness include program evaluation and total quality management (TQM). The term *program evaluation* is often used generically for all types of organizational and program assessment studies (Murray and Tassie 1994). It is also used, as noted later, for a specific category of assessment studies (Kettner, Moroney, and Martin 1999). Program evaluation seeks to measure overall program performance against measurement criteria that have been previously selected (Murray and Tassie 1994; Thomas 1994).

Total quality management is an alternative form of effectiveness assessment, in which the service experience of individuals is assessed on a continuous basis. TQM is intended to be an ongoing program of service production assessment and continuous improvement. TQM also gives particular attention to consumer satisfaction as one of the measures of service effectiveness (Gunther and Hawkins 1996).

Program Evaluation

Program evaluation may be viewed as one element in a rational and systematic approach to quality control and planned change through which the analysis of results from a service program can provide information to guide changes in program design, program technology, and staff organization (Thomas 1994; Rossi, Freeman, and Lipsey 1998). Program evaluations are also mandated, in many instances, as a condition of funding from governmental sources, with an expectation that such evaluations will contribute to systematic improvements in legislation and administrative policy as well as in improved program operation. The GPRA of 1993, for example, makes this assumption.

Studies of service program operation may take several different forms, including what Kettner, Moroney, and Martin describe as "Performance measurement; monitoring; and program evaluation" (1999:217). As these authors point out, the design of such studies should be an integral part of initial program planning rather than being an effort to measure the results of a program that has already been well established. Such studies require an initial definition of program purposes and evaluation purposes, and the creation of systematic methods for gathering information as part of the plan for program operation. The design of any effective evaluation must also be shaped by the underlying design of the service program (see chapter 4). Without the evaluation elements being included in the original planning and design of a service program, the persons responsible for a program evaluation study often find themselves attempting, after the fact, to reach an agreement as to the initial definition of objectives and to bring together the information required for a program assessment.

PERFORMANCE MEASUREMENT Performance measurement includes an ongoing series of reports, primarily for external audiences or stakeholder constituencies (including funding sources), and for organizational managers. Performance measurement includes quantitative measures of service provision, or *outputs*, and *intermediate outcomes*, and the relationship of expenditures to outcomes: cost–benefit and cost-effectiveness results.

Outputs include the service units actually provided—for example, the number of adoption home studies. Kettner, Moroney, and Martin (1999) suggest that outputs should also include a "quality output" measure— that is, a measurement of the degree to which the specific service provided meets service quality definitions established by the organization—for example, the timeliness of initial service provision, or the completeness of a determination of the service user's objectives in seeking the service. Outputs also include service completions—for example, the number of completed adoptions.

Intermediate outcomes are defined as the results, or outcomes, of service provision at the time of service completion. The evaluation of intermediate program outcomes measures the immediate consequences of completed service delivery outputs for the service user. Such measurements could include the perspective of both the service provider and the service user. A child protective services intermediate outcome could be the psychological status of an abused child at the end of an initial period of time in a foster home, or the intellectual and psychological status of a child under state guardianship at age eighteen. Intermediate outcomes in education could include measurements of educational achievement at the end of an educational cycle, such as graduation from high school. Health-care intermediate outcomes could include the wellness status of a patient at the end of a period of surgical recovery as defined by the service user and the service providers. Martin (2000a) describes the use of such intermediate outcomes in budgeting processes of state human service agencies, providing legislators with information about the relative cost of achieving particular outcome levels. Final outcomes and program impacts are viewed as part of comprehensive program evaluation (see later).

MONITORING Monitoring is a systematic assessment of whether a service program is being implemented in a manner consistent with the original plan for the program operation, and whether it is serving the intended constituency of service users. It may also be thought of as a form of preliminary program auditing. Monitoring is a systematic attempt to measure both "*program coverage*, the extent to which a program is reaching its intended target population, and *program process*, the extent to which the service being provided matches what was intended to be delivered" (Rossi, Freeman, and Lipsey 1998:141).

Monitoring studies may be particularly focused either on a small-scale pilot program or on the early stages of a fully developed program, providing information to be shared with program personnel as soon as information becomes available, making it possible to make program changes before the program is fully implemented (Rossi, Freeman, and Lipsey 1998). Monitoring may also be a form of corrective feedback intended to maintain consistency between the ongoing program operation and the original design of the program, as embodied either in an organizational plan or in enabling legislation. Such feedback assessments may also be identified as "process evaluation" or "formative" evaluation research (Rossi, Freeman, and Lipsey 1998). These feedback assessments are designed primarily for program and organizational managers, and for organizational policy makers such as boards of directors of nonprofit service organizations and legislative bodies. Grasso and Epstein (1992) use the term *developmental evaluation* to describe data-gathering processes intended primarily to improve the quality of ongoing service provision. Recently, methods have been developed using data envelopment analysis (Nyhan and Martin 1999) for carrying out the comparative monitoring of several different service organizations providing similar services, or the several local offices of a state-wide service organization.

Monitoring may, in actual practice, directly affect the characteristics of service provision by focusing attention on a limited number of the characteristics of service provision. This is particularly critical if organizational rewards or penalties are attached to the monitoring outcomes.

A highly visible example is the intense attention being given to the testing of elementary and secondary students to determine their achievement levels in reading and mathematics to the exclusion of other significant curriculum elements. Reports of "teaching to the test" also note diminished attention to other curriculum subjects. Assessments of job placement results and caseload reduction have dominated the monitoring reports on TANF services, with limited attention to any assessment of the short-term outcomes for children in the TANF households.

Monitoring may also influence user selection by encouraging "creaming"—that is, the deliberate recruitment or selection of potentially high-achievement, or positive-outcome, service users and the "cooling out" or exclusion of potentially unsuccessful service users. For example, given the public attention that is devoted to standard test scores, secondary school administrators may find it possible to classify low-achieving students as special education students, excused from standard tests, and to accept a higher level of drop-outs among other low-achieving students, as trade-offs for a higher average in the test scores of the remaining students.

PROGRAM EVALUATION Program evaluation, as more narrowly defined by Kettner, Moroney, and Martin (1999), is primarily concerned with *program outcomes*, both intermediate and final; Mullen and Magnabosco (1997) used the term program *impacts*. Such outcome evaluation research may also be identified as *summative* evaluation research. Program evaluation studies are primarily intended for program planners and policy makers who are involved in shaping the design of future programs. *Intermediate outcomes*, as noted, include the condition of the service user at the completion of services—for example, the level of reported adjustment and satisfaction when an adoption placement is finalized.

Final outcomes involve the condition of the service user at some established time after service completion. Final outcomes could include the condition of an interracially adopted child five years after adoption, the recovery status of an individual with alcohol addiction five years after completing an addiction treatment program, or the situation of a young adult ten years after receiving services as a child through a child guidance clinic. Educational institutions might assess the academic, social, and economic position of their students five years after graduation.

The measurement of final outcomes is often difficult and expensive. Service users may be difficult to locate and may be reluctant to participate.

Other life developments may have had an equal or greater impact on the life course of the individual. Service users and service providers may have very different perspectives on the relationship of the services that were provided to such final outcomes.

Program impacts (Kettner, Moroney, and Martin 1999) are defined as those changes in the condition of the service user that can be directly and specifically attributed to the specific service provided. That is, a direct cause-and-effect relationship can be seen between the service and the changes in the condition of the service user. The establishment of the actual level of service impact, in particular, requires an experimental research design that can control for other factors that could have had an effect on the service outcomes. Without such experimental controls, the final outcomes that are discovered may, in fact, be a consequence of other changes in the life situation of the service user, unrelated to service provision.

The evaluation of final, or long-term, outcomes and impacts might well be considered the most significant measure of service effectiveness (Rossi 1999). However, the costs and technical difficulties involved in determining the connection between service inputs and long-term outcomes, except in the most rigorously controlled clinical studies, means that most efforts to identify effectiveness focus on outputs—that is, the number of completed services—or on intermediate, or short-term, outcomes. Moreover, as efforts to determine effectiveness intensify, service programs may focus on those particular forms of intervention that are most likely to produce high output levels or positive short-term, or intermediate, effects (Casalino 1999).

Intense emphasis on output measures such as high school graduation rates can intensify efforts to hold students in the high school system by controlling truancy and efforts to develop procedures that enable all students to demonstrate high school completion, regardless of the real level of academic achievement. Since high school graduation is treated as the primary criterion for admission to many programs of post–high school education, very high levels of high school graduation may be reflected in high numbers of students requiring remedial education at the next academic level. Similarly, job training and placement programs (for example, under the TANF program) may focus on completed placements in low-skill, low-wage employment settings that also have a high turnover, providing a continuous supply of new employment placement opportunities for TANF participants, without any information being provided on the final outcomes for the particular individuals involved.

The assessment of service outcomes in human service programs is complicated by the necessity of distinguishing between person-to-person interaction effects in human service programs and program technology effects (Selber and Streeter 2000). Much of what happens in any type of service encounter is shaped by the distinctive characteristics of the person-to-person interaction between the particular service user and a particular service provider—that is, the level of interpersonal trust—regardless of the methods or technology being used. This includes interactions between a patient and a physician, between students and a teacher, between a recovering alcoholic and an addiction counselor, or between the parents of a child who has experienced abuse and a child protective services worker.

The service user assessment of outcomes may, therefore, be an assessment of the level of trust relationships rather than of the outcomes of the specific form of treatment being provided. Experimental or demonstration programs that clearly demonstrate effectiveness may have selected service providers who bring particular interpersonal skills, or particular skills in the application of a distinctive treatment methodology, together with a personal commitment to making the program a success. The result may be a high level of trust between service users and service providers. As Schorr (1997) points out, these personal traits are often not characteristic of the larger group of service providers who may be involved in implementing a full-scale, standardized application of the demonstration program. The result may be a less effective program even though technically the service procedures are similar.

Total Quality Management

The search for effectiveness measures is linked to systematic efforts to improve the actual quality of service production, what Kettner, Moroney, and Martin (1999) describe as "quality outputs." TQM is associated with a particular emphasis on user satisfaction in the definition of quality outputs (Martin 1993; Gunther and Hawkins 1996; Boettcher 1998). TQM emphasizes the establishment of error-free production methods and a continuous effort to improve production processes, with the use of statistical sampling to check on the maintenance of such standards (Martin 1993). After W. Edward Deming (1986) introduced TQM procedures into Japanese industrial production processes, many Japanese products that had been identified as inexpensive and of poor quality came to be considered high-quality goods. This was particularly important as Japan sought to become a producer for a worldwide market.

TQM began with a focus on the production of goods such as automobiles, home appliances, and computers. Statistical systems for sampling production outputs were established to determine if production was essentially error free. Traditional goods production quality control procedures identified defective units through an inspection process at the end of the production cycle and then recycled them for correction. This required examination of every unit produced, and if seriously defective units were not caught in the final inspection process, a high level of consumer dissatisfaction could result. The application of TQM to establish error-free production methods reduced both the cost of inspection (as a sample was used instead of a 100 percent inspection) and the cost of the corrective action required for defective units.

TQM also involved detailed studies of consumer satisfaction as an essential feedback element in the continuous process of quality improvement. Deming defined the consumer as being part of the organizational system rather than external to it: "The consumer is the most important part of the production line. Quality should be aimed at the needs of the consumer present and future" (1986:5).

In the current application of TQM methods, consumers are viewed as including current consumers, former consumers, potential consumers, indirect consumers such as regulatory agencies and advocacy groups, vendors and suppliers, and ultimately the community (Harnish 1993). Consumers also include "internal" consumers—that is, those individuals within the organization who use materials and information produced by other organizational staff members.

Advocates for quality management in human service programs point out that most programs for improving organizational effectiveness are productivity driven (the primary emphasis being on the number of service units provided) rather than on the quality of such services (Gunther and Hawkins 1996). Management by objectives (MBO) is an example of an organizational assessment model that is productivity driven, with objectives defined and measured primarily in terms of production units, an approach that Deming (1986) defined as inconsistent with quality improvement.

The application of TQM to human services is more complex than its application to goods production (Murray and Tassie 1994; Gummer and McCallion 1995; Brannen and Streeter 1995). The production process for an industrial product is separate from its use. The evidence as to whether an industrial product functions correctly is often very distinct. Moreover, if a defective unit is found by a consumer, it is possible to replace it with another unit from a supply of identical units. However, services are used as they are produced—a medical procedure, a counseling interview, a home visit to a household reported for child abuse. Mistakes in service provision have an irretrievable effect; another unit of service can never be exactly substituted. This increases the importance of establishing quality standards for service provision (Hawkins and Gunther 1998).

The effort to introduce quality management into service production requires two steps (Martin 1993). The first step is detailed attention to the service production process. TQM places an emphasis on *fact-based change*, change that begins with a thorough examination of how the organization functions and the potential impact of each step in that process on the likelihood of satisfactory completion of the service cycle. Part of the TQM approach is using statistical sampling procedures to monitor the accuracy and quality of service production, rather than attempting to apply a 100 percent supervision model or a 100 percent review of service activities. Another element in the review of service production processes is benchmarking—that is, the comparison of actual service production procedures with best-practice standards. This places more emphasis on improving poor-quality service procedures than on developing innovative procedures. TQM also emphasizes team-based guidance systems rather than hierarchical systems, with teams having responsibility for monitoring, correcting, and improving production activities.

The second step is using feedback information from service consumers about the service production experience and about the intermediate or short-term outcomes from service utilization. "The central and most important tenet in the TQM paradigm is the commitment to consumer service" (Gunther and Hawkins 1996:18). The results from production monitoring and user feedback provide a stimulus for improvements in the service production process. However, to be truly useful, the user-satisfaction feedback process must be continuous (Gunther and Hawkins 1996).

User feedback in human services has to distinguish between the quality of the service itself and the quality of the distinctive interaction between the service user and a specific service provider (Selber 1997). As noted, the level of satisfaction reported by service users may be, in part, a result of positive human relationships between a service user and a service provider. The level of satisfaction may or may not be directly associated with the quality of the treatment intervention. Provider and user may also have very different perceptions of the relative importance of each of these two elements. Users may, in some instances, consider the respect that they receive from the service provider as more important than the actual content of the service transaction. Service providers may give more weight to what they perceive as the quality of the content and the technical skill involved.

Global satisfaction reports by internal users, or by vendors and other network participants, may also reflect satisfaction with interpersonal relationships as much as satisfaction with the value of the service provided. User satisfaction reports are also influenced by the extent to which users have choices. The reported level of satisfaction with the only available service may be quite different from a situation in which the user has a choice among providers and has relevant information about comparisons among providers. Both of these assumptions are part of the original assumptions underlying the use of TQM in industrial production.

TQM is not simply a technical strategy. Its adoption must become an organization-changing process (see chapter 12) to be truly effective. Zbracki (1998) and Cole (1998) document the difficulties encountered in implementing TQM when there is not a comprehensive organizational change process. User satisfaction evaluations can strengthen the role of service users in the organization-changing process, providing systematic feedback that has often been missing in human service programs. However, to the extent that TQM is driven by the concept of user satisfaction, it differs from a goal attainment model of evaluation in which organization policy makers establish social impact mission statements and program goals that are independent of individual user priorities. It also differs from the multiple constituency model of evaluation in which the objectives of funders and other stakeholder constituencies are included as assessment criteria. Priority attention to user satisfaction in defining service quality is also inconsistent with the concept of merit goods—that is, that service objectives are defined by third parties, as in the TANF program, or in the permanency requirements established by legislation in child protection services, rather than by the immediate service users. This becomes a particularly complex issue in the instance of services for children, in that the satisfaction preferences of the child and of the parents may be quite different from the service objectives that were established through legislation.

The ability of a service organization to adopt, implement, and maintain a TQM process may be affected by its relative financial and power independence—that is, by its ability to diversify its income sources and to generate income that is not controlled by any single funding source. Otherwise, there is a strong tendency for the funding source, rather than the service users, to have the final word in defining organizational and program component objectives, and in defining *quality* in the assessment of program outcomes.

Moreover, the application of TQM in industrial and technical services production is expected to be reinforced by some form of economic reward—reduced costs, increased market share, increased level of profit. Such economic reinforcements of quality production for human services are seldom available. Even for-profit service businesses are likely to be operating under fixed price contracts with a governmental funding source. Quality of services becomes only one of several variables that may enter into contract negotiation processes, negotiations in which the trade-off between unit costs and quality production is a much less precise measure than in the production of industrial hard goods. Moreover, the implementation of any single innovation such as TQM may be subject to "innovation weariness," which is the tendency for organizational and individual commitment to new procedures to diminish over time, particularly if there is no reward or systematic form of positive feedback.

SUMMARY

The search for evidence of organizational and program effectiveness has become an increasingly important accountability issue for human service organizations. Questions raised by funders, competition for funding, and internal concerns about improving the quality and effectiveness of services have brought a sense of urgency to the determination of effectiveness. This requires increased attention to the service outcomes for individual service users and to the level of user satisfaction. The application of program assessment procedures in service-providing organizations is much more complex than the use of such procedures in goods-producing firms. Different assessment procedures may be required for different, and distinctive, program components rather than an inclusive effort that assesses the effectiveness of the total organization.

The determination of the analytic framework for evaluation studies is shaped by the dynamics of the political economy context of the service organization. This often means that the evaluation criteria are largely determined by funding sources, by larger institutional systems in the instance of accreditation, or by stakeholder constituencies other than the actual service users, whose interests may, or may not, coincide with other stakeholder constituencies. This is particularly significant when it is third parties, other than service providers and service users, who determine organizational purposes and objectives. TQM brings a distinctive perspective to the quality evaluation process, in part because of its emphasis on the continuous assessment of effectiveness. The implementation of a true TQM process also requires establishing a continuous process of organizational adaptation.

TWELVE

DEALING WITH CHANGE

Change masters: Those people and organizations adept at the art of anticipating the need for, and of leading, productive change.
—Rosabeth Moss Kanter (1983:13)

Change-adept organizations cultivate the imagination to innovate, the professionalism to perform and the openness to collaborate.
—Rosabeth Moss Kanter (1997:7)

IN CONTEMPORARY SOCIETY, change is pervasive, both in the larger society and within individual organizations. Many of the writings about *social* change deal with processes of bringing about particular changes in the larger society—public policy changes, changes in the culture. The focus in this chapter, however, is on changes within individual human service organizations, changes that are often responses to changes taking place in the larger society.

Many writers equate *organizational change*, or the introduction of "innovation" (Delbecq 1978), with *progress*. Current organizational performance is not fully satisfactory—change should be an improvement. However, in human service programs, there are also negative changes, changes that harm service users or that harm service providers. Funding sources disappear; restrictive legislation is passed that limits access to services. Innovative changes may provide benefits for one set of stakeholders but impose costs on other stakeholders. Merit-goods policies are adopted that impose particular costs or limitations on service users in the name of community values.

The following discussion does not assume that all change is beneficial. It does assume that human service organizations face constant changes in the organizational environment and therefore must give constant attention to the processes of internal change. This chapter deals with the following:

- Societal changes that are changing the social/political/economic environment within which human service organizations are functioning
- Local and internal forces for change
- Organizational change processes
- Dynamics of organizational change
- Alternative models of change processes
- Change decision making
- Change-adept organizations

SOCIETAL CHANGES

Much of the literature dealing with organizational change focuses on the initiation of change from within the organization and on overcoming internal resistance to change (Delbecq 1978).

> If an organization is functioning satisfactorily, innovative proposals threaten attachments to old ways, introduce the uncertainties of new practices, and may disrupt the comfortable balance. A change may violate the culture or ethos that provides the foundation for organizational cohesion and financial support. . . . Some alterations may be resisted primarily because they seem to require subordination of the organization to the will of outsiders.
>
> Morris and Binstock (1966:95)

Organizational changes may involve costs for service users, who may face changes in their pattern of service usage, as well as for policy makers, who may have to develop new understandings of the pattern of organizational activities. The tendency within human service organizations is to avoid changes in organizational procedures, except at the most incremental level, even when there is a perception that changes are needed. Inertia is an organizational phenomenon as well as a principle of physics.

However, a series of societal changes are underway in the United States at the beginning of the twenty-first century that are forcing changes in individual human service organizations and in service networks. Some of these changes have already been referred to in earlier chapters. These changes are creating what Emery and Trist (1965) identify as a "turbulent" environment, in which rapid changes are occurring not only among the organizations in a given field of activity but also in the characteristics of the field itself. These changes may be imposed by formal policy action at an inclusive level of societal organization such as the federal government. Other societal changes are the result of unplanned, unstructured change processes—in particular, demographic changes and economic marketplace processes.

Current societal change processes affecting human service organizations usually fall into one or more of the following eight categories.

Changes in the Ethnic Characteristics of the U.S. Population

One of the most dramatic shifts is in the characteristics of the current school-age population. In a number of states, more than 50 percent of the public school children are from African American, Latino, and Asian American backgrounds, and this group includes a large number of first-generation immigrant children. These changes are also reflected in the demographic pattern of service users in other services for children. This population shift results in increased diversity among service users in language, in child-rearing practices, in cultural attitudes about physical health care and mental health care, and in attitudes toward the use of nonfamily forms of assistance. These changes are also reflected in increased diversity in the ethnic/cultural characteristics of direct service personnel in many types of human service programs, and increasingly in the characteristics of professional and administrative personnel. Still, members of the boards of directors and other policy-making bodies in nonprofit, quasi-governmental, and for-profit service organizations, and elected public officials, continue to be predominately White men.

"Devolution" of Responsibility for Funding and Policy Making

Beginning with the Depression and the 1935 Social Security Act and through the 1960s and 1970s, there was a major expansion of the federal role in a wide variety of domestic policy areas dealing with economic security, civil rights, the development of health-care services and social services, and the redevelopment of urban communities. The presidency, the Supreme Court, and the Congress were all involved in creating a more powerful role for the federal government in domestic policy. Some of the new programs reflected political ambivalence about such centralization of public authority by providing for a combination of federal authority and state authority in the Aid for Families with Dependent Children (AFDC) and Medicaid programs, as well as a combination of decentralized administration but detailed federal oversight for community action, Model Cities, and community mental health programs, among others.

The beginnings of substantial devolution came during the 1980s with the consolidation of some specialized, targeted, categorical federal funding programs into "block grants" to states and cities with reduced federal oversight authority. This was combined with cutbacks in the level of staffing in federal departments, further reducing federal monitoring of the use of federal funds. The most dramatic example of policy devolution in the 1990s was the welfare reform shift from the federal–state AFDC program to the state-administered, state-controlled Temporary Assistance to Needy Families (TANF) program. In turn, federal subsidy funds for the TANF program were sent to state treasuries as a block grant, rather than directly to the TANF program administrators. This process of devolution has been reinforced by a shift in recent Supreme Court opinions toward limiting the power of the federal government to enforce social policy initiatives on state governments (Lens 2001).

In part, this devolution has involved a process of cost-shifting, through which a more inclusive, or higher, level of government avoids the cost pressures of such services on the tax system at that level by moving to lower levels of government the financial risks of (as well as responsibility for and control of) such services. It is also a process through which a higher level of government avoids dealing with contentious social policy choices by shifting that responsibility to lower, and more dispersed, levels of government. Devolution also makes it possible for there to be a variety of program structures across the states rather than a single program structure for the entire nation. Unless there is a very large-scale national emergency, the process of devolving control over domestic social programs to state and local authorities is likely to persist.

Increasing Distinctions Between Collective
Policy Making and Collective Administration

Distinctions between the function of government as an institution of collective policy making, including the allocation of tax funds, and the function of government as the administrator of service programs are often described as the separation of authority functions from provider functions (see chapter 8). Governmental bodies have a long history of being the administrator of such collective services as the National Guard and police and fire departments. These are services that provide public goods that benefit the entire community. A separation between the authority function and the provider function has existed for a long time within public child welfare systems, in which state and county child welfare organizations have contracted with nonprofit residential children's institutions rather than being the administrators of such institutions. In the child-care field, governmental funds have traditionally been used to purchase child-care services from nongovernmental day-care centers rather than to fund day-care centers operated directly by governmental authorities. In both of these instances, services are primarily being provided to individuals and households rather than being primarily collective, public-goods services for the entire community.

The separation of authority and provider functions has also existed, since the 1960s, in health care, where governmental authorities or funding systems—Medicaid and Medicare, and health care for military dependents—are separate from the operation of health-care programs. This separation of functions in health care has now been extended through the closure of many publicly administered general hospitals or their sale to managed health-care firms, with public authorities paying only for the health-care costs of particular individuals.

This separation of authority and provider functions is now taking place in public mental health services that have traditionally included large-scale service operations by state governments. The governmental policy-making and fund-allocation role is being separated from the function of actually providing mental health services to individuals. A similar move has been initiated in some states in the field of public education through the creation of publicly funded charter schools, together with further proposals for replacing direct governmental operation of public school systems with educational vouchers.

The results of this pattern of separating authority and provider functions include a greater diversity in service provision but with reduced control by governmental bodies over the characteristics of such services, while continuing to spread the costs of such services across the entire taxpaying constituency. One of the other consequences of this separation of authority and provider functions is a marked reduction in the role of government as a large-scale, direct employer of human service personnel.

Commercialization of the Provision of Human Services

There has always been a variety of for-profit, marketplace human service providers, including independent private practice professional providers and for-profit hospitals, educational institutions, and child-care centers. However, during the latter decades of the twentieth century, a large expansion of for-profit businesses occurred in health care, mental health care, education, and criminal justice, as well as in private practice arrangements in many related professions. The expansion of commercialization began in the 1970s with the entrance of commercial insurance companies into the provision of health-care insurance and the recognition under federal law of for-profit health maintenance organizations (HMOs). This was accompanied by the development of large-scale, for-profit operations of residential and in-patient facilities, including nursing homes, residential treatment centers for children and adolescents, Intermediate Care Facilities–Mental Retardation under the Medicaid program, and psychiatric hospitals. During the 1990s, for-profit HMOs combined the health-care insurance function with the operation of large-scale health-care service networks (Shindul-Rothschild 2001).

The combination of devolution and privatization has led to the creation of for-profit service organizations in all of the fields in which purchase-of-service contracts (POSCs) are being used. These for-profit businesses include employee assistance programs in which individual businesses and governmental departments contract for services for their employees, a variety of child welfare services, substance abuse treatment programs, and home health-care programs. Some business corporations operate schools under contracts with local school boards, and operate jails and prisons under contracts with state and local governments. There are extended debates in every field about the comparisons between the operation of specific types of service programs by commercial firms and the operation of similar programs by nonprofit, quasi-governmental, and governmental organizations. Although there are important differences in governance and financial dynamics, there is no indication that any one group of organizations, either nonprofit, governmental, or for-profit, has a clear-cut advantage in the provision of high-quality, responsive, and effective services.

However, the development of for-profit firms has had certain general consequences for other types of human service programs (Shindul-Rothschild 2001). The for-profit service organizations have one group of stakeholders—general public shareholders—that nonprofit and governmental service organizations do not have. General public shareholders, including those who manage the investments for large retirement funds and mutual funds, as distinguished from those shareholders who are officers of the corporation, have one primary interest—the level of corporate profits (and the resultant value of the stock as determined by the stock market).

Competition for service contracts, particularly with governmental authorities, is based primarily on costs. For-profit organizations, in general, have higher administrative costs, including marketing costs, the costs associated with managing shareholder relations, and higher salaries for senior executives. This makes control of service delivery costs a priority focus for organizational management (Wernet 1999; Shindul-Rothschild 2001). One major focus for cost control is professional decision making, with organizational guidelines replacing some of the traditional individual decision making by professional specialists.

The increasing scale of for-profit human service provision has had an impact on policy and program decision making in nonprofit organizations that are competing for service contracts (Alexander 2000). In competitive bidding, a common set of cost expectations and outcome effectiveness criteria (see chapter 11) is applied to all service providers. Such criteria may highlight user benefits and user satisfaction, but they are unlikely to include the public-goods benefits that may be included in the mission statement of the nonprofit service organization. In the health-care field, the process of marketplace competition has resulted in the large-scale absorption of nonprofit health-care providers by for-profit corporations.

Nonprofit service organizations that are competing for service contracts in other fields, including child welfare services and addiction treatment (Wernet 1999), often require additional administrative personnel for proposal preparation, financial accounting, and market development. One result has been a series of mergers and acquisitions among nonprofit organizations in order to create larger organizational bases. Overall, the competition dynamics have often resulted in nonprofit organizations, including quasi-governmental nonprofits, that resemble for-profit organizations.

Blending of Human Service Organizations in a "Mixed Economy" Pattern

Governmental bodies create quasi-governmental nonprofit corporations to operate specialized service programs. For-profit firms create nonprofit subsidiaries in order to enter particular service markets, with the nonprofit subsidiary contracting to pay the parent firm for management services or to pay for the use of a building that was built by the for-profit firm. Governmental service organizations contract out specialized service functions to nonprofit service organizations. Governmental service organizations also contract out specialized administrative functions, such as data processing, to for-profit firms. Nonprofit organizations create wholly owned for-profit subsidiaries to handle the sale of particular goods and services to the general public, with the "profits" accruing to the nonprofit organization. As Kramer states, "A new paradigm is needed in which social policy questions are reformulated in terms of the reality of a mixed welfare economy where sectoral lines are blurred and there is extensive interdependence and interpenetration" (1998:4). Dramatic examples of the new paradigm are multisectoral, collaborative service programs that have been established under the TANF program. These include programs that combine employment training and job placement with social support programs that blend funding streams and combine adult and child welfare programs (Prince and Austin 2001).

Absorption of Professional Specialists into Restricted Positions

Absorption of professional specialists into restricted positions is, in part, a consequence of a continuing replacement of individual payment systems for professional services by third-party payment systems, including both governmental funding programs and for-profit insurance systems. This has always been characteristic of the nursing and education professions, and, generally, of social work in the public sector. Private practice practitioners in social work are now also being absorbed into a variety of managed care systems (Wernet 1999; Reamer 2001). However, this absorption into structured organizational systems is a recent development for most physicians (McArthur and Moore 1997). The forced incorporation of professional specialists into "managed" human service systems is being driven by the complex funding arrangements for all forms of health care, including employment-related insurance plans, and governmental programs including Medicare, Medicaid, and the Department of Defense programs for military dependents.

Under a system of managed professional services, the result has often been an emphasis on containing the costs of professional services, increased complexity in reimbursement procedures, and imposition of organizational treatment guidelines. One consequence of these changes in the position of professional practitioners has been an increasing level of confrontation between professional associations in many different fields and the management policies in large-scale for-profit settings that restrict the independence, or autonomy, of the professional specialist (Nieves 2000:2). This has also taken the form of political coalitions between organized professions and service user constituencies to limit the power of for-profit human service corporations.

Emergence of the Low-Profile, Flexible Production Organization

The low-profile, loosely linked, flexible production organization, often with time-limited employment arrangements, has emerged as the organizational model for the future. Such organizations are composed of "clusters of activity sets." "Projects" rather than "positions" are central to the pattern of activity within the organization (Kanter, Stein, and Jick 1992). Interactions with other organizations are as important as internal interactions. Vertically organized, hierarchical organizations were originally established to maintain stability, predictability, and rule conformance. Decisions were made centrally. Newer organizational forms decentralize decision making, as segments of the organization, or program components, interact with different external constituencies. This requires personnel who are self-reliant and professionally competent. Central oversight is maintained through accountability of the components for results, and through organization-wide, interactive communication systems rather than through structured, hierarchal control systems.

Such low-profile, flexible organizations, including many human service organizations, must maintain a constant process of organizational adaptation—that is, they must become "change-adept" organizations (Kanter 1997), or "learning" organizations (Senge 1990). The limited ability in traditional, large, bureaucratic organizations, including many governmental human service organizations, to create low-profile change-adept internal structures is one factor in the shift toward the contracting out of specialized program operations.

Development of Computer Network Systems as a Universal Form of Communication

The installation of computer systems becomes a recurrent capital cost for many service organizations. Computer use competencies become an essential element in staff requirements. Computerization also changes many traditional aspects of mid-management and staff support positions in large human service organizations. The Internet makes traditional definitions of organizational channels of communication and organizational boundaries obsolete as it becomes increasingly easy to have direct communication with other individuals within the organization as well as with individuals in other organizations.

LOCAL AND INTERNAL FORCES FOR CHANGE

In addition to the pressures for organizational changes that may result from these macro societal changes, pressures for change may be set in motion as a result of changes within the local task environment that directly impact individual service organizations. These may include expansions or contractions in the local economy, changes in the balance of political forces at state or local levels, changes in local funding patterns, local changes in the characteristics of the service population, changes in authorizing legislation for governmental organizations, and changes in the pattern of services in other organizations that are part of a service delivery network. These local external changes together with the societal changes create pressures for change and adaptation within individual human service organizations. Organizational ecology theorists, in particular, focus attention on the effect of changes in the task environment on the growth, or disappearance, of particular service organizations in the local ecology of organizations (Singh and Lumsden 1990).

Some organizational changes may be *imposed* by an external source, such as when a funding source terminates program funding, or by an internal policy board, or by an individual with administrative authority— for example, a new executive. Many of the changes currently taking place in hospitals and other health-care organizations are examples of imposed changes, changes over which organizational participants have little or no control. Changes that are imposed on the members of an organization may lead to organized opposition, as well as unorganized, "underground" efforts to resist the changes. However, in some situations, externally imposed changes may actually be consistent with an underlying, but unexpressed, consensus among organizational constituencies, and thus may result in support for far-reaching organizational transformation.

Forces for change can also come from *within* organizations. A series of small, internally initiated changes or adaptations may take place over time that are never the focus of a deliberate decision to change the organization. Older staff members leave and newer staff members with a different educational background replace them. New building facilities result in changes in staff interactions. New referral sources result in a different mix of service users.

However, the focus here is on decisions that come from within the service organization and that are intended to bring about specific changes. Specific change initiatives may come from a board of directors or other policy-making bodies or from the executive. Organizational staff members may initiate innovations (Delbecq 1978; Kanter 1983).

Some internal change initiatives may be a response to specific requirements from external constituencies, including funding and legitimation sources—for example, changes needed to meet the requirements of national accreditation bodies. A program evaluation study may be undertaken because it is a requirement of an external funding source. Other initiatives may emerge from a systematic process of strategic planning that focuses on the full range of changes taking place in the organizational environment (Bryson 1994).

Internal change initiatives may also result from information that individual staff members receive about changes in service technology or about research results from alternative program structures, or from the perceptions of individual staff members about the unmet needs of service users. Internal change initiatives may also result from perceptions of the comparative organizational advantage or disadvantage resulting from changes in other organizations, particularly organizations that are part of a shared service delivery network. Nearly all internally initiated change efforts are, in reality, linked ultimately to changes in the environment—knowledge changes, funding changes, user demographic changes, changes in the political environment. Moreover, change usually involves significant costs for organizational participants, including time costs, disruption of established routines and procedures, and disruption of working relationships. Internally initiated change is often viewed as something to be avoided if at all possible.

ORGANIZATIONAL CHANGE PROCESSES

Organizational change processes in human service organizations are often described either as proactive, or "anticipatory" (Wernet and Austin 1991) (that is, as being purposively initiated by someone from within an organization), or as reactive (that is, as being initiated only as a response to changes in the organizational environment). There has often been an implication that the initiation of proactive changes is a positive, or progressive, action and that reactive changes are less significant. Such distinctions are largely artificial. Many "proactive" change initiatives are, in fact, reactive, as they are a response to changes in the opportunity mix in the environment, such as a new funding opportunity, the availability of a new technology that may improve the quality of service, or an increase or a decrease in the general incidence of a social or health problem. Many "reactive" changes may, in reality, be proactive, involving the development of new, and innovative, conceptions of the character of service provision because of changes in the task environment. The management of organizational change processes has many similar characteristics regardless of whether the initiation of change action is viewed as proactive or reactive.

The rate of change in the environment has increased the importance of the role of the executive and, in particular, of the externally oriented roles of the executive (see chapter 9). Many different individuals may be involved in change processes in the organization, including the members of the policy board. Indeed, it is action by a board of directors that formalizes change decisions. However, it is the executive who has the ultimate responsibility for the process of monitoring changes in the organizational environment in order to determine potential consequences for the organization. The executive has the final responsibility for the processes of making organizational-change operational decisions, and for implementation. "It is our assumption that . . . executives, indeed, bear final responsibility for the decisions made in their organization" (Perlmutter and Gummer 1994:227).

Fundamentally, organizational change processes require three elements: (1) one or more individuals, including those whom Kanter (1983) identifies as "organizational entrepreneurs," who have ideas about the form and direction of change; (2) an explicit decision to make a change; and (3) the process of change implementation. Kanter (1983:290–300) also identifies five necessary conditions for productive change: (1) the ability to depart from tradition; (2) the presence of an external force such as a crisis or a galvanizing event; (3) carefully developed strategic decisions by organizational managers; (4) the presence of an individual who becomes the prime mover of the change; and (5) a number of "action vehicles" that make it possible for staff members to carry out changes.

A key factor in any change process is leadership, primarily executive leadership. "Change requires leadership, after all, a 'prime mover' to push for implementation of strategic decisions" (Kanter 1983:125). "While managers are seen as key actors in determining all aspects of organizational life, it is in the area of organizational change that the role of the manager has been apotheosized in the notion of 'champions' of change" (Gummer 1992:206). Schorr, in her study of successful program innovations, states, "Successful programs are well managed by competent and committed individuals with clearly identifiable skills" (1997:9). Leadership also includes responsibility for "vision"—that is, a projection of a positive image of the ultimate consequences of proposed changes for the service organization and for the organizational stakeholders.

There is no single successful method of implementing change. The consequences of different change processes may be different under different circumstances. Changes that have a high degree of involvement of interested constituencies may result in a general "buying in" to a change process. But change proposals that attempt to accommodate the interests of all the concerned constituencies may also be limited to marginal or incremental changes that do not match the scale of the changes taking place in the organizational environment that are creating new demands on the organization. As Schorr (1997:18–19) reports,

> It is now absolutely clear that the attributes of effective programs are undermined by their systems' surroundings, especially when they attempt to expand to reach large numbers.
>
> The mismatch between the attributes of effective programs and the imperatives of prevailing systems is what stands in the way of successful demonstrations becoming part of the mainstream. . . .
>
> The history of efforts to replicate, sustain, and scale up from effective programs is dismal. The single most important reason, in my view, is the failure to understand that the environment with which these programs have to operate, and which these programs depend on for long-term funding, skilled professionals, and public support, is profoundly out-of-sync with the key attributes of success.

THE DYNAMICS OF ORGANIZATIONAL CHANGE

A strategic approach to analyzing change processes involves identifying proposed changes as either incremental or "transformational" (Perlmutter and Gummer 1994), and as uncontested or contested (Austin 1965). This involves the extent of the disruption of positions and relationships within the organization, and therefore the degree to which the interests of individuals may be perceived as being affected by those changes. These relationships may involve not only the members of the staff but also the members of the board of directors as well as relationships between service users and the organization. Internal administrative changes may have no consequences for user relationships, whereas reorganization may disrupt established connections between service providers and particular service users and members of their family. Within the service delivery network changes in one organization may have positive or negative consequences for other organizations within the network. A perception of potential negative consequences may result in varying degrees of resistance to proposed changes or even organized opposition.

Incremental Change

The term *incremental change* involves changes at the margins of existing policy or program structure, changes that do not require significant modifications in basic organizational assumptions or in the patterns of power or resource allocation. Incremental change often takes place through the adaptation of particular organizational units to changes in their immediate task environment. As Quinn (1978) points out, organizations often deal with changes in the organizational environment, not through a formal planning process but through "logical incrementalism," or a series of piecemeal adaptations that may result over time in a "strategic" change. Such incremental changes may include the expansion of an existing service program as a result of increased funding, the opening of a new service location to provide ongoing services, or the addition of a new, but familiar, service activity without changing the existing service structure. Even the elimination of a service program that has been funded with time-limited special-purpose funds may constitute an incremental change.

Many incremental organizational changes may be *uncontested*, although in a given situation, what appears to be an incremental change may become *contested* because of the particular sets of interests that may be involved. These may be the interests of particular staff members or of board members who identify with a particular organizational tradition. However, a contested incremental change is unlikely to involve interests beyond the organization, and the issue can normally be determined by policy action by a board of directors or administrative action by an executive.

Transformational Change

"Transformational" changes (Perlmutter and Gummer 1994) may include changes in legitimacy, sector, professionalism, technology, mission, basic structure, or funding relationships; realignment of budgetary resources that changes status and power relationships among program elements; or changes in service priority criteria that change the characteristics of the service population, and, in turn, the criteria for staff selection and promotion. Similar types of transformational changes take place in for-profit corporations as well as in nonprofit organizations. The term *reengineering* has often been used to describe a process through which a for-profit business is reinvented—that is, the basic structure and production process of the firm is totally recreated (Lowenthal 1994).

A series of incremental changes may result in internal contradictions within an organization that may require the consideration of more fundamental changes, such as promoting the development of fee charges as a significant income source for the entire organization after one program component has successfully implemented such a policy. That decision may take on the characteristics of a fundamental, far-reaching, or transformational change as staff members and board members, and even members of the general public, begin to define such a change as a substantive shift in the identity of the organization and how it relates to its community.

Some transformational changes may be far-reaching, but largely *uncontested*, particularly when major sources of authority, legitimation, and funding support the changes. Much of the organizational change literature focuses on processes of stakeholder involvement and, in particular, staff involvement, which can result in uncontested transformational changes. Much of the organizational development (OD) literature deals with bringing about transformational change without confrontation.

But many transformational changes are *contested*. Examples include decisions about the provision of abortion services, a policy change from favoring same-race adoptions to giving equal support to transracial adoptions, the initiation of a POSC program, or a decision on an organizational merger. Contested transformational changes require political change strategies, since they involve, in some way, changes in fundamental organizational assumptions and, in turn, changes in power relationships (Perlmutter and Gummer 1994). The choice between a change strategy involving a series of incremental, uncontested change initiatives, and a strategy of selecting a transformational, likely-to-be-contested model of organizational change requires a "force-field" or political analysis of the interests involved as well as an analysis of the substantive change proposals.

Contested changes may involve a contest between different visions of the change that is being considered. They may also involve mobilized resistance to any substantial form of change. Such resistance may come from organizational staff members or from other constituencies. Many proposals for change fail to include any benefits/rewards for those persons who may be negatively affected by the change. And those persons negatively affected by a proposed change are more likely to work together to oppose the proposed change than are the potential beneficiaries of the change to work together to support it. In the world of legislative decision making, proposals for change often include provisions for buying out sources of resistance.

Objections to change proposals may also come from stakeholder constituencies that view the proposals as being, in reality, token and insignificant, primarily put forward for public relations purposes. Some stakeholders may have experienced recurrent cycles of ritualistic change proposals, frequently associated with the appointment of a new executive, who may assume that the initiation of changes is automatically required to justify the appointment. Stakeholders may have also experienced a cyclical process of centralization–decentralization structural changes that consistently fail to deal with underlying difficulties that limit service effectiveness.

Contested transformational change initiatives may involve power contests that are resolved by a demonstration of sufficient power to impose a particular form of change on an organization. Technical analysis and rational arguments may be part of the process in such a politicized change decision process, but values and ideological commitments may be as important, or more important, than the analyses. The resolution of contested change conflicts may follow specific rules and procedures that are recognized by all the stakeholder interests—for example, in the decision-making process by a board of directors. However, in some instances, the decision process may, in reality, violate such rules but still be imposed on the organization. On rare occasions, such conflicts over change proposals may end up in the courts. These contested transformational change processes may include intense conflicts among stakeholder constituencies, as well as the use of negotiations and compromises in efforts to find a solution that has broad support. This process is similar to those involved in developing, and gaining approval of, legislation that ultimately has strong majority support.

In reality, the change decision that is established through a political power process that follows the rules may or may not turn out to be a correct or even a viable solution for the future of the organization. Indeed, much of the ultimate result may depend on the processes of implementation, which, in some instances, may continue to be shaped by political forces. Indeed, the final outcome for a service organization of a contested transformational change initiative may, in practice, depart substantially from the intent of the original change decision. Moreover, the decision to pursue a far-reaching, contested transformational organizational change objective without the political/power resources to ensure its implementation may only result in an extended period of conflict and struggle.

ALTERNATIVE MODELS OF CHANGE PROCESSES

Planned Change

One approach to transformational change that seeks to find the most effective and efficient way to accomplish particular change objectives is to initiate a systematic process of planned change (Mayer 1985:103–108). Many funding sources require evidence of some form of systematic planning to support a request for funding a new program. A variety of formal, analytic planning models have been described by various authors for use in a planned change model; the key elements in these planned change processes include the following:

- Identification of a need for change
- Establishment of a goal to be sought through the change, stated in general, and often value-based, terms
- Establishment of operational and measurable objectives and a time period within which to achieve them
- Evaluation of alternative service methods and organizational structures for achieving the objectives, including estimates of the probable cost–benefit ratios of the alternatives
- Selection of a specific form of change action
- The making of a "binding decision" to initiate the change, including the possibility of an initial pilot, or experimental, implementation
- Implementation of the change
- Evaluation of the results of the plan for change
- A comparison of the results of the implementation with the stated objectives
- Reconsideration of the original goal and of the operational objectives

Such a formal and comprehensive approach to planned change may involve the use of planning specialists, either staff members or consultants from academic centers or from specialized consulting firms. The planning specialist gathers information about the relevant experience of other organizations and communities; organizes the participation of interested constituencies through, for example, surveys, hearings, and reviews by technical panels; and develops specific proposals. The service organization may then turn to such planning specialists for assistance in implementing the change plan that is selected. One important element of the implementation process is the early involvement of evaluation specialists (see chapter 11), so that plans for evaluation are consistent with the original change plans.

A study of actual experiences with planning for change suggests that in practice, the exploration of change alternatives does not include the examination of all possible alternatives, an approach that may be both time consuming and expensive. The examination of alternatives often proceeds only until a "satisficing" alternative is identified—that is, an alternative that meets a set of minimal criteria that have been explicitly, or implicitly, adopted by a decision body.

Another structured and systematic approach to planned change is the development of multiple scenarios through which alternative "stories about the future that are plausible and based on analysis of the interaction of a number of environmental variables" (Kloss 1999:73) are constructed by interactive groups or teams. Such scenarios are focused on the organizational environment rather than on internal factors. They provide a framework through which organization members can explore the potential effects of emerging forces in the organizational environment. Such scenario construction increases the attention to strategic thinking rather than to rational analytic planning (Shoemaker 1993).

Organizational Development

Examinations of actual planning/implementation processes in society suggest that analytic, systematic, comprehensive planning procedures are not the only way in which change decisions are made (Goldberg 1995). Organizational Development (OD), a widely recognized approach to the process of organizational change, originated in the group dynamic theories of Kurt Lewin and the National Training Laboratories Institute. OD is part of a broader movement identified as "participatory management" (Gummer 1979). OD focuses on internal organizational processes and team building—that is, the development of patterns of collaborative interaction directed toward resolving internal problem conditions or achieving organizational goals (Grasso and Epstein 1992). Substantive change objectives emerge from interactive group processes, primarily among organizational personnel.

Common elements in OD include the use of an external consultant for the OD process, feed-back by the consultant to the process participants on strengths and weaknesses of the team-building process, and a consensus-focused decision process. OD case histories identify success in resolving internal process problems and in improving organizational morale. However, OD approaches to change do not, inherently, change the hierarchical structure of authority and control of bureaucratic organizations. That limits the degree of empowerment, or "internal commitment" to proposed changes, that organizational personnel are likely to experience in comparison to "external commitment," or formal, contractual compliance.

Nonplanned Change Processes

Other change decision processes may involve spur-of-the-moment initiatives in response to either internal or external events that create pressures for action. Such initiatives may involve limited forms of consultation and then a "binding decision" by a policy-making body or an executive. Such ad hoc decision making is sometimes characterized as "garbage can" decision making—that is, a random selection of one option among several possible change options, without a systematic analysis of alternatives, on the grounds that "any action is preferable to inaction."

Another analysis of change processes suggests that actual change processes often proceed through a process of "mutual partisan adjustment" involving adaptive negotiations among the several stakeholder constituencies involved. The interests of various constituencies and related organizations are accommodated in a step-by-step political process of developing a solution that results in at least minimal satisfaction on the part of the involved interests. A major limitation in such incremental-change decision making is that the decision process is largely shaped by interactions among constituency interests, sometimes, but not always, including user interests, without firm information as to the future feasibility of implementing the negotiated changes or the probability that the changes agreed on will actually achieve intended objectives.

CHANGE DECISION MAKING

All change processes involve a series of decisions. The outcome of such decision processes may be influenced as much by the decision-making procedures as by the merits of the substantive issues involved. At least three different methods of explicit decision making may be relevant for use in a particular change decision process. The most traditional approach is the use of *parliamentary procedures*, or *Robert's Rules of Order*. Such procedures are most likely to be used for decisions that may be viewed as having potential legal consequences, requiring a formal record of the actual decision procedures. Parliamentary procedures, however, are most relevant when organized interests are in conflict so that a set of formal rules is required to establish the legitimacy of the decision ultimately arrived at. Indeed, the original development of parliamentary procedures was an effort to establish an alternative to live combat to settle political issues. Parliamentary procedures are used most frequently in quasi-governmental and governmental boards and commissions that may have divided votes and that are required to have a public record of decision making.

Parliamentary procedures do not provide for a free give-and-take in discussion, since relevant discussion at any particular time is intended to deal with only the one specific motion or amendment that is before the decision-making body. Given the general lack of familiarity with the details of parliamentary procedure among the general public, the power in a given decision process often rests with a presiding officer who has the authority and responsibility for determining conformance with the formal decision-making rules. Moreover, parliamentary procedures, in particular, are responsive to the most active and assertive individuals in the decision-making body and to those individuals who represent powerful constituencies.

The second, and most widely used, decision-making procedure is *interactive discussion* (Delbecq, Van de Ven, and Gustafson 1975). Interactive discussion involves a guided discussion process through which a general consensus or agreement emerges from extended exploration of the issues involved, the significance of relevant information, and the implications of proposed actions. Guided interactive discussion is most relevant when there is not a structured or polarized conflict, when there is a shared set of interests, and when members of the group have roughly equal status and power. It is also relevant, for example, for a nonprofit board of directors, when support of all or most of the members of the decision-making body for a policy decision is important for successful implementation. The ability of any given group to arrive at an agreed-on decision is often dependent on the ability of the group leader, chairperson, or presiding officer to focus the interactive discussion without suppressing an exploration of the relevant issues involved.

However, interactive discussion has a number of serious limitations as a decision-making process. One is that the discussion of alternatives may go on indefinitely without arriving at a clear-cut decision. Alternatively, the ability of the group leader to move the discussion to a conclusion may also mean exercising control over the result. Assertive individuals frequently dominate the discussion. Individuals who have less influence or power, or who represent interests with less power, may depend on opinion leaders for guidance. Unpopular points of view may be ignored and the persons presenting such perspectives may withdraw from the discussion. In the course of the discussion, opinions may become polarized around competing perspectives, increasing the difficulty of arriving at a decision that can ultimately be supported by all the members of the decision-making group.

A third form of decision making has been set forth by Delbecq, Van de Ven, and Gustafson (1975)—nominal group technique (NGT). NGT represents an effort to provide a more balanced form of participation and an effort to give attention to a full range of choices. It is an approach that provides an opportunity for individuals who are not normally part of the policy-making group—for example, representatives of service users—to have equal access to the decision process. It also provides a framework for a diverse group—for example, an interdisciplinary team that includes different professional perspectives—that provides equal access for all the group members to the decision process, regardless of differences in the power status of individual group members.

After a presentation of the decision issue, the NGT process in a formal decision session involves the following steps:

- Preparation of a written list of alternative decision recommendations by each participant without discussion
- The listing of all suggested recommendations, which may be done so that the author of each item remains anonymous

- Informational discussion of each alternative for clarification but without debate
- Rank ordering in writing of the preferred alternatives by each member of the group
- Consolidation of the rank ordering statements to provide a summation rank ordering of the alternatives, based on the preferences expressed by each of the members of the group

Delbecq, Van de Ven, and Gustafson (1975) point out that decision processes involve both development of information and decision making about, or evaluation of, that information. NGT separates these two steps and provides equal status for the information contributions and the evaluative opinions of each member of the decision group. Major benefits of NGT include the opportunity to put nontraditional or innovative proposals before the entire group in the information stage, separate from the power status of the person making a suggestion, and the equal weighting, in the evaluation phase, of each participant's preferences among the proposed alternatives.

CHANGE-ADEPT ORGANIZATIONS

Much of the literature dealing with organizational change addresses change as a series of discrete steps moving from a current organizational pattern to some new pattern of organizational activities, sometimes described as a process of "unlocking" the organization, and later "locking in," or institutionalizing, a discrete change in organizational procedures. However, recent perspectives assume that change is a constant for many contemporary organizations, including human service organizations. Kanter writes of the "change-adept organization" (1997). Senge (1990, 1999) writes of the "learning organization." Both authors emphasize that such organizations must have a continuous process of gathering information, reviewing the meaning of that information for the organization, and adapting organizational processes in a manner consistent with that information, a process that has been identified as "strategic management" (Bryson 1994) or "strategic planning" (Stone, Bigelow, and Crittenden 1999).

Strategic planning, or strategic issue management (Eadie 1998), is an effort to establish a focus for the ongoing processes of change in change-adept organizations. The focus is on a continuous organizational reexamination process, rather than on a single planning episode. Emphasis is placed on reexamining organizational mission and vision, an analysis of environmental forces affecting the organization and of internal strengths and weaknesses, identification of key strategic issues that require systematic attention, and the selection of specific future-oriented strategies for dealing with those issues. Such a strategic planning process requires the involvement of key stakeholder constituencies both as sources of critical information and as participants in the process of selecting future-oriented developmental strategies. The translation of such strategies into specific action recommendations then becomes the responsibility of the executive and members of the service staff, in consultation with the board of directors or with specific oversight bodies that have been established.

Change-adept organizations are marked by an openness to information from the environment, individual initiatives, innovation, flexible organizational structures, and by emphasis on project teams and self-managed work teams rather than on hierarchical staff structures and job titles (Kanter 1993). Such an organizational change and development pattern, however, requires that the service organization be able to establish a high degree of control over the legitimacy resources and the economic resources that are required for continued operation. Without such control over input resources, abrupt changes may be forced on the organization without significant participation by any of the organizational stakeholder constituencies.

SUMMARY

Change is pervasive in the environments of human service organizations, creating pressures for organizational changes. Change initiatives also come from within organizations, including program evaluation studies. The organizational executive is particularly responsible for dealing with change processes within an organization, including the implementation actions that follow a change decision. Change processes are affected by the scope of the proposed change, ranging from essentially technical, uncontested incremental changes to highly politicized transformational changes. A number of different change processes may be used, including systematic planning approaches, ad hoc change decisions, and participatory developmental approaches such as organizational development. Within these change processes, there are several alternative methods of making the critical decisions that determine the nature of the change. The rate of change in organizational environments requires that the development of organizational change strategies become an ongoing part of the functioning of the human service change-adept organization.

REFERENCES

Abbott, Andrew D. 1988. *The System of Professions: An Essay on the Division of Labor*. Chicago: University of Chicago Press.

———. 1995. Boundaries of social work or social work of boundaries? *Social Service Review* 69, no. 4:545–562.

Abbott, Pamela, and Claire Wallace. 1990. *The Sociology of the Caring Professions*. London: Palmer Press.

Abercrombie, Nicholas. 1980. *Class, Structure and Knowledge: Problems in the Sociology of Knowledge*. Oxford: Basil Blackwell.

Abramson, J. S., and T. Mizrahi. 1996. When social workers and physicians collaborate: Positive and negative interdisciplinary experiences. *Social Work* 41, no. 3:270–283.

Agranoff, R., and A. Pattaos. 1970. Dimensions of service integration: Service delivery, program linkages, policy management, organizational structure. *Human Services Monograph Series 13*. Washington, D.C.: Project SHARE.

Aiken, M., and J. Hage. 1968. Organizational interdependence and intraorganizational structure. *American Sociological Review* 33:912–930.

Akers, R. L., and R. Quinney. 1968. Differential organization of health professions: A comparative analysis. *American Sociological Review* 33, no. 1:104–121.

Aldrich, H., and D. Herker. 1977. Boundary spanning roles and organization structure. *Academy of Management Review* 2:217–228.

Aldrich, Howard. 1978. Centralization versus decentralization in the design of human service delivery systems. In R. Sarri and Y. Hasenfeld, eds. *The Management of Human Services*, pp. 51–79. New York: Columbia University.

Alexander, C. A. 1976. What does a representative represent? *Social Work* 21, no. 1:3–9.

Alexander, C. A., and A. McCann. 1956. The concept of representativeness in community organization. *Social Work* 1, no. 1:48–52.

Alexander, J. 2000. Adaptive strategies of nonprofit human service organizations in an era of devolution and new public management. *Nonprofit Management & Leadership* 10, no. 3:287–303.

Alexander, Leslie B., and Toba S. Kerson. 1980. Room at the top: Women in social administration. In F. Perlmutter and S. Slavin, eds. *Leadership in Social Administration*, pp. 195–215. Philadelphia: Temple University Press.

Alexander, R., Jr. 1997. Social workers and privileged communication in the federal legal system. *Social Work* 42, no. 4:387–391.

Ammerman, Nancy T. 1997. *Congregation and Community*. New Brunswick, N.J.: Rutgers University Press.

Anderson, Albert. 1996. *Ethics for Fundraisers*. Bloomington, Ind.: Indiana University Press.

Arguello, D. F. 1984. Minorities in administration: A review of ethnicity's influence in management. *Administration in Social Work* 8, no. 3:17–28.

Argyris, Chris. 1962. *Interpersonal Competence and Organizational Effectiveness*. Homewood, Ill.: Dorsey Press.

——. 1964. *Integrating the Individual and the Organization*. New York: John Wiley.

Ashley, W. G., and A. Van de Ven. 1983. Central perspectives and debates in organizational theory. *Administrative Science Quarterly* 28:245–273.

Au, C. 1996. Rethinking organizational effectiveness: Theoretical and methodological issues in the study of organizational effectiveness for social welfare organizations. *Administration in Social Work* 20, no. 4:1–22.

Austin, C. D., D. Kravetz, and K. L. Pollock. 1985. Experiences of women as social work administrators. *Social Work* 30, no. 2:173–179.

Austin, David M. 1958. The special youth program approach to chronic problem families. In *Community Organization*, pp. 101–108. New York: Columbia University Press.

——. 1965. "Community Planning for Critical Issues." Paper presented at the 1965 National Conference of Social Welfare.

——. 1972. Resident participation: Political mobilization or organizational cooptation. *Public Administration Review* 32 (special):409–420.

——. 1978. The politics and organization of services: Consolidation and integration. *Public Welfare* 36, no. 3:20–28.

——. 1979. *Improving Access in the Human Services: Decision Issues and Alternatives*. Washington, D.C.: American Public Welfare Association.

——. 1981. The political economy of social benefit organizations: Redistributive services and merit goods. In H. D. Stein, ed. *Organization and the Human Services: Cross-Disciplinary Reflections*, pp. 37–88. Philadelphia: Temple University Press.

——. 1983a. Administrative practice in human services: Future directions for curriculum development. *Journal of Applied Behavioral Science* 19, no. 2:141–161.

——. 1983b. The Flexner myth and the history of social work. *Social Service Review* 57, no. 3:357–377.

——. 1986. *A History of Social Work Education*. Austin: School of Social Work, University of Texas at Austin.

——. 1988. *The Political Economy of Human Service Programs*. Greenwich, Conn.: JAI Press.

——. 1989. The human service executive. *Administration in Social Work* 13, nos. 3/4:13–36.

——. 1991. Understanding the service delivery system. In R. L. Edwards and J. A. Yankey, eds. *Skills for Effective Human Services Management*, pp. 27–43. Silver Springs, Md.: National Association of Social Workers.

——. 1995. Management in social work. In R. L. Edwards and J. G. Hopps, eds. *Encyclopedia of Social Work*, 19th edition, pp. 1642–1658. Washington, D.C.: National Association of Social Workers.

——. 1997. The institutional development of social work education: The first 100 years. *Journal of Social Work Education* 33, no. 3:599–614.

——. 2000. Social work and social welfare administration: A historical perspective. In R. J. Patti, ed. *The Handbook of Social Welfare Management*, pp. 27–54. Thousand Oaks, Calif.: Sage.

Austin, Michael J., et al. 1982. *Evaluating Your Agency's Programs*. Beverly Hills, Calif.: Sage.

Axelrod, Nancy R. 1994. Board leadership and board development. In R. D. Herman and Associates, eds. *The Jossey-Bass Handbook of Nonprofit Leadership and Management*, pp. 119–136. San Francisco: Jossey-Bass.

Backman, E. V., and S. R. Smith. 2000. Healthy organizations, unhealthy communities. *Nonprofit Management & Leadership* 10, no. 4:355–373.

Bailey, Darlene. 1998. Designing and sustaining meaningful organizational teams. In R. L. Edwards, J. A. Yankey and M. A. Altpeter, eds. *Skills for Effective Management of Nonprofit Organizations*, pp. 185–199. Washington, D.C.: National Association of Social Workers.

Baltzell, Edward D. 1964. *The Protestant Establishment: Aristocracy and Class in America*. New York: Random House.

Barker, Robert L. 1992. *Social Work in Private Practice: Principles, Issues and Dilemmas*, 2nd edition. Washington, D.C.: National Association of Social Workers.

Barko, W., and W. Pasmore. 1986. Sociotechnical systems: Innovations in designing high-performing systems. *Journal of Applied Behavioral Science* 22, no. 3:195–200.

Bartlett, H. M. 1958. Towards a clarification and improvement of social work practice. *Social Work* 3, no. 2:3–9.

Begun, J. 1986. Economic and sociological approaches to professionalism. *Work and Occupations* 13, no. 1:113–129.

Bell, Daniel. 1973. *The Coming of Post-Industrial Society: A Venture in Social Forecasting*. New York: Basic Books.

Bell, James, and Associates. 1994. *Evaluation of HHS Services Integration Pilot Projects*, vol. II. Arlington, Va.: James Bell Associates.

Bendick, Michael. 1985. "Privatizing the Delivery of Social Welfare Service." Working Paper 6, Privatization. Washington, D.C.: National Conference of Social Welfare.

Benson, J. K. 1975. The interorganizational network as a political economy. *Administrative Science Quarterly* 20:229–249.

Berkowitz, Edward D. 1987. *Disabled Policy: America's Programs for the Handicapped*. London: Cambridge University Press.

Blake, Robert, and Jane Mouton. 1964. *The Managerial Grid*. Houston: Gulf.

Blythe, Betty J., and Tony Tripodi. 1989. *Measurement in Direct Practice*. Newbury Park, Calif.: Sage.

Boettcher, R. E. 1998. A study of quality-managed human service organizations. *Administration in Social Work* 22, no. 2:41–56.

Boje, David M., Robert P. Gephart, Jr., and Tojo J. Thatchenkery. 1996. *Postmodern Management and Organizational Theory*. Thousand Oaks, Calif.: Sage.

Bok, D. 1984. Needed: A new way to train doctors. *Harvard Magazine* 86, no. 5:32–43, 70–71.

Boulding, Kenneth E. 1973. *The Economy of Love and Fear: A Preface to Grants Economics*. Belmont, Calif.: Wadsworth.

Bowen, D. E., and B. Schneider. 1988. Service marketing and management: Implications for organizational behavior. In L. L. Cummings and B. M. Staw, eds. *Research in Organizational Behavior*, pp. 43–80. Greenwich, Conn.: JAI Press.

Bozeman, Barry. 1987. *All Organizations Are Public: Bridging Public and Private Organizational Theories*. San Francisco: Jossey-Bass.

Brannen, Stephen J., and Cal Streeter. 1995. Doing it with data: Total quality management and the evaluation of human services. In B. Gummer and P. McCallion, eds. *Total Quality Management in the Social Services: Theory and Practice*, pp. 59–88. Albany, N.Y.: School of Social Welfare, State University of New York at Albany.

Brilliant, Eleanor L. 1990. *The United Way: Dilemmas of Organized Charity*. New York: Columbia University Press.

Brodkin, E. Z. 1997. Inside the welfare contract: Discretion and accountability in state welfare administration. *Social Service Review* 71, no. 1:1–33.

Bruno, Frank. 1957. *Trends in Social Work 1874–1956: A History Based on the Proceedings of the National Conference of Social Work.* New York: Columbia University Press.

Bryson, John M. 1994. Strategic planning and action planning for nonprofit organizations. In R. D. Herman and Associates, eds. *The Jossey-Bass Handbook of Nonprofit Leadership and Management*, pp. 154–183. San Francisco: Jossey-Bass.

Buchanan, James, and Gordon Tullock. 1962. *The Calculus of Consent: Logical Foundations of Constitutional Democracy.* Ann Arbor: University of Michigan Press.

Buell, Bradley, and Associates. 1952. *Community Planning for Human Services.* New York: Columbia University Press.

Buxbaum, C. B. 1981. "Cost-benefit analysis": The mystique versus the reality. *Social Service Review* 55, no. 3:453–471.

Caplow, Theodore. 1954. *The Sociology of Work.* New York: McGraw-Hill.

Carroll, Glenn, ed. 1988. *Ecological Models of Organizations.* Cambridge, Mass.: Ballinger.

Carr-Saunders, Alexander M. 1928. *Professions: Their Organization and Place in Society.* Oxford: Clarendon Press.

———. 1966. Professionalization in historical perspective. In W. M. Vollmer and D. L. Mills, eds. *Professionalization*, pp. 2–6. Englewood Cliffs, N.J.: Prentice-Hall.

Carver, John. 1990. *Boards That Make a Difference.* San Francisco: Jossey-Bass.

Carver, John, and Miriam Carver. 1996. *Basic Principles of Policy Governance.* San Francisco: Jossey-Bass.

Casalino, L. P. 1999. The unintended consequences of measuring quality on the quality of medical care. *New England Journal of Medicine* 341, no. 15:1147–1150.

Chait, Richard P., Thomas P. Holland, and Barbara E. Taylor. 1996. *Improving the Performance of Governing Boards.* Phoenix: Oryx Press.

Chamberlin, Judi. 1978. *On Our Own: Patient-controlled Alternatives to the Mental Health System.* New York: McGraw Hill.

Cherin, D., and W. Meezan. 1998. Evaluation as a means of organizational learning. *Administration in Social Work* 22, no. 2:1–21.

Chernesky, Roslyn H. 1983. The sex dimension of organizational processes: Its impact on women managers. *Administration in Social Work* 7, nos. 3/4:13.

———. 1998. Advancing women in the managerial ranks. In R. L. Edwards, J. A. Yankey, and M. A. Altpeter, eds. *Skills for Effective Management of Nonprofit Organizations*, pp. 200–218. Washington, D.C.: National Association of Social Workers.

Child, John. 1995. Follett: Constructive conflict. In P. Graham, ed. *Mary Parker Follett—Prophet of Management*, pp. 87–96. Boston: Harvard Business School Press.

Chisholm, Donald. 1989. *Coordination Without Hierarchy*. Berkeley: University of California Press.

Chism, Shirley K. 1997. "Measuring Customer Perceptions of Service Quality in Human Services." Dissertation, University of Texas, Austin.

Chisolm, L. B. 1995. Accountability of nonprofit organizations and those who control them: The legal framework. *Nonprofit Management & Leadership* 6, no. 2:141–156.

Chung, Soondol. 1996. "A Study of Interorganizational Relationships in Elderly Service Delivery Systems." Dissertation, University of Texas, Austin.

Clotfelter, Charles T., and Thomas Ehrlich, eds. 1999. *Philanthropy and the Nonprofit Sector in a Changing America*. Bloomington, Ind.: Indiana University Press.

Cloward, Richard, and Irwin Epstein. 1965. Private welfare's disengagement from the poor: The case of the family adjustment agencies. In M. N. Zald, ed. *Social Welfare Institutions*, pp. 623–643. New York: Wiley.

Cohen, Helen A. 1981. *The Nurses' Quest for a Professional Identity*. Menlo Park, Calif.: Addison-Wesley.

Cole, R. E. 1998. Learning from the quality movement: What did and didn't happen and why. *California Management Review* 41, 3:43–73.

Compher, J. V. 1987. The dance beyond the family system. *Social Work* 32, no. 2:105–108.

Congress, E. 1997. Is the *Code of Ethics* as applicable to agency executives as it is to direct service providers? Yes. In E. Gambrill and R. Pruger, eds. *Controversial Issues in Social Work Ethics, Values and Obligations*, pp. 138–142. Boston: Allyn and Bacon.

Connor, J. A., S. Kadel-Taras, and D. Vinokur-Kaplan. 1999. The role of management support organizations in sustaining community collaborations. *Nonprofit Management & Leadership* 10, no. 2:127–136.

Cordes, Joseph, and Burton Weisbrod. 1997. "Differential Taxation of Nonprofits and the Commercialization of Nonprofit Revenues." Working Paper 97-15. Evanston, Ill.: Institute for Policy Research, Northwestern University.

Csikai, E. L., and E. Sales. 1998. The emerging social work role on hospital ethics committees: A comparison of social worker and chair perspectives. *Social Work* 43, no. 3:233–242.

Cullen, John B. 1978. *The Structure of Professionalism—A Quantitative Examination*. New York: Petrocelli Books.

Cutlip, Scott M. 1965. *Fund Raising in the United States: Its Role in American Philanthropy*. New Brunswick, N.J.: Rutgers University Press.

Dahlberg, Jane. 1966. *The New York Bureau of Municipal Research: Pioneer in Government Administration.* New York: New York University Press.

Dart, R., P. Bradshaw, V. Murray, and J. Wolpin. 1996. Boards of directors in nonprofit organizations: Do they follow a life-cycle? *Nonprofit Management & Leadership* 6, no. 4:67–80.

D'Aunno, Thomas. 1992. The effectiveness of human service organizations: A comparison of models. In Y. Hasenfeld, ed. *Human Services as Complex Organizations*, pp. 341–361. Beverly Hills, Calif.: Sage.

Davis, King E. 1975. *Fund Raising in the Black Community: History, Feasibility and Conflict.* Metuchen, N.J.: Scarecrow Press.

Delbecq, Andre L. 1978. The social political process of introducing innovation in human services. In R. Sarri and Y. Hasenfeld, eds. *The Management of Human Services*, pp. 309–339. New York: Columbia University Press.

Delbecq, Andre L., Andrew H. Van de Ven, and David H. Gustafson. 1975. *Group Techniques for Program Planning.* Glenview, Ill.: Scott, Foresman.

Deming, W. Edward. 1986. *Out of the Crisis.* Cambridge, Mass.: Massachusetts Institute of Technology, Center for Advanced Engineering Study.

Demone, Harold, Jr., and Dwight Harshberger. 1974. *Handbook of Human Service Organization.* New York: Behavioral Publications.

Dorsey, Eugene C. 1992. *The Role of the Board Chairperson.* Washington, D.C.: National Center for Nonprofit Boards.

Dressel, Paula L. 1992. Patriarchy and social welfare work. In Y. Hasenfeld, ed. *Human Services as Complex Organizations*, pp. 205–223. Newbury Park, Calif.: Sage.

Drucker, Peter F. 1990a. Lessons for successful nonprofit governance. *Nonprofit Management & Leadership* 1, no. 1:7–14.

——. 1990b. *Managing the Nonprofit Organization: Principles and Practices.* New York: Harper Collins.

——. 1996. Introduction. In F. Hesselbein, M. Goldsmith, and R. Beckard, eds. *The Leader of the Future*, pp. 1–5. San Francisco: Jossey-Bass.

——. 1998. Management's new paradigms. *Forbes* October 5:152–175.

——. 2001. The next society. *The Economist* 361, no. 8246:3–20.

Dunst, Carl J., Carol M. Trivette, and Angela G. Deal. 1988. *Enabling and Empowering Families.* Cambridge, Mass.: Brookline Books.

Eadie, Douglas C. 1998. Planning and managing strategically. In R. L. Edwards, J. A. Yankey, and M. A. Altpeter, eds. *Skills for Effective Management of Nonprofit Organizations*, pp. 453–468. Washington, D.C.: National Association of Social Workers.

Edwards, Richard L., David M. Austin, and M. A. Altpeter. 1998. Managing effectively in an environment of competing values. In R. L. Edwards, J. A. Yankey, and M. A. Altpeter, eds. *Skills for Effective Management of Nonprofit*

Organizations, pp. 5–24. Washington, D.C.: National Association of Social Workers.

Edwards, Richard L., Elizabeth A. S. Benefield, Jeffrey A. Edwards, and John A. Yankey. 1997. *Building a Strong Foundation: Fundraising for Nonprofits.* Washington, D.C.: National Association of Social Workers.

Edwards, R., P. Cooke, and P. N. Reid. 1996. Social work management in an era of diminishing federal responsibility. *Social Work* 41, no. 5:468–479.

Edwards, R. L., S. R. Faerman, and M. R. McGrath. 1986. The competing values approach to organizational effectiveness: A tool for agency administrators. *Administration in Social Work* 10, no. 4:1–14.

Edwards, Richard L., and John A. Yankey, eds. 1991. *Skills for Effective Human Service Management.* Washington, D.C.: National Association of Social Workers.

Emery, F. E., and E. L. Trist. 1965. The causal texture of organizational environments. *Human Relations* 18, no. 1:21–32.

England, Hugh. 1986. *Social Work as an Art.* London: Allen and Unwin.

Epstein, Irwin, and Kayla Conrad. 1978. The empirical limits of social work professionalization. In R. C. Sarri and Y. Hasenfeld, eds. *The Management of Human Services*, pp. 163–183. New York: Columbia University Press.

Etzioni, Amitai. 1964. *Modern Organizations.* Englewood Cliffs, N.J.: Prentice-Hall.

——. 1969. Preface. In A. Etzioni, ed. *The Semi-Professions and Their Organization*, pp. v–xviii. New York: Free Press.

Evan, W. 1966. The Organization Set: Toward a Theory of Interorganizational Relations. In J. D. Thompson, ed. *Approaches to Organizational Design*, pp. 173–191. Pittsburgh: University of Pittsburgh Press.

Ewing, T. N. 1974. Racial similarity of client and counselor and client satisfaction with counseling. *Journal of Counseling Psychology* 21:446–449.

Fallon, K. P. 1978. Participatory management: An alternative in human service delivery systems. In S. Slavin, ed. *Social Administration*, pp. 169–176. New York: Haworth Press.

Felty, D. W., and M. B. Jones. 1998. Human services at risk. *Social Service Review* 72, no. 2:192–208.

Fine, A. H., C. E. Thayer, and A. T. Coghlan. 2000. Program evaluation in the nonprofit sector. *Nonprofit Management & Leadership* 10, no. 3:331–339.

Fitzsimmons, James A., and Mona J. Fitzsimmons. 1994. *Service Management for Competitive Advantage.* New York: McGraw-Hill.

Fletcher, Kathleen. 1997. *Building Board Diversity: A Case Study of the Western Region Affiliates of the Planned Parenthood Federation of America.* Washington, D.C.: Aspen Institute.

Flexner, Abraham. 1910. *Medical Education in the United States* (reprint edition, 1972). New York: Arno Press.

——. 1915. "Is Social Work a Profession?" *Proceedings of the National Conference of Charities and Correction, 1915*, pp. 576–590. Chicago: Hildmann.

Frankel, Arthur J., and Sheldon R. Gelman. 1998. *Case Management: An Introduction to Concepts and Skills*. Chicago: Lyceum Books.

Frankfurter, Felix. 1915. Social work and professional training. *Proceedings of the National Conference of Charities and Correction, 1915*, pp. 591–596. Chicago: Hildmann Printing.

Freidson, Eliot. 1970. *Professional Dominance*. New York: Atherton.

Friedman, Charles P., and Elizabeth F. Purcell, eds. 1983. *The New Biology and Medical Education: Merging the Biological, Information and Cognitive Sciences*. New York: Josiah Macy, Jr., Foundation.

Froland, Charles, et al. 1981. *Helping Networks and Human Services*. Beverly Hills, Calif.: Sage.

Gambrill, E. 2001. Social work: An authority based profession. *Research on Social Work Practice* 11, no. 2:166–175.

Gans, Sheldon and Gerald Horton. 1975. *Integration of Human Services*. New York: Praeger.

Geismar, Ludwig L. 1972. Thirteen evaluative studies. In E. J. Mullen, J. R. Dumpson, eds. *Evaluation of Social Interventions*, pp. 15–38. San Francisco: Jossey-Bass.

Geller, J. 1988. *Racial Bias: The Evaluation of Patients for Psychotherapy in Clinical Guidelines in Cross-Cultural Mental Health*. New York: Wiley.

Gibbs, P., B. L. Locke, and R. Lohmann. 1990. Paradigm for the generalist–advanced generalist continuum. *Journal of Social Work Education* 26, no. 3:232–243.

Gibelman, Margaret. 1995. *What Social Workers Do*. Washington, D.C.: National Association of Social Workers.

——. 2000a. The nonprofit sector and gender discrimination: A preliminary investigation into the glass ceiling. *Nonprofit Management & Leadership* 10, no. 3:251–269.

——. 2000b. What's all the fuss about? Executive salaries in the nonprofit sector. *Administration in Social Work* 24, no. 4:59–74.

Gibelman, M., S. R. Gelman, and D. Pollack. 1997. The credibility of nonprofit boards: A view from the 1990s and beyond. *Administration in Social Work* 21, no. 2:21–49.

Gil, David G. 1998. *Confronting Injustice and Oppression: Concepts and Strategies for Social Workers*. New York: Columbia University Press.

Gilbert, N., and H. Specht. 1974. Advocacy and professional ethics. *Social Work* 21, no. 6:288–293.

Gilligan, Carol. 1982. *In a Different Voice: Psychological Theory and Women's Development*. Cambridge, Mass.: Harvard University Press.

Glaser, John S. 1994. *The United Way Scandal: An Insider's Account of What Went Wrong and Why*. New York: Wiley.

Glisson, Charles. 1992. Structure and technology in human service organizations. In Y. Hasenfeld, ed. *Human Services as Complex Organizations*, pp. 184–202. Newbury Park, Calif.: Sage.

Glisson, C., and L. James. 1992. The interorganizational coordination of services to children in state custody. *Administration in Social Work* 16, nos. 3/4:65–80.

Goddeeris, John H., and Burton A. Weisbrod. 1997. "Conversion from Nonprofit to For-Profit Legal Status: Why Does It Happen and Should We Care?" Working Paper 97-14. Evanston, Ill.: Institute for Policy Research, Northwestern University.

Goldberg, G. S. 1995. Theory and practice in program development: A study of the planning and implementation of fourteen social programs. *Social Service Review* 69, no. 4:614–655.

Goldman, S., and W. M. Kahnweiler. 2000. A collaborator profile for executives of nonprofit organizations. *Nonprofit Management & Leadership* 10, no. 4:435–450.

Goode, William. 1969. The theoretical limits of professionalization. In A. Etzioni, ed. *The Semi-Professions and Their Organization*, pp. 266–313. New York: Free Press.

Gordon, W. E., and M. Schutz. 1977. A natural basis for social work specialization. *Social Work* 22, no. 5:422–427.

Gortner, Harold F., Julianne Mahler, and Jeane B. Nicholson. 1987. *Organization Theory: A Public Perspective*. Chicago: Dorsey Press.

Graham, Pauline, ed. 1995. *Mary Parker Follett—Prophet of Management*. Boston: Harvard Business School Press.

Grasso, A. J., and I. Epstein. 1992. Towards a developmental approach to program evaluation. *Administration in Social Work* 16, nos. 3/4:187–203.

Green, J. C., and D. W. Griesinger. 1996. Board performance and organizational effectiveness in nonprofit service organizations. *Nonprofit Management & Leadership* 6, no. 4:381–402.

Green, J. C., F. Madjidi, T. J. Dudley, and F. L. Gehlen. 2001. Local unit performance in a national nonprofit organization. *Nonprofit Management & Leadership* 11, no. 4:459–476.

Green, Ronald K. 1998. Maximizing the use of performance contracts. In R. L. Edwards, J. A. Yankey, and M. A. Altpeter, eds. *Skills for Effective Management of Nonprofit Organizations*, pp. 78–97. Washington, D.C.: National Association of Social Workers.

Greenwood, E. 1957. Attributes of a profession. *Social Work* 2, no. 3:45–55.

Grønbjerg, Kirsten A. 1993. *Understanding Nonprofit Funding: Managing Revenues in Social Services and Community Development Organizations*. San Francisco: Jossey-Bass.

Grønbjerg, K., L. Harmon, A. Oikkonen, and A. Raza. 1995. The United Way system at the crossroads: Community planning and allocation. Paper presented at the Annual Meeting of the Association for Research on Nonprofit Organizations and Voluntary Action (ARNOVA), Cleveland, Ohio, November 1995.

Gummer, Burton. 1979. "Participatory management"; Social change or chimera? *Administration in Social Work* 3, no. 2:241–246.

——. 1990. *The Politics of Social Administration: Managing Organizational Politics in Social Agencies*. Englewood Cliffs, N.J.: Prentice-Hall.

——. 1992. Organizational change: The breakfast of champions. *Administration in Social Work* 16, nos. 3, 4:205–214.

——. 1996. Ethics and administrative practice: Care, justice, and the responsible administrator. *Administration in Social Work* 20, no. 4:89–106.

——. 1997. Is the *Code of Ethics* as applicable to agency executives as it is to direct service providers? No. In E. Gambrill and R. Pruger, eds. *Controversial Issues in Social Work Ethics, Values and Obligations*, pp. 143–148. Boston: Allyn and Bacon.

Gummer, Burton, and Philip McCallion, eds. 1995. *Total Quality Management in the Social Services: Theory and Practice*. Albany N.Y.: Rockefeller College of Public Affairs and Policy, State University of New York at Albany.

Gunther, John, and Frank Hawkins, eds. 1996. *Total Quality Management in Human Service Organizations*. New York: Springer.

Gutiérrez, L., L. GlenMaye, and K. DeLois. 1995. The organizational context of empowerment practice: Implications for social work administration. *Social Work* 40, no. 2:249–258.

Hage, Jerald. 1986. Conceptualizing mental health delivery systems: Organizational theory applied. In W. R. Scott and B. L. Black, eds. *The Organization of Mental Health Services: Societal and Community Systems*, pp. 53–75. Beverly Hills, Calif.: Sage.

Hammack, D. C. 1995. Accountability and nonprofit organizations: A historical perspective. *Nonprofit Management & Leadership* 6, no. 2:127–140.

Hall, Richard H. 1968. Professionalization and bureaucratization. *American Sociological Review* 33:92–104.

——. 1969. *Occupations and the Social Structure*. Englewood Cliffs, N.J.: Prentice-Hall.

——. 1986. Interorganizational or interprofessional relationships: A case of mistaken identity. In W. R. Scott and B. L. Black, eds. *The Organization of*

Mental Health Services: Societal and Community Systems, pp. 147–158. Beverly Hills, Calif.: Sage.

Hall, R. H., J. P. Clark, P. C. Giordano, P. V. Johnson, and M. Van Roekel. 1977. Patterns of interorganizational relationships. *Administrative Science Quarterly* 22:457–474.

Halliday, Terence C. 1987. *Beyond Monopoly*. Chicago: University of Chicago Press.

Handler, Joel. 1992. *Dependency and Discretion*. In Y. Hasenfeld, ed. *Human Services as Complex Organizations*, pp. 276–298. Newbury Park, Calif.: Sage.

———. 1996. *Down from Bureaucracy: Ambiguities in Privatization and Empowerment*. Princeton: Princeton University Press.

Harlan, S. L., and J. R. Saidel. 1994. Board members' influence on the government nonprofit relationship. *Nonprofit Management & Leadership* 5, no. 2:173–196.

Harnish, V. 1993. *Implementing Total Quality Management*. Boulder, Colo.: CareerTrack.

Hartman, A. 1993. The professional is political. *Social Work* 38, no. 4:365–366, 504.

Hasenfeld, Yeheskel. 1983. *Human Service Organizations*. Englewood Cliffs, N.J.: Prentice-Hall.

———. 1986. Community mental health centers as human service organizations. In W. R. Scott and B. L. Black, eds. *The Organization of Mental Health Services: Societal and Community Systems*, pp. 133–146. Beverly Hills, Calif.: Sage.

———. 1992a. The nature of human service organizations. In Y. Hasenfeld, ed. *Human Services as Complex Organizations*, pp. 3–23. Newbury Park, Calif.: Sage.

———. 1992b. Power in social work practice. In Y. Hasenfeld, ed. *Human Services as Complex Organizations*, pp. 259–275. Newbury Park, Calif.: Sage.

———. 2000. Organizational forms as moral practices: The case of the welfare departments. *Social Service Review* 74, no. 3:329–351.

Hasenfeld, Yeheskel, and Richard English, eds. 1974. *Human Service Organizations: A Book of Readings*. Ann Arbor: University of Michigan Press.

Hasenfeld, Yeheskel, and Rino Patti. 1992. The utilization of research in administrative practice. In A. Grasso and I. Epstein, eds. *Research Utilization in the Social Services*, pp. 221–239. New York: Haworth Press.

Hasenfeld, Y., and H. Schmid. 1989. The life cycle of human service organizations: An administrative perspective. *Administration in Social Work* 13, nos. 3/4:243–269.

Hasenfeld, Yeheskel, and Daniel Steinmetz. 1981. Client-official encounters in social service agencies. In C. T. Goodsell, ed. *The Public Encounter: Where*

State and Citizen Meet, pp. 83–101. Bloomington, Ind.: Indiana University Press.

Hasenfeld, Y., and D. Weaver. 1996. Enforcement, compliance and disputes. *Social Service Review* 70, no. 2:235–256.

Hawkins, Frank, and John Gunther. 1998. Managing for quality. In R. L. Edwards, J. A. Yankey, and M. A. Altpeter, eds. *Skills for Effective Management of Nonprofit Organizations*, pp. 525– 553. Washington, D.C.: National Association of Social Workers.

Haynes, Karen S. 1989. *Women as Managers in Human Services*. New York: Springer.

Herman, Robert D., and Richard Heimovics. 1994a. Executive Leadership. In R. D. Herman and Associates, eds. *The Jossey-Bass Handbook of Nonprofit Leadership and Management*, pp. 137–153. San Francisco: Jossey-Bass.

——. 1994b. *Board Practices, Board Effectiveness, and Organizational Effectiveness in Local Nonprofit Organizations*. Washington, D.C.: Aspen Institute.

Hernandez, C. M., and D. R. Leslie. 2001. Charismatic leadership: The aftermath. *Nonprofit Management & Leadership* 11, no. 4:493–498.

Hillery, George. 1968. *Communal Organizations: A Study of Local Societies*. Chicago: University of Chicago Press.

Hirschman, Albert. 1970. *Exit, Voice and Loyalty*. Cambridge, Mass.: Harvard University Press.

Hjern, B., and D. O. Porter. 1981. Implementation structures: A new unit of analysis. *Organization Studies* 2, no. 3:211–228.

Hoefer, R. 2000. Accountability in action: Program evaluation in nonprofit human service agencies. *Nonprofit Management & Leadership* 11, no. 2:167–177.

Holland, Thomas P. 1998. Strengthening board performance. In R. L. Edwards, J. A. Yankey, and M. A. Altpeter, eds. *Skills for Effective Management of Nonprofit Organizations*, pp. 425–452. Washington, D.C.: National Association of Social Workers.

Houle, Cyril O. 1997. *Governing Boards*. San Francisco: Jossey-Bass.

Howe, E. 1980. Public professions and the private model of professionalism. *Social Work* 25, no. 3:179–191.

Howell, William C. 1976. *Essentials of Industrial and Organizational Psychology*. Homewood, Ill.: Dorsey Press.

Huber, R., and B. P. Orlando. 1995. Persisting gender differences in social workers incomes: Does the profession really care? *Social Work* 40, no. 5:585–591.

Hudson, Walter W. 1997. Assessment tools as outcome measures in social work. In E. J. Mullen and J. L. Magnabosco, eds. *Outcomes Measurement in the Human Services: Cross-Cutting Issues and Methods*, pp. 68–80. Washington, D.C.: National Association of Social Workers.

Hughes, Everett C. 1958. *Men and Their Work*. Glencoe, Ill.: Free Press.

Hunt, J. M. 1948. Measuring movement in casework. *Journal of Social Casework* 29, no. 9:343–351.

Hyde, Cheryl. 1992. The ideational system of social movement agencies: An examination of feminist health centers. In Y. Hasenfeld, ed. *Human Services as Complex Organizations*, pp. 121–144. Newbury Park, Calif.: Sage.

——. 2000. The hybrid nonprofit: An examination of feminist social movement organizations. *Journal of Community Practice* 8, no. 4:45–68.

Iglehart, Alfreda P., and Rosina M. Becerra. 1995. *Social Services and the Ethnic Community*. Boston: Allyn & Bacon.

Inglis, S., and L. Weaver. 2000. Designing agendas to reflect board roles and responsibilities. *Nonprofit Management & Leadership* 11, no. 1:65–77.

Jacobs, D. 1974. Dependency and vulnerability: An exchange approach to the control of organizations. *Administrative Science Quarterly* 19:45–58.

Jacoby, S. M. 1999. Are career jobs headed for extinction? *California Management Review* 42, no. 1:123–145.

Jeavons, J. T. 1992. When management is the message: Relating values to management practice in nonprofit organizations. *Nonprofit Management & Leadership* 2:403–417.

Johnson, P. J., and A. Rubin. 1983. Case management in mental health: A social work domain? *Social Work* 28, no. 1:49–55.

Kagan, Sharon L., and Peter R. Neville. 1993. *Integrating Human Services: Understanding the Past to Shape the Future*. New Haven, Conn.: Yale University Press.

Kahn, Robert L., et al., in collaboration with Robert Rosenthal. 1964. System boundaries. In *Organizational Stress: Studies in Role Conflict and Ambiguity*, pp. 99–124. New York: John Wiley and Sons.

Kanter, Rosabeth M. 1977. *Men and Women of the Corporation*. New York: Basic Books.

——. 1983. *The Change Masters*. New York: Simon and Schuster.

——. 1995. Preface. In P. Graham, ed. *Mary Parker Follett: Prophet of Management*, pp. xiii–xix. Cambridge, Mass.: Harvard Business School Press.

——. 1996. Restoring people to the heart of the organization. In F. Hesselbein, M. Goldsmith, and R. Beckard, eds. *The Leader of the Future*, pp. 139–150. San Francisco: Jossey-Bass.

——. 1997. *On the Frontiers of Management*. Boston: Harvard Business School Press.

Kanter, Rosabeth M., Barry A. Stein, and Todd D. Jick. 1992. *The Challenge of Organizational Change: How Companies Experience It and Leaders Guide It*. New York: Free Press.

Kanter, Rosabeth M., and David V. Summers. 1987. Doing well while doing good: Dilemmas of performance measurement in nonprofit organizations and the need for a multiple-constituency approach. In W. W. Powell, ed. *The Nonprofit Sector: A Research Handbook*, pp. 154–166. New Haven, Conn.: Yale University Press.

Kaplan, R. S. 2001. Strategic performance measurement and management in nonprofit organizations. *Nonprofit Management & Leadership* 11, no. 3:353–370.

Katan, J. 1984. Role formation and division of work in multiprofessional human service organizations. *Administration in Social Work* 8, no. 1:73–80.

Kearns, Kevin P. 1996. *Managing for Accountability: Preserving the Public Trust in Public and Nonprofit Organizations*. San Francisco: Jossey-Bass.

Kemp, Susan P., James K. Whittaker, and Elizabeth M. Tracy. 1997. *Person-Environment Practice: The Social Ecology of Interpersonal Helping*. Hawthorne, N.Y.: Aldine de Gruyter.

Kettner, P. M., and L. L. Martin. 1985. Issues in the development of monitoring systems for purchase of service contracting. *Administration in Social Work* 9, no. 3:69–82.

——. 1996. The impact of declining resources and purchase of service contracting on private, nonprofit agencies. *Administration in Social Work* 20, no. 3:21–38.

Kettner, Peter M., Robert M. Moroney, and Lawrence L. Martin. 1999. *Designing and Managing Programs: An Effectiveness-Based Approach*, 2nd edition. Thousand Oaks, Calif.: Sage.

Kingman, B. R. 1995. Do profits crowd out donations, or vice versa? *Nonprofit Management & Leadership* 6, no. 1:21–38.

Kirk, Stuart, and Herb Kutchins. 1992. *The Selling of DSM: The Rhetoric of Science in Psychiatry*. New York: Aldine de Gruyter.

Kloss, L. L. 1999. The suitability and application of scenario planning for national professional associations. *Nonprofit Management & Leadership* 10, no. 1:71–83.

Knoke, David. 1990. *Organizing for Collective Action: The Political Economies of Associations*. New York: Aldine de Gruyter.

Koroloff, N. M., and H. E. Briggs. 1996. The life cycle of family advocacy organizations. *Administration in Social Work* 20, no. 4:23–43.

Kramer, Ralph M. 1975. Ideology, status, and power in board–executive relationships. In R. M. Kramer and H. Specht, eds. *Readings in Community Organization*, pp. 307–314. Englewood Cliffs, N.J.: Prentice-Hall.

——. 1998. *Nonprofit Organizations in the 21st Century: Will Sector Matter?* Washington, D.C.: Aspen Institute.

Kravetz, D., and C. D. Austin. 1984. Women's issues in social service administration: The views and experiences of women administrators. *Administration in Social Work* 8, no. 4:25–37.

Lamb, H. R. 1980. Therapist-case managers: More than brokers of services. *Hospital and Community Psychiatry* 11, no. 11:761–764.

Larson, Magali S. 1977. *Rise of Professionalism: A Sociological Analysis.* Berkeley, Calif.: University of California Press.

Lawrence, Paul, and Jay Lorsch. 1967. *Organization and Environment: Managing Differentiation and Integration.* Boston: Harvard Business School Press.

Lawry, R. P. 1995. Accountability and nonprofit organizations: An ethical perspective. *Nonprofit Management & Leadership* 6, no. 2:181–180.

Leduc, R. F., and S. R. Block. 1985. Conjoint directorship: Clarifying management roles between the board of directors and the executive director. *Journal of Voluntary Action Research* 14, no. 1:67–76.

Leiby, James. 1984. *A History of Social Welfare and Social Work in the United States.* New York: Columbia University Press.

Lens, Sidney. 1966. *Radicalism in America.* New York: Thomas Y. Crowell.

———. 1969. *Poverty: America's Enduring Paradox: A History of the Richest Nation's Unwon War.* New York: Thomas Y. Cromwell.

Lens, V. 2001. The Supreme Court, federalism and social policy. *Social Service Review* 75, no. 2:318–336.

Levin, H. 1985. The board–executive relationship re-visited. In S. Simon, ed. *An Introduction to Human Services Management,* 2nd edition, vol. 1, pp. 25–211. New York: Haworth Press.

Levine, Daniel S. 1982. Cost-effectiveness evaluation in mental health care. In G. J. Stahler and W. R. Tash, eds. *Innovative Approaches to Mental Health Evaluation,* pp. 277–304. New York: Academic Press.

Levine, S., and P. E. White. 1961. Exchange as a conceptual framework for the study of interorganizational relationships. *Administrative Science Quarterly* 5:583–601.

Levy, Charles S. 1982. *Guide to Ethical Decisions and Actions for Social Service Administrators: A Handbook for Managerial Personnel.* New York: Haworth Press.

———. 1983. Client self-determination. In A. Rosenblatt and D. Waldfogel, eds. *Handbook of Clinical Social Work,* pp. 904–919. San Francisco: Jossey-Bass.

Lewis, Judith, Michael Lewis, and Frederick Souflee, Jr. 1991. *Management of Human Service Programs,* 2nd edition. Pacific Grove, Calif.: Brooks-Cole.

Lipsky, Michael. 1980. *Street-level Bureaucracy: Dilemmas of the Individual in Public Service.* New York: Russell Sage Foundation.

Littell, J. H., L. B. Alexander, and W. W. Reynolds. 2001. Client participation: Central and underinvestigated elements of intervention. *Social Service Review* 75, no. 1:1–28.

Lohmann, Roger A. 1980. *Breaking Even: Financial Management in Human Service Organizations.* Philadelphia: Temple University Press.

——. 1999. Has the time come to reevaluate evaluation? Or who will be accountable for accountability? *Nonprofit Management & Leadership* 10, no. 1:93–101.

Lowell, Josephine. 1884. *Public Relief and Private Charity.* New York: G. P. Putnam's Sons.

Lowenthal, Jeffrey N. 1994. *Reengineering the Organization.* Milwaukee, Wisc.: Quality Press.

Macdonald, Keith M. 1995. *The Sociology of the Professions.* London: Sage.

Martin, Lawrence L. 1993. *Total Quality Management in Human Service Organizations.* Newbury Park, Calif.: Sage.

——. 2000a. Budgeting for outcomes in state human service agencies. *Administration in Social Work* 24, no. 3:71–88.

——. 2000b. The environmental context of social welfare administration. In R. J. Patti, ed. *The Handbook of Social Welfare Management,* pp. 55–67. Thousand Oaks, Calif.: Sage.

Martin, Lawrence L., and Peter M. Kettner. 1996. *Measuring the Performance of Human Service Programs.* Thousand Oaks, Calif.: Sage.

——. 1997. Performance management: The new accountability. *Administration in Social Work* 21, no. 1:17–29.

Martin, Patricia. 1985a. Multiple constituencies, dominant social values and the human service administrator: Implications for service delivery. In S. Slavin, ed. *Social Administration: The Management of the Social Services,* vol. I, 2nd edition, pp. 72–84. New York: Haworth Press.

——. 1985b. Group sex composition in work organizations: A structural-normative model. In S. Bachrach and S. Mitchell, eds. *Research in the Sociology of Organizations,* vol. 4, pp. 311–349. Greenwich, Conn.: JAI Press.

——. 1988. Multiple constituencies and performance in social welfare organizations: Action strategies for directors. In R. Patti, J. Poertner, and C. A. Rapp, eds. *Managing for Service Effectiveness in Social Welfare Organizations,* pp. 223–254. New York: Haworth Press.

Martin, P., and R. H. Chernesky. 1989. Women's prospects for leadership in social welfare: A political economy perspective. *Administration in Social Work* 13, nos. 2/3:117–141.

Marx, J. D. 1997. Corporate philanthropy and the United Way: Challenges for the year 2000. *Nonprofit Leadership & Management* 8, no. 1:19–30.

Mattessich, P. W., and B. R. Monsey. 1992. *Collaboration: What Makes It Work: A Review of Research Literature on Factors Influencing Successful Collaboration.* St. Paul, Minn.: Amherst H. Wilder Foundation.

Matusow, Allen J. 1984. *The Unraveling of America: A History of Liberalism in the 1960s.* New York: Harper & Row.

Mayer, Robert R. 1976. *Utilization of Social Research Findings in Programs Effecting Institutional Change*. Washington, D.C.: Department of Health, Education and Welfare/National Institute of Mental Health.

——. 1985. *Policy and Program Planning: A Developmental Perspective*. Englewood Cliffs, N.J.: Prentice-Hall.

Mayer, Robert R., and Ernest Greenwood. 1980. *The Design of Social Policy Research*. Englewood Cliffs, N.J.: Prentice-Hall.

Maynard, G. F., III, and D. L. Poole. 1998. Stewardship: The distinguishing characteristic of not-for-profit health care. *Health and Social Work* 23, no. 4:243–247.

Mayo, Elton. 1933. *Human Problems of an Industrial Civilization*. New York: Macmillan.

McArthur, J. H., and F. D. Moore. 1997. The two cultures and the health care revolution. *Journal of the American Medical Association* 277, no. 12:985–989.

McDonald, C. 1997. Government funded nonprofits and accountability. *Nonprofit Leadership & Management* 8, no. 1:51–64.

McGregor, Douglas. 1960. *The Human Side of Enterprise*. New York: McGraw-Hill.

McManus, J. M., and D. E. Leslie. 2000. Resignation or dismissal? When CEO and a president clash. *Nonprofit Management & Leadership*. 11, no. 2:225–230.

Menefee, D. T. 1997. Strategic administration of nonprofit human service organizations: A model for executive success. *Administration in Social Work* 21, no. 2:1–20.

Menefee, D. T., and J. J. Thompson. 1994. Identifying and comparing competencies for social work management: A practice driven approach. *Administration in Social Work* 18, no. 3:1–25.

Meyer, Carol H. 1983. *Clinical Social Work in the Eco-systems Perspective*. New York: Columbia University Press.

——. 1993. *Assessment in Social Work Practice*. New York: Columbia University Press.

Meyers, M. K. 1993. Organizational factors in the integration of services for children. *Social Service Review* 67, no. 4:547–575.

Mills, P. K., J. L. Hall, J. K. Leidecker, and N. Margulies. 1983. Flexiform: A model for professional service organizations. *Academy of Management Review* 8, no. 1:118–131.

Minahan, A. 1976. Generalists and specialists in social work: Implications for education and practice. *Areté* 42, no. 2:62.

Minahan, A., and A. Pincus. 1977. Conceptual framework for social work practice. *Social Work* 22, no. 5:347–352.

Mintzberg, Henry. 1979. *The Structuring of Organizations: A Synthesis of the Research*. Englewood Cliffs, N.J.: Prentice-Hall.

———. 1983. *Power In and Around Organizations*. Englewood Cliffs, N.J.: Prentice-Hall.

Mondros, Jacqueline B., and Scott M. Wilson. 1994. *Organizing for Power and Empowerment*. New York: Columbia University Press.

Montes, Guillermo. 1997. Public funding and institutional reorganization: Evidence from the early kindergarten movement. *Nonprofit Management & Leadership* 7, no. 4:405–420.

Moore, S. 1992. Case management and the integration of services: How service delivery systems shape case management. *Social Work* 37, no. 5:418–423.

Moore, S. T., and M. J. Kelly. 1996. Quality now: Moving human services organizations toward a consumer orientation to service quality. *Social Work* 42, no. 1:33–40.

Morgan, Gareth. 1986. *Images of Organizations*. Beverly Hills, Calif.: Sage.

Morris, R. 1977. Caring for vs. caring about people. *Social Work* 22, no. 5:353–359.

Morris, Robert, and Robert H. Binstock. 1966. *Feasible Planning for Social Change*. New York: Columbia University Press.

Morton, M. J. 1998. Cleveland's child welfare system and the "American Dilemma," 1941–1964. *Social Service Review* 72, no. 1:112–136.

Mullen, Edward J., and Jennifer L. Magnabosco, eds. 1999. *Outcomes Measurement in the Human Services: Cross-Cutting Issues and Methods*. Washington, D.C.: National Association of Social Workers.

Mullen, Edward J., and John R. Schuerman. 1990. Expert systems and the development of knowledge in social welfare. In L. Videka-Sherman and W. Reid, eds. *Advances in Clinical Social Work Research*, pp. 67–83. Washington, D.C.: National Association of Social Workers.

Munson, C. E. 1976. Professional autonomy and social work supervision. *Journal of Education for Social Work* 12, no. 3:95–102.

Murray, Vic, and Bill Tassie. 1994. Evaluating the effectiveness of nonprofit organizations. In R. D. Herman and Associates, eds. *The Jossey-Bass Handbook of Nonprofit Leadership and Management*, pp. 303–324. San Francisco: Jossey-Bass.

Musgrave, Richard. 1959. *The Theory of Public Finance*. New York: McGraw-Hill.

Najam, A. 1996. Understanding the third sector: Revisiting the prince, the merchant and the citizen. *Nonprofit Management & Leadership* 7, no. 2:203–220.

National Association of Social Workers. 1996. *Code of Ethics*. Washington, D.C.: National Association of Social Workers.

———. 1997. NASW joins a lawsuit charging some managed care companies with antitrust violations. *NASW News* 42, no. 7:1.

National Child Welfare Resource Center for Organizational Improvement. 2001. New child and family service reviews. *Managing Care for Children and Families* 3, 2:1–2.

Nieves, J. 2000. Social work collective bargaining? *NASW News* 45, no. 1:2.

Nugent, W. R., and C. Glisson. 1999. Reactivity and responsiveness in children's service systems. *Journal of Social Service Research* 25, no. 3:41–60.

Nyhan, R. C., and L. L. Martin. 1999. Comparative performance measurement: A primer on data envelopment analysis. *Public Productivity and Management Review* 22, no. 3:348–364.

O'Brien, Gregory St. L., and Jon L. Bushnell. 1980. Interorganizational behavior. In S. Feldman, ed. *The Administration of Mental Health Services*, 2nd edition, pp. 196–234. Springfield, Ill.: Charles C. Thomas.

O'Connell, Basil. 1985. *The Board Member's Book*. New York: Foundation Center.

Okten, Cagla, and Burton A. Weisbrod. 1999. "Determinants of Donations in Private Nonprofit Markets." Working Paper 10. Evanston, Ill.: Institute for Policy Research, Northwestern University.

Oliver, A. L. 1997. On the nexus of organizations and professions: Networking through trust. *Sociological Inquiry* 67:227–245.

Oliver, C. 1988. The collective strategy framework: An application to competing predictions of isomorphism. *Administrative Science Quarterly* 33:543–561.

——. 1990. Determinants of interorganizational relationships: Integration and future direction. *Academy of Management Review* 15, no. 2:241–265.

Olson, Mansour. 1971. *The Logic of Collective Action: Public Goods and the Theory of Groups*. Cambridge, Mass.: Harvard University Press.

Onken, Steven J. 2000. "Facilitating Consumer Voice in Public Mental Health: Exploring Congruence in Conceptualizing and Prioritizing Services and Supports." Dissertation, University of Texas, Austin.

Organ, D. W. 1971. Linking pins between organizations and environment. *Business Horizons* December, pp. 73–80.

Orlin, M. 1995. The Americans with Disabilities Act: Implications for social services. *Social Work* 40, no. 2:233–239.

Ostrower, Francie. 1995. *Why the Wealthy Give: The Culture of Elite Philanthropy*. Princeton, N.J.: Princeton University Press.

Ouchi, William G. 1978. Coupled versus uncoupled control in organizational hierarchies. In M. Meyer and Associates, eds. *Environments and Organizations*, pp. 264–289. San Francisco: Jossey-Bass.

——. 1981. *Theory Z: How American Business Can Meet the Japanese Challenge*. Menlo Park, Calif.: Addison-Wesley.

Padgett, D. L. 1993. Women and management: A conceptual framework. *Administration in Social Work* 17, no. 4:57–76.

Parker, M., and L. J. Secord. 1988. Private geriatric case management: Current trends and future directions. In K. Fisher and E. Weisman, eds. *Case Management: Guiding Patients Through the Health Care Maze*. Chicago: Joint Commission on Accreditation of Healthcare Organizations.

Parsons, Talcott. 1954. The Professions and the Social Structure. In T. Parsons, ed. *Essays in Sociological Theory*, revised edition, pp. 185–199. Glencoe, Ill.: Free Press.

Patti, Rino J. 1983. *Social Welfare Administration: Managing Social Programs in a Developmental Context*. Engelwood Cliffs, N.J.: Prentice-Hall.

——. 1988. Managing for service effectiveness in social welfare: Towards a performance model. In R. J. Patti, J. Poertner, and C. A. Rapp, eds. *Managing for Service Effectiveness in Social Welfare Organizations*, pp. 7–22. New York: Haworth Press.

Paulson, R. I. 1984. Administering multiple treatment modalities in social service agencies. *Administration in Social Work* 8, no. 1:89–98.

Pearl, N. A., and D. M. Bryant. 2000. "Bringing reality to the table": Contributors to the lack of parent participation in an early childhood service program. *Administration in Social Work* 24, no. 4:21–37.

Peat, B., and D. L. Costley. 2000. Privatization of social services: Correlates of contract performance. *Administration in Social Work* 24, no. 1:21–38.

Perlman, Robert. 1975. *Consumers and Social Services*. New York: John Wiley and Sons.

Perlmutter, Felice D., and Burton Gummer. 1994. Managing organizational transformation. In Robert D. Herman and Associates, eds. *The Jossey-Bass Handbook of Nonprofit Leadership and Management*, pp. 227–246. San Francisco: Jossey-Bass.

Perrow, Charles. 1986. *Complex Organizations: A Critical Essay*, 3rd edition. New York: McGraw-Hill.

Peters, J. B., and J. Masaoka. 2000. A house divided: How nonprofits experience union drives. *Nonprofit Management & Leadership* 10, no. 3:305–317.

Peters, Thomas J., and Robert H. Waterman, Jr. 1982. *In Search of Excellence*. New York: Warner Books.

Pfeffer, Jeffrey, and Gerald R. Salancik. 1978. *The External Control of Organizations: A Resource Dependence Perspective*. New York: Harper & Row.

Pinderhughes, E. B. 1983. Empowerment for our clients and for ourselves. *Social Casework* 64, no. 6:331–338.

——. 1989. *Understanding Race, Ethnicity, and Power: The Key to Efficacy in Clinical Practice*. New York: Free Press.

Polsky, H. W. 1978. From claques to factions: Subgroups in organizations. *Social Work* 23, no. 2:94–99.

Poole, D. L., J. K. Davis, J. Reisman, and J. E. Nelson. 2001. Improving the quality of outcome evaluation plans. *Nonprofit Management & Leadership* 11, no. 4:405–421.

Poole, Dennis L., Joan Nelson, Sharon Carnahan, Nancy G. Chepenik, and Christine Tubiac. 2000. Evaluating performance measurement systems in nonprofit agencies: The program accountability quality scale. *American Journal of Evaluation* 21, no. 1:15–26.

Popple, P. 1985. The social work profession: A reconceptualization. *Social Service Review* 59, no. 4:560–577.

Powell, D. 1986. Managing organizational problems in alternative service organizations. *Administration in Social Work* 10, no. 3:57–70.

Powell, Thomas J. 1995. Self-help groups. In In R. L. Edwards and J. G. Hopps, eds. *Encyclopedia of Social Work*, 19th edition, pp. 2116–2123. Washington, D.C.: National Association of Social Workers.

Powell, Walter W., and Paul J. DiMaggio, eds. 1991. *The New Institutionalism in Organizational Analysis*. Chicago: University of Chicago Press.

Prince, J., and M. J. Austin. 2001. Innovative programs and practices emerging from the implementation of welfare reform: A cross-case analysis. *Journal of Community Practice* 9, no. 3:1–14.

Pruger, R. 1973. The good bureaucrat. *Social Work* 18, no. 4:26–32.

Quinn, J. B. 1978. Strategic change: "Logical incrementalism." *Sloan Management Review* Fall, 1978:7–21.

Quinn, Robert E. 1988. *Beyond Rational Management: Mastering the Paradoxes and Competing Demands of High Performance*. San Francisco: Jossey-Bass.

Quinn, R. E., and K. Cameron. 1983. Organizational life cycles and shifting criteria of effectiveness: Some preliminary evidence. *Management Science* 29, no. 1:33–51.

Quinn, R. E., and J. Rohrbaugh. 1983. A spatial model of effectiveness criteria: Towards a competing values approach to organizational analysis. *Management Science* 29:363–377.

Radin, Beryl A. 1998. The Government Performance and Results Act (GPRA): Hydra-headed monster or flexible management tool? *Public Administration Review* 58, no. 4:307–316.

Raiff, N. R., and B. K. Shore. 1993. *Advanced Case Management: New Strategies for the Nineties*. Newbury Park, N.J.: Sage.

Rapp, C. A., and R. Wintersteen. 1989. The strengths model of case management: Results from twelve demonstrations. *Psychosocial Rehabilitation Journal* 13, no. 1:22–32.

Rapp, Charles, and John Poertner. 1988. Moving clients center stage through the use of client outcomes. In R. Patti, R. Poertner, and C. Rapp, eds. *Managing for Service Effectiveness in Social Welfare Organizations*, pp. 23–37. New York: Haworth Press.

——. 1992. *Social Administration: A Client-Centered Approach.* New York: Longman.

Reamer, Frederic G. 1993. Liability issues in social work administration. *Administration in Social Work* 17, no. 4:11–26.

——. 1994. *Social Work Malpractice and Liability.* New York: Columbia University Press.

——. 1995. Ethical dilemmas in social work: Indirect practice. *Social Work Values and Ethics*, 2nd edition, pp. 130–164. New York: Columbia University Press.

——. 2001. Ethics and managed care policy. In N. W. Veeder and W. Peebles-Wilkins, eds. *Managed Care Services: Policy, Programs and Research*, pp. 74–96. New York: Oxford University Press.

Reich, Robert B. 1983. *The Next American Frontier.* New York: Times Books.

Reitan, T. C. 1998. Theories of interorganizational relations in the human services. *Social Service Review* 72, no. 3:285–309.

Richan, Willard. 1984. Professional dissonance in public welfare. In F. Perlmuter, ed. *Human Services at Risk*, pp. 213–227. Lexington, Mass.: D. C. Heath.

Rincon, Erminia Lopez, and Christopher B. Keys. 1985. The Latina social service administrator: Developmental tasks and management concerns. In S. Slavin, ed. *An Introduction to Human Services Management*, 2nd edition, vol. I, pp. 237–250. New York: Haworth Press.

Rivard, J. C., M. C. Johnson, J. P. Morrisey, and B. E. Starett. 1999. The dynamics of interagency collaboration: How linkages develop for child welfare and juvenile justice sectors in a system of care demonstration. *Journal of Social Service Research* 26, no. 3:61–82.

Robins, A. J., and C. Blackburn. 1985. Governing boards in mental health: Roles and training needs. In S. Simon, ed. *An Introduction to Human Services Management*, 2nd edition, vol. 1, pp. 127–138. New York: Haworth Press.

Romo, Harriet, and Toni Falbo. 1996. *Latino High School Graduation: Defying the Odds.* Austin, Tex.: University of Texas Press.

Rose, Stephen M., ed. 1992. *Case Management and Social Work Practice.* New York: Longman.

Rosenberg, Marvin, and Ralph Brody. 1975. *Systems Serving People: A Breakthrough in Service Delivery.* Cleveland: School of Applied Social Sciences, Case Western Reserve University.

Rosenthal, M. 2000. Public or private children's services? Privatization in retrospect. *Social Service Review* 74, no. 2:281–305.

Rosenthal, Seymour J., and James E. Young. 1980. The governance of the social services. In F. D. Permutter and S. Slavin, eds. *Leadership in Social Administration*, pp. 86–102. Philadelphia: Temple University Press.

Rossi, Peter H. 1978. Issues in the evaluation of human services delivery. *Evaluation Quarterly* 2, no. 4:573–599.

———. 1999. Program outcomes: Conceptual and measurement issues. In E. J. Mullen and J. L. Magnabosco, eds. *Outcomes Measurement in the Human Services: Cross-Cutting Issues and Methods*, pp. 20–34. Washington, D.C.: National Association of Social Workers.

Rossi, Peter H., Howard E. Freeman, and Mark Lipsey. 1998. *Evaluation: A Systematic Approach*, 6th edition. Beverly Hills, Calif.: Sage.

Roth, J. A. 1974. Professionalism—The sociologist's decoy. *Sociology of Work and Occupations* 1, no. 1:6–23.

Rothman, Jack. 1994. *Practice with Highly Vulnerable Clients: Case Management and Community-Based Services*. Englewood Cliffs, N.J.: Prentice-Hall.

Rubin, Allen, and Earl Babbie. 1997. *Research Methods for Social Work*, 3rd edition. Pacific Grove, Calif.: Brooks-Cole.

Rubin, A., Jose Cardenas, Keith Warren, Cathy King Pike, and Kathryn Wambach. 1998. Outdated practitioner views about family culpability and severe mental disorders. *Social Work* 43, no. 5:412–422.

Saidel, Judith R., and Alissandra M. D'Aquanni. 1999. *Expanding the Governance Construct: Functions and Contributions of Nonprofit Advisory Groups*. Washington, D.C.: Aspen Institute.

Saidel, J. R., and S. L. Harlan. 1998. Contracting and patterns of governance. *Nonprofit Management & Leadership* 8, no. 3:243–259.

Salamon, Lester M. 1989. The voluntary sector and the future of the welfare state. *Nonprofit and Voluntary Sector Quarterly* 18, no. 1:11–24.

———. 1993. *The Marketization of Welfare: Changing Nonprofit and For-Profit Roles in the American Welfare State*. Baltimore: Johns Hopkins University Press.

———. 1995. *Partners in Public Service: Government-Nonprofit Relations in the Modern Welfare State*. Baltimore: Johns Hopkins University Press.

Sandfort, J. 1999. The structural impediments to human service collaboration: Examining welfare reform at the front lines. *Social Service Review* 73, no. 3:314–339.

Sayles, Leonard R. 1979. *Leadership: What Effective Managers Do, and How They Do It*. New York: McGraw-Hill.

Schatz, M. S., L. E. Jenkins, and B. W. Sheaford. 1990. Milford redefined: A model of initial and advanced generalist social work. *Journal of Social Work Education* 26, no. 3:217–231.

Schaufeli, Wilmar, Christina Maslach, and Tadeusz Marek. 1993. *Professional Burnout*. Washington, D.C.: Taylor and Francis.

Schorr, A. L. 2000. The bleak prospect for child welfare. *Social Service Review* 74, no. 1:124–135.

Schorr, Lisbeth B. 1997. *Common Purpose: Strengthening Families and Neighborhoods to Rebuild America*. New York: Anchor Books, Doubleday.

Schwartz, S. R., H. H. Goldman, and S. Churgin. 1982. Case management for the chronic mentally ill: Models and dimensions. *Hospital and Community Psychiatry* 33, no. 12:1006–1009.

Scott, W. Richard, and Bruce L. Black, eds. 1986. *The Organization of Mental Health Services: Societal and Community Systems*. Beverly Hills, Calif.: Sage.

Segal, L. M., and B. A. Weisbrod. 1997. "Interdependence of Commercial and Donative Revenues." Working Paper 27. Evanston, Ill.: Institute for Policy Research, Northwestern University.

Segal, S. P., C. Silverman, and T. Temkin. 1993. Empowerment and self-help agency practice for people with mental disabilities. *Social Work* 38, no. 6:705–712.

Selber, K., and D. M. Austin. 1997. Mary Parker Follett: Epilogue to or return of a social work management pioneer. *Administration in Social Work* 21, no. 1:1–14.

Selber, K., and C. L. Streeter. 2000. Managing service quality in human services. *Administration in Social Work* 24, no. 2:1–14.

Selznick, Philip. 1957. *Leadership in Administration*. New York: Harper & Row.

Senge, Peter. 1990. *The Fifth Discipline: The Art and Practice of the Learning Organization*. New York: Doubleday.

——. 1999. *The Dance of Change: The Challenge of Sustaining Momentum in Learning Organizations*. London: Nicholas Beasley.

Senor, J. M. 1963. Another look at the executive–board relationship. *Social Work* 8, no. 2:19–25.

Shanley, Mark T., and Michael Lounsbury. 1996. "Network Interpretations of Non-market Bureaucracies: The Case of a State Children's Services Agency." Working Paper 96-31. Evanston, Ill.: Center for Urban Affairs and Policy Research, Northwestern University.

Shenhav, Y. 1995. From chaos to systems: The engineering foundations of organizational theory, 1879–1932. *Administrative Science Quarterly* 30:557–585.

Shindul-Rothschild, Judith. 2001. The macroeconomic impact of managed care. In N. W. Veeder and W. Peebles-Wilkins, eds. *Managed Care Services: Policy, Programs and Research*, pp. 15–30. New York: Oxford University Press.

Shoemaker, P. J. H. 1995. Scenario planning: A tool for strategic thinking. *Sloan Management Review* Winter: 25–40.

Siciliano, J., and G. Spiro. 1992. The unclear status of nonprofit directors: An empirical survey of director liability. *Administration in Social Work* 16, no. 1:69–80.

Silk, T. 1994. The Legal Framework of the Nonprofit Sector in the United States. In R. D. Herman and Associates, eds. *The Jossey-Bass Handbook of Nonprofit Leadership and Management*, pp. 65–82. San Francisco: Jossey-Bass.

Silverman, Phyllis R. 1978. *Mutual Help Groups*. Washington, D.C.: Department of Health, Education and Welfare.

Simpson, Richard P., and Ida H. Simpson. 1969. Women and bureaucracy in the semi-professions. In A. Etzioni, ed. *The Semi-Professions and Their Organization*, pp. 196–265. New York: Free Press.

Singh, J. V., and C. J. Lumsden. 1990. Theory and research in organizational ecology. *Annual Review of Sociology* 16:161–195.

Siporin, M. 1988. Clinical social work as an art form. *Social Casework* 69, no. 3:177–183.

Skocpol, Theda. 1994. *Social Policy in the United States: Future Possibilities in Historical Perspective.* Princeton, N.J.: Princeton University Press.

Smith, Page. 1966. *As a City upon a Hill.* New York: Knopf.

Smith, Steven R., and Michael Lipsky. 1993. *Nonprofits for Hire: The Welfare State in the Age of Contracting.* Cambridge, Mass.: Harvard University Press.

Solomon, Barbara. 1976. *Black Empowerment: Social Work in Oppressed Communities.* New York: Columbia University Press.

Sorenson, J. E., and T. L. Sorenson. 1974. The conflict of professions in a bureaucratic organization. *Administrative Science Quarterly* 19:98–106.

Specht, Harry, and Mark E. Courtney. 1994. *Unfaithful Angels: How Social Work Has Abandoned Its Mission.* New York: Free Press.

Springer, D. W., D. S. Sharp, and T. A. Foy. 2000. Coordinated service delivery and children's well-being: Community resource coordination groups of Texas. *Journal of Community Practice* 8, no. 2:39–52.

Starr, Paul. 1982. *The Social Transformation of American Medicine.* New York: Basic Books.

——. 1985. "The Meaning of Privatization." Working Paper 6, Privatization. Washington, D.C.: National Conference of Social Welfare.

Stein, Herman D. 1968. Professions and universities. *Journal of Education for Social Work* 4, no. 4:53–65.

——. 1981. The concept of human service organization: A critique. In H. D. Stein, ed. *Organization and the Human Services*, pp. 24–36. Philadelphia: Temple University Press.

——. 1985. Board, executive, and staff. In S. Simon, ed. *An Introduction to Human Services Management*, 2nd edition, vol. 1, pp. 191–204. New York: Haworth Press.

Steiner, Jesse F. 1925. *Community Organization: A Study of Its Theory and Current Practice.* New York: Century.

Stoesz, D., and D. Saunders. 1999. Welfare capitalism: A new approach to poverty policy? *Social Service Review* 73, no. 3:380–400.

Stone, M. M., B. Bigelow, and W. Crittenden. 1999. Research on strategic management in nonprofit organizations. *Administration and Society* 31, no. 3:378–423.

Strauss, Anselm, et al. 1985. *Social Organization of Medical Work.* Chicago: University of Chicago Press.

Street, David, George T. Martin, Jr., and Laura K. Gordon. 1979. *The Welfare Industry: Functionaries and Recipients in Public Aid.* Beverly Hills: Sage.

Streeter, C. L., and D. Gillespie. 1992. Social network analysis. *Journal of Social Service Research* 16, nos. 1/2:201–222.

Task Force on Social Work Research. 1991. *Building Social Work Knowledge for Effective Services and Policies: A Plan for Research Development.* Austin: School of Social Work, University of Texas at Austin.

Taylor, Frederick W. 1947. *Principles of Scientific Management.* (First published in 1913.) New York: Harper & Row.

Thomas, John C. 1994. Program evaluation and program development. In Robert D. Herman and Associates, eds. *The Jossey-Bass Handbook of Nonprofit Leadership and Management,* pp. 342–365. San Francisco: Jossey-Bass.

Thompson, James D. 1967. *Organizations in Action.* New York: McGraw Hill.

Thompson, Victor. 1961. *Modern Organizations.* New York: Knopf.

Timberlake, E. M., C. A. Sabatino, and J. A. Martin. 1997. Advanced practitioners in clinical social work: A profile. *Social Work* 42, no. 4:374–385.

Tremper, C. 1994. Risk Management. In R. D. Herman and Associates, eds. *The Jossey-Bass Handbook of Nonprofit Leadership and Management,* pp. 485–508. San Francisco: Jossey-Bass.

Trice, Harrison M. 1993. *Occupational Subcultures in the Workplace.* Ithaca, N.Y.: ILR Press.

U. S. Department of Health and Human Services. 1995. *Performance Measurement in Selected Public Health Programs.* Washington, D.C.: Public Health Service.

Vandenberg, Henry. 1996. "Organizational Deviance in For-Profit Psychiatric Hospital Business Practices." Dissertation, University of Texas, Austin.

Vinokur-Kaplan, Diane, and Daniel Bogin. 2000. Motivating work performance in social services. In R. J. Patti, ed. *The Handbook of Social Welfare Management,* pp. 169–193. Thousand Oaks, Calif.: Sage.

Vourlekis, B. S., K. Ell, and D. Padgett. 2001. Educating social workers for health care's brave new world. *Journal of Social Work Education* 37, no. 1:177–191.

Wakefield, J. C. 1993. Is altruism part of human nature? Towards a theoretical foundation for the helping professions. *Social Service Review* 67, no. 3:406–458.

Wallis, A. 1994. *The Challenge of Coordination in Human Service Networks.* Washington, D.C.: Aspen Institute.

Walmsley, Gary L., and Mayer N. Zald. 1976. *The Political Economy of Public Organizations.* Bloomington, Ind.: Indiana University Press.

Wasserman, H. 1971. The professional social worker in a bureaucracy. *Social Work* 16, no. 1:89–95.

Weaver, D. 2000. Organizational technology as institutionalized ideology: Case management practices in welfare-to-work programs. *Administration in Social Work* 24, no. 1:1–20.

Weick, Karl E. 1976. Educational organizations as loosely coupled systems. *Administrative Science Quarterly* 21:1–19.

——. 1981. Evolutionary theory as a backdrop for administrative practice. In H. D. Stein, ed. *Organization in the Human Services: Cross Disciplinary Reflections*, pp. 106–141. Philadelphia: Temple University Press.

Weil, Marie, James M. Karls, and Associates, eds. 1985. *Case Management in Human Service Practice*. San Francisco: Jossey-Bass.

Weiner, Myron E. 1990. *Human Services Management: Analysis and Applications*. Belmont, Calif.: Wadsworth.

——. 1991. Motivating employees to achieve. In R. L. Edwards and J. A. Yankey, eds. *Skills for Effective Human Services Management*, pp. 302–316. Washington, D.C.: National Association of Social Workers.

——. 1993. Managing the transition to new systems. In *Human Services Management: Analysis and Applications*, 2nd edition, pp. 421–439. Belmont, Calif.: Wadsworth.

Weirich, Thomas W. 1985. The design of information systems. In S. Slavin, ed. *Social Administration: The Management of the Social Services*, 2nd edition, vol. II, pp. 315–328. New York: Haworth Press.

Weisbrod, Burton. 1977. *The Voluntary Nonprofit Sector*. Lexington, Mass.: D. C. Heath.

Weisbrod, Burton A., ed. 1998. *To Profit or Not to Profit: The Commercial Transformation of the Nonprofit Sector*. Cambridge: Cambridge University Press.

Wells, K. B., and R. H. Brook. 1988. Historical trends in quality assurance for mental health services. In G. Stricker and A. R. Rodriguez, eds. *Handbook of Quality Assurance in Mental Health*, 39–63. New York: Plenum Press.

Wernet, Stephen. 1988. "Relationships Between Characteristics of Nonprofit Human Service Organizations and Organizational Adaptation." Dissertation, University of Texas, Austin.

Wernet, Stephen P., ed. 1999. *Managed Care in Human Services*. Chicago: Lyceum Books.

Wernet, S., and D. M. Austin. 1991. Decision making style and leadership patterns in nonprofit human service organizations. *Administration in Social Work* 15, no. 3:1–17.

Westby, D. L. 1966. The civic sphere in the American city. *Social Forces* 45, no. 2:161–169.

Wilensky, H. 1964. The professionalization of everyone? *American Journal of Sociology* 70:142–146.

Williamson, O. E. 1996. Economics and organizations: A primer. *California Management Review* 38:131–146.

Wilson, W. J. 1985. Cycle of deprivation and the underclass debate. *Social Service Review* 59, no. 4:541–559.

Wilson, Woodrow. 1978. The study of administration (1887). In J. M. Shafritz and A. C. Hyde, eds. *Classics of Public Administration*, pp. 3–6. Oak Park, Ill.: Moore.

Witkin, S. L. 1998. Mirror, mirror on the wall: Creative tensions, the academy and the field. *Social Work* 43, no. 5:389–391.

Wolch, Jennifer. 1990. *The Shadow State: Government and Voluntary Sector in Transition.* New York: Foundation Center.

Woodard, K. L. 1994. Packaging effective community service delivery: The utility of mandates and contracts in obtaining administrative cooperation. *Administration in Social Work* 17, no. 2:17–43.

———. 1995. Introduction and acceptance of inter-organizational agreements: The experience of seventy-five administrators in one county. *Administration in Social Work* 19, no. 4:51–83.

Zald, Meyer N. 1969. The power and functions of boards of directors: A theoretical synthesis. *American Journal of Sociology* 75, no. 1:97–111.

———. 1970. Political economy: A framework for comparative analysis. In M. N. Zald, ed. *Power in Organizations*, pp. 221–261. Nashville: Vanderbilt University Press.

———. 1972. *Occupations and Organizations in American Society.* Chicago: Markham.

Zbracki, J. J. 1998. The rhetoric and reality of total quality management. *Administrative Science Quarterly* 43, no. 3:602–636.

Zelman, W. N. 1977. Liability for social agency boards. *Social Work* 22, no. 4:270–274.

Zimbalist, Sidney E. 1977. *Historic Themes and Landmarks in Social Welfare Research.* New York: Harper & Row.

Zinman, S., H. T. Harp, and S. Budd. 1987. *Reaching Across: Mental Health Clients Helping Each Other.* Riverside, Calif.: California Network of Mental Health Clients.

Zucker, Lynne G., ed. 1988. *Institutional Patterns and Organizations: Culture and Environment.* Cambridge, Mass.: Ballinger.

INDEX

DATE DUE
